D0207731

Critical Essays on
Walker Percy

Critical Essays on Walker Percy

J. Donald Crowley and Sue Mitchell Crowley

G. K. Hall & Co. • Boston, Massachusetts

Library of Congress Cataloging in Publication Data

Crowley, J. Donald (Joseph Donald)
Critical essays on Walker Percy / J. Donald Crowley and Sue
Mitchell Crowley.
     p. cm. — (Critical essays on American literature)
    Includes index.
    ISBN 0-8161-8880-7 (alk. paper)
    1. Percy, Walker, 1916— Criticism and interpretation.
  I. Crowley, Sue Mitchell. II. Title. III. Series.
  PS3566.E6912Z64 1989
  813'.54—dc19   89-1787
                                                 CIP

This publication is printed on permanent/durable acid-free paper
MANUFACTURED IN THE UNITED STATES OF AMERICA

TICAL ESSAYS ON
ERICAN LITERATURE

This series seeks to anthologize the most important criticism on a wide variety of topics and writers in American literature. Our readers will find in various volumes not only a generous selection of reprinted articles and reviews but original essays, bibliographies, manuscript sections, and other materials brought to public attention for the first time. *Critical Essays on Walker Percy* is the most comprehensive collection of criticism ever assembled on this important writer and the first to reflect the historical development of critical opinion about him. It contains both early reviews and comments and a broad selection of more modern scholarship. Included are reviews by Stanley Edgar Hyman, Joyce Carol Oates, John Gardner, Benjamin DeMott, and others. Among the authors of reprinted articles are Alfred Kazin, Cleanth Brooks, Thomas LeClair, and Simone Vauthier. There is also an important interview with Walker Percy on "Questions They Never Asked Me." In addition to an extensive introduction that traces the history of Percy scholarship are three original essays, commissioned specifically for publication in this volume, by Sue Mitchell Crowley, Lewis A. Lawson, and J. Donald Crowley. We are confident that this book will make a permanent and significant contribution to American literary study.

JAMES NAGEL, GENERAL EDITOR

Northeastern University

For Roy and John and Don:
friends and fathers, wayfarers all

CONTENTS

INTRODUCTION

THE WORK, THE WRITER, THE LIFE

Walker Percy is known widely now among readers of contemporary American fiction as the author of six novels, the most recent being *The Thanatos Syndrome* (1987), and another volume very difficult to file under any single heading — *Lost in the Cosmos* (1983), a crafty, antic mixture of satire, language theory, multiple-choice questionnaire, comic postapocalyptic jeremiad, and numerous other items, mostly pensées, all of it cast parodically, as his subtitle has it, in the form of *The Last Self-Help Book*. This proto-fiction, a rich fusion of Percy's characteristic storytelling and nonfictional instincts and tropes, is still another new American — that is, "organic" — testament of wit and wisdom. Like several of the novels themselves, it is a reminder of the extent to which Percy's interests, thinking, and art are centered in decidedly mixed and oftentimes offbeat forms of fabulation — a reminder, as the criticism at times suggests, that the term "novel" is for one reason or another a not altogether adequate name for much of Percy's fiction.

To a significantly smaller number of readers, generalists and specialists alike, Percy is known too, first, for a collection of essays — *The Message in the Bottle* (1975) — addressing for the most part many of the very questions about the nature of language, metaphor, communication — naming and being — that his fiction explores. Also, for perhaps fewer readers, Percy has become a familiar presence because of other, uncollected essays some of which are belletristic, others of which are exercises in cultural criticism and commentary about what he calls the postmodern, post-Christian world of our time. Percy's journalistic topics range from a local-color appreciation of the ambience of New Orleans and an apologia declaring his preference for bourbon ("drinking Scotch is like looking at a picture of Noel Coward") to scientific arguments against abortion and mercy killing; from the form of the murder mystery and the decline of the "western" movie to the current state of the novel; from roughly a dozen reviews and review-essays of fiction and nonfiction he clearly wished to have his say about to his personal attitudes about the desegregating Sunbelt South and what he sees as "The Coming Crisis of Psychiatry."[1]

Taken all around Percy's is an impressive corpus making up in height

1

and depth what it might be seen to lack in length. Without the prolific nature of a Joyce Carol Oates or John Updike, Percy has the craftly care and patience, the intense detachment of the Artist of Kouroo. And if Henry James's praise of Hamlin Garland's genius as "the soaked sponge of his air and time"[2] is justified, much the same, without any regional strictures, might be claimed for Percy. As both his fiction and his essays demonstrate, the range and deftness of his topical allusions to contemporary culture, from clichéd "pop" to the profoundly philosophical, as well as his ability to make them vibrate in harmony or disharmony with the past, are the match of Scott Fitzgerald's. The growing interest in his work and the spirited commentary on it leave no doubt that he is perceived far more often than not to have a sensitively diagnostic finger on the pulse of the age. To be sure, Percy has his detractors, but they stand in the face of this sort of assessment of his significance: "the basic themes of Percy's novels are certainly not to be regarded as the privileged crankiness of a somewhat eccentric Roman Catholic intellectual; and they are not merely the private and special insights of an important novelist. . . . they have a close relationship to a powerful and searching criticism of the world . . . which in the last decade has begun to claim the attention and the endorsement of an increasing number of modern scholars."[3]

Percy fairly sprang upon the literary scene in 1962 when his first novel published—the third one he had tried out, *The Moviegoer* (1961)—earned him the National Book Award for Fiction. His second, *The Last Gentleman*, a near miss for the same prize, was, like almost all his books, a long time coming and did not appear until 1966. *Love in the Ruins*—anticly subtitled *The Adventures of a Bad Catholic at a Time Near the End of the World*—was not published until 1971.[4] The fifteen essays collected in *The Message in the Bottle* (1975), all but one of them reprinted pieces published periodically over two decades in a variety of journals with at best small circulation, gave additional testimony to what Percy calls his "recurring interest [in] . . . the nature of human communication and, in particular, the consequences of man's unique discovery of the symbol."[5] It testified as well to the long, arduous initiation into the craft of writing that lay behind his fiction—and to his penchant for the wry subtitle: *How Queer Man Is, How Queer Language Is, and What One Has to Do with the Other*. Although the shortest of his novels, *Lancelot* was equally time-consuming in the composition and did not appear until 1977. The fifth novel, *The Second Coming*, was published in 1980—after Percy made the many careful revisions required by his discovery, more than two-hundred pages into the typescript, that the story he was telling really belonged to Will Barrett, the young amnesiac protagonist of *The Last Gentleman* now facing his terrors of middle age.[6] Three years later came *Lost in the Cosmos*, whose working title, "Novum Organum," hints of Percy's keen interest in and astute knowledge of science, the scientific method, the history of science; it suggests too that some part of the form of that book (not yet traced by the criticism) stems from Percy's satire of latter-day reincarnations of Francis Bacon's old Idols — of the Tribe, the Cave, the Marketplace, the Theater.[7] *The Thanatos Syndrome* (1987) is both Percy's second sequel and, like *Love in the Ruins*, futuristic as it takes up the farther adventures of Dr. Tom More in the mid-1990s and immerses him in the pop-art conventions of the mystery story.[8]

Virtually all of Percy's writing to date has set about diagnosing — and engaging the reader actively to diagnose — the elemental malaise of postmodern consciousness, the question as he phrased it in "The Delta Factor" (1975), of "Why does man feel so sad in the twentieth century?" He is by no means the only one of our major contemporary writers to have assumed the pertinence of the question, but, as both the popular and the critical receptions of his work make clear, no others have pursued that pressing dilemma more powerfully or relentlessly. Woven throughout Percy's investigation of the question is his belief that man is still perched to be open to the redemptive right uses of language even though living now in a world where, given the gross and terrifying debasement of language itself, he is everywhere exposed to the threat of the total debasement of man. Language itself is at once for Percy the index to and the instrument of man's entire range of possibilities: the great good of saying and knowing and doing truth, the evil of erecting Towers of Babel all over the landscape.

Walker Percy was born in Birmingham, Alabama, on 28 May 1916, the oldest of three sons, into a lineage whose Southern American roots date from 1776.[9] The family's saga — the lives of the successive generations of Percy males — reads, in Lewis Baker's biographical account, rather like Peter Taylor's story "Dean of Men," the aggressively public, political, and entrepreneuring energies of the earlier generations gradually being re- or displaced by an ideal of domestic life and of literary pursuits much more retiring if no less demanding. Percy's early life was, to say the least, marked by severe trauma of the sort that, in the absence of fuller biographical facts, tends to mythologize the terms of a writer's career. He was at the critical age of eleven when his father, an attorney, committed suicide, and only several years older when, in 1931, his mother died in an automobile accident. Percy and his brothers were fortunate, however, for their father's cousin — William Alexander Percy, a lifelong bachelor dedicated to literature, the arts, and a stoical conduct of the good life — adopted them and made his Greenville, Mississippi, home theirs. Details of Percy's youth are sketchy, but it appears that he took up reading as a steady, serious habit, became early on the sort of devoted and rather abstracted moviegoer that Binx Bolling of *The Moviegoer* is, and spent some large part of his adolescence fretting not only the question of vocation but the melancholier one still of what life was really all about. Fascinated by the elegance and beauty of the scientific method, Percy took a degree in chemistry at the University of North Carolina at Chapel Hill and immediately, without quite knowing just why, went off to New York to study medicine at Columbia College of Physicians and Surgeons. For three years there he underwent psychoanalysis (to little avail) while continuing his practice of going to movies and cocking his eye at other moviegoers. In 1941, a resident surgeon at Bellevue Hospital in New York City, Percy was stricken with tuberculosis as a result of performing an autopsy. He had hardly begun his long convalescence in the first of two sanitaria (an experience he later tried to translate into the second of his attempted novels) when word reached him, in January 1942, of the death of his adoptive father, "Uncle Will."

Percy's convalescence took virtually the duration of World War II: in the sanitarium, within the grip of the dreadful disease, and outside the spectacle of the world's war, the physician was missing, like Rip Van Winkle, the latest revolution. Percy's spectating habit, one surmises, must have been severely tested along with his physical health. That his two brothers were out there up and doing — Leroy with many air force missions over Germany, Phinizy, just turned twenty, serving in the South Pacific on the same patrols as John F. Kennedy — lends to Percy's own situation the sort of private fable surrounding, say, Henry James and the Civil War. By all available accounts Percy literally read his way through disease and war together, the French existentialists and the Russian realists serving as his private European theater. Recovering and then suffering a relapse, Percy this time retired to a Connecticut sanitarium and learned that he was occupying the same bed that Eugene O'Neill had been a patient in. As the war out there ended, Percy's inner struggle continued. The dislocation, perhaps disorientation, were multifaceted and seemed to shape themselves as a dark homelessness at once literal and metaphorical, physical and spiritual. And it continued, clearly, a classic American crisis of identity and vocation. As Ralph Waldo Emerson had discovered that one must leave the ministry to be a good minister, so Percy found as it were that to be a good physician one must first be a good patient and then leave medicine conventionally defined in favor of other modes of diagnosis.

Released from the sanitarium, Percy returned to Greenville only briefly before setting out for New Mexico, the Grand Canyon, Santa Fe. There he stayed for just over a year, living alone (except for about a month when his friend from boyhood Shelby Foote joined him) in an old barn. Then, again without quite knowing just why, he resolved to return to Greenville. Still adrift, with little notion of what he would replace a medical career with or how he would make use of the wide reading he had continued, Percy finally declared his thoughtful desire to place himself in his world. Robert Coles — to whom Percy dedicated *The Thanatos Syndrome* — gives the fullest account of these life-defining events:

> For the young physician there was no dramatic "conversion": rather, a
> deeply introspective and somewhat withdrawn man gradually began to

> make commitments, and affiliation to a particular faith was one of them. On November 7, 1946, in a Baptist church in New Orleans, . . . Dr. Percy married Mary Bernice Townsend. . . . He had first met her five years before, when he worked briefly in a Greenville clinic. She had worked there, too, as a medical technician. . . . They had intermittently kept in touch, but only a few months before their marriage did the man feel in any way inclined to propose. Next they had to find a place to live. Uncle Will had owned a country house, a lovely but unpretentious place up in the hills near Sewanee, Tennessee. They went there and lived a quiet, rural life. The reading continued. There were walks, and occasional trips back to Greenville or into nearby Nashville. There were also religious discussions — eventually culminating in a decision to take instruction in the Catholic faith. Six months after they were married they became Catholics, and have remained so, believing ones, to this day. (68)

This brief narrative strikes me as an indispensable piece of critical equipment for any reader who would hope to understand with any fullness Percy's writing and thinking. The events simply touched on here trace Percy's movement existentially from the solitariness and — what was for him — the unreality of "I think" to the metaphysics of Gabriel Marcel's "we are." And they find in indirect and unsentimental ways their expression as varied themes in much of his work. They exist for him as Archimedan points, not of fixed, known, certain ends, but recovered beginnings from which to live — passionately, quietly, attentively — and to engage reality with something resembling wholeness of sensibility and being. Percy's comments to Coles suggest the steady pressures of further quest and search to come that have since been part and parcel of both the living and the writing: "After the war, when I guess I made reading a full-time occupation, I kept asking myself what is *believable* in these days, not just for me, but for others: my family, my friends, the people I knew. Dostoevski knew how hungry we all are for faith, but how hard it is to find — and to keep" (72).

After living several years near the Garden District in New Orleans following their brief stay in Tennessee, the Percys planted themselves in Covington, Louisiana, a small town on the north edge of Lake Pontchartrain where they live today close to their two daughters and their growing families.[10] It is here that Percy plunged with discipline into an apprenticeship as a writer, concerned from the first, really, with a humanity suffering from a crisis in culture, a crisis in language. This long foreground issued only very slowly, beginning in the mid-1950s, in essays that found their way to philosophical, religious, psychiatric, and "academic" journals. During these years Percy gradually persuaded himself that fiction, or fabulation, was a possibility of form more communicable to the wider audience he obviously wished to reach. He was not to this manor born, however, and subsequently endured writing two decisively unpublishable novels.[11] The watching, waiting, and listening motifs that have proven to be so large in his writing, however, he patiently persevered at, and the writing of unpublishable novels was his studiously cognitive route to writing more than publishable ones. And recognition came at last, in the National Book Award citation of Lewis Gannett, Herbert Gold, and Jean Stafford: "*The Moviegoer*, an intimation rather than a statement of mortality and the inevitability of that condition, is a truthful novel with shocks of recognition and spasms of nostalgia for every — or nearly every — American. Mr. Percy, with compassion and without the sentimentality or the mannerisms of the clinic, examines the delusions and hallucinations and the daydreams and the dreams that afflict those who abstain from the customary ways of making do."

THE CRITICISM

Since 1962 Percy's writing has prompted what is oftentimes a distinguished body of critical commentary, analysis, and interpretation. Not the least tribute to the freshness and power, the incisiveness and the vision of his work is the fact that the past quarter century has seen far more written about him than he has written himself. The critical literature has so far had several distinct features. It expresses, even for Americans, an unusually intense interest in the life of the writer "behind" and "within" the writing. If, as has been said, American literature is an enterprise of creating or establishing a "voice," Percy has been found out as having more than one such voice deserving of response; and, indeed, a number of rich, controversial misreadings arise out of mistaking Percy's voice for those of his characters. Given his wide reading and his persistently allusive style, source and influence studies have been, not surprisingly, abundant, and the best of them have often been at the forefront of elucidating his art. The difficulty of placing Percy with any precision and completeness has been for much of this time an inevitable if not always happy preoccupation with his critics: in what ways is he to be understood as a Southern novelist? a Catholic one? Is he most of all a Christian existentialist who bends the novel to serve eschatological concerns, or is he basically a chronicler of cultural ideas generally, one who has difficulty fleshing out his characters and plots with ample drama? Another perennial question asked is whether his writing diverges into two distinct streams — fiction and nonfiction — or whether it is, if complicatedly so, all one and continuous. Studies explicating individual works and analyzing the relationships between and among works — particularly the latter — are now quite numerous, as are those addressing specific aspects of his vision of the human condition.

Several critics have distinguished themselves as first among a larger number of equals: Lewis A. Lawson, Simon Vauthier, Martin Luschei come first to mind, and more recently Jerome Taylor and William Rodney Allen. Together with Walker Percy himself, one of his own best commentators, since his essays on the reading and writing of fiction and his many interviews with critics contribute one of the identifiable threads in the developing response. There are no doubt readers whom Percy either does not reach, or, reaching, puts off, but busily engaged detractors are few when one considers that Percy's satiric thrusts are regularly armed with the power to offend virtually almost everyone. When it comes to Percy's dramatized assessments of our contemporary world, it is Binx Bolling of the first novel who makes the most restrained objections: and he lives, he says, in "the great shithouse of scientific humanism where needs are satisfied, everyone becomes an anyone, a warm and creative person, and prospers like a dung beetle, where one hundred percent are humanists and ninety-eight percent believe in God, and men are dead, dead, dead" (228). The meaning of Percy's Catholicism has variously been misinterpreted, failed to win consent, and not even been caught in the act. His techniques of satiric-fantastic realism have confused some reviewers and been questioned by other critics. A foreign visitor examining a current bibliography of the criticism might very well get the impression, what with all the essays published in the likes of the *Southern Review*, the *Mississippi Quarterly*, and other Southern academic journals, magazines, and newspapers, and the book-length titles issued by Louisiana State University Press, that Percy is nothing more than the darling of the delta, a coterie writer offering up postpartum consolations to folks mourning the passing of the Southern Agrarians. A second glance will inform him, though, that Percy's readership has long since been widespread, is in fact a phenomenon with its own fascination, his American correspondents being spread out all around the territory. Of serious contemporary American writers, moreover, Percy is one of the most translated into what Twain called the awful German language and others. One or another, several, sometimes most, of his novels now exist in German, French, Japanese, Norwegian, Spanish, Swedish, Hungarian, Portuguese, Italian, Serbo Croat, Rumanian, and Turkish; and all of his works are much reprinted here at home.[12] His best readers have included both established critics and younger ones who have written publishable dissertations. And his writing has already generated the sort of coherent critical tradition that declares his voice to be a major one, one to be contended with. His vision is sufficiently distinctive that each of his works after *The Moviegoer* has come to be awaited with the sort of great expectations that make an edge of disappointment almost inevitable.

REVIEWS

With comparatively few exceptions the initial reviews of Percy's works have been positive — engaged, for the most part enthusiastic — but only rarely can they be said to be truly substantive. They have also been numerous: whereas *The Moviegoer* attracted only several dozen reviews in major periodicals, his later works have prompted, on average, roughly twice that many. For the just-published *Thanatos Syndrome* I already have in hand over twenty. Major critics, practicing writers, recognizable reviewers who have written on Percy include Malcolm Bradbury, Peter Butenhuis, Frederick Crews, Benjamin DeMott, James Dickey, George Garrett, Granville Hicks, Stanley Edgar Hyman, Richard Lehan, Joyce Carol Oates, Reynolds Price, V. S. Pritchett, John Wain, Jonathan Yardley. One reason for the smaller number of *Moviegoer* reviews is, no doubt, its being a first novel by an unknown writer. Another is that Alfred Knopf, the original publisher, did not himself like the book or the idea of its winning the Book Award and, so the story goes, did not push it in the press.[13]

Hyman praises the novel's creation of character and subtle symbols, Percy's knack for catching varieties of speech, most of all "its clear firm line of action," but he objects to what he calls "pretentious attempts to make [Binx's] search seem not neurotic but deeply spiritual."[14] In a longer and more substantial review Brainard Cheney puts the novel in the context of Dostoyevski's *Notes from the Underground* and Camus's *The Fall* in explicating approvingly those very dimensions of meaning Hyman finds objectionable.[15] Malcolm Bradbury cites the novel as being "in a particularly American way, a very good book," but he fails to say exactly how.[16] The back-handed compliment of the *Times Literary Supplement* review is rather more representative of British statements: the novel "fails by a narrow margin [and] is [only] nearly very good indeed" largely because Percy "can write a little too glibly of despair."[17] Opinions voiced in the American Catholic press, on the other hand, have been from time to time almost embarrassingly uncritical: though the rest of his review is not unintelligent, Harold C. Gardiner's conclusion that Binx "will go far in realizing the best of the traditions in which he had been raised" is not only piously reductive but flatly wrong if it implies that Binx will conform to his Aunt Emily's unbending stoicism.[18] Virtually all the reviews, like those of Percy's later work, focus on bits and snippets of character, plot, setting, theme, but collectively they give the impression that Percy's portrayal of Binx as suffering from "everydayness" and embarking on a "search" had touched a nerve and caught the attention. Generally, if not with equal eloquence, they reaffirm the views of Gannett, Gold, and Stafford; but they in no way solidly anticipate either the vigor, insight, and complexity of the sustained commentary to come or the continuing sales and popularity of the story nearly three decades later.

Reviewers of *The Last Gentleman* were at once somewhat less uniformly complimentary and more pointed in their criticisms. Some clearly did not recognize the book's deliberately episodic structure, and some of those who did expressed displeasure; a larger number found Dr. Sutter Vaught's notebook entries so intrusive and unamalgamated into the charting of Will Barrett's amnesiac displacement as to seriously mar the book; several commented negatively about the irresolution of the story's ending. Marcus Klein accuses Percy not only of embracing a myth of the Southern hero-gentleman long defunct but of far too much "philosophical discursiveness" on the one hand and "mythicizing" on the other.[19] John Wain, however, calling Percy a "breathtakingly brilliant writer," admonishes the reader: "This isn't just any old novel, but a novel written for very alert people" because everything "is prismatic, discrete, a matter of half-conveyed hints."[20] Wain's willingness to recognize Percy's subtle stylistic indirections is that general point separating the many positive reviews from those that chiefly complain. R. G. G. Price, writing in *Punch*, for example, simply refuses to grant Percy his donnée: "The American love for the Innocent as hero has never spread to our more sardonic climate and anyway this particular Innocent is interesting only clinically."[21] American reviews generally show themselves to be much more easily conversant with the novel's metaphysical conception of the immanence / transcendence conflict and at home with Barrett's plight being a comment on the human condition rather than solely on him. Stanley Trachtenberg finds Percy's initiation fable sustained because of Barrett's "sympathetic intelligence,"[22] and Peter Butenhuis, in one of the very best early statements on any of the novels, makes the telling point that "a writer who can find a hero who is inadequate not only to the demands of his plot but also to the requirements of his complex civilization, of which the plot should be some kind of imitation, has found the way to write a distinguished work of art."[23] Retrospectively it can be seen that Butenhuis uncovered a crux that much of the most incisive later criticism of this novel would elaborate. *The Last Gentleman*, whatever similarities it shares with its predecessor, announces a great many differences: its rambunctious picaresque mode, the vast spread of the American landscape it makes Percy's descriptive powers responsible for, its much greater number of characters, its device of simultaneity of scene, the far more aggravated consciousness first of Will Barrett but then, too, of other characters, the style itself being necessarily more oblique in order to register Will's lapsing into and reviving from his fugue states. If finally neither more complex nor profound than Binx's story, Will's is much denser and more complicated, and it has required more commentary than *The Moviegoer* to suggest how it yields up the meanings of its textural richness.

Love in the Ruins was sufficiently different from both the first two novels — and its comic-apocalyptic satire sufficiently controversial — that it took a few lumps in various of the initial reviews. A British reviewer was discombobulated enough to end on this declaration: "Mr Walker [*sic*, I guess] is plainly worried about his country, but one of the reasons the rest of us are even more worried is the *way* he worries: he just doesn't seem to see that it is not the business of politics to produce a new man."[24] Here at home J. Mitchell Morse accused Percy of lacking a "certain moral courage" and writing in fact "banalities."[25] That the book is preoccupied with banalities virtually all reviewers recognized, but Morse is alone in associating them with the author or what others saw as his comic but steadily compassionate vision. David C. Anderson sees Percy as reaching if anything a wider audience since his satire "makes explicit the relationship of his . . . philosophy to our wider problems as a society."[26] Percy's views embrace his Catholic belief, of course, and Wilfred Sheed uses the occasion to comment that "Percy's greatest technical problem is that he does want his Christian allegory to show" but in such a way, obviously, to be available to readers other than complacent Catholics.[27] It was generally recognized that Percy, in blowing his religious cover, portrayed the state of the Catholic Church in this country as no less hilariously divided and, except for a sociologically negligible remnant, as destructive as every other dimension of life—government and politics, medicine, racial and sexual relations, and so on. Even so, many of the reviews seemed oblivious, if not to its Faustian strands, to the religious fabric it wove, and saw Percy's interests as "chiefly sociological."[28] Others, aware of the "Christian allegory" there, could still drop such conclusions as this one—"Unhappily, no one believes More, who can measure spiritual malaise in a materialist age"[29]—when his Lapsometer is the very mark of his participation in the gnostic world being satirized. Anatole Broyard's review, on the other hand, is typical of the best of the positive reviews in that it names accurately the book's setting as a world turned into "a wholly idle experiment without a goal or even a guiding hypothesis" because of scientism, "a belief that everything is measurable—and manipulable."[30] And it is Melvin E. Bradford's "Dr. Percy's Paradise Lost: Diagnostics in Louisiana" that deserves description as the most intelligent and balanced of those reviews expressing ambivalence, even though what he finds "at the bottom of" the mischief he sees responsible for the book's "considerable formal shortcomings" is nothing less than a " 'Christian existentialism' " that he thinks Percy far too confident about.[31] Generally, Martin Luschei's comment— "Some reviewers . . . showed an instinct to hedge, as if in recognition that Percy was onto something best treated with respect whether or not one could really follow it" (16)—has its truth not just for this work but others as well.

The reviews of *The Message in the Bottle*, surprisingly numerous given the difficult and technical nature of many of the essays, were again engaged, affirmative, even enthusiastic—though far too brief to comment substantively on more than an aspect or two of Percy's thought. A general preference declared itself for the more personal and concrete essays such as "The Loss of the Creature," "The Man on the Train," "Notes for a Novel about the End of the World" over those addressing in technical and abstruse terms various linguistic issues—"Toward a Triadic Theory of Meaning," "Semiotic and a Theory of Knowledge," "Symbol as Hermeneutic in Existentialism." Hugh Kenner, as eager as Percy himself to get beyond both B. F. Skinner and Noam Chomsky, calls the collection a

"Copernican . . . breakthrough" in praising Percy's ideas about the nature of man's "Naming Faculty."[32] Whereas Kenner sees "abstracted ghosts" of Percy's first two novels in the essays, which he calls "the record of his real preoccupation," James Torrens speaks of the continuity between the theory and the fiction: Percy "wants to stress in theory what he has amply illustrated in practice as a novelist, the great mystery of naming, the symbolic power of language as 'the medium through which we see the world,' and which we have so much trouble seeing in its own intersubjective reality, and not just as a trigger of behavior or a logical system locked up in itself."[33] In another of the most substantial reviews Thomas LeClair pronounces the volume "ambitious, dense, and difficult" and correctly identifies Percy's efforts to move toward a new theory of man by starting from "the singularity of language." He too finds the essays "amplifying . . . ideas dramatized in the fiction."[34] Calling only Bellow and Gass the equal of Percy in "learning, precision and passion for concepts both in and out of fiction," LeClair, wondering out loud just who Percy's readers are, answers that the specialists—"Psycholinguists, transformationalists, semioticists, structuralists, phenomenologists, behaviorists, and those in the interstices"—would do well to take note of where Percy differs from them. But the essays are also, he insists, for any astute general reader capable of a sense of wonder. Clearly an admirer of Percy, LeClair nonetheless refers to the three later novels as "a promise unfulfilled, or, more accurately, a promise not quite made yet still somehow unkept." It's only in *The Moviegoer*, he says, that Percy "comes close to achieving a style that registers [his] profound thinking about language," and he wishes that Percy would imagine a novelistic mode that would transform "his enormous intelligence into some supreme verbal fiction."

Although *Lancelot* was likewise received in a generally favorable way, numerous reviews made it clear that novels of ideas invariably come under considerable native American suspicion. Christopher Lehmann-Haupt, for instance, contends that Percy has trouble controlling his narrative manner in registering Lance's Southern broad-sword rant, and as a result some of the novel's ideas are "downright upsetting"; he ends by reminding himself, not too confidently, that they are "not necessarily Walker Percy's" and that the novel "is, after all, a portrait of a philosophical quest rather than an argument for the quest's objectives."[35] John Gardner's review, reprinted here, is even more expansively condemnatory. Joyce Carol Oates also expresses dissatisfaction that the novel consists "for the most part of a lengthy and crotchety denunciation of what Percy sees to be the sickness of contemporary society," is beset by a "confusion of tones" and a "mixture of genres." Her conclusion—"If *Lancelot* is one of the most disappointing novels I have read in recent years, it is perhaps a tribute to the promise that Percy's earlier works have made"[36]—constitutes a sentiment present in several basically negative reviews. The positive reviews of Peter Prescott,

Philip French, and Robert D. Daniel were more typical of the majority of early statements.[37]

The Second Coming, obviously Percy's most intense effort to create something like an old-fashioned story of romantic love, a new-fangled variation on the novel of manners about courtship and marriage with none of the comic-parodic elements of his previous fiction bearing directly on the lovers themselves, prompted extravagant disagreement about the credibility of the Allie-Will Barrett relationship. Walter Clemons found the novel's "schematic symbolism [to] deaden credence," the novel itself Percy's "worst," though "still more interesting than most other writers' best shot."[38] Gene Lyons laments "how this extraordinarily gifted writer expects his readers to attend seriously to a conclusion in which Barrett and Allison get themselves a motel room and become lovers after a spate of dialogue whose inanity only underscores the improbability of all that has transpired to that point," and he longs for the old ambiguities of *The Moviegoer*.[39] William Koon, John Romano, Daphne Merkin, Robert Towers, and Benjamin DeMott, however, are representative of those reviewers, the majority, who think of the novel as Percy's best since *The Moviegoer*.[40] Percy's depiction of Allie was frequently noted as a grand improvement, and it muted earlier charges that Percy had some misogyny in his veins. Towers's review, like DeMott's (reprinted here), praises Allie's "greenhouse fable" as "one that continues to flourish magically when the book is closed."[41] Romano's charge that Percy's disdain for the everyday can be, in its tenor, morally unpleasant, even antisocial" and that his characteristic concerns lead to the doubt whether "a transcendent religious conviction and an ultimate attachment to other people are not finally incompatible" will strike many Percy readers as curious, wrongheaded; but it is typical of the kinds of questions Percy's fiction sometimes prompts. And Towers seems to repeat the basic attitude of many reviewers when he terms Percy "a kind of literary sport, one who imposes his own terms."

The extent to which Percy provokes controversy is nowhere proved more loudly than in the reviews of *Lost in the Cosmos*. Again, positive assessments outnumbered negative ones, but virtually all were somewhat quizzical even when paying tribute to the "devastatingly funny, devastatingly relevant"[42] nature of the satire. Many cite his deft wit in this or that section — in the manner of the *Newsweek* reviewer who noted "the good-humored rejoinder to the 'unmalicious, even innocent scientism' of Carl Sagan's popular book and PBS series 'Cosmos.' "[43] The judgment of R. G. Sheppard — "name another voice in American writing that is as beguiling and as civilized as Walker Percy's"[44] — is similar to sentiments in various reviews. But some ranged from negative through hostile to condemnatory. Jack Beatty complains that Percy "repeatedly posits the reality he would like to reveal. He conjures; he does not . . . capture."[45] The book's oddball structure irritated and incensed some as did the multiple-choice answers in the self-help quiz. Others confessed boredom. It is perhaps Peter Clecak, writing in *Commonweal*, who took greatest offense: the book's "condemnation of the world" is "simply too facile, too sweeping, too final. . . . Percy's dismissal of the human enterprise . . . [is] structured by a mean-spirited apprehension of his own religious norm," which turns out to be, in spite of "Catholic trappings, [a] classically Protestant vision of salvation of the self through the shed blood of Jesus."[46] The most distinctive feature of these reviews is their diversity in coming to grips with Percy's voice: for some there is genial humor, for others a supercilious misanthropy, and we are given a choice between a dogmatic Roman Catholicism and a down-home post-Puritan Protestantism.

The Thanatos Syndrome has so far inspired much the same disparate opinion as *Lancelot* and *Lost in the Cosmos*. Michiko Kakutani states flatly that this book, unlike *Love in the Ruins*, has such a "creaky plot machinery" that Percy neglects his genius for lyrical language as well as his talent for dramatizing "the inner life of angst-ridden individuals"; it is, in short, "one of the weakest efforts of one of our most talented and original authors."[47] Gail Godwin, on the other hand, hails the work as a "perceptive mirror of Right Now and an entertaining assault on our society's besetting sins: the manipulative and reductionist practice of social science, the zeal and self-righteousness of ultra-conservatives, the splintering of the Government into clandestine groups, often working at cross purposes inside the same organization."[48] And once more the majority of reviews are favorable to enthusiastic. George Garrett finds the story line to have "all the machinery of good old-fashioned plot fiction" as well as approaching "something very close to fable, the purely fabulous," and he sees in the book's Christianity and Catholicity attitudes that "will challenge and delight everyone."[49] Douglas Bauer does likewise and notes "Percy's brilliance" in delineating "the droll Dixie anthropology, the pitch-perfect comic dialogue, the sheer intelligence alive on every page."[50]

Taken as a whole, the "history" of reviews of Percy shows a principle of entropy at work, born of a repetition of expectations and preferences covering only a narrow range of considerations stereotypical of popular (and elite) journalism. That history demonstrates more than anything else that the format of the review is ill-designed to address fictions as singular as Percy's. For one thing, Percy's prose is too dense and elaborate of texture and idea to be absorbed immediately in a single close reading. As often as not what the reviews yield up is a preferential taste, either well- or ill-informed, and not the sort of being steeped in and mulling over the figures in the fictional carpet that have come only with the more studious and sustained dialogue generated by the explorations of critics largely academic rather than journalistic. Still, as Philip French noted, "Percy is an acquired taste,"[51] and the reviews of his work have played a significant role in helping to establish — particularly for a writer given to putting such burdens on his reader — something of the large audience he has striven for.

ESSAYS AND BOOKS,
COLLECTIONS OF ESSAYS, INTERVIEWS

On the score of the relationship between the literature of reviews and what I will call more sustained and penetrating criticism, a wag might say that "Southern Literature is now a thriving small industry within English departments and must have its geniuses to serve as the subjects of monographs and doctoral dissertations. We critics have to have our Southern Novelist as well, and a Southern Catholic Novelist offers topical opportunities not to be missed." And then such a wag might go on to wonder whether Percy "can actually put a novel together in a manner that readers who are not disarmed by regional or religious enthusiasm can take entirely seriously from beginning to end."[52] My calculations are that Percy is a large or singular subject in now over a hundred dissertations — as well as almost countless essays, several monographs, multiple brief mentions — and that divers hands in academe have been pursuing his matter and meanings for reasons more ennobling than tenure and promotion. Commentary on Percy is now quite mature and sophisticated, enough so that it is in a third stage or phase of revaluation and reinterpretation after having gone through the first customary two of exploration and tentative, speculative assertion and then consolidation (if not consensus). It "takes such an accumulation of history and custom, such a complexity of manner and types, to form a fund of suggestion for the novelist," said Henry James, lamenting the paucity of Hawthorne's materials: and it has taken an analogous sort of "funding" for the serious Percy critic to catch up with him. Beginnings, origins are always arbitrary, I suppose, and there is more than a little of serendipity in the way Percy criticism had its real, auspicious beginnings. Tony Tanner's *The Reign of Wonder: Naivety and Reality in American Literature* (1965), citing *The Moviegoer* and Bellow's *Dangling Man* as contemporary novels that "could . . . only be American," grouped Percy with a whole string of classical American writers — Emerson, Whitman, Thoreau, Melville, Hawthorne, James, Fitzgerald, Anderson, others — because of "their predilection for the strategy of the naive vision, that deliberate attempt to regard reality with minimum reference to previous familiarity and interpretive knowledge, that enduring preference for wonder over analysis" (11). Tanner's work marks nothing less than the "discovery" of Percy by a literary critic who turned out to be a major one. And it is remarkable on three counts: that, given the general deprecation of Percy's work in England, the critic should have been British; that Tanner, knowing little of Percy's medical and scientific background, should turn out to be as dead wrong as he is, on other counts, suggestively illuminating; and, finally, that what Tanner with his English eyes saw as Percy's essential "Americanness" came to be virtually ignored by most American critics themselves.[53]

Tanner notes that his "aim is not to extol an undiscovered masterpiece but simply to take a recent, talented first novel and show how unmistakably it relates itself to" what he defines as the characteristic American "habit of wonder" and the American denigration of scientific modes of inquiry (349). The developing criticism has left no doubt that Tanner's description is unduly modest and hedged; and it has made amply clear that Percy's quiver arms him not only with wonder but with keen analytical powers—perhaps too keen for popular American taste—of diagnosis at once scientific, philosophical, and, in the American way, linguistic. When one adds to Tanner's work that of the French critic Simone Vauthier, whom Percy himself thinks one of his most insightful readers, we have reason to view Percy as another of those native American writers appreciated abroad earlier than he came to be widely recognized at home. Vauthier's "Le Temps et la Mort Dans *The Movie-Goer*,"[54] though it did not appear until 1971, is still one of the earliest substantive commentaries; what is most memorable today about the essay is Vauthier's eagerness to distinguish Binx Bolling's secret fascination with death from that typical of the French existentialist hero (Camus's Merseault of *The Stranger* is insinuated throughout) and to see Binx himself as a definitively American type.

Here on native grounds there were at least two, perhaps three, other beginnings of criticism that mark enduring motifs in our understanding of Percy's basic concerns and themes. In all of them there is a lag time that bespeaks not a slowness in warming to Percy but a recognition of the difficulties of coming to grips with the complexities of his style and content. Thus, with just a few exceptions the essays published in scholarly-critical journals before the late 1960s have little current merit, and it has been only in more recent years that the most illuminating critiques of Percy's early work have been done.[55] Four early essays that all Percy students have to take account of are Lewis A. Lawson, "Walker Percy's Indirect Communications," "Walker Percy's Southern Stoic," "Walker Percy: The Physician as Novelist," and Jim Van Cleave, "Versions of Percy."[56] Lawson's earliest essay represents a dramatic critical breakthrough on several fronts, first in uncovering the degree to which Percy's thinking was steeped in Kierkegaardian existentialism and, second, in discussing so deftly the interrelationships between the essays (his "direct communications") and the first two novels ("indirect communications"). Dense and allusive, Lawson's study demonstrates how Percy's fictional method successfully filters through Binx's consciousness "a considerable amount of existentialist . . . statement" in a way at once novelistically enlivened and faithful, too, to an abstractive age and audience. Likewise in his second essay Lawson was the first to isolate Percy's central concern, both in his first two novels and in "Stoicism in the South,"[57] with the rigorous idealism embodied for him in William Alexander Percy. "It may be," he concludes, "that the vision of such a noble man's failure has been the single most powerful stimulus to Walker Percy's continued writing"

(31). Van Cleave's essay is also a reading of the fiction through William Alexander Percy, his *Lanterns on the Levee* and his friends' "affectionate memoirs" of him: what *The Moviegoer* gives us, then, is a measurement of the vast "distance between the Old South and the contemporary South, between a serene and deeply willed idealism and a tortured existential psychological and social realism" (991). One of the best indices to the sophistication and the insight of Percy criticism is the subtlety with which his own essayistic ideas and other literary "pre-texts" have been brought to bear on the clarification of his own fiction. Numerous of Percy's early commentators as well as some of his more recent ones have used the essays rather mechanically as convenient handles—because earlier, simpler statements—for grasping the more complex fiction. The danger is that Percy's fiction has at times been read as illustrations merely of concepts presented more schematically elsewhere. And on occasion the result has been that the artistic integrity of the novels themselves has been ignored or given second place. Not so with Lawson and Van Cleave, whose essays are models of critical strategy. In his third essay Lawson turns from specula-tion to accurate prediction: "in some future novel, if there are future novels, Dr. Percy will devote his full attention to the physician who recognizes his own illness and admits that he cannot alone heal himself" (62), and shortly after the writing of the essay (though prior to its publication) Percy's *Love in the Ruins* and the troubled Dr. Tom More appeared. Lawson's later essays, like these early ones, are lessons in how to move gracefully back and forth between the life and the work.[58]

Enter Percy himself as one of those writers whose collaborative spirit conspires profitably with readers interested in interviewing him. "Art lives upon discussion, upon experiment, upon curiosity, upon variety of at-tempt, upon the exchange of views and the comparison of standpoints," intoned James in "The Art of Fiction," and Percy would be one to agree that while "the successful application of any art is a delightful spectacle, . . . the theory too is interesting." Various of Percy's own essays—"From Facts to Fiction," "Notes for a Novel about the End of the World," "The State of the Novel: Dying Art or New Science?," and more recently "The Diagnostic Novel"[59] as well as numerous reviews and remarks made about fiction in his essays on language theory—attest to Percy's James-like belief that fiction "must take itself seriously for the public to take it so." Interviews with Percy have been a continuous dimension of the author's reception from the beginning. In the first phase of critical interest the interviews of Ashley Brown, Carlton Cremeens, and John C. Carr were instrumentally informative on a score of topics ranging from the biographical and southern-sociological to the literary, philosophi-cal, and religious.[60] Happily, these have been collected with two dozen others, mostly later ones some of which are equally penetrating, and are now easily available in Lewis A. Lawson and Victor A. Kramer's *Conver-sations with Walker Percy*.[61]

Related to the interviewing impulse and pivotal here at home in attracting a wider attention to Percy's life, art, and thinking is Alfred Kazin's "The Pilgrimage of Walker Percy," a keenly personal but not uncritical essay still representative of one of the major qualities informing the unfolding criticism.[62] This essay and William Dowie's "Walker Percy: Sensualist Thinker,"[63] a general but perceptive discussion of the delicate balance between idea and raw sensation and experience in Percy's first three novels, are included here as examples of the best statements on the typical issues addressed in the early criticism. It was in Martin Luschei's *The Sovereign Wayfarer: Walker Percy's Diagnosis of the Malaise,*[64] however, that this criticism can be said to have come of age. Percy had by this time published three novels, and the monograph's timing is indicative of the slow process of accretion and accumulation that has continued to guide the most enlightened commentary on the writer. Luschei sets out to redress the reality that, Percy being so "multifaceted" a writer, "no one to date has assembled all his writings to give anything like a measure of the man" (vii). Rightly convinced that he had to know Percy's "metaphysics before evaluating his fictional technique," Luschei proceeds to close explications of Percy's fictions by way of an intellectual biography and a second chapter that, drawing on previous criticism, discusses pertinently a range of existential ideas in order to outline the "newness" — neither Southern nor Catholic nor, finally, in any conventional sense, American — of Percy's voice. The book defined one lasting dimension of Percy criticism by analyzing Percy's first novels as a kind of Kierkegaardian trilogy, as "a gloss on Kierkegaard" (241; a footnote adds that Percy "said he would never write another like them"). Many of the best of the subsequent essays in scholarly-critical journals elaborated upon or modified Luschei's interpretations of Percy's work: his drawing on Camus's *The Stranger* and Sartre's *Nausea;* Heidegger's Alltäglichkeit ("everydayness") and inauthenticity; Gabriel Marcel's notion of intersubjectivity and religious conception of alienation as an inevitable and normal human plight, his view of man as castaway and exile — as Homo Viator — and his assessment of the dangers embedded in the postmodern self's spirit of abstraction; perhaps most especially — after Lawson — Kierkegaard's aesthetic, ethical, and religious "stages" of life, his definition of indirect communication, of experience construed as involving patterns of rotation, repetition, and return, his exploration of man's need for what he calls "the infinite passion."

Luschei's study catches Percy at mid-career, and its last chapter — "Toward a Rediscovery of Being" — speculates about just how Percy will proceed, whether with more fiction or further essays, in his exploration of man's postmodern predicament in which, citing Percy, "a new breed of person in whom the potential for catastrophe — and hope — has suddenly escalated. . . . The psychical forces presently released in the postmodern consciousness open unlimited possibilities for both destruction and liberation, for an absolute loneliness or a rediscovery of community and reconcilation" (240–41). Whatever, "His pilgrimage bears watching," Luschei concludes, "for who else do we have in America who writes superlative novels out of a considered philosophical position and a professional knowledge of medicine? And what contemporary who *is* our contemporary speaks to our predicament from a sense of his own sovereignty as this man does?" (243).

As this first phase of the criticism closed, several characteristics had declared themselves: British and continental readers saw an indelible Americanness in Percy, and his best American readers were defining him as a supremely talented translator of European ideas into facts and fictions that bore on native conditions; many of the essential terms and issues for an unfolding evaluation—such as the proper uses of Percy essays—had been set in place, and the work of Lawson and Luschei in dredging up those early essays from little-known journals had mandated their publication in collected form in *The Message in the Bottle* (1975); the intensely personal interest that Percy's thinking had aroused in many readers, academic and otherwise, was a fact in our literary landscape; and the sense of the shape of Percy's career and the direction of his writing was beginning to be formulated. The following second phase of the criticism, roughly the next decade and closing—if it can be said to have closed—with Percy's *The Second Coming*, which, though a sequel, came to be perceived as a new departure for him, builds on the first's interests in sources, influences, and terms central to his basic vision by asking where he might be headed in his pilgrimage. There are many more diverse hands at work in these years, and studies in critical journals, interviews, special issues of journals abound—and have a generally high quality; another book-length study and a first collection of essays appear, and brief mentions of Percy in large thematic studies relating him to other contemporary writers become commonplace. In a collection such as this, the purpose of which is to create at least the outlines of the critical reception and recognition, editors confront an embarrassment of riches and the limitations of space. Five of the essays reprinted here are the result, then, of incredibly difficult choices: Thomas LeClair's "The Eschatological Vision of Walker Percy's Novels" (1974), Richard Pindell's "Basking in the Eye of the Storm: The Esthetic of Loss in *The Moviegoer*," Mark Johnson's "The Search for Place in Walker Percy's Novels" (1975), Cleanth Brooks's "Walker Percy and Modern Gnosticism" (1977), and J. P. Telotte's "A Symbolic Structure for Walker Percy's Fiction" (1980).[65] Original plans to include Percy's own "Questions They Never Asked Me" (Esquire, 1977) to represent the large part played by interviews in the criticism still prevailed even after the writer's parody was made available in *Conversations with Walker Percy*.[66]

Whereas Luschei virtually discontinued his engagement with Percy's development, Lawson wrote eight more superb essays by 1983 and a ninth—"Walker Percy's Prodigal Son"—expressly for this volume. In the first of these he speculates—accurately, I think—that "in a future novel, acting upon his contention that consciousness is a collaboration, that thinking is symbolization resulting from intersubjectivity, that the self cannot know itself through symbolization, Percy will create a new first-person narration that will offer a radical complexity—and truthfulness—to the rendering of consciousness in fiction."[67] He touches here on the interests of Simone Vauthier in the complexity of Percy's narrative principles, which she addressed in four essays, the most recent of which is reprinted here. Vauthier's analysis of what she calls Percy's patterns of triangulation offers up insights constituting a critique of the misreadings of various other critics.[68] Other studies appearing in scholarly journals during these years that might justifiably have a place in such a collection as this include work by Eugene Cheswick, Anthony Quagliana, Lewis P. Simpson, and Thomas LeClair.[69]

Two books—Robert Coles, *Walker Percy: An American Search* and Panthea Reid Broughton (ed.), *The Art of Walker Percy: Strategems for Being*—could not be more different from one another, and yet together they throw a stark light on the curiosity that is Walker Percy's audience—or audiences. The Harvard child psychiatrist, well-known for his five-volume *Children of Crisis* studies, is quoted on the dust-jacket: "I have relied upon Dr. Percy's ideas constantly . . . to the point that I can scarcely imagine how I would have thought about either my own life or the lives of the children, parents, teachers I have met, were he to have decided, long ago, to keep his important and instructive thoughts to himself." By no means a literary critic, Coles writes his appreciation with so much personal attachment as to be offensive to many of various critical persuasions. His real subject seems to be an impressionistic comprehension of the man behind the works—his life and values—and Coles's own abiding relationship to him. He has little to say of great freshness to the reader with formal literary or philosophical interests, but his book is a reminder that Percy's audience includes many another kind of general reader who, in an age as Gerald Graff says of *Literature Against Itself*, profits from a humanistic sensibility and sympathetic imagination that clearly finds in Percy's writing some of his own equipment for living.[70] Thoreau had to question the sanity of a mere telegraph connecting Maine and Texas; Percy has felt duty bound to object that in our telecommunicative age, when theory and technique are at a level of "sophistication" Thoreau could never have foretold, all of us seem to be talking more and both saying and hearing less and that, as our artists remind us, we seem to have lost our capacity to communicate. It might be claimed, to make use of Graff's latest title, that the transactions between Percy and Coles are acts that ring, however unorthodoxly, of a true *Professing Literature*.

Broughton's collection of fifteen essays (thirteen of them written for the volume) is designed to treat at least suggestively central themes and questions in all the Percy works then published. The essays are by no means of equal use and value, but most have at least some memorable insights and the best are indispensable statements.[71] The book has a rare quality of familiarity between writer and critics: it is "For Walker," "Each [of the contributors] is a Walker Percy fan," and Broughton's hope is that it "will find an audience not only in Percy fans and Percy students but in Walker Percy himself" (xv). Still the collection is more than true to her claim that it "assesses [not only] the charms, the achievements, the strengths" but also "the weaknesses of Percy's art" (xv). There are two points of scenic interest here. One is that Percy seems to be viewed as a Charles Dickens redivivus who can be counted on to chart his next installment in compliance with suggestions received in readers' "correspondence." And there is indeed in this question of the fullness of Percy's collaborative art a most serious subject yet unexamined. Second, if there is deep sentiment but no sentimentality in Coles's study, one suspects the presence of the latter in Broughton's collection: it is as if tender familiarity is qualified by its cousin, zealous toughness and critical overkill, in some of the essays. I refer here not just to Broughton's radical misreading in her own essay but to those of J. Gerald Kennedy, Thomas LeClair, and, if to a lesser extent, Ted R. Spivey. Kennedy's "The Sundered Self and the Riven World: *Love in the Ruins*" attacks the very heart of Percy's art and thinking when it claims that his satiric diagnosis of twentieth-century man is "the product of Percy's scientific training, his passion for ideas, and his pursuit of a 'theory of man' within the context of Christian belief, [and] comes to us finally not as the confession of a fellow-sufferer but as the clinical diagnosis of an angel orbiting the earth" (136). Regular readers of Percy will see this charge as perhaps the most unkindest cut of all, unless they consider still more damaging Thomas LeClair's accusation in "Walker Percy's Devil" that this novel is Percy's "sell-out." "More," he argues, "is philosopher Percy tempted by the literary sure thing—the futuristic and satiric adventure," and "in *Love in the Ruins* Percy tends toward popularity, edification, and conventionality of form" (167). Fortunately, William Leigh Godshalk's "Thomas More's Distorted Vision" is in effect a rebuttal of both these objections. The Tom More Godshalk sees as decidedly distinct from Percy is (though Godshalk does not use the term) the gnostic described by Cleanth Brooks in an essay reprinted in both the Broughton volume and here. Percy's analysis of the contemporary forms of gnosticism, as large as they are in his last three works, is another subject future criticism must attend to. The Broughton, Kennedy, and LeClair essays are neither the first nor the last whose insights are vitiated by a failure to locate Percy's own voice in his fiction, nor are the LeClair and the Ted R. Spivey studies the only ones in Percy criticism to refuse to grant him his données and to realize that, finally, however attentive he is to his critics, he writes what he himself is disposed to write—as if, as he has said, he were the first person to take pen in hand.

The volume's other essays are admirable and instructive. Simone

Vauthier's "Narrative Triangulation in *The Last Gentleman*" — her structuralist analysis of "the trinity of narrator, narration, and narratee — should be required reading as a clarification of Percy's handling of narrative points of view. It anticipates her "Story, Story-teller and Listener" of the present volume. Lawson's "The Fall of the House of Lamar" is a richly contextual reading that traces Percy's heightened treatment of the opposition between stoical and Christian values in *Lancelot*, and William J. Dowie's "*Lancelot* and the Search for Sin" elucidates the ways "Percy has shown us the complexity of the difficulty in reestablishing moral responsibility through the irony of a hero who, though explicitly concerned about moral irresponsibility, is himself a victim of it" (252). Martin Luschei comments on Percy's use of a cinematic device as both technique and theme in "*The Moviegoer* as Dissolve," and Max Webb ("Binx Bolling's New Orleans: Moviegoing, Southern Writing, and Father Abraham") and Richard Pindell ("Toward Home: Place, Language, and Death in *The Last Gentleman*") comment astutely on the wide and resonant meanings of Percy's depiction of place. Two essays on Percy's interest in language theory — Weldon Thornton's "Homo Loquens, Homo Symbolificus, Homo Sapiens: Walker Percy on Language" and William H. Poteat's "Reflections on Walker Percy's Theory of Language" — provide a neatly balanced and speculative assessment. Thornton's critique ends by praising Percy's attempt to "win certain basic questions about language, about meaning, about human nature back from the specialists [such as Skinner and Chomsky] who have claimed them but neglected them" (190); Poteat, more abstruse and technical, describes Percy's philosophy of language appreciatively as "*profoundly* confused (193)." His discussion of Percy's definition of humanity as distinguished dually by "*our power to speak*," our "*symbolmongering*," and our "*alienation*" and "*our feeling bad*" is lively, pertinent (216–18). His provocative thesis that Percy's contribution to a theory of man is not in "A Theory of Language," where he "is dialectically most explicit and rigorous," (194) but in "The Delta Factor," where he is more anecdotal, will lead later to what I fear is a badly mistaken and overblown book — Patricia Lewis Poteat's *Walker Percy and the Old Modern Age: Reflections on Language, Argument, and the Telling of Stories* (1985).[72]

A special issue of *The Southern Quarterly* (18 [Spring 1980]) edited by Jac Tharpe prints ten new essays focusing particularly on *The Message in the Bottle* and *Lancelot*.[73] It also includes a superb primary and secondary Percy bibliography (137–57) by Joel Weixlmann and Daniel H. Gann, a compilation that reflects the extraordinary growth of Percy criticism through 1979. This collection too has much to recommend it. It is the richest single source of statements on Percy's language theory and his aesthetics. Charles P. Bigger's "Walker Percy and the Resonance of the Word" speculates judiciously about the ways in which the novels "celebrate human strangeness" vis-à-vis the "queerness" of man and his language referred to in the subtitle of *The Message in the Bottle*. In "Art as Symbolic Action: Walker Percy's Aesthetic" Michael Pearson evaluates sensitively Percy's dramatization of his theory of symbolization in the closing action of *Lancelot*, where Percy, "no longer content with the reader's viewing genuine naming between two characters," presses him "to enter into the struggle to name his own experience" (63). And J. P. Telotte addresses a central but relatively neglected topic in "Charles Pierce and Walker Percy: From Semiotic to Narrative," an investigation of Percy's adaptations of Pierce's triadic theory that establishes what I take to be a first principle of Percy's work not yet sufficiently recognized by all his critics: for Percy, "at no time does the act of writing or using words to tell a story ever become the major concern of his narratives" (77–78). Jerome C. Christenson makes a related point in "*Lancelot*: Sign for the Times," which finds that "the monstrous excellence of this book, hardly a novel," involves the reader "in a repetition of Lancelot's catastrophe, a repetition that is the limit and the possibility of readerly action and knowledge" (119). The whole issue of the extraordinary burdens Percy loads upon his reader is one that will surely provoke further critical comment; in this direction lies one of the major clarifications yet to be made fully.

Likewise readable and typical of another strain in Percy criticism is Corinne Dale's "*Lancelot* and the Medieval Quests of Sir Lancelot and Dante," which argues engagingly that Percy's network of allusions to myth and romance informs the book's strategy of silence in the conclusion. Another essay, part Christenson and part Dale, is Richard H. Brinkmeyer, Jr.'s "Percy's Bludgeon: Message and Narrative Strategy," which compares Percy to Flannery O'Connor in his willingness to assault his readers' "rational sensibilities to prepare them for the larger Christian vision that permeates" his fiction (80). Though the issue he addresses is a real one, many readers, friend and foe alike, will find Brinkmeyer's Percy coercively didactic and bent on edification. Another essay in this vein, Susan S. Kissel's "Voices in the Wilderness: The Prophets of O'Connor, Percy, and Powers," must be mentioned, regrettably, only because it is another misreading that unconscionably equates the views of Percy himself with those of his very sick protagonist Lance. Percy's sense of place has been a continuing fascination, and John Edward Hardy's "Percy and Place: Some Beginnings and Endings" is an attempt, not vigorous enough, to survey the extent to which Percy's opening-scene settings predict and embody the situations of his protagonists at the ends of four novels. Cecil L. Eubanks's "Walker Percy: Eschatology and the Politics of Grace" is, as Huck Finn might say, "interesting but tough." The question of Percy's willing omissions from his novelistic contexts has been a subject of debate from time to time, and Eubanks finds Percy lacking the substance of a political component: "Percy's vision of individual authenticity or salvation or escape from the malaise is so imbued with the notion of the 'sovereign pilgrim' and so highly critical of abstract solutions that attempts at political or social reform, institutional or revolutionary, seem by comparison to be gnostic" (127–28). Eubanks's evaluation is thoughtful, complex — but where he says "politics" he seems to mean "utopian politics," and he overlooks Percy's insistently communal intentions. And besides, the Percy he writes of may be one who agrees with the Robert Frost who said that politics is merely an expression about grievances, poetry an expression of grief. The collection's most immediately rewarding study is Lawson's "Moviegoing in *The Moviegoer*," in which he carefully tracks Binx's movies seen and actors and actresses referred to in countering Kazin's view that Percy's title is misleading in establishing moviegoing as a primary unity in the novel: in the end "Binx Bolling has come out of the movies, to chance acting himself" (40).

The publication of *The Second Coming* occasioned still another special issue on Percy, this one of *Delta* (13 [November 1981]), at Université Paul Valerie in Montpellier, France, and coedited by Ben Forkner and J. Gerald Kennedy. It can be recommended for five of its eight essays and its bibliography, which is complete on primary sources and usefully selective on the criticism. From that issue J. Gerald Kennedy's "The Semiotics of Memory: Suicide in *The Second Coming*" is reprinted here. In "*Love in the Ruins*: Percy's Metaphysical Thriller" Max Webb points out "how thoroughly Percy understood, explored, and exploited the literary conventions of a particular, recognizable, popular genre" to create a work that "fittingly develops from the interest in popular culture evident in *The Moviegoer*" and "fittingly leads to *Lancelot*, a new confabulation of disparate literary genres" (66). Lawson's "Tom More: Cartesian Physician" is a penetrating analysis of Percy's protagonist as at once gnostic and Cartesian, at once Don Juan and Faust, this novel being the deepest investigation Percy has made into the "idolatries" of scientific humanism. His is one of the essays that will provide a basis for critiques on Percy's sequel study of More in *The Thanatos Syndrome*, in which the phenomena of institutionally approved euthanasia for infants and elderly on the one hand and systematic child molestation on the other make the Gerry Rehab clinic of *Love in the Ruins* look innocuous. In "Violence and Mimesis in *Lancelot*" Simone Vauthier employs Rene Girard's theory of mimetism to construct an intricate analysis: Lancelot's abortive efforts to overcome the "undifferentiation" of his world by resorting to his homemade movies in order to expose the pornography that has invaded his Belle Isle home lead him, instead, only to achieve the novel's ultimate pornography. "Walker Percy: An Interview" by the editors has since been reprinted in Lawson and Kramer's *Conversations with Walker Percy*.

The criticism since 1980 has taken for granted that Percy's works have been accepted into the canon of our most serious literature, and it oftentimes has both the sort of contextuality and specialization that mature commentary always possesses. It is also recognizable as something of a growth industry and prone, like others, to a certain amount of repetition and, here and there, a tad too little insight or a straining after originality. But in general it has the quality of continuing dialogue that has generated real and lively differences of opinion proving that Percy's works offer up an enormous amount worth talking about. Two general studies, for example, confirm Percy's preeminence among Southern writers. Thomas Daniel Young's *The Past in the Present: A Thematic Study of Modern Southern Fiction*[74] (Baton Rouge: Louisiana State University Press, 1981) tests the thesis of Lewis P. Simpson's *The Dispossessed Garden*[75] (Athens: University of Georgia Press, 1975) that after World War II the Southern renaissance, entering a second phase, found writers no longer, like their forebears Faulkner, Tate, Warren, Welty, and O'Connor, struggling to rediscover viable meanings in a viable past but abandoning that search in favor of exclusively existential presuppositions the effect of which is that "the literature produced in the South has lost its unique regional flavor" (xvi). The freshness of Young's "Intimations of Mortality: Walker Percy's *The Moviegoer*" seems severely limited by his singular design "to demonstrate the validity of my thesis" (xvii). Of more immediate purpose in explicating Percy is J. Madison Davis's "Walker Percy's *Lancelot*: The Shakespearean Threads."[76] Davis tracks Percy's allusions to Shakespeare and others sensitively if not exhaustively to show that his purpose (and here lies a counterstatement to Young's hard-driving thesis) is to dramatize "a character and a society tangled in a web of mythologies" (171). And Rowland A. Sherrill puts *Love in the Ruins* in the much larger context of "The Bible and Twentieth-Century American Fiction."[77] Throughout the 1970s and after, influence studies and contextual ones in scholarly journals have been steady fare: essays on Percy's drawing from Dante, T. S. Eliot, Doestoyevski, Camus, and Sartre, on points of comparison between Percy and Hemingway and Faulkner, most of all, Flannery O'Connor. At their best they issue in insights such as Mary G. Land's "Three Max Gottliebs: Lewis's, Dreiser's, and Walker Percy's View of the Mechanist-Vitalist Controversy," and Sally McFague's "The Parabolic in Faulkner, O'Connor, and Percy,"[78] which we reprint here as representative of the type.

Whereas most of these contexts are expansive in that they enlarge the range of Percy's interests and references, that of Robert H. Brinkmeyer, Jr., *Three Catholic Writers of the Modern South*[79] rather contracts and artificializes at the same time in grouping Percy with only Tate and Gordon; as in his earlier essay Brinkmeyer finds Percy elementally didactic, and here he asserts insistently, without justification, that even "Binx has become a believing Catholic" (133) by the the epilogue. The way for Brinkmeyer's views had been more than prepared for by Jac Tharpe's 1983 Twayne Authors Series monograph, *Walker Percy*. That Percy criticism is in a third phase now — of revaluation and reinterpretation, a going back round again to earlier works through insights offered by studies of the later — is evidenced, sadly, in Tharpe's radical revisionism. For Tharpe "misinterpretation" of Percy's work began on a grand scale with the National Book Award citation for *The Moviegoer*, the most important "misapprehension" being "the failure to see that the novel was by a Roman Catholic novelist writing about immorality" and "attempting to recall the nation (not the irrevocably lost world) back to God, much as the American Puritans wished to do with more naive and sanguine hope" (preface). Consequently, he contends, the criticism since 1962 "seems to derive from the false hopes that he encouraged by the manner of his first novel" so that "Disappointment with his latest novel, *The Second Coming*, derives for the most part from the failure to realize that Percy's subjects were never rebellion and philosophy or epistemology but religion" [vi]. One senses that Tharpe is correct when he finds that Percy's fifth novel "quite as neatly rounds out a career as if it had been designed for that purpose back in the fifties when Percy was trying to sort out the differences between his own romantic self and his cultural interests" [v]. But the series of judgments that has *The Moviegoer* "a somewhat pretentious edifying discourse" (46) and Percy always verging on being an evangelical tractarian makes the study a terribly reductive, monistic one; Tharpe's footnotes and very thin bibliography make clear that he has not availed himself of much of the range of the criticism; and, perhaps because of the Twayne format, his chapters are too broken up into discontinuous mini-essays on discrete topics.

Still, we now have at least several versions of Percy, and Tharpe's is only one recent title that points to the problematic reception Percy faces in various quarters as a religious writer. If Tharpe seems to hedge uneasily in his assessment, Harold Bloom does not. In his *Modern Critical Views: Walker Percy*,[80] Bloom's introduction (1–7) has it that "*The Moviegoer* alone of Percy's fictions, to date, is a permanent American book" and that "the waste of Percy's authentic talents is a lamentable instance of art yielding to moralism, of storytelling subverted by religious nostalgias" (3). The quickness with which religious belief is relegated to the status of a nostalgia is moralistically peremptory here, the judgment shorn of any capacity for suspension of belief or disbelief. And the sentiment makes for a curious volume. The two reviews and eight essays included are all reprints, and six of these latter are from books and thus already easily available: Tony Tanner's very early statement, a chapter from Luschei, the Pindell and Vauthier essays in Broughton and the Christenson one from Tharpe's *Art & Ethics*, and a chapter from Patricia Poteat. Though several of the essays do go against the grain of Bloom's response (Luschei, Pindell, Vauthier, Poteat) and thus create incoherence rather than dialectic, the collection's bias makes his claim that it is "the best criticism published upon the novels" (vii) seem farfetched. The bibliography, for example, listing just eighty-seven items roughly forty of which are reviews, ignores also, like the contents, even more of the finest essays published in scholarly journals than does Tharpe's Twayne monograph.

Bloom's collection closes with Poteat's "Percy as Storyteller," the second chapter of her *Walker Percy and the Old Modern Age,* a longer study whose essential thesis is intricate in part but repetitious and belabored. Percy succeeds brilliantly at every turn in all of his novels, she says, but fails at every point in his philosophical essays taking up the same epistemological issues. The reason: "his conceptual vision becomes progressively more blurred as his style and vocabulary become progressively less anecdotal or narrative and more analytical and abstract" (2). Whereas the characters in all the novels are compelling because immersed in "the concrete particulars of persons in predicaments," Percy's voice in the essays sounds like the plague of "Anyone Anywhereness" he takes such pains to have his fictional characters avoid. Poteat's thesis, like Broughton's in "Gentlemen and Fornicators," would hoist Percy on his own petard, but her errors seem larger and more real than her arguments. Metaphor seems for her to embrace only literary, "predictamental" tropes and to exclude all other words, signs, and symbols — as well as nature itself. Virtually any abstraction uttered without benefit of a novelistic or storytelling concreteness she equates with a spirit of Cartesian abstractedness. Finally, so eager is she to prove the irreversible flaw of the philosophical essay form that she does not really demonstrate her claims for the novels' unqualified successes. Surely storytelling, even for the literary critic, is only one of many modes of discourse capable of sighting truths. If not, and if Percy's own essayistic sophistication is itself to be rejected, what remains to be said of those essays like Poteat's own — unnarrative and unanecdotal themselves — except that they prove the case against themselves?

Four remaining recent books are as a whole much fresher, more balanced, and useful than these last. Given what relatively little we know about Percy's life, *Conversations with Walker Percy* (1985) makes ready at hand a potpourri of anecdote and opinion that relates the biograhical and the fictional. And Lewis Baker's *The Percys of Mississippi: Politics and Literature in the New South* (1983), though saying nothing new about Percy's own life, offers up familial and historical data that suggest that Percy's life, art, and thinking are rooted in a rich relationship, often dialectical, with ancestral values and incidents in the family saga beyond those having to do with his adoptive father's stoical virtues. Uncle Will's boyhood passion for Catholic belief, the fact that he himself had an older brother die from an accidental gunshot, the words used by Senator LeRoy Percy in addressing hostile Klansmen at a Greenville rally (108) are but a few points of family history that might lead to further clarification of Percy's conversions of facts into fictions.

Jerome Taylor's *In Search of Self: Life, Death & Walker Percy*[81] is at once the culmination of studies that have seen Percy through Kierkegaardian eyes and proof that there are several Percys because there are several Percy audiences — literary, philosophical, and religious at least by turns. Percy himself has provided one of the book's blurbs (back cover): "Quite brilliant, both in its unerring dead aim on my characters, but also in his treatment of Kierkegaard." An elaborated version of his "Walker Percy's Knights of the Hidden Awareness,"[82] the monograph has a philosophy-in-literature clarity and thoroughness. Knowledgeable about Kierkegaard himself, Taylor demonstrates Percy's keen command of existentialism. His explications of Percy's fictional situations lead to a perceptive commentary on many of Percy's characters — particularly Will Barrett and Sutter Vaught but also such minor ones, examples all of Percy's "dead," as Walter Wade, the Lovells, Doris Thigpen, Jules Cutrer, Sam Yerger, and Elgin. Most recently, William Rodney Allen's *Walker Percy: A Southern Wayfarer*[83] takes account of the best criticism, especially Lawson's, to argue persuasively that "the key to understanding Percy's 'Americanness' and 'southernness' — as well as his denial of these affinities — lies in an understanding of his tragic childhood and his consequent ambivalence toward his southern heritage" (xvi). Allen marshalls formidable evidence that Percy's works must be seen as a steady, continuous effort to "transcend the weight of his southern past" and to defeat "an inordinate number of 'fathers' " — "his literal suicidal father, his stoical, melancholy adopted father; Freud (against whom he struggled in three years of psychoanalysis); Faulkner, whose influence he has too insistently denied; and, finally, American literary precursors like Twain, Warren, and Hemingway" (xviii). One could well quarrel with the Freudian–Harold Bloomian (*The Anxiety of Influence*) term "defeat" here, but Allen's study is a superbly sensitive psychoanalytic reading that, agreeing with others but on different grounds, finds in *The Second Coming* "a sense of closure, . . . a rounding off of . . . [Percy's entire] imaginative world" (xii). Allen's chapters address thorough interpretations of each of the first five novels' father-son themes, and his strategy of viewing both the essays and the fiction as a total text unfolding only gradually is one that is pronounced in the most recent, and frequently the most perceptive, critical assessments. Still, given the number of essays appearing in scholarly journals, that criticism has not yet achieved a completely holistic reading.

Let me suggest the range of perspectives taken in the best of these essays. In "The Lebenswelt of Lancelot Lamar,"[84] Joseph P. Natoli uses Husserl, Heidegger, and Merleau-Ponty's terminology to explore for signs of hope in Lancelot's "life-world." Cleanth Brook's "The Southernness of Walker Percy"[85] treats suggestively but all too briefly Percy's deft distinctions among a variety of southern female characters. In the same issue Jan Nordby Gretlund's "Walker Percy: A Scandinavian View" (18–27) is a lively survey of Percy's reception in Norway, Sweden, and Denmark. John W. Stevenson's "Walker Percy: The Novelist as Poet"[86] is a timely reminder, in spite of its own lack of sustained close analysis, that Percy's lyricism, his vocal and visual elements of style, have been much praised but still need closer explication. Percy's radical experiment in dialogue between Lancelot and the silent Percival "provides an analogue for the relationship between author and reader which Percy strives to establish in his fiction": such is Bill Oliver's arresting conclusion in "A Manner of Speaking: Percy's *Lancelot*."[87] And in the same issue Mark Johnson gives, for one thing, a crisp answer to John Gardner (see his review of *Lancelot* reprinted here) in "*Lancelot*: Percy's Romance,"[88] a study with numerous provocative insights about Percy's formal intentions that suggest that each Percy fiction is another self-reflexive design in the basic question of how to read. The fullest treatment so far of Percy's concern with apocalypse is in Gary Ciuba's penetrating study, "The Omega Factor: Apocalyptic Visions in Walker Percy's *Lancelot*."[89] Equally insightful is John Churchill's "Walker Percy, Wittgenstein's *Tractatus*, and The Lost Self,"[90] which concludes that Percy's attack on the traditional Cartesian categories of mind / body, subject / object, immanence / transcendence is to deny — properly — "that we must in some profound sense know our *selves* before we can live our lives" (281). Finally, to pick just the best posey, since there seem to be no endings to the commentary any more than there are to Percy's fictional closures, I cite Malcolm O. Magaw's "Certitude Be Not Proud: Percy's View of Will Barrett's Extended Stay in Ambivalence,"[91] an essay that contains extrapolated answers to single-minded complaints or doubts about Percy — those of Bloom and Gardner, of Doreen Fowler, of Broughton and Poteat, of from way back now John F. Zeugner:

> The chronic incertitude of Will Barrett represents one of the many speculations offered by Percy in his novels on the idiosyncracies and diversities of the American collective consciousness. There are ironies and moral implications tied in with most of Percy's speculations, but never in a doctrinaire sense. There are questions raised, considered, tentatively answered or left unanswered, but never with an irresponsible, cavalier or hedging authorship. Indeed, Percy invites the reader to speculate along with him. In the words of Simone Vauthier, reading a Percy novel "impels us not only to participate in the construction of its meaning but to do some thinking of our own about language, about the relationship between words and things and people and being. . . . The narration leaves the reader wondering about 'what happened,' free to resonate or not to 'the unspoken word' within the written word." (88)

Thus would Percy, in creating his fictions, also create the demanding conditions for the reader's astute reading of those fictions. Magaw and Vauthier emphasize here the same idea that Oliver settles upon: "There is no such thing as a final question in Percy" (18), not, at least, within the bounds of fiction. Percy's sixth novel, *The Thanatos Syndrome*, "ends" just as its predecessors have done, on the open-ended note of positioning characters and readers alike before the need for still another new beginning — this one, for characters and readers alike, beyond the book itself. It ends, that is, at least for the reader of Jay Martin's recent masterful study, *Who Am I This Time: Uncovering the Fictive Personality*,[92] with the quiet admonition that "the profusion of fictions is central to

[both] the creativity—and the crisis—of our modern condition" and that the sole mark of Good Books is that they let us know them thoroughly enough that we can declare our freedom from them.

I am deeply grateful to the University of Missouri–Columbia Research Council for the Summer Research Fellowship awarded to me for this project. I am grateful as well to my co-editor and wife, Sue Mitchell Crowley, whose help in library research and in all editorial decisions has been indispensable to me. Both of us here thank Paul Taylor, our research assistant, Jeaneice Brewer of the University of Missouri libraries and staff members at both the Ohio State University and the University of Iowa libraries for their generous help.

The editors have silently corrected obvious errors in the reprinted essays.

J. Donald Crowley

University of Missouri–Columbia

Notes

1. "New Orleans Mon Amour," *Harper's Magazine* 237 (September 1968):80–82, 86, 88, 90; "Bourbon," *Esquire* 84 (December 1975):148–49; "The Mercy Killing," *New York Times Book Review*, 6 June 1971, 7; "The Willard Huntington Wright Murder Case," *Carolina Magazine* 64 (January 1935): 4–6; "Decline of the Western," *Commonweal* 68 (16 May 1958):181–83; "The State of the Novel: Dying Art or New Science?" *Michigan Quarterly Review* 16 (Fall 1977):359–77. For two of his most interesting reviews, see "The Fire This Time," *New York Review of Books* 4 (1 July 1965):3–5, and "Walter M. Miller, Jr.'s *A Canticle for Leibowitz*," in *Rediscoveries*, ed. David Madden (New York: Crown, 1971), 262–69. For statements on other social and political issues see "A Southern View," *America* 97 (20 July 1957):428–29; "The Southern Moderate," *Commonweal* 67 (13 December 1957):279–82; "Mississippi: The Fallen Paradise," *Harper's* 230 (April 1965):166–72. The essay on psychiatry is from *America* 96 (January 1957):391–93, 415–18.

2. "American Letter," *Literature* 2 (9 April 1898):422–32.

3. Cleanth Brooks, "Walker Percy and Modern Gnosticism," *Southern Review* 13 (1977):687. The essay is reprinted here.

4. Percy's working title—"How to Make Love in the Ruins"—suggests that he has more than once been tempted to exploit the possibilities of the instruction manual.

5. "Author's Note," *The Message in the Bottle* (New York: Farrar, Straus and Giroux, 1975), [vii]. Listed here are the essays in the order of their original appearance in that collection and the sources of their original publication: "The Delta Factor," *Southern Review* 11 (January 1975):29–64; "The Loss of the Creature," *Forum* 2 (Fall 1958):6–14; "Metaphor as Mistake," *Sewanee Review* 66 (Winter 1958); "The Man on the Train: Three Existential Modes," *Partisan Review* 23 (Fall 1956):478–94; "Notes for a Novel about the End of the World," *Katallagete* (Winter 1967–68):7–14; "The Message in the Bottle," *Thought* 34 (Autumn 1959):405–33; "The Mystery of Language," titled "The Act of Naming," *Psychiatry* 35 (February 1972):1–19; "The Symbolic Structure of Interpersonal Process," *Psychiatry* 24 (February 1961):39–52; "Culture: The Antinomy of the Scientific Method," *New Scholasticism* 32 (October 1958):443–75; "Semiotic and a Theory of Knowledge," *Modern Schoolman* 34 (May 1957):225–46; "Symbol, Consciousness, and Intersubjectivity," *Journal of Philosophy* 55 (17 July 1958):631–41; "Symbol as Hermeneutic in Existentialism," *Philosophy and*

Phenomenological Research 16 (June 1956):522–30; "A Theory of Language," first printed in *The Message in the Bottle.*

6. Percy had burned hundreds of pages of his original draft of *The Last Gentleman*, in which he had tried to treat the assassination of President Kennedy, and so had been forced to rewrite most of the novel. The shift in the subject of *The Second Coming* was suggested to Percy, as he told me several years ago, by the appearance on his doorstep of an old friend who had days earlier left his wife after a church service several states away and, in an amnesiac condition, hopped aboard a bus that took him to Covington, Louisiana.

7. This is the one book by Percy that has so far failed to prompt developed commentary beyond the reviews.

8. The best study of Percy's interest in this subliterary form is Max Webb, "*Love in the Ruins*: Percy's Metaphysical Thriller," *Delta* (Montpellier, France) 13 (November 1981):55–66.

9. In this biographical sketch I rely on the facts made available in three sources: Martin Luschei, *The Sovereign Wayfarer: Walker Percy's Diagnosis of the Malaise* (Baton Rouge: Louisiana State University Press, 1972); Robert Coles, *Walker Percy: An American Search* (Boston: Little, Brown & Co., 1978); and Lewis Baker, *The Percys of Mississippi: Politics and Literature in the New South* (Baton Rouge: Louisiana State University Press, 1983).

10. Too infrequently noted in the criticism is the fact that Percy's interest in language stems in some large part from his second daughter's having been born deaf. See Coles, *An American Search*, 72.

11. "The Charterhouse," as Percy called the first of these, used a country club as the cultus of its contemporary world; the second, untitled, focused on a dying tubercular patient in a sanitarium at Lake Saranac (see Luschei, *Sovereign Wayfarer*, 14–15). I have read this second effort in typescript; curiously, it has in it something of the plot — and the sensibility — of Hawthorne's *Fanshawe* and few hints indeed of *The Moviegoer.*

12. I am indebted to Mary Alice Moore of Farrar, Straus and Giroux for verifying this information.

13. See Alfred Kazin, "The Pilgrimage of Walker Percy," reprinted in this book, for a brief account of these events.

14. Hyman's review is reprinted in this book.

15. "To Restore a Fragmented Image," *Sewanee Review* 69 (Autumn 1961):691–700.

16. "New Fiction," *Punch* 244 (17 April 1963):573–74.

17. "Self-Sacrifice," (London) *Times Literary Supplement* 29 (March 1963):221.

18. *America* 105 (17 June 1961):448.

19. "Melted into Air," *Reporter* 36 (9 February 1967):61–62.

20. "The Insulted and the Injured," *New York Review of Books* 7 (28 July 1966):23–24.

21. "New Novels," *Punch* 252 (8 February 1967):210.

22. "Beyond Initiation: Some Recent Novels," *Yale Review* 56 (Autumn 1966):131–38.

23. "A Watcher, A Listener, a Wanderer," *New York Times Book Review* 26 (June 1966):5.

24. "Lapsed from Grace," (London) *Times Literary Supplement*, 1 October 1971, 1165.

25. "Fiction Chronicle," *Hudson Review* 24 (Fall 1971):526–40.

26. "Mr. Percy's Positive Statement," *Wall Street Journal*, 17 May 1971, 12.

27. "The Good Word: Walker Percy Redivivus," *New York Times Book Review*, 4 July 1971, 2.

28. Anon., "Notes on Current Books," *Virginia Quarterly Review* 47 (Summer 1971):xcvi.

29. Anon., "Reservations," *Antioch Review* 31 (Summer 1971):283.

30. "Apocalypses and Other Ills," *New York Times*, 15 May 1971, 29.

31. *Sewanee Review* 81 (Autumn 1973):839–44. For a rejoinder, see Brainard Cheney, "Correspondence," *Sewanee Review* 82 (Winter 1974):194–96.

32. "On Man the Sad Talker," *National Review* 27 (12 September, 1975):1000–2.

33. "Walker Percy's Bicentennial Message," *America* 133 (25 October 1975):256–58.

34. "For Walker Percy Man is the Naming Animal," *New York Times Book Review*, 8 June 1975, 6–7.

35. "Camelot Lost," *New York Times*, 17 February 1977, 37.

36. *New Republic* 176 (5 February 1977):32–34.

37. Peter S. Prescott, "Unholy Knight," *Newsweek* 89 (28 February 1977):73–74; Philip French, "Communing with Camus," (London) *Times Literary Supplement*, 28 October 1977, 1259; Robert D. Daniel, "Walker Percy's *Lancelot*: Secular Raving and Religious Silence," *Southern Review* 14 (Winter 1978):186–94.

38. "Lay Preacher," *Newsweek*, 6 July 1980, 66.

39. "Deep Hidden Meaning," *Nation* 231 (16–23 August 1980):157–58.

40. William Koon, *South Carolina Review* 13 (1981):109–11; John Romano, "A Novel of Powerful Pleasures," *New York Times Book Review*, 29 June 1980, 1, 28, 31; Daphne Merkin, "Lost Souls," *New Leader*, 28 July 1980, 15–16; Robert Towers, "To the Greenhouse," *New York Review of Books*, 14 August 1980, 39–41; Benjamin DeMott, "A Thinking Man's Kurt Vonnegut," *Atlantic Monthly* 246 (July 1980):81–84.

41. Percy thinks of the novel as a complete departure from his earlier fiction because of its joyfully happy ending: "It seems to me that these two characters achieve their lives in a way no other characters I've written about have. I consider this my first unalienated novel." See James Atlas, "A Portrait of Mr. Percy," *New York Times Book Review*, 29 June 1980, 1, 30, 31.

42. Dannye Romine, "Walker Percy Writes to Help Us Recognize Our Malaise," *Charlotte* (North Carolina) *Observer*, 5 June 1983, 10.

43. Anon., *Newsweek*, 13 June 1983, 72–73.

44. "Aliens," *Time*, 20 June 1983, 78–79.

45. "Travels with My Angst," *New Republic*, 11 July 1983, 38–39.

46. "Condemnation and Catharsis," *Commonweal*, 17 June 1983, 373.

47. "Books of the Times," *New York Times*, 1 April 1987, 19.

48. "The Devil's Own Century," *New York Times Book Review*, 5 April 1987, 1, 22–23.

49. "Reflections of America," *Chicago Tribune*, 29 March 1987, 1, 5.

50. "To Live and Die in Dixie," *Newsweek*, 16 April 1987, 76.

51. "Communing with Camus," (London) *Times Literary Supplement*, 28 October 1977, 1259.

52. The wag is Gene Lyons, "Deep Hidden Meaning," *Nation* 231 (16–23 August 1980):158.

53. The lateness with which American critics picked up on Tanner's thesis is indicated by the date of Panthea Reid Broughton's astute "Walker Percy and the Myth of the Innocent Eye," *Literary Romanticism in America* 20 (1979):94–108, which concludes that if Tanner is correct in fixing on "a continuing American tendency to value the innocent eye, . . . Percy does not continue it, [but] satirizes it and thus takes his place in a long line of Christian satirists whose art judges the world and its devices and finds them wanting" (108). For still more recent attempts to qualify Tanner's reading, see my "Walker Percy: The Continuity of the Complex Fate" in the present volume and William Rodney Allen, *Walker Percy: A Southern Wayfarer* (Jackson: University Press of Mississippi, 1986), the fullest treatment yet of Percy's quite self-conscious allusions to the work of various American predecessors.

54. *Recherches Anglaises et Americaines*, no. 4, 98–115.

55. Besides the criticism already mentioned those exceptions are: Michael T. Blouin, "The Novels of Walker Percy," *Xavier University Studies* 6 (February 1967):29–42, for his analysis of Percy's use of family as symbolic matrix in his first two novels; Anselm Atkins, "Walker Percy and Post-Modern Search," *Centennial Review* 12 (1968):73–95, for his clarification of earlier critical efforts to define the Kierkegaardian terms of Binx's search; Richard Lehan, "The Way Back: Redemption in the Novels of Walker Percy," *Southern Review* 4 (1968):306–19, if only as an example of the critical difficulties of being unaware that Percy is indeed using Kierkegaard's terms in describing his protagonists' actions; and Ellen Douglas, *Walker Percy's "The Last Gentleman": Introduction and Commentary* (New York: Seabury Press, 1969), largely for its biographical sketch.

56. *Texas Studies in Literature and Language* 11 (1969):867–900; *Southern Literary Journal* 3 (1970):5–31; *South Atlantic Bulletin* 37 (1972):58–63; *Southern Review* 6 (197):990–1010.

57. *Commonweal* 64 (6 July 1956):342–44.

58. See "Walker Percy as Martian Visitor," *Southern Literary Journal* 8 (1976):102–13; "The Gnostic Vision in *Lancelot*," *Renascence* 32 (Autumn 1979):52–64; "Walker Percy's Silent Character," *Mississippi Quarterly* 33 (Spring 1980):123–40; "William Alexander Percy, Walker Percy and the Apocalypse," *Modern Age* 24 (Fall 1980):396–406; "The Allegory of the Cave and *The Moviegoer*," *South Carolina Review* 13 (Spring 1981):13–18; "Time and Eternity in *The Moviegoer*," *Southern Humanities Review* 41 (Spring 1982):129–41; "Gnosis and Time in *Lancelot*," *Papers on Language and Literature* 19 (Winter 1983):72–86.

59. "From Facts to Fiction," *Book Week* 4 (25 December 1966): 6, 9; "Notes for a Novel about the End of the World," *Katallagete* (Winter 1967–68):7–14; "The State of the Novel: Dying Art or New Science?" *Michigan Quarterly Review* 16 (Fall 1977):359–73; "The Diagnostic Novel," *Harper's* 272 (June 1986):39–45.

60. Ashley Brown, "An Interview with Walker Percy," *Shenandoah* 18 (Spring 1967): 3–10; Carlton Cremeens, "Walker Percy, The Man and the Novelist: An Interview," *Southern Review* 4 (Spring 1968): 271–90; John C. Carr, "An Interview with Walker Percy," *Georgia Review* 25 (Fall 1971): 317–32.

61. *Conversations with Walker Percy* (Jackson: University Press of Mississippi, 1985).

62. "The Pilgrimage of Walker Percy," *Harper's* 242 (1971):81–86.

63. "Walker Percy: Sensualist Thinker," *Novel* 6 (1972):52–65.

64. *The Sovereign Wayfarer: Walker Percy's Diagnosis of the Malaise* (Baton Rouge: Louisiana State University Press, 1972).

65. Thomas LeClair, "The Eschatological Vision of Walker Percy's Novels," *Renascence* 26 (1974):115–22; Richard Pindell, "Basking in the Eye of the Storm: The Esthetic of Loss in *The Moviegoer*," *Boundary* 2 4 (1975):219–30; Mark Johnson, "The Search for Place in Walker Percy's Novels," *Southern Literary Journal* 8 (1975):53–81; Cleanth Brooks, "Walker Percy and Modern Gnosticism," *Southern Review* 13 (1977):677–87; J. P. Telotte, "A Symbolic Structure for Walker Percy's Fiction," *Modern Fiction Studies* 26 (1980):227–40.

66. Walker Percy, "Questions They Never Asked Me," *Esquire* 88 (1977):170, 172, 184, 186, 188, 190, 193–94. See my review of the *Conversations* volume in *Studies in American Fiction* 14 (Autumn 1986):241–43.

67. "Walker Percy's Indirect Communications," *Texas Studies in Literature and Language* 11 (1969):867–900.

68. Besides her "Narrative Triangulation in *The Last Gentleman*," in Panthea Reid Broughton, ed., *The Art of Walker Percy: Stratagems for Being* (Baton Rouge: Lousiana State University Press, 1979), 69–95, see also her "Narrative Triangle and Triple Alliance: A Look at *The Moviegoer*," in *Les Américanistes: New French Criticism on Modern American Fiction*,

ed. Ira D. Johnson and Christiane Johnson (Port Washington, N.Y.: Kennikat Press, 1978), 71–93.

69. Eugene Cheswick, "Novel's Ending and the World's End: The Fiction of Walker Percy," *Hollins Critic* 10 (1973):1–11; Anthony Quaglia, "Existential Modes in *The Moviegoer*, *Research Studies* (Washington State University) 45 (1977):214–23; Lewis P. Simpson, "The Southern Aesthetic of Memory," *Tulane Studies in English* 23 (1978):207–27; Thomas LeClair, "Death and Black Humor," *Critique* 17 (1975):5–40.

70. Gerald Graff, *Literature Against Itself: Literary Ideas in Modern Society* (Chicago: University of Chicago Press, 1979). For a fine review of Coles, see Lewis A. Lawson, "Walker Percy's Wonder-Working Powers," *Southern Literary Journal* 12 (Fall 1979):109–14. See also my discussion of Walt Whitman's remarks on the nature of an authentic American literature and the proper burdens of the American reader in "Walker Percy: The Continuity of the Complex Fate" in the present volume.

71. The weaker essays strike me as being Janet Hobbs's "Binx Bolling and the Stages on Life's Way," which has little new to say about Kierkegaard's aesthetic, ethical, and religious stages and flies in the face of the statements both by Percy and others that Binx simply skips past the ethical phase; Ted R. Spivey's "Walker Percy and the Archetypes," an otherwise provocative essay which becomes too insistently prescriptive and peremptory and not a little jargon-ridden in seeming to urge Percy into a pursuit of Jung's archetypes of mandala and shadow; and Panthea Reid Broughton's own "Gentlemen and Fornicators: *The Last Gentleman* and a Bisected Reality," the thesis of which is that "Walker Percy places his faith in triads, but speaks in twosomes" (114) — surely a radical misreading arising out of a simplistic confusion of Percy's voice with those of his characters. That it is printed immediately following Vauthier's essay makes its argument the more astonishing.

72. Patricia Lewis Poteat, *Walker Percy and the Old Modern Age* (Baton Rouge: Louisiana State University Press, 1985).

73. The issue was reprinted as *Walker Percy: Art and Ethics* (Jackson: University Press of Mississippi, 1980) with the omission of Randolph Bates's "Writing about Percy: Reviews" (158–63) and its critiques of the Coles and Broughton volumes.

74. Thomas Daniel Young, *The Past in the Present: A Thematic Study of Modern Southern Fiction* (Baton Rouge: Louisiana State University Press, 1981).

75. Lewis P. Simpson, *The Dispossessed Garden* (Athens, Ga.: University of Georgia Press, 1975.)

76. In Philip C. Kolin, ed., *Shakespeare and Southern Writers: A Study in Influence* (Jackson: University Press of Mississippi, 1985). The collection includes essays on eight southern writers.

77. In Giles Gunn, ed., *The Bible and American Arts and Letters* (Philadelphia: Fortress Press, 1983), 58–59.

78. Mary G. Land, "Three Max Gottliebs: Lewis's, Dreiser's, and Walker Percy's View of the Mechanist-Vitalist Controversy," *Studies in the Novel* 15 (Winter 1983):314–41; Sally McFague, "The Parabolic in Faulkner, O'Connor, and Percy," *Notre Dame English Journal* 15 (Spring 1983):49–66.

79. Robert H. Brinkmeyer, Jr., *Three Catholic Writers of the Modern South* (Jackson: University Press of Mississippi, 1985).

80. Harold Bloom, ed., *Modern Critical Views: Walker Percy* (New York: Chelsea House Publishers, 1986).

81. Jerome Taylor, *In Search of Self: Life, Death & Walker Percy* (Cambridge, Mass.: Cowley Publications, 1986).

82. Jerome Taylor, "Walker Percy's Knights of the Hidden Awareness," *Anglican Theological Review* 56 (1974):125–51.

83. William Rodney Allen, *Walker Percy: A Southern Wayfarer* (Baton Rouge: Louisiana State University Press, 1986).

84. Joseph P. Natoli, "The Lebenswelt of Lancelot Lamar," *Journal of Phenomenological Psychology* 12 (Spring 1981): 63–74.

85. Cleanth Brooks, "The Southernness Of Walker Percy," *South Carolina Review* 13 (1981):34–38.

86. John W. Stevenson, "Walker Percy: The Novelist as Poet," *Southern Review* 17 (Winter 1981):164–74.

87. Bill Oliver, "A Manner of Speaking: Percy's *Lancelot*," *Southern Literary Journal* 15 (Spring 1983):7–18.

88. Mark Johnson, "*Lancelot*: Percy's Romance," *Southern Literary Journal* 15 (Winter 1983):19–28.

89. Gary Ciuba, "The Omega Factor: Apocalyptic Visions in Walker Percy's *Lancelot*," *American Literature* 57 (March 1985):98–112.

90. John Churchill, "Walker Percy, Wittgenstein's *Tractatus*, and the Lost Self," *Soundings* 67 (Fall 1984):267–82.

91. Malcolm O. Magaw, "Certitude Be Not Proud: Percy's View of Will Barrett's Extended Stay in Ambivalence," *Southern Quarterly* 25 (Winter 1987):76–88.

92. Jay Martin, *Who Am I This Time? Uncovering the Fictive Personality* (New York: W. W. Norton & Co., 1988).

REVIEWS

Moviegoing and Other Intimacies

Stanley Edgar Hyman*

I missed *The Moviegoer* by Walker Percy . . . when it came out last spring. It was Percy's first published novel, although he was 45 and had written two earlier novels, unpublished and, he says, "very bad." I was not the only person who missed it, since Knopf did not push the book very hard, reportedly because the head of the firm was "baffled and somewhat irritated" by it. When *The Moviegoer* received the National Book Award as the "most distinguished" work of fiction published in 1961, there were howls of rage, as though the umpire had made a bum call against the home team.

I am not fully able to evaluate the choice, since I have not read all the 11 books nominated. Of the ones I know, some seem unsuitable because too successful to need the award, such as J. D. Salinger's *Franny and Zooey*, others the work of promising young writers who have not yet demonstrated their staying power, such as Joan Williams' *The Morning and the Evening*. In my view, the award should recognize a distinguished book by the author of a body of work deserving recognition. On that basis, had I been a judge, I should have voted for William Maxwell's *The Chateau* or Isaac Bashevis Singer's *The Spinoza of Market Street*. But I have now read Percy's novel, and there is no question but that the judges — Lewis Gannett, Herbert Gold and Jean Stafford — made a responsible and defensible choice. Probably the solution is, as Lewis Nichols suggested in the New York *Times*, to turn the award formally into a first-novel prize, or else to have two awards, as was done once in the past, one for the year's most distinguished work of fiction and one for the best first novel.

In any case, in calling *The Moviegoer* to the attention of a wider public, the National Book Award has performed a service. Like George P. Elliott's *David Knudsen*, Percy's book is a detailed pathology of modern neurosis, but unlike Elliott's it embodies its pathology in a realized fictional form. The book's narrator-protagonist, Jack Bolling, is a young Louisiana stockbroker of good family, undergoing very considerable emotional difficulties. Although he has a wallet full of identity cards, he

*Reprinted by permission from the *New Leader* 45 (30 April 1962):23–24. © 1962 by the American Labor Conference on International Affairs, Inc.

has no sense of identity, and much of the time he has no sense of inhabiting a real place at a real time. Only four activities give him any illusion of meaningfulness, and he has reduced his life to them: "I spend my entire time working, making money, going to movies and seeking the company of women." "What do you think is the purpose of life—to go to the movies and dally with every girl that comes along?" his aunt asks him. "No," Jack answers, but only because he doesn't think that there is any purpose of life.

Women stir him, particularly their beautiful bottoms or "splendid butts," and he spends quite a lot of time chasing them, but he does not appear anxious to catch any. When, after an elaborate campaign, a girl fends him off, he seems more relieved than not. "The truth is that nowadays one is hardly up to it," he concludes unhappily at another point. In an experience that Percy has said is autobiographical, Jack spent his college years "propped on the front porch of the fraternity house, bemused and dreaming." He suffers from what he calls "invincible apathy," combined with periodic severe depression. He is obsessed with death, not the fear of death, but the sense "that everyone is dead," himself particularly. It is visibly the wish for death, and Jack thinks of "the grandest coup of all: to die."

On this neurotic disturbance Jack erects a sizable mystique. One of its features is the concept of "the search," which transforms his aimless and apathetic rambling into a quest for identity and value. Another is a concept of "repetition," a deliberate "re-enactment of past experience toward the end of isolating the time segment which has lapsed." The third is a concept of "rotation," defined as "the experiencing of the new beyond the expectation of the experiencing of the new."

All of these heady ideas result in moviegoing. "The movies are onto the search," Jack says, "but they screw it up." Seeing a western film in the same seat in the same theater in which one saw a western film 14 years before, in the same season, is "a successful repetition." Seeing a western film in the company of the invalid half-brother one loves *and* a girl one is pursuing, a "fine big sweet piece," is "a good rotation." Once Jack drove into a Louisiana village to see a movie in which the characters drive into a Louisiana village to see a movie, a triumphant "repetition within a rotation."

Jack sees all experience, even the death of his brother, in terms of remembered movies, and he acts in the stances of movie heroes. Movies "certify" the reality of places they show. Jack goes to see them alone, or if he goes with anyone, "it is understood that we do not speak during the movie." In his mind, Jack explains and justifies his behavior in dialogues with movie actors. He sometimes identifies a person he meets as "a moviegoer, though of course he does not go to the movies."

Pleased to learn "that a significantly large percentage of solitary moviegoers are Jews," Jack becomes a metaphoric Jew: "Anyhow it is true that I am Jewish by instinct. We share the same exile. The fact is, however,

I am more Jewish than the Jews I know. They are more at home than I am. I accept my exile." Jack insists that his life is so unreal that he goes to the movies to find reality, but his descriptions of the experience make it clear what special reality he is searching for, what major event requires repetition — it is the uterine state, and the book's title translates as *The Womb-Returner*.

The heroine of *The Moviegoer* is Jack's cousin Kate Cutrer, a thin girl with a "marvelously ample" behind. She is more desperately neurotic than he, although she repeatedly denies it, insisting "You're like me, but worse. Much worse," or "You're nuttier than I am." After an automobile accident in which she was unhurt and her fiancé was killed, Kate had a breakdown. Now she is a secret wino and an addict of barbiturates. Where Jack is sunk in apathy, Kate has periods of despair and terror, where he longs dreamily for death, she has true suicidal impulses, and makes a try at it once in the book.

The Moviegoer is more than pathology because Jack and Kate are not only case histories but complex human beings. Percy's talent for the creation of character brings the minor characters just as vividly alive: gentle Uncle Jules, "whose victory in the world is total and unqualified"; bluestocking Aunt Emily, who expects more of Jack because he and she used to read the *Crito* together: Jack's formidable, beautiful secretary Sharon Kinkaid, a comic masterpiece; half-brother Lonnie in his wheelchair, like Jack "a moviegoer."

The book's language is sometimes quite fancy, as when Jack's neck manifests "eschatological prickling," or a train corridor has a "gelid hush" and "the peculiar gnosis of trains." Some sentences are elaborately Jamesian. For the most part, however, the language is spare and effective, and Percy has a superb ear for speech. He hears a Negro servant turn the word "is" into a diphthong "Harlem-style," or Alabama-raised Sharon protest "Ho no, you son," report "I said nayo indeed," and euphemize "God damn" as "Got dog."

Percy's use of symbolism shows a sure touch. The symbol that dominates the book is New Orleans Carnival Week culminating in the Mardi Gras parade, and its monstrous and mechanical gaiety is the background against which the drama of neurotic quest is performed. Some lesser symbols are subtler yet equally powerful: the elderly married authors of a *Technique in Marriage* manual, imagined "at their researches, solemn as a pair of brontosauruses, their heavy old freckled limbs twined about one another" — a vision of the enlightened joylessness of our world; Aunt Emily lecturing Jack with a paperknife in her hand, its tip bent by him as a child — an image of the inclined tree in the bent twig; a deserted ocean wave in a playground, on which Jack often sits, that is recognizably some life rhythm that has been stilled in him; Kate's nervous habit of tearing at the flesh around her thumbnail, which might as readily be her heart.

More than character, language or symbol, the strength of *The Moviegoer* is its clear strong line of action. Jack's Aunt Emily, Kate's stepmother, puts him in the essentially false and crippling role of Kate's keeper. He breaks out of it by taking her to Chicago and going to bed with her on the train, the two of them just barely managing it under "the cold and fishy eye of the malaise," both terrified, both shaking like leaves. On their return, Jack stands up to his aunt and answers her question, "Were you intimate with Kate?" with the marvelous phrase, "Not very." He is then free to create a valid relationship with her, a marriage in which they pool their neuroses democratically. At the end of the book, with Jules and Lonnie sacrificially dead, there is some hope that each, with the help of the other, will be better able to function in the world. At least they have no illusions about how hard the world really is.

There are flaws in *The Moviegoer*, certainly. One character, Sam Yerger, a figure of superhuman wisdom who imitates Amos 'n' Andy, is preposterous from start to finish, and a mistake. Sometimes Jack's philosophy, as when he meditates on "the genie-soul," is just blather. There are occasional pretentious attempts to make Jack's search seem not neurotic but deeply spiritual, along the lines of Percy's unfortunate statement on receiving the National Book Award that his novel shows Judaeo-Christian man as "a wayfarer and a pilgrim." These are minor failings in a considerable success. I think that *The Moviegoer* is a better novel than the work it most readily brings to mind, Albert Camus' *The Stranger*. It is patronizing and ridiculous to say of a 46-year-old man who has been late publishing his excellent first novel that he shows "promise." Walker Percy shows performance.

Gentleman without a Past   Joyce Carol Oates*

Walker Percy's second novel, *The Last Gentleman*, is altogether richer and more intriguing than his first, *The Moviegoer*, which won him the National Book Award in 1962. It is a highly whimsical kind of picaresque tale that puts one in mind of both Faulkner and Camus, though only peripherally: the Faulknerian concern for the South, the "problem" of the South, the land, the engaging domesticity of a past tradition however past, and above all the traumatic suicide of a philosophically inclined father; and the floating, detached, "Existential" world of Camus that is rendered to us through the amnesia-plagued hero who cannot quite connect but who advances no titanic anguish because of his condition.

Percy's moviegoer was a man of a modern sort, addicted to public, commercial fantasies, and trying however numbly to break through to

*Reprinted by permission from the *Nation*, 8 August 1966, 129–30.

"reality"; his "last gentleman" is clearly kin, represented as he is by his telescope and his attachment to both love and death in an attempt to find his destiny, a man in whom something is mysteriously missing. The dissociated hero, subject to distressing attacks of *déjà vu* that render all reality suspect, taken up by an upper-middle-class Southern family of a comic-page type, in love with a pretty cipher of a girl, is a recognizable fictional type: a man without a soul, without an essence because he is without a sensible environment or past.

The young hero encounters a dying boy and his family, and the bulk of the novel concerns his being companion to and rendering up to the dying boy the attention that the dignity of death demands. The death of Jamie, which finally occurs in the concluding pages of the novel, is the central event of the work but it is not a very important event, strangely enough, because it works so obviously as a symbol, as theme. Percy's use of the naturalistically approached and staged death is out of keeping with his lovely and brilliant whimsy. This novel is one no critic should want to snipe at, for it is rare to encounter a work engaging in nearly every line; but Percy's strength simply does not extend to the naturalistic. Or perhaps it is beyond the naturalistic. His success with the country-club golfers, the pseudo-Negro who is really a white man working on a behind-the-scenes Negro piece, the Southern ladies who outlive their men by fifty years and 35,000 hearty meals, the Negro butler boy who falls "sappily" between Negro and white styles of living, are triumphs that suggest that Percy's power is in the reaction against the naturalistic, the half-comic half-horrified reflection of the naturalistic through a whimsical temperament.

But, how are we to take the apparently sincere love the hero feels for his brainless Chi Omega, and how are we to reconcile it with other graver, deeper pronouncements of his? The phrase "holding her charms in his arms" recurs enough to invoke in us the faintly sickish sensation we hope Percy intends, but we cannot believe that Normal Love and Life are exclusively Kitty Vaught. And how are we to reconcile the unforgettable and deeply moving death of Jamie with the ease with which he gets into college a few months before, apparently in one day, without medical examination, without the usual clutter of transcripts, applications, etc.? Trivial criticism indeed, but this inconsistency of vision mars the novel's dreamlike (though never nightmarish) logic.

Percy's writing is strangely similar to the highly gifted but rather hallucinatory pieces of Janet Frame: the more closely one looks at each sentence, each glimpse of a detail or image, the more hypnotic is the spell; but when one stands back for a larger view something has failed. Between Percy's main character and his excellent walk-on people there is an unhappy wasteland of secondary characters who just do not work. Percy can handle language in a way strictly his own, though at times parodied Faulkner, but as one starts moving out to larger units like the paragraph and the chapter, something is missing. The crankish and quackish journal of a discredited doctor ("We are doomed to the transcendence of abstraction and I choose the only reentry into the world which remains to us. What is better than the beauty and exaltation of the practice of transcendence . . . and of the delectation of immanence . . . lewd love?") becomes quite important near the end of the novel, but it is to be hoped that Percy is not advancing Dr. Vaught's verbose Lawrentian theology with any more seriousness than he is advancing the novel's other fragmentary concerns.

The Hero as "Case"   Frederick C. Crews*

The American novelist who would appear up-to-date must go through certain familiar motions. He must assure us at once that he isn't recounting a story but establishing a style, an adequate manner of coping with the zany modern world. He must replace characterization with caricature, and stamp "Artifact" on every page lest we mistake him for, say, Sinclair Lewis. He must be horrible and cool, morbid and funny, sex-ridden and bored with sex. And he must never look inward, for it is understood that the personal psyche has been thoroughly explored and found uninteresting. With luck the talented writer who follows these rules will puzzle Orville Prescott with his obscurity, please Leslie Fiedler with his courageous negativism, and begin to nudge the older-style bestsellers off the list.

If Walker Percy disdains this path to success, it is not because he is slower-witted than the pop novelists. He too thinks that America is weird, sex largely comic, and the dead just plain dead. But there is a difference: these ideas *matter* to him and to his characters, and they must be painfully learned rather than decoratively embodied in grotesqueries of plotting. Thus, though Percy's second novel does aim at making a broad statement about the modern condition and has its moments of heavyhanded symbolism, it does no great violence to the conventions of realistic fiction. Like most good novels before the present era, it assumes that characters have souls to be won or lost, or at any rate to be lost in better or worse ways.

Percy's uniqueness is genuine but hard to pin down. The thematic trappings of *The Last Gentleman* are so familiar — Civil War nostalgia, religious zeal, racial tension, the vulgar New South and the anonymous North — that it might be mistakenly regarded as belonging to the school of lapsed-Baptist regionalism. In fact, Percy is a remarkably fastidious writer who would never permit himself a cliché of any sort. His manner as a storyteller is that of his hero: "the amiable and slightly ironic air which Southerners find natural away from home." And the story he has to tell is

*Reprinted by permission from *Commentary* 42 (September 1966):100–2. All rights reserved.

only incidentally regional; its three locales of New York, Alabama, and New Mexico are meant almost as the steps of a philosophical proof. Perhaps this abstraction is Percy's keynote. Brilliant though he is in satirizing what lies before him, his attention is fixed on the absoluteness of death and the impossibility of genuine intimacy. The proof to which he submits his hero is that these ultimate facts can be temporarily mitigated only if one accepts a limited role and pretends to be immersed in it. When the hero finally heads back toward his native Alabama to sell Chevrolets, it is not at all because he has discovered that he belongs there, but because he has seen that the alternative is suicide.

Percy's demonstration requires that all his major characters illustrate the same underlying predicament. All are Southerners maladapted to the hustling, secular world of urban America. The most confused and malleable of them is naturally the hero, Will Barrett. He does excellently on aptitude tests but can't think what to do between tests, and sometimes he quite literally forgets who he is. Suffering alternately from *déjà vus* and amnesia, haunted by the Civil War and by the suicide of his antiracist father, unable to stomach his ordained role as Princeton man, waiting for a sign that will narrow the seemingly infinite possibilities of his life, he attaches himself to the Vaught family in New York, routinely falls in love with the younger daughter, follows them all to Alabama, and watches the younger brother die of an incurable disease in Santa Fe. Each character he meets and each station of his passive pilgrimage bring him closer to the wry but serviceable disillusion he possesses at the end.

The most important of Barrett's teachers, the one who frames Percy's dilemma most articulately, is Sutter Vaught, a gifted physician who is slowly destroying himself because (so he believes) scientific theory has made all his human relations "transcendent." He epitomizes the refined Southerner who can neither accept the present nor forget the past; he is obsessed in particular with the breakdown of courtship, and he takes private revenge on the emancipated ladies of America by seducing them perfunctorily. Such forays into the "immanence" of the flesh only feed his cynicism. His sister, Val, equally disoriented by consumer democracy, has taken refuge in Catholic sacramentalism and missionary work; she is waiting irrelevantly for an apocalypse that is not forthcoming. Sister Kitty, Barrett's fiancée, would like to be a coy belle, and Barrett himself approves of this stereotype; but she is even more anxious to prove her sexual capacity. As Sutter writes in his notebook, "Now one begins with genital overtures instead of a handshake, then waits to see what will turn up (e.g., we might become friends later)." And another brother, Jamie Vaught, is mentally sound but drifting toward an ugly death that will show Barrett conclusively that he had better cease trusting in destiny. When he finally decides to marry the conformist Kitty and join the Chevrolet agency of her suffocatingly beneficent father, it is clear that he has Percy's endorsement. If life is mysterious, lonely, and terrible, the novel seems to say, the thing to do is to find a convenient way of blotting out the truth.

The power of *The Last Gentleman* doesn't depend on the validity of this disappointing syllogism. In most respects the book is solid and admirable, full of brilliant observation and subtle thought. Though Percy has a certain difficulty maneuvering his characters from one suitably meaningful backdrop to another, the general development is patient and coherent. And the closing episode of Jamie's death, with its gruesome hassle over baptism and its wrenching combination of sympathy and clinical detail, is stronger than anything in Percy's notable first novel, *The Moviegoer.*

Yet the total effect is somehow pale. Because it is finally a literal story, *The Last Gentleman* depends heavily on the felt intensity of Will Barrett's plight, and Barrett never comes across very emphatically. Though he feels constantly dissatisfied, suffers sudden lapses, and allows himself to be molded by every chance occurrence, he remains oddly insulated from his conflicts. Some of his emotional substance, as with Hawthorne's Robin Molineux or James Purdy's Malcolm, has been drained off into the symbolic vicissitudes he undergoes, so that we can puzzle out his "case" in a detached way by interpreting his various mishaps; but such an understanding is no substitute for the existential anguish Percy would like us to feel.

Indeed, I am not sure that Percy would approve of our regarding Will Barrett as a "case" at all. His explicit psychological remarks as a narrator are designedly superficial; he really prefers to see Barrett as Modern Man, or at any rate to play off his apparent symptoms against the more serious unhealthiness of the times. Barrett's amnesia, which disappears as soon as he has decided to begin selling Chevvies, is meant as nothing more than a device to underline his identity crisis, and his *déjà vus* are likewise devices for bringing the past thematically to bear upon that crisis. His New York psychoanalyst learns virtually nothing about his mind in five years of expensive banter, and Percy hints that after all there is nothing worth learning.

Yet the "case" is nonetheless there to be discerned. Barrett is an orphan in search of a surrogate family, and his attitudes are in some respects those of an adolescent scandalized by sex. He is an eavesdropper by temperament; even when he falls in love it is while spying with his telescope in Central Park. His habitual indecision is related to this streak of voyeurism: "he had to know everything before he could do anything." He is disgusted by the ease with which he has seduced Kitty, yet, as he confesses to Sutter, he has yearned for "the coarsest possible relations" with women generally. And Sutter, whom he is excessively anxious to obey, perceives why Barrett is so sheepish with him: "You either want me to tell you to fornicate or not to fornicate, but for the life of me I can't tell which it is." These and many other details fit into a classic Oedipal pattern, whether or not Percy intends them to.

There should be nothing either surprising or damaging in the possibility that a novelist has not fully calculated the inner consistency of his hero's behavior; so far as I can tell, this is the rule with interesting fiction. A difficulty arises only if the author, taking a superficial view of his handiwork, mistakes the hero for an Everyman whose problems are the exigencies of universal reality. Percy does not seem aware that the moral extremes to which Barrett and Sutter are drawn — lewdness versus saintliness, suicide versus salesmanship — are appropriate only to a particular adolescent crisis. Dostoevsky, it may be said, had the same predilection for seeing the decisions of his driven heroes as metaphysical imperatives; but in Dostoevsky the suffering that precedes those decisions is a primary reality that does not have to be established by symbolism or theory. If *The Last Gentleman*, despite its substantial virtues, finally fails to make a deep impression, the reason may be that Percy does not care either to inspect Will Barrett's conflicts at close range or to understand them much more clearly than Barrett does himself.

Ravening Particles of Anxiety   Wilfrid Sheed*

Let's christen this thing right, with a quote from the panjandrum, Edmund Wilson: "The Northerner is apt to underestimate the degree to which the Southern writer — however intuitive, intelligent, imaginative, well-travelled, well-read — may fail to accept our assumptions or to sympathize with our aims. We do not realize that he lives in a world in which planning, reform, progress, making the world safe for democracy, laying the foundations of a classless society, promoting the American way of life do not really mean anything at all."

This lack of concern is not necessarily villainous. Mr. Percy, for one, is not the kind of Southerner who sets his face against the great Yankee abstractions (you might as well battle the wind), any more than he minds their overgrown children — psychiatry, sociology, high-level ecumenism. What puzzles him is a world in which the abstraction comes first: the conceptualized Yankee world where plans are always proceeding for this and that but where nobody asks the serious questions such as what does the neighborhood feel like, how does it sound in the afternoons, can you get a decent nap, how do the children look, etc. — the questions that the poet puts to the schoolman concerning the texture of life.

Mr. Percy is above all a student of textures (even his lovers "rub dorsal

*Reprinted by permission from the *Critic*, 25 (1966):92–93.

surfaces") and *The Last Gentleman* is a fantastically intuitive report on how America feels to the touch. He uses for probe a Southern Gulliver named Williston Bibb Barrett, who for some years has been trying to suck nourishment out of the thin Northern air. Barrett has no objection to joining groups and interrelating with his peers, if those are the things one does (this is the sense of the word "gentleman"); but he regards them mainly as cultural pastimes, like attending games or sitting on the porch with his aunts. To worry first about their intellectual validity would be to approach life backwards.

Unfortunately, Barrett's psyche tends to collapse on this diet. He learns group-therapy like a young gentleman learning to dance, but he might as well be chewing on air. It does nothing for the sense of emptiness and obliteration in New York, the awareness that the Great Disaster has already occurred. The important landmarks of the imagination, i.e., the sense of time and place, have become so pale in the North that at moments they wash away completely, and Barrett forgets who he is and wanders off arbitrarily to Ohio or Virginia. (In Mississippi you can tell a Tuesday afternoon from a Thursday; here he is always forgetting what month it is.) Other times he finds himself being bombarded by "ravening particles" of collective anxiety which obstruct vision, and which Barrett can only fend off by straining everything through a giant telescope.

The answer would seem to be to return to the South, and this in a roundabout way he does. But all is not well here either. For he finds that in some ways he now prefers the sad self-consciousness of the North to the pointless good cheer of the South. He catches himself saying "hi" to people before they are in earshot. His trick knee jumps so often that he has to hold it down and hobble like a spastic. When he discovers his uncle and colored servant cackling over Cap'n Kangaroo he realizes that time and place are being washed away here too, that the Madison Avenue bulldozer has already begun to work. And beyond all this, the unsolved question of race has left the South a blank, a fixed grin at an old joke. So Barrett lights out West where the air is empty of both memory *and* ravening particles.

Mr. Percy looks at Barrett through both ends of Barrett's own telescope. Through the small, comic end he is the last of a line of Southern gentlemen who have passed from bravery through irony to ironic helplessness — culminating, in Barrett's case, in a sensibility so fine that you can't use it any more: a perfect instrument that snaps in your fingers. Through the other end, he looks rather different. There he becomes the robust American naif, a little like George Brush in *Heaven's My Destination* — the gypsy-missionary on pilgrimage through America. Oddly enough, the two halves match: one of several truths that Mr. Percy is on to. It is all a question of context.

Mr. Percy in fact does so many things so well that he managed to accordion several types of novel into one. There are semiparodies of the hectic on-the-road novel (where the hero keeps waking with mysterious bumps on the back of his neck), of the mysterious-gothic-family novel (this he has more trouble with, and small wonder) and of the novel of galloping-disaster (models: *Candide, A Cool Million*). He even manages to pull off a deathbed baptism scene exactly the way Evelyn Waugh should have done it in *Brideshead Revisited*.

This fiendish dexterity has annoyed a critic or two, who feel that too much cleverness can be a formal defect. But on the whole the book is seamlessly designed. The set-pieces are knitted from the same material as the others, and come in the right places. The only jarring note is a casebook kept by one of the characters in which ideas are discussed explicitly. This offends against one's Northern taste for smoothness and technical efficiency; worse, it substitutes for the rendering of an important character, and this hurts.

But it is gentlemanly to make at least one mistake, and Mr. Percy doesn't make many others. Page-for-page and line-for-line this is certainly one of the best-written books in recent memory. As a Southern writer, Percy inherits the remains of a sonorous musical language. But beyond that, his unique point of view forms beautiful sentences like a diamond cutting glass.

Most writers nowadays are like the advertisers who have to stress marginal differences to conceal basic similarities. But with Percy, the problem would seem to be the reverse. He must make concessions in order to sound even a little like the others. As a Southern Catholic and as a comparatively late-blooming novelist, he sees everything his own way. Like his hero, who feels at his best in thunderstorms, his reactions are bizarre and effortlessly unexpected. By a constant play of metaphor and acute literalness — seeing the thing as something else, seeing it as precisely itself, a whipsaw arrangement — he recreates the world, and gives the readers the run of a brand-new sensibility. His humor, which is considerable, consists largely of this breaking-down of received categories. (E.g. The old Chestertonian question: If you saw a man eating and didn't know what eating was, what would you suppose he was up to? Percy sees things that way all the time.)

A review can only touch on one or two aspects of this remarkable book. To use Henry James' simile: Mr. Percy has woven too rich a rug for the pattern to be easily detached; the figure must remain in the carpet. If things seem to go a little awry toward the end, it may be that the reader has taken his eye off the thread for a moment. The riddles are not meant to be solved in one sitting.

One of them, for reasons of complexity and difficulty of paraphrase, has not been mentioned at all; so let's use it to end the ceremony. On top of its other distinctions, *The Last Gentleman* is one of the few serious religious novels of recent years. The question, among others, that concerns

Mr. Percy is the one that fretted Albert Camus—why do we not commit suicide? But Percy, characteristically, does not answer the question with a formula. Like a good Christian, he writes a novel instead.

Clowns

V. S. Pritchett*

The hero as the clown. It is not a new idea, but it can be given a new twist if he is sick and if the "normal" world is more absurd, more dangerous, and sicker than he is. *That* sickness comes from the normal man's refusal to face the facts; the clown's sickness comes from a morbid awareness of them. Having gone through so much he is clever and stoical. He pesters himself to the point of laughter. After all, he is the comedian of the clinic; and, in Walker Percy's novels, the clinic is sex-mad, science-mad, pleasure-mad contemporary life.

Why is the clown sick? After reading *Love in the Ruins*, which is a satirical fantasy set in the United States twenty or thirty years ahead, one sees that the basic reasons have been developed since that very seductive first novel *The Moviegoer*. In this work the clown is a prosperous young broker and lapsed Catholic in New Orleans, pursuing happiness in a civilization which has stretched that piece of elastic until it snaps back on him. Caught by the itch for instant sex, new things, and the general go-go, he is unaccountably trapped by malaise. Buy a new car, try a new girl, and there is the instant "pain of loss." He is "no longer able to be in the world than Banquo's ghost." He becomes—in the later novels—"abstracted from reality" and can be said to be "orbiting in limbo" between "angelism and bestiality." In *The Moviegoer*, he is a nice, clever, unreliable young man. The movie ideal of the car and the girl never quite works:

> I discovered to my dismay that my fine new Dodge was a regular incubator of malaise. Though it was comfortable enough, though it ran like a clock, though we went spinning along in perfect comfort and with a perfect view of the scenery like the American couple in the Dodge ad, the malaise quickly became suffocating. We sat frozen in gelid amiability. Our cheeks ached from smiling. . . . In despair I put my hand under her dress, but even such a homely little gesture as that was received with the same fearful politeness. I longed to stop the car and bang my head against the curb. We were free, moreover, to do that or anything else, but instead on we rushed, a little vortex of despair moving through the world like the still eye of a hurricane.

In *The Last Gentleman*, the sense of loss becomes literal amnesia. He has lost identity, but that is rooted of course in the past and there, somewhere lying about, was the religion he no longer believes in; also the

*Reprinted by permission from the *New York Review of Books*, 1 July 1971, 15. © 1971 by Nyrev, Inc.

security of a shady but settled way of life in the South. To devote oneself blindly to another's pain is worth a try; but shy of a moral so schematic, he turns this into a wandering adventure all the way from New York to Louisiana with the bizarre family of a dying youth. The sick make good picaresque figures, for sickness gives one the sharp eyes and freedom of fever.

Walker Percy's gift is for moving about, catching the smell of locality, and for a laughing enjoyment between his bouts with desperation and loss. As in pretty well all intelligent American novels, the sense of America as an effluence of bizarre locality is strong. The hero is liable to sexual hay fever. This book ends with him racing after his sinful psychiatrist, in desperation. Case unsolved, but he has traveled like mad, his eyes starting out of his head: a comedian.

In *Love in the Ruins*, the sick hero is older. He is in his disgraceful forties, a brilliant alcoholic and girl-chasing doctor, liable to depression and bowel trouble most of the week. But war and general disaster have an appeasing or stimulating effect upon neurotics. The sense of a loss beyond his own wakes up his eccentric faculties; he now sees that the world is more farcical than he is. For the America of (I suppose) the 1990s is breaking up. There have been outbreaks of civil war for years, brought on by Negro risings and the fifteen-year war in Ecuador:

> our beloved old U.S.A. is in a bad way. Americans have turned against each other; race against race, right against left, believer against heathen, San Francisco against Los Angeles, Chicago against Cicero. Vines sprout in sections of New York where not even Negroes will live. Wolves have been seen in downtown Cleveland.

Poison ivy grows up the speaker-posts in drive-in movies, vegetation grows through the cracks in the highways, and — greatest of all symbols of disaster — many a Howard Johnson motel has gone up in flames. Of course there has been nuclear fallout here and there. The hero has hives.

A disastrous story, but not very tragic for the doctor, although his wife has run off with an English Buddhist and his daughter has died. A shrewd irony, helped by a mixture of bourbon and self-interest, pulls him together. Not only that: he is lucky to live in a suburban town which survives in a state of respectable paranoia on the edge of a swamp inhabited by murderers and other disaffected people. Occasionally the murderers come out for the kill, but golf staggers along. In the Fedvil complex, the hospital still stands, the Masters-and-Johnson-style Love Clinic — now run by a lapsed Irish priest — is packed every day with experimental copulators who earn fifty dollars a go; the Geriatric Rehab buildings keep people alive until they are a hundred, and euthanasia does well at Happy Isles. You press the Euphoria button.

The American way carries on, but the evasions, the unaccountable rages, and the tendency to be abstracted from reality and orbit in limbo and to alternate between bits of meaningless idealism and bestiality have increased. Cunningly the doctor has patched up a corner of a wrecked Howard Johnson where he plans to store three girls he will save in the next wave of destruction. Sniping has begun again, there are rumors of a new rising of blacks, and there is a sodium cloud in the distance.

The doctor, known to be a crackpot genius and no more than a nuisance when in drink, has a consolation. The study of sodium and encephalogy has led him in the course of years to create an instrument called the lapsometer. It measures the electrical activity of the separate centers of the brain. Can the readings be correlated with the causes of the woes of the Western World, its terrors, rages, and impulses, even the perturbations of the soul? Up to a point they can be. There are comic successes with the impotent, the frigid, the angry, the passive: the medical comedy is very good. The hospital suspects the metaphysical turn of its drunk genius, but the Director sees what a political weapon the lapsometer can be. What a gift for Washington, this machine that can, at any rate, manipulate people if it can do no more.

This theme of science fiction is crossed with the drama of the community's situation. The riots are beginning, murders increase, the sodium cloud comes nearer, the sand in the golf bunkers is on fire. Saved by his lapsed Presbyterian secretary, the lapsed Catholic stays on in the wrecked community, now largely taken over by the blacks who copy English accents from their English golf pros on the course. The intellectual blacks have fled to Berkeley, Harvard, and the University of Michigan, to scowl at the mixed-up population who, as well as they can, get on with ordinary life. The doctor is nearly off the bottle and nearly off chasing girls.

To satirize the present one pretends it is the future. Mr. Walker Percy's present is limbo; a scene of wicked comedy, sharp portraits of types, and awful habits of mind. The religious and political mix-up is very funny. He is a spirited and inventive writer and there is a charred hell-fire edge to his observation. Exactly what, as a moralist, he wants us to do, I'm not sure. Join the remains of the church, get back to the doctor's ancestor Sir Thomas More? Or simply rejoin ordinary life? Or is middle age the ideal to be aimed at? He is more interested in the state of sex than in the state of the Union: but isn't sex just the latest item of conspicuous waste in Western society? I am afraid that in the eye of this hurricane of laughing anger, there is a sentimentalist. Still, a very clever one, full of ideas. As always in American novels, the impediments are good. Sears Roebuck has made its contribution to literature.

Logos and Epiphany: Walker Percy's Theology of Language

Charles P. Bigger*

No matter how close our sympathy and our shared concern, it is almost impossible to imagine an American writer making a serious and sustained contribution to the living fabric of existential and phenomenological philosophy. European writers seek to reclaim and to make authentic a mode of human being whose roots are classical and medieval, to reveal and defend the ontological roots of human transcendence into a world of intrinsic, spiritual achievement against those scientific, positivistic, economic, technological, and utilitarian demonic powers which would alienate us from ourselves, make us into commodities, trends, and interests to be vectored, disposed of, and otherwise dealt with. Either man is a mystery or he is a problem. If he is a problem, he can be solved by some appropriate methodological or technical notation and means. If he is a mystery, he stands outside of the whole system of intramundane priorities, is the archaic light that reveals rather than something to be brought into the light, is the being through whom there is a world rather than something in the world.

Americans live in a world self-fabricated by eighteenth-century Rationalism. If one teaches technology to a savage, one can imagine its savage use. So, too, for us a curious gaucherie of rationalism has led to a self-fabricating view of culture; while we are quite willing to look for models and to take all sorts of proffered advice, we can make what we want and make it new and, in so doing, create a human world. This is the New Jersey landscape that flashes by Walker Percy's traveller on a train, the symbol of a rootless culture. European experience is that of man as historical being, in the sense expressed by a Hegel, a Nietzsche, a Marx, or a Heidegger, that history is something we are and live and that through a participation in and interpretation of its spiritual form we achieve self-definition and self-understanding. The European faces the threat that his tradition will be Americanized, that he will stand to himself as a strange object to be understood, self-distanced by the threat of an imperialism of objects and their manipulative techniques. He must recover a spiritual mode of being which can overcome the threat of a nihilistic culture. Since the eighteenth century the European intellectual has rebelled against that rationalism that would isolate the phenomena as within a closed system, a sort of Skinner box, *and* which would seek to understand it in its absolute foreignness—the way it relates to lived experience. Bacon, Descartes, and Locke, phases in the life of the spirit, become for us grounds for spirit. Here this larger heritage is the subject of a technique, a method of breaking up its continuities into monuments and documents and poems and institutions to be understood scientifically, in the spirit of a social

*Reprinted by permission from the *Southern Review* 13 (1977):196–206.

science of man not a science of the human spirit. Protestantism, capitalism, barren distances, and the social and behavioral sciences all conspire with our history to alienate us from the mystery of human presencing, its ontological depths. Our alienation takes the form of psycho-neurosis. We lack that spiritual form which makes community possible. We train. Education is a luxury we cannot understand and cannot afford. Students stream into the deserts of career education through life adjustment programs, ignorant of the Bible, the history of Christian doctrine, Plato, Aristotle, Homer, Shakespeare, Marx, Hegel, Henry Adams, Moliere, Shaw, Adam Smith, Hume, Jefferson, Dante, architectural history, or anything else that might transform life by bringing one to grasp through the tradition its foundation on what really is and how it shows itself in history. Along the way, we humanists try to provide a few humanizing experiences, show a few slides of Chartres, read a page or two of Dante, talk of Plato's influence on Shelley or Spenser, provide perhaps a happening or two. We might arrange a tour of "London Bridge" in Arizona on the way to Disneyland or a bowl game. We package, label, and pass on a product that no one really will, or even should, buy.

Perhaps we should remember that the *logos* showed itself in Bethlehem, not Athens, Rome, and Alexandria. Walker Percy lives in Covington, Louisiana, and he mostly writes about the epiphany of the *logos* in Tuscumbia, Alabama, where Helen Keller discovered that "w-a-t-e-r" was water, out by the pump in the back yard. Through him we can almost forget every other monument and document to the magnificence of being human which has come to be in places far more resonant with human history: *The Message in the Bottle* is a series of reflections on the birth of a human world through the mystery of language.

As an American writer, Percy can hardly lay claim to something called "the tradition" in and through which we encounter Being. Our tradition for understanding man is provided by the social and behavioral sciences, a reductive hermaneutics wherein nothing spiritual is what it seems but is always the expression of something more or less primitive, the id, the chauvinism of sex or race, and so forth. We have bought the whole fabric of scientism as our ideology. American criticism is either a vast *ad hominem* argument or the celebration of an autonomy of feeling and technique, of a sensitivity which is sensitivity to literature alone, reality having been won by the positive sciences. We can sing psychic unsuccess, make a pure music, or perpetrate the latest variant of a scientific ideology. Percy has taken on this scientific tradition and subjected it to the searching light which is the coming-into-being of the *logos* itself and has, on the whole successfully, showed its inherent incapacity to yield understanding. Perhaps in freeing ourselves from the dimensions which constrain us to think of ourselves as this or that, we open ourselves to Being and human reality.

The major hero of Walker Percy's series of essays is the American mathematician-physicist-philosopher Charles S. Peirce. Best known for the pragmatic tradition he founded and repudiated, Peirce was the first to become concerned with semiotics, the way the world enters into the being of language through the mystery of naming. Naming is not an event in the world, the passing on from one to another of a sound or inscription (sign) which serves by association or habit to stimulate attention to that of which it is a name. After Hume and Pavlov, we have been apt to think of a name as an element in a stimulus-response network, not something which through its assertory character makes a claim of truth (and the attendant risk of falsity) in the naming act. Symbols reveal what is while signs produce responses.

Percy shows through the act of naming that the truth conditions for the sciences of man are other than what is assumed to be the case on their positivistic and naturalistic foundations. These conditions lie within the dimension of meaning explored by the existential and phenomenological philosophers. I am the being who encounters the world as meaning in virtue of the constituting act of the transcendental ego, an act which reveals its ideality only when I through the *epoché* withdraw from the standpoint of the naturalistic sciences and discover brute facticity as itself an intentional structure of meaning. The world is itself a constituted horizon grounded on the transcendence (ecstasy) of the self wherein it in turn meets itself in its local concern with this or that. The world is a spiritual formation. But the existential and phenomenological philosopher leaves the world of the other in his otherness, the vestige of the Kantean thing-in-itself with its worth and dignity, as entirely problematic. Neither you nor I am persuaded that we are constituted by the other except when grasped by Sartre's powerful images. Also we should like to think that being is not something we merely intend. Otherwise we have sophistry on top of solipsism. In spite of those well-intentioned escapes from the loneliness of transcendental subjectivity to be found in such dialectical categories as authentic and inauthentic, finite and infinite, self and other, I-it and I-Thou, *pour soi* and *en soi*, are these not made from within the Cartesian ego? What sort of ontological claim can that ego make short of the lamented ontological proof? Insofar as there is a real world of conformal necessity and transpersonal powers, this is handed over to the physical scientist. When those versed in the jargon of science complain that the existentialist records his private feelings, themselves artifacts of an artifactual ego, in the face of the real world of functional structure and causal efficacy, and that, as such, these feelings have no epistemic status, we are often prone to agree. Aren't we all inclined to strongly urge those who wallow in the self-intoxication of despair, who seem to be out of their depth in a foot of water, "Why on earth don't you stand up?" Naturalism must be broken from within, not opposed by contrary dogma. Then we shall be free to explore the full richness of the world of culture itself and effectively participate in the creation of a human world.

Walker Percy learned his thesis about the intentionality of consciousness, not from Husserl and Sartre, but from such masters as Wittgenstein and Heidegger who found it in the nature of language itself. Beyond this lurks the realism of Aristotle and Aquinas. For Wittgenstein there can be no realm of private meaning and private language; for us reality is the public world of linguistic meaning, meanings which are shared forms of life. For Heidegger transcendental subjectivity is a distortion and perversion of our original prethematized self-understanding of Being. When this understanding is thematized, first as substance and then as transcendental subject, there is a progressively instrumental and technological feeling (mood) toward beings, a feeling which justifies itself in a science that strips objects and ourselves of ontological mystery and makes of them problems for a technique. We are creatures who constitute a world out of a primordial understanding of Being, and the intentionality founded on this structure gives the world its form. Being, not the I, is the ground of a world: it is this, not subjectivity, which is intended or meant in all our cultural and linguistic formations.

Percy intends to cut through Cartesian dualism and its idealistic and materialistic variants by close attention to the act of naming. This is first of all a public act. I am given the name by him who has for me the authority to name, acts Plato associated with the legislator and dialectician. When something or other is given for me a name, in this original experience of self, world, and other, I encounter a being in its beingness. The *is* of naming, "This or that *is* so and so," or coupling of word and thing, raises an experience of———from the level of natural and egological flux to the enduring and shareable presence of "whatness." The naming act asserts of a being its beingness, revealing in the thing its structure (*logos*) through the word (*logos*). There is no question of isomorphism between language and beings, whether this is understood formally or in terms of an image theory of thinking. How an arbitrary sound can raise things to essence and order them to mind is a mystery that no technical vocabulary can gloss over. The symbol "somehow contains within itself the thing it means," which accounts for the word magic of archaic and scientistic people. "What took place when the first man uttered a mouthy little sound and the second man understood it, not as a sign to be responded to, but as 'meaning' something they beheld in common?"

The great scholastic truth, gained through reflection on the "word made flesh," that through the imposition of names the thing becomes intensionally present in its act, that there is in naming an apprehension of a whatness in a being itself, so that existence becomes our spiritual theme is the lesson we can relearn through Walker Percy from Helen Keller. The thing in itself and subjectivity are fictions. It is through this epiphany of the *logos* that Percy extends the discoveries of phenomenology to the anthropological sciences; this marks *The Message in the Bottle* as a unique contribution to what has hitherto been a European phenomenon. The mystery of the symbolic event discloses that the problem for man is that he has come to think of himself as a problem, not a mystery. And what have the human sciences done, insofar as they are true to their positivistic foundations, which has taught us anything much worth knowing? Should we not at least try to follow up Percy's lead? Where might we expect it to take us?

If man is, in Percy's paraphrase of Heidegger, "That being in the world whose calling is to find a name for being, to give testimony to it, and to provide for it a clearing," then our responsibility for our world, our relations to nature, to our fellows and to ourselves, must be a function of the way we talk about Being. That being itself is not much talked about is evident if we look at how we have come to think about talk itself, both in the formal disciplines in linguistics and philosophy wherein speech is made into an object for us, and in more concrete disciplines in anthropology, sociology, psychology, and philosophy where talk enters into our concern for worldly structure and human behavior. In the first sense, it is evident that this talk is always construed as a system of signs which is regimented by logic as a calculus, as a set of rules for judgment and argument wherein words function as terms having a precisely defined range of signification. Other uses may be recognized; but in its primary role as a calculus, it converts the given contents of private experience into the public form of propositions, statements which assert of something what that thing is in some categorial or syntactical aspect. Being is the copula. The power of the calculus predisposes us, just as the magic of names predisposed archaic man, to identify what we say with that of which it is said, to reify the formal order of discourse as the structure of the world. The demand for univocity and the fact that this calculus is itself the formal condition for knowing, means that in its semantical dimension (the attribution of conditions for meaning and truth to the formal signs, the predicates and individual variables of the calculus), such a calculus is in fact the language of science. It is up to the sciences to determine the predicates and those features which fit an individual to be an instance thereof, and the univocity of this assignment is secured if by measurement we can map this formal system into and onto nature. The meanings determined by science and the form prescribed by logic and syntax determine what it is to be and be a something or other. Behavioristics is concerned with establishing the correlation between stimulus meaning and the resulting behavioral disposition through artificial sign-object stipulation or conventions. We then insist that these conditions impose upon experience a necessary conformity through our rule-governed linguistic procedures, that we cannot conceive of nature as being otherwise than as it appears through these necessities of thought. This hubristic myth in the end, I believe, is a function of Aristotle's categories as the canonical form of discourse, and leads to the notion that metaphor is a "surplus," meaning, an infestation of univocity by poetic irresponsibility.

The fact that scientific change is founded on the way new metaphors reschematize our grasp of Being and thus break conformal, sedimented patterns of expectation and response is overlooked by that positivistic tyranny of mind by little facts. The thing freshly seen and grasped through metaphor generates a concept, the manner in which the things are represented to mind. In the shock of recognition through metaphor we transcend the "little facts" which are the outcome of the regimentation of experience to an artificial language of terms, not words, designed for use in computation within the limits of current capacity to produce algorithms and hardly meant as itself a metaphysics. Man interprets and computes, but human recognition through metaphor is an interpretation which is utterly different in kind and degree from algorithms, human or mechanical. Experience is for us creative. To exploit a Buddhist proverb, must we always mistake the finger for the moon?

Language is metaphorical. In perhaps the finest essay in this collection, "Metaphor as Mistake," Percy tells of hunting with his father and a black guide in Mississippi.

> At the edge of some woods we saw a wonderful bird. He flew as swift and straight as an arrow, then all of a sudden folded his wings and dropped like a stone into the woods. I asked what the bird was. The guide said it was a blue-dollar hawk. Later my father told me the Negroes had got it wrong; It was really a blue darter hawk. I can still remember my disappointment at the correction. What was so impressive about the bird was its dazzling speed and the effect of alternation of its wings, as if it were flying by a kind of oaring motion. . . .

The first notable moment occurred when he saw the bird. What struck him at once was the extremely distinctive character of the bird's flight — its very great speed, the effect of alternation of the wings, the sudden plummeting into the woods. This so distinctive and incommunicable something — the word which occurs to one is Hopkins's "inscape" — the boy perceived perfectly. It is this very uniqueness which Hopkins specifies in inscape: "the unspeakable stress of pitch, distinctiveness, selving."

The next moment is, for our purposes, the most remarkable of all, because it can receive no explanation in the conventional sign theory of meaning. The boy, having perfectly perceived the flight of the hawk, now suffers a sort of disability, a tension, even a sense of imminence! He puts the peculiar question, *What is that bird?* and puts it importunately. He is really anxious to know. But to know what? What sort of answer does he hope to hear? What in fact is the meaning of his extraordinary question? Why does he want an answer at all? He has already apprehended the hawk in the vividest, most plenary way — a sight he will never forget as long as he lives. What more will he know by having the bird named? (No more, say the semioticists, and he deceives himself if he imagines that he does.)

One recognizes the situation in one's own experience, that is, the metaphorical part of it. Everyone has a blue-dollar hawk in his childhood, especially if he grew up in the South or West, where place names are so prone to poetic corruption. Chaisson Falls, named properly after its discoverer, becomes Chasin' Falls. Scapegoat Mountain, named after some Indian tale, becomes Scrapegoat Mountain — mythic wheels within wheels.

So far so good. But the question on which everything depends and which is too often assumed to be settled without ever having been asked is this: Given this situation and its two characteristics upon which all agree, the peculiar presence or distinctiveness of the object beheld and the peculiar need of the beholder — is this "need" and its satisfaction instrumental or ontological? That is to say, is it the function of metaphor merely to diminish tension, or is it a discoverer of being? Does it fit into the general scheme of need-satisfactions? — and here it doesn't matter much whether we are talking about the ordinary pragmatic view or Cassirer's symbolic form; both operate in an instrumental mode, one, that of biological adaptation; the other, according to the necessities of the mythic consciousness. Neither provides for a real knowing, a truth-saying about what a being is. Or is it of such a nature that at least two sorts of realities must be allowed: one, the distinctive something beheld; two, the beholder (actually *two* beholders, one who gives the symbol and one who receives the symbol as meaningful, the Namer and the Hearer), whose special, if imperfect, gift it is to know and affirm this something for what it actually is? . . . In this primitive encounter which is at the basis of man's cognitive orientation in the world, either we are trafficking in psychological satisfactions or we are dealing with that unique joy which marks man's ordainment to being and the knowing of it.

The ontological thesis implicit in the naming act restores the world, reveals our original participation in Being and shows that the real task of the human sciences lies in the domain of the humanities, that of understanding man through this symbolic dimension. Metaphor is an *epoché* which reveals that, rather than being founded on the "I" of transcendental idealism, meaning is founded on the intention to Being.

Between a transcendental ego which *pace* Kant gives to experience a prescribed epistemic bias and then reads itself out of the resulting materialistic picture it constructs and a transcendental ego which *pace* Kierkegaard finds in this materialism a condition for *angst* there is really very little to choose. To which fiction shall we surrender our autonomy? What shall the poet do? Despair is rather more interesting than classical mechanics. When we confront experience through formulas, surrendering the dignity of the creature to a jargon which prescribes what we can say, whether it be naturalistic or existential, we are clearly absent from our own experience. Percy shows us that the originary presencing of self to itself is with and to another through the naming act, the assertion of a word that raises Being to being known. Being is doubtless inexhaustible, but we shall exhaust ourselves and the creative roots of culture itself in avoiding the ontological issue.

When we abrogate our common right to participate in Being and in one another through the *logos* and bind ourselves to some abstractive scheme which renders experience possible (Kant), or at least respectable, we shall fail to note that our own experience is not the dreary, tiresome repetition of saying and knowing the same thing about the same sorts of things. We become programmed calculators. Socrates in the paradigm case of Meno's slave taught that experience is not so much conformal (for Meno was himself so wrapped up in technical jargon derived from Gorgias that he could not recognize a color when he saw one but had to have it "explained" in the nonsense terminology of Empedoclean effluences) as it is negating, a break away from the customary and conventional into an openness for Being. Language is the instrument of this continual re-creation of the world. In talking to one another in serious, passionate pursuit of what is there, so Beautiful and true, in trying to get right about things, we can follow the power of language itself to lead us from our banal and orthodox subjectivity into a participatory encounter, an epiphany. This human act, not Skinner boxes, might well be the proper paradigm for the human sciences. The truth conditions for the human sciences lie within those conditions of language, essentially spiritual, which constitute knower and known, self and other, man and world. This is the great theme of the *logos* itself.

If one is to pick a nit with Walker Percy it is that he has, in freeing us from naturalistic jargon of the social sciences, unwittingly laid claim to the sterile jargon of despair we have inherited from Kierkegaard and romantic existentialism. Granted that the intolerable banality of our culture is endurable only through irony, through the hubris of distancing: were there no community with saints and sages, how in God's name could any humanist bear the burden of trying to represent his values in such a world as we are called to serve? And it is the positive value of this participation in the historic fabric of our tradition which Percy ignores. One can in fact read Plato on a train. It is easy enough to pick away at the social sciences and to demonstrate their bizarre consequences for human self-understanding; but the real issue of a hermaneutical philosophy, as we are now learning from Hans-Georg Gadamer, Paul Ricoeur, and Charles Taylor, is the possibility of a meaningful involvement in culture and the recovery of effective freedom within the scope of ontologically grounded, inherited values. We can now see a way of avoiding historicism, relativism, and subjectivism in the nature of language itself. Given this understanding, despair seems to be a limit situation, not a norm, and we can begin to see the possibilities of a rebirth, a recovery of effectiveness, duration, and power, the marks of human being in a human world. We can develop the human sciences on their spiritual foundations as sciences of meaning.

The final essay, "A Theory of Language," makes a fundamental contribution to our understanding of linguistics. Percy demonstrates that on his account of naming, which says of something what it is, the basic syntactical structure is implicit. To the dispute between Chomsky and Skinner, which as far as it goes is clearly in Chomsky's favor, he proposes an empirical theory of the origin of "deep structure." The asserting structure of the original naming act is rich enough for that structure which Chomsky has to account for on occult grounds, for oddly he recognizes only those semantical and syntactical features which have been handed over by the formal logicians, not the semiotic dimension itself. There is abundant evidence in various studies of how children learn speech to show how syntax develops out of semiotic activities. A semological-phonological model is "transsyntactical," founded on "the science of the relations between people and signs and things — which specifies syntax as but one dimension of sentential theory"; it accords with the data of language acquisition and provides a model for the ontogenesis of speech; it allows the possibility of looking for a neurophysiological correlate of such a model; and it permits the assimilation of linguistic theory to a more general theory of all symbolic transaction, "a theory which in turn must accommodate such nonsyntactical 'sentences' as metaphor, a painting, a sculpture, a piece of music." I think it works.

Most of the essays have been previously published. They should have been rewritten to avoid what becomes when taken together the tiresome repetition of catch words, stock examples, and identical arguments. Also a good index would make this badly produced book even more valuable, for believe me it is very valuable indeed. It is an important work by a major novelist who is also even more impressive as a philosopher, one who lovingly seeks and strives for wisdom in and out of the conditions here and now with us in America. One is reminded of greater ages when culture was in the hands of amateurs, not prostitutes, of a Jefferson or a Hume. Walker Percy is a member of that community of saints and sages without whom life would be unbearable indeed.

The Quest for the Philosophical Novel
John Gardner*

Thanks — to "The Moviegoer," "The Last Gentleman" and "Love in the Ruins" — readers have come to expect a good deal of Walker Percy. His virtues, in this age of mostly terrible fiction, are notable. Though he cares about plot and character, making fictions that easily translate into movies, he is a serious, even moderately philosophical novelist not at all ashamed of his seriousness. Nor should he be: the familiar philosophical questions he raises, and his ways of raising them, are as interesting as his characters and plots, or anyway they would be if he had any idea of how to answer them. He cares about technique, enough so that — as is often the case in the very best fiction — technique is one of the things we watch with interest, though here sometimes with dismay. He's clever, witty, efficient, concerned, and his fictions pass one of the two or three most important esthetic tests: they're memorable. All this I say without much reservation, which is to say I think he's a novelist people ought to read, as they will anyway, since he's caught on.

"Lancelot" is the story of a man, Lancelot Andrews Lamar, who, after years of happy marriage, learns that his beautiful, voluptuous wife has been unfaithful to him. The wife is Texas rich, low-born, a bad movie actress, originally attracted to Lancelot because he is of an old Louisiana family, owner of a huge declining mansion. She took on his class as she takes on accents. From the beginning there was no hope that she would be faithful. Out of his disappointment and jealousy — and out of his sophisticated modern sense that perhaps there are no evil acts, no good acts either, only acts of sickness, on one hand, and acts flowing from unrecognized self-interest, on the other — Lancelot turns his wife's sexual betrayal into a central philosophical mystery. Question: Is all good mere illusion? — in which case, seemingly, there can be no God — or can we at least affirm that evil exists, so that (as Ivan Karamazov saw) we see God by His shadow? This question sets off Lancelot Lamar's "quest," as he tells his old school chum, now father-confessor, Percival. (The whole novel is Lancelot's "confession," though it reads like writing, not speech.) Lancelot says, "We've spoken of the Knights of the Holy Grail, Percival. But do you know what I was? The Knight of the Unholy Grail. In times like these when everyone is wonderful, what is needed is a quest for evil." A good start for a philosophical novel. One begins to read more eagerly.

In his pursuit of evil, Lancelot first tries voyeurism, making absolutely certain of what he already knows, that his wife — and nearly everyone around him — is betraying all traditional values, turning life to garbage. Predictably the proofs do not satisfy, and Lancelot takes the next step. He turns himself into a monster to find out how evil feels — if it feels

*Reprinted by permission from the *New York Times Book Review*, 20 February 1977, 1, 16, 20. © 1977 by the New York Times Company.

like anything. Even as he commits his most terrible crime, Lancelot feels nothing, so for him as for Nietzsche there can be no such thing as good or evil in the Christian sense, only strength, on one hand, and, on the other, "milksopiness."

The events that dramatize Lancelot's transformation are typical of the Southern Gothic novel at its best, grotesque but sufficiently convincing to be chilling. They flow from the potential of character and situation with deadly inevitability, supported by brilliant descriptions of place and weather — the climax comes during a hurricane, or rather two hurricanes, one real, one faked by a film crew — and supported by the kind of intelligence, insight and wit that make the progress of the novel delightful as well as convincing. A quick example: Lancelot's huge Louisiana mansion is full of people who are making a typically stupid modern movie about, in fact, promiscuity as freedom. Nearly all of them are slightly crazy, in the way many movie people really are, and Lancelot, eagerly on the watch for evil, catches precisely what's wrong with these new Californians. On the night of the hurricane, one of them, an actress called Raine, talks mystically about "fields of force":

> "I feel the convergence of all our separate lines of force. Can't you feel something changed in the air between all of us?"
> "Well . . ."
> "There's a force field around all of us, waxing and waning," said Raine absently, suddenly waning herself, losing interest. She spoke a little more, but inattentively.
> "Maybe you're right, Raine." I could never figure out the enthusiasm of movie folk. It was as if they were possessed fitfully by demons, but demons of a very low order to whom one needn't pay strict attention.

I've said that technique is one of the things one watches with interest as one reads "Lancelot." Percy uses, throughout the novel, the conventional device of regular rotation from motif to motif, incrementally building toward the dramatic and intellectual climax. Lancelot tells, for a while, the story of his wife's unfaithfulness, then breaks off to speak of Elgin, the brilliant young black who turns out to be, in effect, a modern slave (without a moral second thought he covertly films the novel's betrayals for his "master"), then shifts to talk of Anna, the raped girl in the hospital room next door — the true "new woman," Lancelot thinks, violated back into innocence — then turns to direct address to his silent confessor, Percival, then to elaborating one or another of the novel's central symbols or to wonderful rant on what's wrong with the modern world. All this is well done, and the rant — much of it true, some of it intentionally crazy — gives the novel rhetorical oomph. For instance, Lancelot rails at his confessor.

> Don't speak to me of Christian love. Whatever came of it? I'll tell you what came of it. It got mouthed off on the radio and TV from the

pulpit and that was the end of it. The Jews knew better. Billy Graham lay down with Nixon and got up with a different set of fleas, but the Jewish prophets lived in deserts and wildernesses and had no part with corrupt kings. I'll prophesy: This country is going to turn into a desert and it won't be a bad thing. Thirst and hunger are better than jungle rot. We will begin in the Wilderness where Lee lost. Deserts are clean places. Corpses turn quickly into simple pure chemicals.

Convinced that Percival's meek Christianity and faith can have no effect and incensed, rightly, by the modern world's obscenity — summed up in the trashy illusions of the film maker, Merlin — Lancelot decides, slipping into madness, to start up, somehow, a new revolution and, like Christ Triumphant, either purify the world or destroy it utterly. We're encouraged to believe that he and others like him might really pull it off. He's a competent murderer. Lancelot's decision is not quite firm, however. He would like to be answered by his priest-confessor, though faith, we're told, has never been sufficient to answer reason. Percy is content to leave it at that. He suggests in his final line that some answer is possible, but he doesn't risk giving it to Percival. Certainly no answer can be deduced from the novel except Kierkegaard's consciously unreasonable "leap of faith" — a blind, existential affirmation of the logically insensible Christian faith. But surely everyone must know by now that Kierkegaard's answer is stupid and dangerous. Why Abraham's leap of faith and not Hitler's? Lancelot himself makes that point.

The reader has come all this way in critical good will — ignoring Percy's errors of scientific and mythic fact, though important arguments hang on them (human females are by no means, as Percy thinks, the only ones that make love face-to-face, and Malory's Guinevere was by no means indifferent to the betrayal). And from interest in the story and argument the reader has put up, too, with quite gross esthetic mistakes on Percy's part. Even granting the funny way Southerners name their children, the allegory is too obviously contrived; it distracts us from drama to mere message. Also, as I've said, the "confession" sounds written, not spoken — a bad fault, since it shows that the writer is not serious about creating a fictional illusion but is after only a moderately successful "vehicle," like the occasions of Chairman Mao's verse.

From interest in the drama and argument, we blinked all this, but when the end comes and we see the issue has been avoided and evaded, as it nearly always is in our stupid, whining, self-pitying modern novels, we hurl away the book. When everyone's talking, as Lancelot does, about the world has no values, it's not a good time to rehash "The Brothers Karamazov" ("Is there evil? Does it imply God?") or offer a sniveling version of Ayn Rand, that is, "Maybe — just maybe — Lancelot is right." Everybody, these days, is thinking and feeling what Walker Percy is thinking and feeling. Lancelot rages, at one point, "I will not have my son or daughter grow up in such a world. . . . I will not have it." Paddy

Chayevsky's mad TV news commentator and his disciples say the same—
only better—in the movie "Network." Everybody says it. Over and over,
film after film, novel after novel, people keep whining about the black
abyss and turning in their ignorance to Nietzsche and Kierkegaard, as if no
one had ever answered them (George Sedgwick, Brand Blanshard, Roman
Ingarten, Paul Weiss, dozens more).

Fiction, at its best, is a means of discovery, a philosophical method.
By that standard, Walker Percy is not a very good novelist; in fact
"Lancelot," for all its dramatic and philosophical intensity, is bad art, and
what's worse, typical bad art. Like Tom Stoppard's plays, it fools around
with philosophy, only in this case not for laughs but for fashionable
groans. Art, it seems to me, should be a little less pompous, a lot more
serious. It should stop sniveling and go for answers or else shut up.

A Thinking Man's Kurt Vonnegut   Benjamin DeMott*

Williston Bibb Barrett, hero of Walker Percy's fifth novel, *The Second
Coming* (Farrar, Straus & Giroux, $12.95), makes it big as a New York
lawyer, marries a handsome fortune, heads home with his wife to the
Southland for early retirement—and is at once overwhelmed with problems. His mate dies. Her religious adviser commences hounding him to
underwrite a "total love-and-faith" retirement village as a monument to
the departed. By accident a neighbor nearly shoots him dead. His
daughter, Leslie, a granny-beglassed Kahlil Gibran fan who's soft on
creative relationships ("Jason and I level") and the expression "You better
believe it," tells him he's never been honest in his life. Mysterious forces
knock him off his feet into *petit mal* trances. An old girlfriend, appearing
from nowhere, bends herself to the enterprise of seducing him. He
contracts an obsession with the circumstances of his father's suicide. He
contracts a determination to prove or disprove—by a "rational" experiment that combines a retreat to a cave, the use of advanced pharmaceuti-
cal technology, and a suicidal gamble—the existence of God. He contracts
a golf slice. Yet despite these and other troubles, frustrations, miscon-
ceived projects, and flat-out disasters, *The Second Coming* is miles
removed from tragedy. At the end of the book Will Barrett isn't a mere
survivor; he's flourishing.

The reason is that, in a central although only gradually emerging
dimension, *The Second Coming* is a love story. At the height of his anguish
Will Barrett chances upon a young female, Allison Hunnicutt Huger by
name—a lieder-singing escapee from a sanitarium for the mentally ill.
Allison is less God-haunted than he, but she shares his hunger for true

*Reprinted by permission from the *Atlantic Monthly* 246 (1980):81–84. © 1980 by the
Atlantic Monthly Company, Boston.

knowledge of the nature of our situation on earth, and of how best to endure it. And this shared longing draws them close, ultimately transforming their responses to the world's contradictions, perplexities, trials. By falling in love they save — or at least freshen — their souls.

It's not quite that simple, of course. For a considerable while after first meeting Allie Huger, the hero remains in thrall to raddling religious uncertainties — and to the experiment he dreams will end them. Seething in alienation, despising the complacencies of liberated skeptics on the one hand and the hypocrisies of the unfaithful on the other — people oblivious to the differences between Christendom and Christianity — he has lost his gift for connection. "I am surrounded by two classes of maniacs," he insists:

> The first are the believers, who think they know the reason why we find ourselves in this ludicrous predicament yet act for all the world as if they don't. The second are the unbelievers, who don't know the reason and don't care if they don't.

The only refuge he can imagine is "a search for the third alternative, a tertium quid — if there is one." And the notion of Allie Huger as belonging to that search — opening his secret, self-immured, God-tormented inner life to new possibilities — is slow in coming. Through pride of mind he hangs back.

As for Allie Huger: while eager from the start for lyrical union, she too has distracting preoccupations. By the time she encounters Will Barrett she has suffered years of institutional infantilization. Chapters interleaved with those detailing the hero's troubles show us Allie Huger's parents and analyst conniving to cheat her out of her inheritance. We watch the young woman struggling to plan an escape — writing extended instructions to her "disturbed" self about how to function on the outside, as a free being, while still partially crippled by electroshock treatment. (Only in the period just after her "buzzing" does sanitarium security ease sufficiently to permit an escape attempt.) Warily, painfully, at length exhilaratingly, in pages as delicately imagined as anything we're likely to have for some seasons from an American fictionist, Allie conceives ambitions of her own — projects infinitely more concrete than Barrett's, but to her not a whit less bemusing. She's engaged in constructing a language, a home (in an abandoned greenhouse), and a personal life. She's learning to see and hear for herself again, to hunt for clues to the insides of the human creatures with whom she's obliged to deal, to begin once more to appreciate:

> ". . . Have a nice day."
> "What?" She was puzzled by the way [the policeman] said it, in a perfunctory way like goodbye. But what a nice thing to say.
> But he only repeated it — "Have a nice day" — and raised a finger to

the place where the brim of his hat would have been. He returned to his street corner.

Her experience in supermarkets and hardware stores echoes the joys of provisioning as they exist in *Robinson Crusoe*; her awakening by the tinkle of a sliced golf ball through her greenhouse roof (Barrett the slicer arrives soon after) shapes a cute meet reminiscent of that between Shakespeare's Ferdinand and Miranda. But everywhere the fascination of her own second coming edges her back from the obvious answer to the brave new longings nascent within her.

And because the elements of her recovered nature — kindness, courage, resourcefulness, candor, sweet sensuality — emerge unselfconsciously, utterly unpolluted by self-promotion, we're impatient with the hesitations and reluctancies. How can the golfing metaphysician hang back? Granted, Will Barrett is a thoughtful chap with a splendidly savage eye for the deceitfulness round about. Granted, his spiritual aspirations deserve respect. Granted, Allie Huger has the whole of the "sane" world to master. But where are these people's eyes? Why can't they recognize their best hope for salvation? How much longer will he go on in her company without junking embitterment and convolution and taking her into his arms?

We're in the presence, in short, of that surest-fire of literary things: deliciously dramatic — deliciously romantic — obtuseness.

Walker Percy enthusiasts will remember Will Barrett from the author's second novel, *The Last Gentleman*, which recounts Barrett's adventures as a twenty-five-year-old Princeton dropout whose precarious perch, after an extended psychoanalysis and much battering by amnesiac spells and other "funks," is a room at the Y and a janitor's job at Macy's. In this earlier work young Will plays a role similar to the one assigned in *The Second Coming* to Allie Huger — that of a vulnerable, innocent *isolato* adrift in settings alternately senseless and hostile. Another continuity between the Barrett books is the care taken in each to insure that their themes of innocence versus experience nowhere dwindle into banal contests between good and evil. Will Barrett, as the "young engineer" of *The Last Gentleman*, is impulsive and unguarded, given (like Allie Huger) to sudden rushes of affection, and altogether unsmutched by sins of knowingness and manipulativeness. But while he's clearly meant to be understood as a person of value, he's never presented as a person whose virtues are without defects. Time and again the young engineer's reflections are played off against those of a strong-minded elder, a doctor named Sutter Vaught, in whose notebook on American events, personalities, and traumas warmth of affection is conjoined with chill perspicuity:

> Kennedy. With all the hogwash, no one has said what he was. The reason he was a great man was that his derisiveness kept pace with his brilliance and his beauty and his love of country. He is the only public

man I have ever believed. This is because no man now is believable unless he is derisive. In him I saw the old eagle beauty of the United States of America. I loved him.

By the light of this intelligence the limits of a youngster's beamishness can be clearly made out.

And Will Barrett grown up, mordantly conscious of the sentimentality of a citizenry self-preeningly awash in "relationships," does for Allie Huger precisely what Sutter Vaught did for him. He creates an atmosphere, that is, in which one can simultaneously value and devalue such thoughts as, say, Allie Huger's on the niceness of "Have a nice day." There's no denying that Will Barrett's creator sometimes seems on the verge of a seizure of Beatlemanic cuteness, but almost invariably he recovers, intervening with a muscular, satiric hand on the side of mind. Walker Percy is a thinking man's Kurt Vonnegut.

What exactly does this mean? Not, certainly, that Percy's books are clogged with complicated puzzles and conundrums of the kind Scholarship lusts to solve. Heavy weather is, to be sure, regularly made about this author in the learned journals, and he himself bears some responsibility for it. Over the years Percy has written many quirkishly brilliant essays on philosophical matters, animadverting on this or that contemporary theory of language, setting straight one or another school of empiricists, idealists, existentialists, or phenomenologists. (A volume of these essays, *The Message in the Bottle*, appeared in 1975.) As a matter of fact, one aspect of *The Second Coming* will probably inspire a further bout of brain-cudgeling among linguistic philosophers. In his essays Percy often takes as a starting point or key illustration Helen Keller's moving account of the hour in which her teacher finally succeeded in explaining words to her — the nature of the relation between the word *water* and the flowing sensation over her wrist. And, as it happens, a number of the most striking chapters of *The Second Coming* are those in which Allie Huger, whose grasp of the nature of language has become shaky, recovers it, bit by bit, working (with Will Barrett's help) from writing to reading to things:

> ". . . You're going to need two ten-inch crescent wrenches and a can of WD-40 to loosen the rusty bolts."
> "Give me the words." She took out pad and pencil. He wrote *Creeper. Ten-inch crescent wrench. WD-40.*
> "Good."
> "I found the word 'block' in the dictionary in the library under the word 'pulley.' So I knew what to ask for in the hardware store."
> "I see."
> "Thank you."
> "You're welcome."

In my view these chapters matter chiefly as a dramatization of the truth that learning depends on connectedness — sympathy, companionship, confidence, in student and teacher alike, of a steady flow of good will. Will Barrett can teach Allie the names of tools she needs to turn her greenhouse into a home because, having known something akin to her disorientation, he can reach into it, caringly and unobtrusively, with a patience so effortless that it's not felt as patience at all.

> They stood in silence. It was not for her like a silence with another person, a silence in which something horrid takes root and grows. . . . perhaps there was no unease with him because he managed to be both there and not there as one required. Is it possible to stand next to a stranger at a bus stop and know that he is a friend? Was he someone she had known well and forgotten?

But while sermons on Noam Chomsky and language acquisition couldn't conceivably clarify the pertinent feelings here, they're bound to be delivered. ("Let us, however," runs one of the plainer sentences in a recent essay on Percy's theory, "Let us, however, show schematically what it is that Percy has hoped to do with the argument from the irreducibly triadic structure of the Delta Factor.") And, to repeat, part of their effect will be to obscure the real source of Percy's ability to please people resistant (unlike Vonnegutians) to mindlessness.

That source, bluntly stated, is Percy's power of rousing unbelief to a sense of the interest — the emotional and intellectual challenge — of belief. Not surprisingly, this power operates erratically. It's least impressive to me when most ambitious — most driven to represent the intensity of religious states. Late in *The Second Coming*, in a bizarre night scene, Will Barrett ecstatically rejects a devil called death-in-life, meanwhile "laughing and hooting *hee hee hooooee* like a pig-caller and kicking the tires" of his Mercedes 450 SL. From now on we gather he'll be proof against this devil's standard guises — old and new Christendom, "isms and asms," "marriage and family and children," and so on. Nobody who remembers his Kierkegaard will have the slightest difficulty comprehending these goings-on. Will Barrett is waging war on passivity, heroically renewing his struggle against despair and for the achievement of spiritual and personal reality.

But these pages are far less effective than the splendid teaching scenes with Allie — moments where, at a reduced noise level, we witness the onset of a subtler self-questioning. And there are a half-dozen other episodes in which, without fuss or tire-kicking, the reader intuits what it might be like to see the human landscape as an array of souls, to read the world as though divinity could be glimpsed by its light. I liked especially a moment in an old folks' home during which two orderlies, a "black mammy" named Rosie, and a lad who reminds Will Barrett of Sugar Ray Robinson, comfort a terror-struck old woman they're taking to the hospital:

> "You be all right, honey," said the black woman, her eyes absent-minded, and put a black-and-pink hand on the patient's swollen leg. "You gon be fine, bless Jesus." . . .

"Listen lady, I'm gerng to tell you something," [said Sugar Ray]. (That was the difference between them, the two orderlies, that *gerng*, his slightly self-conscious uptown correction of the black woman.) "The doctors know what they know, but I have noticed something too. I can tell about people and I'm gerng to tell you. We taking you to the hospital in Asheville and we coming to get you Tuesday and bringing you back here and that's the truth, ain't that right, Rosie?" And he smiled, a brilliant white-and-gold Sugar Ray smile, yet his eyes had not changed because they didn't have to. The patient couldn't see his eyes.

"Sho," said Rosie, her eye not quite meeting Sugar Ray's eye and not quite winking. "You gon be fine, honey."

Percy's hero asks himself how the "economy of giving and getting" adds up for these two speakers. He acknowledges that "even in the very act of their offhand reassurances to [the terror-struck lady] they were probably cooking up something between themselves. . . ." Was their reason for giving that "it was so little to give and so much for her to get? . . . Does goodness come tricked out so as fakery and fondness and carrying on and is God himself as sly?" The casual assumption, here and elsewhere, that experience can be inspected for signs of Presence, gathers force from chapter to chapter; by its magic the most commonplace human exchanges are more than once metamorphosed into shadow plays of ideas.

I admit to a preference for fiction in which everyday life — ordinary scraping for social power, ordinary civic-secular concern — comes off better than it's allowed to by Walker Percy. And I'm prepared to admit that, while this book's love scenes are as charming as any I've read since odd snippets in J. D. Salinger, they can't be promoted as flawless: now and then affectation defaces a phrase.

But only now and then — and none but the professionally hard-nosed will be seriously discomforted. The case is, ladies and gentlemen, that we have before us a novel in which a woman of grace, beauty, talent, and wit falls believably in love with a man who's vigorous, athletic, competent, sensitive, funny, unillusioned, and loving at his core. A novel in which, when the author steps forward as though persuaded of his capacity for consecutive thought, there's no need to roll one's eyes skyward or to commit (covering one's mouth) a little cough of embarrassment. A work in which fresh imaginings occur of a wide range of human experiences — including striving for ascent from despair — and in which human kindness as well as human idiocy receives its due. I wonder what, at this hour, such a work could reasonably be called except an enchantment.

A Pop-Socratic Survey of Despair

Francine Du Plessix Gray*

If I've managed to decipher this problematic book — Walker Percy's second venture into nonfiction — its subject is summed up in the following words: "How you can survive in the Cosmos about which you know more and more while knowing less and less about yourself."

The waning of our self-knowledge and clear identity, the roots of this malaise in the decline of religious faith and the cult of technology, has been a central theme in most of Mr. Percy's work. His protagonists are well-bred Southern gentlemen who, although endowed with all the trappings of contemporary comfort, are haunted by the fear that they lead meaningless and inauthentic lives. They are all the more doomed because their gentility curbs them from that searing self-questioning which might jolt them into admitting their despair and exploring its roots. "The specific character of despair is that it is unaware of its despair" — so reads Kierkegaard's epigraph to Mr. Percy's novel "The Moviegoer."

However familiar this topic — contemporary man as stranger to himself — the best of Mr. Percy's novels have modulated it with an irony and compassion matched by few current authors. And the religious dimension he has added to the theme of self-estrangement makes him, to my mind, our greatest Catholic novelist alongside Flannery O'Connor. So it is my very infatuation with Mr. Percy's fictions that makes me so disappointed by his forays into nonfiction. His first collection of essays — "The Message in the Bottle" (1975) — was a dense, ambitious book that centered on the importance of language in understanding the human predicament. It offered several ill-digested summaries of contemporary theories of semiotics, lashed out at fashionable behaviorist views that reduce man to an organism reacting solely to its environment and attempted to provide a respiritualized ethos (the only redeeming sections of the book) based on those Christian existentialists who have most deeply influenced Mr. Percy's work: Kierkegaard, Heidegger, Gabriel Marcel.

"Lost in the Cosmos" is more playful, less ambitious, less turgid than "The Message in the Bottle." But I find it, alas, equally exasperating. Its oddball structure can best be described as pop-Socratic. Two-thirds of the volume consists of 20 long-winded questionnaires with multiple-choice answers, a parody of magazine quizzes and self-help books that plumbs different modes of despair allegedly suffered by contemporary Americans. The quiz headings include "The Self as Nought (II): Why Most Women, and Some Men, are Subject to Fashion," "The Fearful Self: Why the Self is so Afraid of Being Found Out" and "The Nowhere Self: How the Self, Which Usually Experiences Itself as Living Nowhere, is Surprised to Find that it Lives Somewhere."

*Reprinted by permission from the *New York Times Book Review*, 5 June 1983, 9. © 1983 by the New York Times Co.

In the "Nowhere Self" quiz, Mr. Percy asks why members of Johnny Carson's studio audience clap when their hometowns are mentioned.

"Question: Do Chicagoans in Burbank, California, applaud at the mention of the word Chicago

"(*a*) Because they are proud of Chicago?

"(*b*) Because they are boosters, Chamber of Commerce types, who appreciate a plug, much as a toothpaste manufacturer would appreciate Carson mentioning Colgate?

"(*c*) Because a person, particularly a passive audience member who finds himself in Burbank, California, feels himself so dislocated, so detached from a particular coordinate in space and time, so ghostly, that the very mention of such a coordinate is enough to startle him into action?"

As in most of the other quizzes, the solemn tone of answer (c) makes us suspect that this is the one we should choose if we wish to earn a clean bill of health in Mr. Percy's moral scheme. This engages the reader at a level of earnestness that jars with the questionnaire's parodic format. Throughout, Mr. Percy offers equally earnest digressions that deplore the reign of the contemporary scientist ("prince of the post-religious age and sovereign of the Cosmos"), express nostalgia for "an age of faith . . . in which men perceived a saving relationship to God, the Cosmos, the world, and each other" and urge us to return to a more mythic cast of mind ("Because there is a need in humans for myth, for symbols, to construe and order a confusing and hostile environment — just as there is a need for food, water, shelter, and sex — and the abstract truths in science do not provide this myth").

Although I share Mr. Percy's Christian, existential and anti-technological convictions, I found his mishmash of satire and seriousness totally confusing. Furthermore, his diatribes against specific aspects of contemporary mores offended me by their priggishness. There is a hostility toward homosexuals in his pages that is particularly odious. And Mr. Percy's stand on women is hardly more palatable. "Are there not still religious folk, women who give their very lives to serve God and their fellowman, all for the love of God?" he asks. "Well some," he answers, "though for every Mother Teresa, there seem to be 1,800 nutty American nuns, female Clint Eastwoods who have it in for men and are out to get the pope."

Also offensive are the excesses of Mr. Percy's pop-Soc style, which inspires him to people his moral fables with a swarm of media personalities — Robert Redford, Al Pacino, Mickey Rooney, Tom Snyder, Phil Donahue. In such passages Mr. Percy's botched attempts at humor make him sound like a hippie clergyman trying to "level" with his audience — turning the author into someone akin to the swinging cleric he parodied so brilliantly in his novel "The Second Coming."

It takes Mr. Percy some 120 pages to get through the 20 questionnaires. The other segments of "Lost in the Cosmos" are less objectionable but equally tedious. They consist of two ineffectual attempts at "Space Odyssey" science fiction and a 40-page "intermezzo" that attempts to define "an elementary semiotical grounding of the theory of self." Its central insight, already elaborated ad nauseum in "The Message in the Bottle," is that "of all the objects in the entire Cosmos which the sign-user can apprehend through the conjoining of signifier and signified (word uttered and thing beheld), there is one which forever escapes his comprehension — and that is the sign-user himself."

And so "Lost in the Cosmos" remains curiously schizophrenic. Percy the satirist tries to make us laugh at some of the excesses of American culture. Percy the twice-converted moralist (from science to art, from agnosticism to the Roman Catholic Church) tries to awaken us to the dangers of those excesses and to uncover the despair he suspects lurks in all of us. Both attempts fail. It would take a considerably broader and more inventive comic gift to satirize successfully such hackneyed subjects as the sexual revolution, the inanity of self-help manuals or the numbing effect of the electronic media. As for my attempt to play along with the author and answer his self-help quizzes, it thrust me into the worst form of despair I know — boredom. I fear that those who are as enamored as I am of Mr. Percy's fictions will feel like jilted lovers while trying to find their way in this particular cosmos.

Percy's Christian Humanist, More Hero Than Saint

Thomas D'Evelyn*

My heroes were always cowboys until I read Walker Percy's novels. His newest stars Dr. Thomas More, named after Sir Thomas More, the humanist saint. Percy's More is a cross between Chevy Chase and Charlton Heston. A tough guy of noble mold somewhat rattled by experience, but charming withal.

Still, can naming your hero after Sir Thomas More be anything but a joke, easy irony, a cheap shot at the old religion?

Walker Percy is a Roman Catholic novelist greatly influenced by the Protestant philosopher Soren Kierkegaard. Thomas More, an early Catholic humanist who practiced irony before Kierkegaard, is clearly important to him.

The original Thomas More, famous as the author of the humanist classic "Utopia," who opposed Henry VIII's divorce and died for it, lent his name to his friend Erasmus's "Encomium Moriae" ("In Praise of Folly"):

*Reprinted by permission from the *Christian Science Monitor*, 8 April 1987, 23. © 1987 by the Christian Science Publishing Society. All rights reserved.

He's the model Christian humanist. Recent scholarship has clarified More's thought on topics of interest to the novelist: on language, on the relationship between religion and secular culture.

As Daniel Kenney shows in volume 15 "The Complete Works of St. Thomas More" (Yale University Press), More's defense of humanism included a vindication of rhetoric over speculative grammar. This coincides with Walker Percy's "The Message in the Bottle."

In general, neither More nor Percy dwells on abstractions, even religious ones. This can cause confusion, but, as Kenney explains, "If revelation is the form of Christian existence, the matter is history; but the matter of history is primarily secular custom."

Each Percy novel has been a virtual update on what's happening in the new South — on the prevailing customs of liberated blacks, Pentecostal Christians, secular liberals, and "knot head" conservatives. Combine this journalistic attitude with Percy's interest in science, and you get novels that don't strike you as "religious."

Still, Percy's Christianity, like More's, provides crucial perspectives. Like More, Percy is fascinated by utopias, by modern concepts of the good life.

In *The Thanatos Syndrome*, it's a conspiracy to reduce street crime and raise SAT scores by adding chemicals to the drinking water. Given his assumptions about man and history, the data lead More in the opposite direction to that of the utopians. Some of his old patients are returning to him, and he gradually gets a handle on what he calls the death — "thanatos" — syndrome. The additive not only affects the inhibitory function of the brain — which leads to the riotously funny and obscene climax to the novel — it affects the major speech center and, worse, the "locus of self-consciousness."

More's patients can't say "I" or construct sentences; they talk in computer commands. Percy's interest in the mysteries of language began when he was convalescing from TB while still in medical school (he soon left medicine for writing) and read the French Catholic existentialist Gabriel Marcel on the devaluation of symbols. In this novel, it's Father Smith who tells More about how words can be deprived of meanings.

"Name it!" he says. "Any words, Tom, U.S.A., God, Simon, prayer, sin, heaven, world."

In these times, Smith tells Tom, Christian concepts don't "signify." As a Catholic novelist, Percy has always used the indirect method of expressing himself, not unlike Thomas More in "Utopia."

Percy has Father Smith explain to More that if you cross a lover of Mankind (Whitman) with a theorist of Mankind (Rousseau or Skinner) "what you've got now is a Robespierre or Stalin or Hitler and the Terror, and millions dead for the good of Mankind. Right?"

Maybe. Anyway, the novel ends with the plot foiled, people returning to normal.

Early on, More said that the way to reach someone who's tied in knots is to ask him to help you with something. Percy has a fine ear and eye for behavior; he has a lot of fun catching different voices and body language gestures. The last sentence of the book echoes an earlier consultation with one of his patients. This time when she comes, the Na-24 has worn off and she meets his gaze:

> She falls silent, but her eyes are softer, livelier, are searching mine as if I were the mirror of her very self. She lets go of her hand. She almost smiles. She ducks her head and touches the nape of her neck as she used to.
> "Well?" I say.
> She opens her mouth to speak.
> Well well well.

And all shall be well? Not exactly. But the good flawed doctor will continue to bear witness to what is truly lovable in his patients and draw it out. Times are bad, the language of love is mute. *Well well well*, we note, is not said by anyone.

Still, Percy's novels (he is proud of his happy endings) do give one a lift, not in the usual way of fiction, perhaps, but in the way of parable. The hero of "The Thanatos Syndrome" is indeed Sir Thomas More, the saint / Dr. Tom More. It's as if without the Christian concept of the cross, the definition of man is open to the deformations of scientism, and man vulnerable to all sorts of nutty schemes. Regardless of its ultimate standing as a novel *The Thanatos Syndrome* bears witness to the validity of Christian humanism in our time.

SELF-INTERVIEW

Questions They Never Asked Me (So He Asked Them Himself)

Walker Percy*

Question: Will you consent to an interview?

Answer: No.

Q: Why not?

A: Interviews always ask the same questions, such as: What time of day do you write? Do you type or write longhand? What do you think of the South? What do you think of the New South? What do you think of southern writers? Who are your favorite writers? What do you think of Jimmy Carter?

Q: You're not interested in the South?

A: I'm sick and tired of talking about the South and hearing about the South.

Q: Do you regard yourself as a southern writer?

A: That is a strange question, even a little mad. Sometimes I think that the South brings out the latent madness in people. It even makes me feel nutty to hear such a question.

Q: What's mad about such a question?

A: Would you ask John Cheever if he regarded himself as a northeastern writer?

Q: What do you think of southern writers?

A: I'm fed up with the subject of southern writing. Northern writing, too, for that matter. I'm also fed up with questions about the state of the novel, alienation, the place of the artist in American society, race relations, the Old South.

Q: What about the New South?

A: Of all the things I'm fed up with, I think I'm fed up most with hearing about the New South.

Q: Why is that?

A: One of the first things I can remember in my life was hearing about the New South. I was three years old, in Alabama. Not a year has passed since that I haven't heard about a new South. I would dearly love

*From *Esquire*, December 1977, 170, 172, 184, 186, 188, 190, 193–94. ©1977 by Walker Percy. Reprinted by permission of McIntosh and Otis, Inc.

never to hear the New South mentioned again. In fact my definition of a new South would be a South in which it never occurred to anybody to mention the New South. One glimmer of hope is that this may be happening.

Q: But people have a great curiosity about the South now that Jimmy Carter is President.

A: I doubt that. If there is anything more boring than the questions asked about the South, it is the answers southerners give. If I hear one more northerner ask about good ol' boys and one more southerner give an answer, I'm moving to Manaus, Brazil, to join the South Carolinians who emigrated after Appomattox and whose descendants now speak no English and have such names as Senhor Carlos Calhoun. There are no good ol' boys in Manaus.

Q: In the past you have expressed admiration for such living writers as Bellow, Updike, Didion, Mailer, Cheever, Foote, Barthelme, Gass, Heller. Do you still subscribe to such a list?

A: No.

Q: Why not?

A: I can't stand lists of writers. Compiling such a list means leaving somebody out. When serious writers make a list, they're afraid of leaving somebody out. When critics and poor writers do it, they usually mean to leave somebody out. It seems a poor practice in either case.

Q: Do you have any favorite dead writers?

A: None that I care to talk about. Please don't ask me about Dostoevski or Kierkegaard.

Q: How about yourself? Would you comment on your own writing?

A: No.

Q: Why not?

A: I can't stand to think about it.

Q: Could you say something about the vocation of writing in general?

A: No.

Q: Nothing?

A: All I can think to say about it is that it is a very obscure activity in which there is usually a considerable element of malice. Like frogging.

Q: Frogging?

A: Yes. Frogging is raising a charley horse on somebody's arm by a skillful blow with a knuckle in exactly the right spot.

Q: What are your hobbies?

A: I don't have any.

Q: What magazines do you read?

A: None.

Q: What are your plans for summer reading?

A: I don't have any.

Q: Do you keep a journal?

A: No.

Q: But don't writers often keep journals?

A: So I understand. But I could never think what to put in a journal. I used to read writers' journals and was both astonished and depressed by the copiousness of a single day's entry: thoughts, observations, reflections, descriptions, snatches of plots, bit of poetry, sketches, aphorisms. The one time I kept a journal I made two short entries in three weeks. One entry went so: *Four p.m. Thursday afternoon — The only thing notable is that nothing is notable. I wonder if any writer has ever recorded the observation that most time passes and most events occur without notable significance. I am sitting here looking out the window at a tree and wondering why it is that though it is a splendid tree, it is of not much account. It is no good to me. Is it the nature of the human condition or the nature of the age that things of value are devalued?* I venture to say that most people most of the time experience the same four o'clock-in-the-afternoon devaluation. But I have noticed an interesting thing. If such a person, a person like me feeling lapsed at four o'clock in the afternoon, should begin reading a novel about a person feeling lapsed at four o'clock in the afternoon, a strange thing happens. Things increase in value.

Possibilities open. This may be the main function of art in this peculiar age: to reverse the devaluation. What the artist or writer does is not depict a beautiful tree — this only depresses you more than ever — no, he depicts the commonplaceness of an everyday tree. Depicting the commonplace allows the reader to penetrate the commonplace. The only other ways the husk of the commonplace can be penetrated is through the occurrence of natural disasters or the imminence of one's own death. These measures are not readily available on ordinary afternoons.

Q: How would you describe the place of the writer and artist in American life?

A: Strange.

Q: How do you perceive your place in society?

A: I'm not sure what that means.

Q: Well, in this small Louisiana town, for example.

A: I'm still not sure what you mean. I go to the barbershop to get a haircut and the barber says: "How you doing, Doc?" I say: "Okay." I go to the post office to get the mail and the clerk says: "What's up, Doc?" Or I go to a restaurant on Lake Pontchartrain and the waitress says: "What you want, honey?" I say: "Some cold beer and crawfish." She brings me an ice-cold beer and a platter of boiled crawfish that are very good, especially if you suck the heads. Is that what you mean?

Q: What about living in the South with its strong sense of place, of tradition, of rootedness, of tragedy — the only part of America that has ever tasted defeat?

A: I've read about that. Actually I like to stay in motels in places like Lincoln, Nebraska, or San Luis Obispo.

Q: But what about these unique characteristics of the South? Don't they tend to make the South a more hospitable place for writers?

A: Well, I've heard about that, the storytelling tradition, sense of identity, tragic dimension, community, history and so forth. But I was never quite sure what it meant. In fact I'm not sure that the opposite is not the case. People don't read much in the South and don't take writers very seriously, which is probably as it should be. I've managed to live here for thirty years and am less well-known than the Budweiser distributor. The only famous person in this town is Isiah Robertson, linebacker for the Rams, and that is probably as it should be, too. There are advantages to living an obscure life and being thought an idler. If one lived in a place like France where writers are honored, one might well end up like Sartre, a kind of literary-political pope, a savant, an academician, the very sort of person Sartre made fun of in *Nausea*. On the other hand, if one is thought an idler and a bum, one is free to do what one pleases. One day a fellow townsman asked me: "What do you do, Doc?" "Well, I write books." "I know that, Doc, but what do you really do?" "Nothing." He nodded. He was pleased that I was pleased.

I have a theory of why Faulkner became a great writer. It was not the presence of a tradition and all that, as one generally hears, but the absence. Everybody in Oxford, Mississippi, knew who Faulkner was, not because he was a great writer but because he was a local character, a little bitty fellow who put on airs, wore a handkerchief up his sleeve, a ne'er-do-well, Count No-count they called him. He was tagged like a specimen under a bell jar; no matter what he wrote thereafter, however great or wild or strange it was, it was all taken as part of the act. It was part of "what Bill Faulkner did." So I can imagine it became a kind of game with him, with him going to extraordinary lengths in his writing to see if he could shake them out of their mild, pleasant inattention. I don't mean he wanted his fellow southerners to pay him homage, that his life and happiness depended on what they thought of him. No, it was a kind of game. One can imagine Robinson Crusoe on his island doing amazing acrobatics for his herd of goats, who might look up, dreamily cud chewing for a moment, then go on with their grazing. "That one didn't grab you?" Crusoe might say, then come out with something even more stupendous. But even if he performed the ultimate stunt, the Indian rope trick, where he climbs up a stiff rope and disappears, the goats would see it as no more or less than what this character does under the circumstances. Come to think of it, who would want it otherwise? There is a good deal of talk about community and the lack of it, but one of the nice things about living an obscure life in the South is that people don't come up to you, press your hand and give you soulful looks. I would have hated to belong to the Algonquin round table, where people made witty remarks and discussed Ezra Pound. Most men in the South don't read and the women who do usually prefer Taylor Caldwell and Phyllis Whitney to Faulkner and O'Connor.

No, it is the very absence of a tradition that makes for great originals like Faulkner and O'Connor and Poe. The South is Crusoe's island for a writer and there's the good and bad of it. There is a literary community of sorts in the North. The best northern writers are accordingly the best of a kind. As different as Bellow, Cheever, Updike and Pynchon are, their differences are within a genus, like different kinds of fruit: apples, oranges, plums, pears. A critic or reviewer can compare and contrast them with one another. But Faulkner, O'Connor, Barthelme? They're moon berries, kiwi fruit, niggertoes.

Q: Niggertoes?

A: That's what we used to call Brazil nuts.

Q: How did you happen to become a writer? Didn't you start out as a doctor?

A: Yes, but I had no special talent for it. Others in my class were smarter. Two women, three Irish Catholics, four Jews and ten WASPs were better at it than I. What happened was that I discovered I had a little knack for writing. Or perhaps it is desire, a kind of underhanded desire.

Q: What do you mean by knack?

A: It is hard to say.

Q: Try.

A: I suspect it is something all writers have in greater or lesser degree. Maybe it's inherited, maybe it's the result of a rotten childhood — I don't know. But unless you have it, you'll never be a writer.

Q: Can you describe the knack?

A: No, except in negative terms. It is not what people think it is. Most people think it is the perfecting of the ordinary human skills of writing down words and sentences. Everybody writes words and sentences — for example, in a letter. A book is thought to be an extended and improved letter, the way a pro ballplayer is thought to do things with a ball most men can do, only better. Not so. Or if you have an unusual experience, all you have to do is "write it up," the more unusual and extraordinary the experience the better, like My Most Extraordinary Experience in *Reader's Digest*. Not so. Psychologists know even less about writing than laymen. Show me a psychologist with a theory of creativity and I'll show you a bad writer.

Q: Can't you say what the knack is?

A: No, except to say that it is a peculiar activity, as little understood as chicken fighting or entrail reading, and that the use of words, sentences, paragraphs, plots, characters and so forth are the accidents, not the substance, of it.

Q: What is it if not the putting together of words and sentences?

A: I can't answer that except to say two things. One is that it is a little trick one gets onto, a very minor trick. One does it and discovers to one's surprise that most people can't do it. I used to know a fellow in high school who, due to an anomaly of his eustachian tubes, could blow smoke out of both ears. He enjoyed doing it and it was diverting to watch. Writing is something like that. Another fellow I knew in college, a fraternity brother and a trumpet player, could swell out his neck like a puff adder — the way the old horn player Clyde McCoy used to do when he played *Sugar Blues*.

The other thing about the knack is that it has theological, demonic and sexual components. One is aware on the one hand of a heightened capacity for both malice and joy and, occasionally and with luck, for being able to see things afresh and even to makes things the way the Old Testament said that God made things and took a look at them and saw that they were good.

The best novels, and the best part of a novel, is a creatio ex nihilo. Unlike God, the novelist does not start with nothing and make something of it. He starts with himself as nothing and makes something of the nothing with things at hand. If the novelist has a secret it is not that he has a special something but that he has a special nothing. Camus said that all philosophy comes from the possibility of suicide. This is probably not true, one of those intellectual oversimplifications to which the French regularly fall prey. Suicide, the real possibility of self-nihilation, has more to do with writing poems and novels. A novelist these days has to be an ex-suicide. A good novel — and, I imagine, a good poem — is possible only after one has given up and let go. Then, once one realizes that all is lost, the jig is up, that after all nothing is dumber than a grown man sitting down and making up a story to entertain somebody or working in a "tradition" or "school" to maintain his reputation as a practitioner of the *nouveau roman* or whatever — once one sees that this is a dumb way to live, that all is vanity sure enough, there are two possibilities: either commit suicide or not commit suicide. If one opts for the former, that is that: it is a *letzte Lösung* and there is nothing more to write or say about it. But if one opts for the latter, one is in a sense dispensed and living on borrowed time. One is not dead! One is alive! One is free! I won't say that one is like God on the first day, with the chaos before him and a free hand. Rather one feels, What the hell, here I am washed up, it is true, but also cast up, cast up on the beach, alive and in one piece. I can move my toe up and then down and do anything else I choose. The possibilities open to one are infinite. So why not do something Shakespeare and Dostoevski and Faulkner didn't do, for after all they are nothing more than dead writers, members of this and that tradition, much-admired busts on a shelf. A dead writer may be famous but he is also dead as a duck, finished. And I, cast up here on this beach? I am a survivor! Alive! A free man! They're finished. Possibilities are closed. As for God? That's his affair. True, he made the beach, which, now that I look at it, is not all that great. As for me, I might try a little something here in the wet sand, a word, a form . . .

Q: What's this about a sexual component?

A: I'd rather not say.

Q: Why not?

A: Because no end of dreary bullshit has been written on the subject, so much as to befoul the waters for good. Starting with Freud's rather stupid hydraulic model of art as the sublimation of libidinal energies: libido suppressed in the boiler room squirts up in the attic. There followed half a century of dull jokes about x orgasms equals y novels down the drain, and so forth and so forth. Freud's disciples have been even more stupid about "creative writing." At least Freud had the good sense to know when to shut up, as he did in Dostoevski's case. But stupider still is the more recent Hemingway machismo number. The formula is: Big pencil equals big penis. My own hunch is that those fellows have their troubles, otherwise why make love with a pencil? Renoir may have started it with a smart-ass statement: "I paint with my penis." If I were a woman, I wouldn't stand for such crap. No wonder women get enraged these days. Some of the most feminine women writers have this same knack, or better, and can use it to a fare-thee-well—southern women like K.A. Porter, Welty, O'Connor—look out for them!

The twentieth century, noted for its stupidity in human matters, is even stupider than usual in this case. And in this case Muhammad Ali is smarter than either Freud or Hemingway. Float like a butterfly, sting like a bee. Ali's exaltation and cunning and beauty and malice apply even more to writing than to fighting. Freud made a mistake only a twentieth-century professor would have been capable of: trying to explain the human psyche by a mechanical-energy model. Take away four hundred fifty psychic calories for love and that leaves you four hundred fifty short for art. Actually it's the other way around. The truth is paradoxical and can't be understood in terms of biological systems. Psychic energy is involved here, but it follows a different set of laws. Like Einstein's theory, it at times defies Newton's law of gravitation. Thus it is not the case that E minus one-half E equals one-half E (Newton, Freud) but rather E minus one-half E equals six E. Or simply, zero minus E equals E—which is more astounding than Einstein's E equals MC squared.

I will give you a simple example. Let us say a writer finds himself at 0, naught, zero, at four p.m. of a Thursday afternoon. No energy, depressed, strung out, impotent, constipated, a poet sitting on the kitchen floor with the oven door open and the gas on, an incarnated nothingness, an outer human husk encasing an inner cipher. The jig is up. The poem or novel is no good. But since the jig is up, why not have another look, or tear it up and start over? Then, if he is lucky—or is it grace, God having mercy on the poor bastard?—something opens. A miracle occurs. Somebody must have found the Grail. The fisher king is healed, the desert turns green—or better still: the old desert is still the old desert but the poet names it and makes it a new desert. As for the poet himself: in a strange

union of polarities — wickedness / good, malice / benevolence, hatred /
/ love, butterfly / bee — he, too, comes together, sticks his tongue in his
cheek, sets pencil to paper: What if I should try this? Uh-huh, maybe . . .
He works. He sweats. He stinks. He creates. He sweats and stinks and
creates like a woman conceiving. Then what? It varies. Perhaps he takes a
shower, changes clothes. Perhaps he takes a swim in the ocean. Perhaps he
takes a nap. Perhaps he takes a drink, flatfoots half a glass of bourbon.
Then, if he is near someone he loves or wants to love or should love or
perhaps has loved all along but has not until this moment known it, he
looks at her. And by exactly the same measure by which the novel has
opened to him and he to it, he opens to her and she to him. Well now, why
don't you come here a minute? That's it. Give me your hand. He looks at
her hand. He is like the castaway on the beach who opens his eyes and sees
a sunrise coquina three inches from his nose. Her hand is like the coquina.
What an amazing sight! Well now, why don't we just sit down here on this
cypress log? Imagine your being here at four-thirty in the afternoon. All
this time I thought I was alone on this island and here you are. A miracle!
Imagine Crusoe on his island performing the ultimate stunt for his goats,
when he turns around and there *she* is. Who needs Friday? What he needs
now is her, or she him, as the case may be.

Such is the law of conservation of energy through its expenditure:
Zero minus E equals E.

Q: If writing is a knack, does the knack have anything to do with
being southern?

A: Sure. The knack has certain magic components that once came in
handy for southern writers. This is probably no longer the case.

Q: Why is that?

A: Well, as Einstein once said, ordinary life in an ordinary place on
an ordinary day in the modern world is a *dreary* business. I mean *dreary*.
People will do anything to escape this dreariness: booze up, hit the road,
gaze at fatal car wrecks, shoot up heroin, spend money on gurus, watch
pornographic movies, kill themselves, even watch TV. Einstein said that
was the reason he went into mathematical physics. One of the few things
that diverted me from the dreariness of growing up in a country-club
subdivision in Birmingham was sending off for things. For example,
sending off for free samples, such as Instant Postum. You'd fill in a coupon
clipped from a magazine and send it off to a magic faraway place (Battle
Creek?) and sure enough, one morning the mailman would hand you a
box. Inside would be a small jar. You'd make a cup and in the peculiar
fragrance of Postum you could imagine an easily fragrant and magical
place where clever Yankee experts ground up stuff in great brass mortars.

That was called "sending off for something."

It was even better with Sears and Roebuck: looking at the picture in
the catalog, savoring it, fondling it, sailing to Byzantium with it, then —
even better than poetry — actually getting it, sending off to Chicago for it,

saving up your allowance and mailing a postal money order for twenty-three dollars and forty-seven cents and getting back a gold-filled Elgin railroader's pocket watch with an elk engraved on the back. With a strap and a fob.

Writing is also going into the magic business. It is a double transaction in magic. You have this little workaday thing you do that most people can't do. But in the South there were also certain magic and exotic ingredients, that is, magic and exotic to northerners and Europeans, which made the knack even more mysterious. As exotic to a New Yorker as an Elgin pocket watch to an Alabama boy. I've often suspected that Faulkner was very much onto this trick and overdid it a bit.

You write something, send it off to a *publisher* in *New York* and back it comes as a — book! Print! Pages! Cover! Binding! Scribble-scratch is turned into measured paragraphs, squared-off blocks of pretty print. And even more astounding: in the same mail that brought the Elgin pocket watch come *reviews*, the printed thoughts of people who have *read* the book!

The less the two parties know about each other, the farther apart they are, the stronger the magic. It must be very enervating to be a writer in New York, where you know all about editing and publishing and reviewing, to discover that editors and publishers and reviewers are as bad off as anyone else, maybe worse. Being a writer in the South has it special miseries, which include isolation, madness, tics, amnesia, alcoholism, lust and loss of ordinary powers of speech. One may go for days without saying a word. Then, faced with an interview, one may find oneself talking the way one fancies the interviewer expects one to talk, talking southern — for example, using such words as "Amon": "Amon git up and git myself a drink." Yet there are certain advantages to the isolation. At best one is encouraged to be original; at worst, bizarre; sometimes both, like Poe.

It was this distance and magic that once made for the peculiarities of southern writing. Now the distance and magic are gone, or going, and southern writers are no better off than anyone else, perhaps worse, because now that the tricks don't work and you can't write strange like Faulkner, what do you do? Write like Bellow? But before — and even now, to a degree — the magic worked. You were on your own and making up little packages to send to faraway folk. As marooned as Crusoe, one was apt to be eccentric. That's why Poe, Faulkner, O'Connor and Barthelme are more different from one another than Bellow, Updike and Cheever are.

The southern writer at his best was of value because he was somewhat extraterrestrial. (At his worst he was overwhelmed by Faulkner: there is nothing more feckless than imitating an eccentric.) He was different enough from the main body of writers to give the reader a triangulation point for getting a fix on things. There are degrees of difference. If the writer is altogether different from the genus *Writer*, which is the only genus the reviewer knows, the reviewer is baffled — as New York reviewers like Clifton Fadiman were baffled by Faulkner; they were trying to compare him with such standard writers as Thornton Wilder, and it can't be done. But if the critic recognizes the value of difference, the possibility of an extraterrestrial point of view, he will be excited. That's why the French went nuts over Poe and Faulkner.

Meanwhile, Mississippians shrugged their shoulders.

Q: Would you care to say something about your own novels?

A: No.

Q: What about your last novel, *Lancelot?*

A: What about it?

Q: What do you have to say about it?

A: Nothing.

Q: How would you describe it?

A: As a small cautionary tale.

Q: That's all?

A: That's all.

Q: It has generally been well reviewed. What do you think of reviews?

A: Very little. Reading reviews of your own book is a peculiar experience. It is a dubious enterprise, a no-win game. If the review is flattering, one tends to feel vain and uneasy. If it is bad, one tends to feel exposed, found out. Neither feeling does you any good. Besides that, most reviews are of not much account. How could it be otherwise? I feel sorry for reviewers. I feel sorry for myself when I write a review. Book reviewing is a difficult and unrewarding literary form and right now no one is doing it. The reviewer's task is almost impossible. A writer may spend years doing his obscure thing, his little involuted sexual-theological number, and there's the poor reviewer with two or three days to figure out what he's up to. And even if the review is good, you're in no mood to learn anything from it. The timing is all bad. You're sick to death of the book and don't even want to think about it. Then, just when you think you're rid of this baby, have kicked him and his droppings out of the nest forever, along come these folks who want to talk about him.

Q: Do you feel bad about a bad review?

A: Moderately bad. One likes to be liked. The curious thing is I always expect people to like me and my writing and am surprised when they don't. I suffer from the opposite of paranoia, a benign psychosis for which there is no word. I say "curious" because there is a good deal of malice in my writing — I have it in for this or that — but it is not personal malice and I'm taken aback when people take offense.

A rave review makes me feel even more uneasy. It's like being given an A plus by the teacher or a prize by the principal. All you want to do is grab your report card and run — before you're found out.

Q: Found out for what?

A: Found out for being what you are (and what in this day and age I

think a serious writer has to be): an ex-suicide, a cipher, naught, zero —
which is as it should be because being a naught is the very condition of
making anything. This is a secret. People don't know this. Even distinguished critics are under the misapprehension that you are something, a
substance, that you represent this or that tradition, a skill, a growing store
of wisdom. Whereas in fact what you are doing is stripping yourself naked
and putting yourself in the eye of the hurricane and leaving the rest to
chance, luck or providence. Faulkner said it in fact: Writing a novel is like
a one-armed man trying to nail together a chicken coop in a hurricane. I
think of it as more like trying to pick up a four-hundred-pound fat lady:
you need a lot of hands to hold up a lot of places at once.

There are four kinds of reviews, three of which are depressing and
one of which is at best tolerable.

The first is the good good review. That is, a review that is not only
laudatory but is also canny and on the mark. One is exhilarated for three
seconds, then one becomes furtive and frightened. One puts it away quick,
before it turns into a pumpkin.

The second is the bad good review. That is, it is the routine
"favorable" review that doesn't understand the book. The only thing to say
about it is that it is better to get a bad good review than a bad bad review.

The third is the bad bad review. It is a hateful review in which the
reviewer hates the book for reasons he is unwilling to disclose. He is
offended. But he must find other reasons for attacking the book than the
cause of the offense. I don't blame this reviewer. In fact he or she is sharper
than most. He or she is onto the secret that novel writing is a serious
business in which the novelist is out both to give joy, and to draw blood.
The hateful review usually means that one has succeeded only in doing the
latter. The name of this reviewer's game is: "Okay, you want to play
rough? Very well, here comes yours." A hateful reviewer is like a street
fighter: he doesn't let on where he's been hit and he hits you with
everything he's got — a bad tactic. Or he lies low and waits for a chance to
blindside you. A bad bad review doesn't really hurt. Getting hit by an
offended reviewer reminds me of the old guy on *Laugh-In* who would
make a pass at Ruth Buzzi on the park bench and get slammed across the
chops by a soft purse. It's really a love tap. I can't speak for Ruth Buzzi but
I can speak for the old guy: all he wants to say is, "Come on, honey, give
me a kiss."

The fourth is the good bad review, a rare bird. It would be the most
valuable if one were in any shape to learn, which one is not. It is the
critical review that accurately assesses both what the novelist had in mind,
was trying to do, and how and where he failed. It hurts because the failure
is always great, but the hurt is salutary, like pouring iodine in an open
wound. Here the transaction is between equals, a fair fight, no blind-
siding. It makes me think of old-movie fistfights between John Wayne and
Ward Bond. Ward lets the Duke have one, racks him up real good. The

Duke shakes his head to clear it, touches the corner of his mouth, looks at the blood, grins in appreciation. Nods. All right. That's a fair transaction, a frontal assault by an equal. But what the hateful reviewer wants to do is blind-side you, the way Chuck Bednarik blind-sided Frank Gifford and nearly killed him. Unlike Chuck Bednarik, the hateful review can't hurt you. He gives away too much of himself. The only way he can hurt you is in the pocketbook — the way a playwright can be knocked off by a *Times* reviewer — but in the case of a book even that is doubtful.

Even so, one is still better off with hateful reviewers than with admiring reviewers. If I were a castaway on a desert island, I'd rather be marooned with six hateful reviewers than with six admiring reviewers. The hateful men would be better friends and the hateful women would be better lovers.

The truth is all reviewers and all your fellow novelists are your friends and lovers. All serious writers and readers constitute less than one percent of the population. The other ninety-nine percent don't give a damn. They watch *Wonder Woman.* We are a tiny shrinking minority and our worst assaults on each other are love taps compared with the massive indifference surrounding us. Gore Vidal and Bill Buckley are really two of a kind, though it will displease both to hear it. Both are serious moralists to whom I attach high value.

Q: Do you see the Jimmy Carter phenomenon as a revival of Protestant Christianity or as a renascence of Jeffersonian populism or the southern political genius or all three, and if so, what is the impact on the southern literary imagination and race relations?

A: How's that again?

Q: Do you —

A: What was that about race relations?

Q: How do you assess the current state of race relations in the South?

A: Almost as bad as in the North.

Q: But hasn't there occurred a rather remarkable reconciliation of the races in the South as a consequence of its strong Christian tradition and its traditional talent for human relations?

A: I haven't noticed it. The truth is most blacks and whites don't like each other, North or South.

Q: But great changes have taken place, haven't they?

A: Yes, due mainly to court decisions and congressional acts and Lyndon Johnson. It was easier for the South to go along than to resist. After all, we tried that once. Anyhow, as Earl Long used to say, the feds have the bomb now.

Q: Can you say anything about the future of race relations?

A: No.

Q: Why not?

A: I'm white. It's up to the blacks. The government has done all it can do. The whites' course is predictable. Like anybody else, they will simply hold on to what they've got as long as they can. When did any other human beings behave differently? The blacks have a choice. They can either shoot up the place, pull the whole damn thing down around our ears — they can't win but they can ruin it for everybody — or they can join the great screwed-up American middle class. Of course what they're doing is both, mostly the latter. It is noteworthy that blacks, being smarter than whites about such things, have shown no interest in the Communist party. Blacks seem less prone than whites to fall prey to abstractions. Comradeship and brotherhood are all very well, but what I really want is out of this ghetto, and if I can make it and you can't, too bad about you, brother. But that's the American dream, isn't it? It will even make them happy like it did us — for a while. It will take them years to discover just how screwed up the American middle class is. I visualize a U.S. a few years from now in which blacks and whites have switched roles. The pissed-off white middle class will abandon suburbia just as they abandoned the cities, either for the countryside, where they will live in r.v.'s, mobile homes, converted barns, log cabins, antebellum outhouses, Revolutionary stables, silos, sod huts, or to move back to the city, back to little ethnic cottages like Mayor Daley's Victorian shotguns, stained-glass boardinghouses, converted slave quarters, abandoned street cars — while the blacks move out to Levittown and the tracts, attend the churches of their choice, P.T.A.'s, Rotary, Great Books. In fact it's already happening. The only danger is that this happy little switch may not happen fast enough and the young blacks in the city who have little or nothing to lose may say the hell with it and shoot up everything in sight.

There is a slight chance, maybe one in a hundred, that blacks and whites may learn the best of each other rather than the worst.

Q: What is the worst?

A: Well, whites in the Western world don't know how to live and blacks don't know how to govern themselves. It would be nice if each could learn the gift of the other. But there are already signs in America that blacks are learning the white incapacity for life. For example, they've almost reached the white incidence of suicide and gastric ulcer and have surpassed them in hypertension. And some white politicians govern like Haitians and Ugandans. I've noticed that more and more blacks act like Robert Young as Dr. Marcus Welby, with that same tight-assed, suspect post-Protestant rectitude, while more and white politicians act like Idi Amin.

Q: Can you describe the best thing that could happen?

A: No. All I can say is that is has something to do with southern good nature, good manners, kidding around, with music, with irony, with being able to be pissed off without killing other people or yourself, maybe with Jewish humor, with passing the time, with small unpretentious civic-minded meetings. Some whites and blacks are sitting around a table in Louisiana, eating crawfish and drinking beer at a P.T.A. fund raiser. The table is somewhat polarized, whites at one end, blacks at the other, segregated not ill-naturedly but from social unease, like men and women at a party. The talk is somewhat stiff and conversation making and highfaluting—about reincarnation in fact. Says a white to a white who has only had a beer or two: "I think I'd rather come back as an English gentleman in the eighteenth century rather than this miserable century of war, alienation and pollution." Says a black to a black who has had quite a few beers: "I'd rather come back as this damn crawfish than as a nigger in Louisiana." All four laugh and have another beer. I don't know why I'm telling you this. You wouldn't understand it. You wouldn't understand what is bad about it, what is good about it, what is unusual about it or what there is about it that might be the hundred-to-one shot that holds the solution.

Q: Why do you leave Christianity out as one of the ingredients of better race relations?

A: Because the Christians left it out. Maybe Jimmy Carter and Andrew Young and a few others mean what they say, I don't know, but look at the white churches. They generally practice the same brand of brotherhood as the local country club. If Jesus Christ showed up at the Baptist church in Plains, the deacons would call the cops. No, the law, government, business, sports, show business, have done more here than the churches. There seems to be an inverse relationship between God and brotherhood in the churches. In the Unitarian Church, it's all brotherhood and no God. Outside the churches the pocketbook has replaced the Holy Ghost as the source of brotherhood. Show me an A & P today that is losing money because it is not hiring blacks and I'll show you an A & P tomorrow that has hired blacks and, what is more, where blacks and whites get along fine.

Q: But aren't you a Catholic?

A: Yes.

Q: Do you regard yourself as a Catholic novelist?

A: Since I am a Catholic and a novelist, it would seem to follow that I am a Catholic novelist.

Q: What kind of Catholic are you?

A: Bad.

Q: No. I mean are you liberal or conservative?

A: I no longer know what those words mean.

Q: Are you a dogmatic Catholic or an open-minded Catholic?

A: I don't know what that means, either. Do you mean do I believe the dogma that the Catholic Church proposes for belief?

Q: Yes.

A: Yes.

Q: How is such a belief possible in this day and age?

A: What else is there?

Q: What do you mean, what else is there? There is humanism,

atheism, agnosticism, Marxism, behaviorism, materialism, Buddhism, Muhammadanism, Sufism, astrology, occultism, theosophy.

A: That's what I mean.

Q: To say nothing of Judaism and Protestantism.

A: Well, I would include them along with the Catholic Church in the whole peculiar Jewish-Christian thing.

Q: I don't understand. Would you exclude, for example, scientific humanism as a rational and honorable alternative?

A: Yes.

Q: Why?

A: It's not good enough.

Q: Why not?

A: This life is much too much trouble, far too strange, to arrive at the end of it and then to be asked what you make of it and to have to answer "Scientific humanism." That won't do. A poor show. Life is a mystery, love is a delight. Therefore I take it as axiomatic that one should settle for nothing less than the infinite mystery and the infinite delight, i.e., God. In fact I demand it. I refuse to settle for anything less. I don't see why anyone should settle for less than Jacob, who actually grabbed aholt of God and wouldn't let go until God identified himself and blessed him.

Q: Grabbed aholt?

A: A Louisiana expression.

Q: But isn't the Catholic Church in a mess these days, badly split, its liturgy barbarized, vocations declining?

A: Sure. That's a sign of its divine origins, that it survives these periodic disasters.

Q: You don't act or talk like a Christian. Aren't they supposed to love one another and do good works?

A: Yes.

Q: You don't seem to have much use for your fellowman or do many good works.

A: That's true. I haven't done a good work in years.

Q: In fact, if I may be frank, you strike me as being rather negative in your attitude, cold-blooded, aloof, derisive, self-indulgent, more fond of the beautiful things of this world than of God.

A: That's true.

Q: You even seem to take a certain satisfaction in the disasters of the twentieth century and to savor the imminence of world catastrophe rather than world peace, which all religions seek.

A: That's true.

Q: You don't seem to have much use for your fellow Christians, to say nothing of Ku Kluxers, A.C.L.U'ers, northerners, southerners, fem-libbers, anti-fem-libbers, homosexuals, anti-homosexuals, Republicans, Democrats, hippies, anti-hippies, senior citizens.

A: That's true—though taken as individuals they turn out to be more or less like oneself, i.e., sinners, and we get along fine.

Q: Even Ku Kluxers?

A: Sure.

Q: How do you account for your belief?

A: I can only account for it as a gift from God.

Q: Why would God make you such a gift when there are others who seem more deserving, that is, serve their fellowman?

A: I don't know. God does strange things. For example, he picked as one of his saints a fellow in northern Syria, a local nut, who stood on top of a pole for thirty-seven years.

Q: We are not talking about saints.

A: That's true.

Q: We are talking about what you call a gift.

A: You want me to explain it? How would I know? The only answer I can give is that I asked for it, in fact demanded it. I took it as an intolerable state of affairs to have found myself in this life and in this age, which is a disaster by any calculation, without demanding a gift commensurate with the offense. So I demanded it. No doubt other people feel differently.

Q: But shouldn't faith bear some relation to the truth, facts?

A: Yes. That's what attracted me, Christianity's rather insolent claim to be true, with the implication that other religions are more or less false.

Q: You believe that?

A: Of course.

Q: I see. Moving right along now —

A: To what?

Q: To language. Haven't you done some writing about the nature of language?

A: Yes.

Q: Will you say something about your ideas about language?

A: No.

Q: Why not?

A: Because, for one thing, nobody is interested. The nature of language is such, I have discovered from experience, that even if anyone had the ultimate solution to the mystery of language, no one would pay the slightest attention. In fact most people don't even know there is a mystery. Here is an astounding fact, when you come to think of it. The use of symbols between creatures, the use of language in particular, appears to be the one unique phenomenon in the universe, is certainly the single behavior that most clearly sets man apart from the beasts, is also the one activity in which humans engage most of the time, even asleep and dreaming. Yet it is the least understood of all phenomena. We know less about it than about the back side of the moon or the most distant supernova — and are less interested.

Q: Why is that? Why aren't people interested?

A: Because there are two kinds of people, laymen and scientists. The layman doesn't see any mystery. Since he is a languaged creature and sees everything through the mirror of language, asking him to consider the nature of language is like asking a fish to consider the nature of water. He cannot imagine its absence, so he cannot consider its presence. To the layman, language is a transparent hum-drum affair. Where is the mystery? People see things, are given the names of things when they are children, have thoughts, which they learn to express in words and sentences, talk and listen, read and write. So where is the mystery? That's the general lay attitude toward language. On the other hand there are the theorists of language, who are very much aware of the mystery and who practice such esoteric and abstruse disciplines as transformational generative grammar, formal semantics, semiotics, and who by and large have their heads up their asses and can't even be understood by fellow specialists. They remind me of nothing so much as the Scholastics of the fifteenth century, who would argue about the number of angels that could dance on the head of a pin.

Q: Haven't you written something about a theory of language?

A: Yes.

Q: Could you summarize your thoughts on the subject?

A: No.

Q: Why not?

A: It is not worth the trouble. What is involved in a theory of language is a theory of man, and people are not interested. Despite the catastrophes of this century and man's total failure to understand himself and deal with himself, people still labor under the illusion that a theory of man exists. It doesn't. As bad and confused as things are, they have to get even worse before people realize they don't have the faintest idea what sort of creature man is. Then they might want to know. Until then, one is wasting one's time. I'm not interested in butting my head against a stone wall. I've written something on the subject. Maybe ten years from now, fifty years from now, some people will be interested. That's their affair. People are not really interested in science nowadays. They are interested in pseudoscientific mysteries.

Q: Like what?

A: Laymen are more interested in such things as the Bermuda Triangle, U.F.O.'s, hypnotic regression, Atlantis, astrology — pseudomysteries. Scientists are more interested in teaching apes to talk than in finding out why people talk. It is one of the peculiarities of the age that scientists are more interested in spending millions of dollars and man-hours trying to teach chimps to use language in order to prove that language is not a unique property of man than in studying the property itself. Scientists tend to be dogmatic about the nature of man. Again they remind me of the Scholastics battling with Galileo. Scholastics spent thousands of man-hours inside their heads trying to prove that Jupiter couldn't have moons and that the earth was at the center of the universe. To suggest otherwise offended their sense of the order of things. Galileo pointed to his telescope: Why don't you take a look?

Today we have plenty of scholastics of language. What we need is a Galileo who is willing to take a look at it.

Q: You still haven't said what you think of Jimmy Carter.

A: No.

Q: There is an extraordinary divergence of opinion. Some say he is the greatest of all southern con artists, that everything he says and does in the way of humility, sincerity, honesty, love, brotherhood and so forth is an act, a calculated living up to an image. Others say that these virtues are real. Which is it?

A: Is there a difference?

Q: Moving right along. . . . This is a pleasant room we're sitting in, overlooking a pleasant bayou.

A: Yes it is. It is still a pretty country, despite the fact that the white man did his best to ruin it, ran the Indians off, cut down all the trees.

Q: Is that a portrait of you over the fireplace?

A: Yes. It was done by an artist friend of mine, Lyn Hill. I like it very much.

Q: I don't quite get it. What's going on there?

A: It shows me — well, not exactly me, a version of me — standing in front of what seems to be another framed painting. A picture within a picture, so to speak.

Q: What does it mean to you?

A: I can only say what I see. The artist may very well disagree, but after all the subject and viewer is entitled to his own ideas — like a book reviewer. I identify the subject of the portrait as a kind of composite of the protagonists of my novels, but most expecially Lancelot. He is not too attractive a fellow and something of a nut besides. As we say in the South, he's mean as a yard dog. It is not a flattering portrait — he is not the sort of fellow you'd like to go fishing with. He is, as usual, somewhat out of it, out of the world that is framed off behind him. Where is he? It is an undisclosed place, a kind of limbo. It's a dark place — look at that background — if one believed in auras, his would be a foreboding one. It is a kind of desert, a bombed-out place, a place after the end of the world, a no-man's land of blasted trees and barbed wire. As for him, he is neither admirable nor attractive. Rather, he is cold-eyed and sardonic. There is a gleam in his eyes, a muted and dubious satisfaction. He is looking straight at the viewer, soliciting him ironically: *You and I know something, don't we? Or do we?* Or rather: *The chances are ninety-nine in a hundred you don't know, but on the other hand you might be the one in a hundred who does — not that it makes that much difference. True, this is a strange world I'm in, but what about the world you're in? Have you noticed it lately? Are we into something, you and I? Probably not.*

But look at this apocalyptic world behind him. Something is going on. Is he aware of it? The dead blasted tree is undergoing a transformation. Into — ? Into what? A bound figure? Figures? A woman? Lovers? The no-man's-land barbed wire is not really wire but a brier and it is blooming! A rose! Behind him there is a window of sorts, an opening out of his dark world onto a lovely seascape/skyscape. A new world! Yet he goes on looking straight at the viewer, challenging him: *Yes, I know about it, but do you? If you do, well and good. If you don't, there's no use in my telling you or turning around and pointing it out.* There's a limit to what writers can tell readers and artists can tell viewers. Perhaps he is Lancelot with the world and his life in ruins around him, but there is a prospect of a new world in the Shenandoah Valley. There was something wrong with the old world, the old things, the old flowers, the old skies, old clouds — or something wrong with his way of seeing them. They were used up. They have to be seen anew. Here is a new sky, a new sea, a new rose. . . .

Q: Could you say something about your debt to Kierkegard?

A: No.

Q: Could you at least explicate the painting in Kierkegaardian terms?

A: If I do, will you leave me alone?

Q: Yes.

A: Very well. I see the painting as depicting the very beginning of the Kierkegaardian stages of life — which can apply to an individual, a people, an age. It is the dawn of the aesthetic stage, the emergence of life from death, of light from darkness, the first utterance of words between people. The desert is just beginning to flower and there is the possibility that there may be survivors after the catastrophe. He, somewhat sardonic and smartassed as usual, knows it but does not want to give away the secret too easily. So he keeps his own counsel, except for the faintest glimmer in his eye — of risibility, even hope? — which says to the viewer: *I doubt if you know what's going on, but then again you just might. Do you? Do you understand?*

Q: No.

ESSAYS

The Pilgrimage of Walker Percy   Alfred Kazin*

> . . . goofy as he was, he knew two things not many people know. He knew how to listen and he knew how to get at that most secret and aggrieved enterprise upon which almost everyone is embarked.
>
> —Walker Percy, *The Last Gentleman*

> Don't think . . . *look!*
>
> —Ludwig Wittgenstein

In 1962 the National Book Award for fiction was awarded to a first novel, *The Moviegoer*, by an unknown writer in Louisiana, Walker Percy, who was a doctor of medicine but had never practiced. The book's publisher, Alfred A. Knopf, was not elated by the news—he had been rooting for another novel on his list, William Maxwell's *The Château*—and more than one editor in his employ heard him exclaim, "They're running the prize into the ground!" "They" could have been that year's fiction jury for the National Book Awards—Jean Stafford, Lewis Gannett, Herbert Gold. But it was no secret that Jean Stafford's husband, the *New Yorker* writer A. J. Liebling, had discovered *The Moviegoer* while in Louisiana doing the series of pieces on Huey Long's brother that became *The Earl of Louisiana*.

The book had not been launched with any great expectations. *The Moviegoer* was indeed published only because one editor at Knopf's had stuck with it. In its first draft this editor had found only forty good pages and a rather evangelical Catholic ending, and under his patient counseling the book was twice rewritten from start to finish. The final draft was the fourth.

Mr. Knopf's open lack of enthusiasm for the prizewinning novel suddenly gave *The Moviegoer* rather more notice than the National Book Award necessarily creates. Mr. Knopf is as famous for the crusty independence of his ways as he is for being the last great individual entrepreneur

*Reprinted by permission from *Harper's* 242 (1971):81–86.

and tastemaker in American publishing who can afford to please only himself. Mr. A. J. Liebling, in his turn, was a man of equally formidable temperament, and a writer who at the moment, already irritated with his old publisher Alfred A. Knopf for not having done at all well by a book of his called *Chicago: The Second City*, became further irritated over what he felt to be Mr. Knopf's failure to cheer a National Book Award-winning novel that he, A. J. Liebling, had initially brought to influential attention. (*The Moviegoer* had had good reviews in *The National Observer* and *The New Leader*, but had been indifferently reviewed in the unencouraging "Other Fiction" columns of the principal Sunday book supplements.) Mr. Liebling's irritation with Mr. Knopf even led him to make some comments about Mr. Knopf at a Columbia seminar held in conjunction with the Book Awards. While Liebling's remarks were reported in the city edition of the *Times* that night, they disappeared from further editions, supposedly because Mr. Knopf called Mr. Arthur Hays Sulzberger on the subject.

Meanwhile, the astonished and grateful author of *The Moviegoer* quietly accepted the award in New York, expressed his thanks to Mr. Knopf for appearing at the ceremony, and returned to his house, wife, and two daughters in Covington, in the parish of St. Tammany, a small town on the other side of Lake Pontchartrain from New Orleans, where he lived a most comfortable and studious existence and wrote in the bedroom. The ladies in their set — the best in Covington — often asked Mrs. Percy how she could bear having her husband around the house all day.

The agitation over the prize in New York was in sharp contrast with Walker Percy himself and with *The Moviegoer* — a sardonic, essentially philosophical novel about the spiritual solitude of a young stockbroker in the New Orleans suburb of Gentilly who eventually marries a tragically vulnerable young woman to whom he is distantly related. *The Moviegoer* was certainly not a book to arouse the usually tired reviewers of "Other Fiction," or even those editors of Sunday book supplements to whom any book on public affairs nowadays seems more immediately newsworthy than any novel not left by Hemingway in a bank vault. Novels these days get written off with dismaying ease, and *The Moviegoer* was in any event a book difficult to place. It was a lean, tartly written, subtle, not very dramatic attack on the wholly bourgeois way of life and thinking in a "gracious" and "historic" part of the South. But instead of becoming another satire on the South's retreat from its traditions, it was, for all the narrator's bantering light tone, an altogether tragic and curiously noble study in the loneliness of necessary human perceptions.

The narrator and protagonist — John Bickerson Bolling, "Binx" — cleverly increases his income every year and carries on in a mechanical way with one of his secretaries after another. But he has become obsessed with the meaninglessness of everything he is just beginning to see, with the despair whose specific character, said Kierkegaard, is precisely that it is unaware of being despair. His father, a doctor, perished during the war;

Binx has a distinct sense of fatherlessness, of traditions he is supposed to carry on that he cannot locate or justify in the cozy ways around him. In the secrecy of his own mind he is excited by the possibility of newly looking at life with the special, hallucinated feeling of discovery that he gives to the movies where he spends many evenings. He has become an enraptured observer of the human face, a man who is training himself to look steadily at the most commonplace things in his path. He has found some tiny chink in the wall of his despair — the act of looking, of seeing and discovering. He is a man who can look and listen, in a world where most people don't. His real life, you might say, is dominated by the excitement of conversion. There is a newness in his life. He is a spiritual voyeur, a seeker after the nearest but most unfathomable places of the human heart. He can listen to the tortured girl Kate, who has a powerful attraction to death and belabors him — his ability to give her all his attention constitutes the love between them. He has become the one man around him who seems to want nothing for himself but to look, to be a spectator in the dark. This clinician and diagnostician of the soul trains himself in the movies. The enlarged, brilliantly lighted and concentrated figures upon the screen have taught him how to focus on the secret human places.

The Moviegoer, essentially a sophisticated search of the search for faith in a world that seems almost bent on destroying it, was not calculated to win great popularity. It was not exactly about going to the movies. It was a brilliant novel about our abandonment, our *Geworfenheit*, as the existentialists used to say — our cast-off state. Yet Binx the narrator and presiding figure was so tart and intractable in tone that one had to be sympathetic to the mind behind it, not impatient with the lack of action, in order to respond. It was, in fact, a book about an outsider for outsiders. Southerners used to call themselves outsiders because they came from the rural, underdeveloped, old-fashioned, defeated South. But as Binx shows, in every passage of his involvement with the sophisticated upper-middle class in New Orleans, it is the South itself that today makes outsiders of its people, breeds a despair that will never know it is despair.

The Moviegoer was, in fact, an odd, haunting unseizable sort of book. It was not "eccentric," did not overplay tone and incident in the current style — it was as decorous as an old-fashioned comedy of manners. But it was evidently and deeply the expression of some inner struggle. The author himself seemed in some fundamentals to feel himself in the wrong, to be an outsider in relation to his society. Southern novelists have made their fame in the twentieth century by proving just how different the South is from the rest of the country. The point of *The Moviegoer* was precisely that Gentilly, New Orleans, the South, had become the representative examples of an America in which people no longer know how to *look* at anything, did not know how or what to look for. They lived with only the most distant intimations of their own pain. One man would have to learn to *see* (as if for the first time) with only the minimum chance of saving himself at all. His bride-to-be, Kate, they both know he cannot save.

The author of *The Moviegoer* was, in every respect, far off the beaten track of the contemporary writing business in New York. He was a Percy, and the Percys of the Deep South—Walker was born in Birmingham, Alabama, and grew up in Greenville, Mississippi—if not ascertainably descended from Hotspur, were definitely descended from a British naval lieutenant, Charles Percy, who by all accounts was an ancestor with some go to him. In 1776 he removed himself from the Dutch West Indies to Wilkinson County in Mississippi where, as one history of the Percy family puts it, "He acquired quite a fortune in lands and slaves." Charles Percy became Don Carlos Percy, something of a Spanish grandee, during the period when Spain controlled the West Florida territory that included the lower third of what is now Mississippi. But, as the Percy family history does not state, he was bedeviled by too many wives—he had had one in England, acquired one in Mississippi—and when the first wife appeared in Mississippi with his son, a full-grown captain in the English Navy, Don Carlos was thoroughly provoked, everybody immediately began suing everybody else, and during the commotion Don Carlos walked down to the creek with a sugar kettle, tied it around his neck, and hopped in. The creek is called Percy's Creek to this day. This ancestor's marital problems are related without sympathy in *Lanterns on the Levee* by the poet-lawyer William Alexander Percy, a life-long bachelor, a painfully dutiful man and generally full of the most immense regard and concern for the Percy family. William Alexander Percy, "Uncle Will,"—*The Moviegoer* is dedicated "in gratitude to W.A.P."—a first cousin of Walker's father LeRoy, became Walker's foster father. His own father died when he was eleven, his mother died two years later, and Walker and his younger brothers LeRoy and Phinizy were brought up by "Uncle Will" in Greenville—in the old Percy house on Percy Street.

W. A. P. was a minor poet (his books were published by Alfred A. Knopf) in the still romantic style of so many minor poets in the Twenties; a graduate of Sewanee and Harvard Law School; a planter without much interest in the family's great cotton plantation, Trail Lake, a noticeable adornment of Greenville; a strong foe of the K. K. K.; sensitive and chivalrous and hot-tempered. By his admission in *Lanterns on the Levee*, the only fun in his life, the only time he broke clear of the Percy family and Greenville, was in the A. E. F. during World War I. Greenville produced some notable literary talents—Shelby Foote, David Cohn, Hodding Carter, Charles Bell—and writers from Mississippi liked to remind the world that Mississippi had produced Faulkner, Eudora Welty, and Tennessee Williams. "Uncle Will" seems to have been proud of Mississippi writers even when his literary tastes were counter to theirs—Faulkner used to play tennis on the Percy court (retiring into the house at regular intervals for the libations that spaced the slow collapse of his game). In some ways William Alexander Percy must have been like Faulkner's lawyer-savant, Gavin Stevens. He was a man almost too sensitive to his family. His father (still another LeRoy Percy) was the last great "aristocratic" figure in Mississippi politics — he was a United States Senator but was replaced by the poor whites' favorite, James Vardaman. Will was so much under the influence of his strict, pure, and burdeningly impressive father that he had the sculptress Malvina Hoffman create over Senator Percy's grave the heroic figure of a medieval knight pensively leaning on his sword. The inscription reads PATRIOT and does not seem to stop the citizenry from leaving empty beer cans around it.

One way to Walker Percy is by way of William Alexander Percy. *Lanterns on the Levee* came out in 1941 (the year W. J. Cash brought out *The Mind of the South*) and is as testily defensive about the South and its traditions as Cash was sardonic. From *Lanterns on the Levee* one gets the impression of a much-harried man, brave, all too responsible to his family and regional heritage, rarely happy, chafing under restrictions that he did not always understand. Since he owned a cotton plantation in the Delta but was bored by business, was a lawyer whose greatest interest was literature, and a man of obviously deep emotions that he could not always find employment for in Greenville, one way out of his many conflicts and dilemmas was to romanticize the South in a way that his cousin Walker has never been tempted to do. In *Lanterns on the Levee* W. A. P. says of the old slaveholders, the landed gentry, the governing class: "Though they have gone, they were not sterile; they have their descendants, whose evaluation of life approximates theirs." In 1965, writing in *Harper's* on "Mississippi: The Fallen Paradise," Walker Percy wrote:

> The bravest Mississippians in recent years have not been Confederates or the sons of Confederates but rather two Negroes, James Meredith and Medgar Evers. . . . No ex-Mississippian is entitled to write of the tragedy which has overtaken his former state with any sense of moral superiority. . . . He strongly suspects that he would not have been counted among the handful . . . who not only did not keep silent but fought hard . . . The Gavin Stevenses have disappeared and the Snopeses have won. . . . Not even Faulkner foresaw the ironic denouement of the tragedy: that the Compsons and Sartorises should not only be defeated by the Snopeses but that in the end they should join them.

William Alexander Percy was perhaps like Gavin Stevens in his love of both the law and literature, but his book shows how completely he lacked the philosophic temper even as he praised it. Everything he says about the struggle between the classes and the races in the South reveals a taste for sentimental abstractions rather than for the facts in social evidence. He of course detested the poor whites who eliminated his father from the United States Senate, and he says proudly of the Delta: "It was not settled by these people; its pioneers were slave-owners and slaves." But as he admits about the descendants of the slaves, "the sober fact is that we understand one another not at all." Despite the usual condescending praise of their "good manners," it is obvious from his book that his black retainers were a constant trial to him, exceeded in their power to annoy him only by the liberals during the New Deal period who were prodding him to expressions of concern for blacks and sharecroppers that he obstinately refused to make. He says of the blacks: "This failure on their part to hold and to pass on their own history is due, I think, not so much to their failure to master any written form of communication as to their obliterating genius for living in the present . . . [The Negro] neither remembers nor plans. The white man does little else; to him the present is the one great unreality."

William Alexander Percy was a romantic agnostic who turned away from his mother's Catholicism; Walker Percy is a Catholic convert — who is by no means romantic about that or about the Church. W. A. P. liked to compare Southerners to Russian aristocrats. Defending the sharecropping system on the Percy cotton plantation, he wrote: "Sharecropping is one of the best systems ever devised to give security and a chance for profit to the simple and the unskilled. It has but one drawback — it must be adminis- tered by human beings to whom it offers an unusual opportunity to rob without detection or punishment. The failure is not in the system itself . . . the failure is in human nature. The Negro is no more on an equality with the white man in plantation matters than in any other dealings between the two." Both *The Moviegoer* and *The Last Gentleman* say some concrete things about money-getting in the South, about the coarsening and thickening of upper-class Southerners, that W. A. P. would surely have found too shocking to swallow.

Yet there is one striking link between these two Percys, quite apart from the fact that one brought the other up, made him financially independent, and that both are Southern gentlemen for whom literature has been an avocation. Will Percy could never feel that he was living up to his father, "The Patriot," whose monument is so out of keeping with the modest gravestones in the Greenville cemetery. Will obviously felt himself to be an inadequate son of the Southern Tradition which finally enclosed him, the small-town litterateur, in wistful gestures of regret, lyric flight, and a nostalgia for a South that perhaps never was. But it has been the genius of Southern writing in our time to keep tradition alive. It has been the South's writers, not its politicians, who have maintained our interest in the South as another country. The Southern writers have in fact perpetu- ated the idea of the South by personalizing its history, by their obstinate moralism, their scorn for corruption, their belief in a true country of the spirit — and their compassion for the Negro.

So Walker Percy seems to me very much a Southern son who believes in the existence of a spiritual tradition, another Southerner orphaned by modern history who still believes in the great cause of Christian truth, not the "lost" cause of the Confederacy. He is a subtle mind and in many respects a hidden one, distinctly different from most American novelists today; Walker Percy becomes clear only when you realize how much he is a pilgrim of faith who believes that there is a true way, a lost tradition, that he will yet discover.

In our time it has been the Southern writer who has been the conscience of the South, who has restored its legends, who has taken on the terror as well as the romance of its history. When Percy was asked at the National Book Awards why the South produced so many good writers, he replied in his usual offhand style, "Because we got beat." But the Byrds as well as the Wallaces rose from "defeat" a long time ago. The Southern writer feels that *he* is still in a state of defeat, of exile, of classic outsidedness and apartness. It is the Southern writer who remains "unreconciled" at a time when dominant elements in the South have become the voice of our spurious Americanism.

Walker Percy belongs with the "defeated" and the "exiled"—one might say that he knows exile and defeat in their purest American state. The story of how he became a writer at all is an important part of it. Percy graduated from the University of North Carolina in 1937 and Columbia's College of Physicians and Surgeons in 1941. He did not particularly like medical school, thought many of his classmates childish—one of their recreations was to fill balloons with water and drop them onto 168th Street—and he still remembers with distaste a box of bones he had to learn to identify. "P" and "S" emphasized the mechanics of disease, and it was in some revolt against this, and because of his interest in psychiatry, that he had himself psychoanalyzed while a medical student. The study of pathology, with its marvelously colored slides, fascinated him. Then, as an intern at Bellevue, he caught pulmonary tuberculosis from one of the many bodies on which he performed autopsies, caught it from "the same scarlet tubercle bacillus I used to see lying crisscrossed like Chinese characters in the sputum and lymphoid tissue of the patients at Bellevue. Now I was one of them."

Two years of physical inactivity followed. America was in the full tide of World War II. His brother LeRoy was a captain in the Air Force, and would get the Bronze Star, his brother Phinizy, an Annapolis graduate, would be on a PT boat in the Pacific with Jack Kennedy. Dr. Walker Percy was in Saranac Lake. But there wasn't any room for him in the famous Trudeau sanitarium, and while waiting to be admitted, Percy lived in a boardinghouse, all alone, reading and beginning to write. He says now, "TB liberated me." His illness, the enforced absence from his family, the solitariness—all seem to have brought out in him one of those religious personalities whom William James in *The Varieties of Religious Experience*, called the "twice-born." His real life, his spiritual and intellectual life, his vocation as a writer, his growing concern with symbolism, the philosophy of language, and those whom James had called "sick souls"— all this began when he found himself cut off from the career he had planned, from the war that was to be decisive for his generation, from the

South that on Percy Street in Greenville he had taken for granted. Typically, it was the religious existentialists Kierkegaard and Dostoevsky, not Faulkner the Southern genius, who influenced him; with his wife Mary, a Mississippi girl who had been a medical technician, he became a Catholic. This was only one of his many actual "conversions." In becoming a writer, as in his professing Catholicism, he declared himself born again, born to a new understanding.

Chekhov, William James, Maugham were also doctors who became writers. But although Percy has in fact never practiced, one feels about him that in becoming a writer he underwent an unusually significant personal change, a change of faith within his change of profession. Although he is a natural writer, downright, subtle, mischievous, his novels seem to me essentially the self-determination of a religious personality, of a seeker who after being ejected from the expected and conventional order of things has come to himself as a stranger in the world.

A disposition to look at things, at oneself, in a radically new way is very much what happens in both *The Moviegoer* and *The Last Gentleman.* The violence of Southern history — the violence you can feel in the streets of Greenville today, where stores advertise "Guns and Ammo," where every truck driver seems to have a rifle with him — is not in Percy's books. In each case the protagonist is someone who feels himself in the grip of a profound disorder, and who as a result cultivates the art of looking, examining, taking things in, with an intellectual intensity that clearly has personal significance. Binx, in *The Moviegoer*, is only subtly, secretly estranged from the life around him. "Whenever I approach a Jew, the Geiger counter in my head starts rattling away like a machine gun . . . I am more Jewish than the Jews I know. They are more at home than I am. I accept my exile." Making money is a game at which he is very good, but living has also become a kind of game with which he must appear outwardly unconcerned. This pose makes him seem frivolous and immoral to his great-aunt (whose opinions, romantic and traditionalist, bear a marked resemblance to those of William Alexander Percy). But Binx is not really in the world he seems to be thriving in. In his usual mock-correct way he says:

> My uncle and aunt live in a gracious house in the Garden District and are very kind to me. . . . It is a pleasure to carry out the duties of a citizen and to receive in return a receipt or a neat styrene card with one's name on it certifying, so to speak, one's right to exist. . . . But things have suddenly changed. My peaceful existence in Gentilly has been complicated. This morning, for the first time in years, there occurred to me the possibility of a search. . . . What are generally considered to be the best of times are for me the worst of times, and that worst of times was one of the best. . . .

The mental refusal, the silent spiritual opposition, the effort to make some countervailing gesture are those of a man who seems to be *here*, with us, but is really out *there*, all by himself. One day he puts the contents of his wallet out on the dresser and suddenly looks at the stuff.

> I stood in the center of the room and gazed at the little pile, sighting through a hole made by thumb and forefinger. What was unfamiliar about them was that I could see them. . . .

Binx complains of Harry Stern, a dedicated biologist he had worked with in the lab, that "he is no more aware of the mystery which surrounds him than a fish is aware of the water it swims in." In the office Binx reads a copy of Doughty's *Arabia Deserta* enclosed in a *Standard & Poor*'s binder; in hotel rooms he reads science.

> There I lay in my hotel room with my search over yet still obliged to draw one breath and then the next. But now I have undertaken a different kind of search, a horizontal search. . . .
>
> Today is my thirtieth birthday . . . and knowing less than I ever knew before, having learned only to recognize merde when I see it, having inherited no more from my father than a good nose for merde, for every species of shit that flies. . . .

This contrast of the here and the there, of the "regular" American world that can never understand the panic it breeds and the self training itself to face despair, to become a microscopist of salvation, gives *The Moviegoer* its special wry charm. Binx does see things in a special light — not God's light, perhaps, but, like the light on a movie screen, the light of hallucination, excessive concentration, obsession, that is given to those who at least turn their faces in the right direction. There emerges, to use a favorite word of Percy's, a hypertrophy of detail. Things become oddly distinct, enlarged on the movie screen we carry in our heads when we make the supreme effort to see the world in a new relation — by this alone may we lift ourselves out of our sickness.

In *The Last Gentleman* the hero — always called "the engineer" — is more obviously sick than Binx in *The Moviegoer*, more publicly in exile, for he is a Southerner who works at night as a maintenance engineer at Macy's in New York so he can spend his days looking through the high-powered telescope on which he has spent his savings. He needs above all to make himself new organs of sight, and from his room at the YMCA he discovers two women sitting on a bench in Central Park who come to have the greatest possible influence on his life.

The point of *The Last Gentleman* is hardly that the hero is a "gentleman"; the point of *The Moviegoer* is hardly the movies. Percy has trouble with his titles; a new novel I have seen in manuscript about the "end of the world" is tentatively entitled *How To Make Love in the Ruins* [published as *Love in the Ruins*]. These are all stories of the effort at cognition, in a mad world, by men who on the surface seem mad but really aren't. Both the "moviegoer" and the "engineer" are the only knights of faith left among people who have given up all knowledge of a "search."

Both have taken on the burden of being declared "sick." As in the classical Russian novels that Percy loves, it is the sick man, the outsider, the "idiot" in Dostoevsky's beautiful sense of the word, who by the sacrifice of his good name may yet teach the others charity. "I'm not well," reflects the engineer, "and therefore it is fitting that I should sit still, like an Englishman in his burrow, and see what can be seen." Even as a college student he saw that the young men around him were "very much with themselves, set, that is, for the next fifty years in the actuality of themselves and their own good names. They knew what they were, how things were and how things should be. As for the engineer, he didn't know. I'm from the Delta too, thought he . . . and I'm Episcopal; why ain't I like them, easy and actual?" With his girl (he discovered her through his telescope) he reflects: ". . . goofy as he was, he knew . . . how to get at that most secret and aggrieved enterprise upon which almost everyone is embarked. He'd give her the use of his radar."

Wilfrid Sheed, an admirer of his, interestingly lists Percy among the "dandys" of contemporary fiction. Certainly the lean, subtle Percy style, the unmistakable breeding behind the style, do put Percy among the "dandys" now writing fiction when there are so many real and would-be roughnecks. A. J. Liebling, a great connoisseur of style in boxing, journalism, and food, must have been delighted by this aspect of *The Moviegoer*. And with his spare, economical, utterly quiet personal style, Walker Percy is himself so impressive an example of the cultivated upper-class Southerner that after going around the French Quarter with him in New Orleans, spending a weekend with him and his family at their house in Covington, accompanying him to Mass, one could easily leave it at that: the upper-class sense of style, fitness, leanness. Percy lives what seems on the surface a wholly typical suburban life in the beautiful house in Covington with his wife Mary and younger daughter Ann—the other daughter, Mary Pratt, is married, has a son, and lives near enough for Walker and Mary Percy to baby-sit frequently with their first grandchild. He is easy to talk to, a great listener but no very enthusiastic talker himself—it was from his brother LeRoy that I learned of threats to Walker from the local K. K. K. after he objected to the Confederate flag's hanging in a school, and when the issue was brought into court in New Orleans, he testified there. It is somehow typical of a certain shyness, reserve, a charming gift in his nature for not bearing down too hard in personal conversation, that he likes to keep the television picture on without the sound. He has cultivated the art of restful sitting and lounging, of looking easy, in a way that keeps conversation with him as casual as drifting through a summer afternoon. He seems a most domesticated creature, intensely devoted to his family, but also at home with himself.

But to one admirer of his novels, it seems clear that Walker Percy, a philosopher among novelists, is just as atypical a Southerner and Catholic. There is a singularity to his life, to his manifest search for a new religious humanism, there is a closeness to pain and extreme situations, that makes him extraordinarily "sensitive"—to the existentialist theme of life as shipwreck—without suggesting weakness. Percy in his novels touches the rim of so many human mysteries and despairs that one criticism I have is that he remains equidistant from many *different* problems—psychological, social, Godly—without his getting near enough to use them. After I left him in Covington and was shown around Greenville and the Percy cotton plantation in the Delta by Walker's brother LeRoy, I wondered why so little of the town and the Delta itself has as yet appeared in his fiction. Walker Percy seems far away from what is near to many Southerners, and he sees the "near" in the light of a symbolism that is almost too speculative. Faith for him seems to express a search rather than something found, a *way* of seeing, not an end. Though Walker Percy of Covington (Dr. Percy in the society page) seems solidly there, one knows from his novels, his history, from the extraordinary *philosophical* poignance of the man, that he remains betwixt and between many things. The madness (very real) of the women in his books signifies their never having attempted the "search." The "madness" of his heroes is a figure of speech for the immense loneliness of looking for a God who, in Nietzsche's phrase, is the great unknown and so cannot be found.

That a *novelist* should make one think of such things says much about Walker Percy. Unlike the United States of America, unlike the bustling bourgeois South of today, Walker Percy does not feel that he is a success. He is still looking. "Looking" as a way of life reminds me of a sentence by Simone Weil: Attentiveness without a "goal" is a supreme form of prayer.

Basking in the Eye of the Storm: The Esthetics of Loss in Walker Percy's *The Moviegoer*

Richard Pindell*

"At its best," writes Flannery O'Connor, "our age is an age of searchers and discoverers, and at its worst, an age that has domesticated despair and learned to live with it happily."[1] Walker Percy's moviegoer, Binx Bolling, every whit a man of our age, operates from both the positive and negative poles of this perspective. In the course of *The Moviegoer* he awakens to the possibility of a search for how he can best place himself in this world. "To become aware of the possibility of the search," he notes, formulating the burden of Miss O'Connor's statement in other terms, "is to be onto something. Not to be onto something is to be in despair."[2] Brought alive by his search, and learning along the way in trust and patience to

*Reprinted by permission from *Boundary 2* 4 (1975):219–30.

practice the arts of openness and to promote kindness, he becomes by the book's end a man like Kierkegaard's knight of faith who is steadfastly involved in the need to radiate the truth of his relationship with the world and his connection with being. But, on the other hand, Binx, to an extraordinary degree, "has domesticated despair and learned to live with it happily." Clearly, as Percy tells us, Binx "enjoys his alienation."[3] This is what interests me. How does Binx contrive to like the corner into which he has painted himself? How does he carry off with such plausibility and aplomb the joke that he is alive and well? Apart from the search (which is, after all, in the course of the book only getting under way and which sometimes falls into dormancy), how does Binx survive our age sufficiently whole to discover the possibility of a search?

In a sense Binx is, as the old black folks down South would say, born knowing. Close at hand is the example of Quentin Compson, Binx's literary father, whose career in the Southern chronicle of the post Romantic death journey Binx often bids fair to emulate. Quentin is in love with the Romantic ideal of innocent power. But he has no faith in it. Bereft, therefore, of the mode of self-transcendence that the ideal demands, he falls into the vortices of solipsism and fixation. He is rent asunder by a racking and pernicious combination of narcissism and self-hatred. But by the grace of history Binx has the advantage of Quentin. He inherits the Romantic tradition not in its decline but in its demise. Although something of the heroic ambience may linger, the heroic occasion is extinct. Nothing ennobles: the tragic nerve is dead. Binx is immunized against the deadly fever of excessive expectations by the distemper of our times. Unlike Quentin, he cannot remember in any clear, attractive, or compelling way what he has lost. He is born the nihilist that Quentin would rather die than become.

The admonitory example of Quentin Compson is brought home to Binx in the character and fate of his natural father, who can find only in war — and a hero's death — a world drawn to the promised godlike scale. Thus Binx can quite early identify a chief adversary of his soul: "That's what killed my father, English romanticism, that and 1930 science" (88). His father, like his father's literary predecessors, Jay Gatsby or Lord Jim or, again, Quentin Compson, is in some way the victim of a too literalistic devotion to the dream of the terrestrial Paradise.[4] Taking heed of this, wary as any cogent close-shave survivor, Binx formulates a preserving truth that Quentin Compson disastrously refuses to recognize: "Beauty is a whore" (196). By promising a kingdom she cannot deliver, beauty breaks down the defenses people need in order to improvise their existence amid the nagging particulars of the day-to-day world. The phrase, "beauty is a whore," is a kind of countercharm Binx devises to dispel the dire contagions of Romanticism's corpse. For the failure of the Utopian dream has enflamed our guilt at not coinciding with ourselves, as the "trees . . . coincide with themselves" (25). We are become paranoically sensitive to the rebuke of beauty. The great danger lies in our readiness somehow to compensate for our proven ontological shortcomings by surrendering again to the seductions of a hope gone wild — to seek, that is, death in the guise of renewal.

The besetting danger of our modern loss, then, Percy realizes, is the temptation to beautify the loss and thereby repeat it. The loss of the old unities and verities can be, in the very size of it, ominously flattering. It may nurture such pride in what was as, in Quentin's case, to demand the proof of martyrdom. In this connection what one calls his loss is important. Quentin calls the loss Caddy — the unattainable — and by that token he, in effect, deifies it. But, unlike Quentin — or, for that matter, Captain Ahab — Binx is no sacrifice looking for a God. Binx calls the loss "the malaise," and the very term is an effort to demystify and detoxify the loss. "What is the malaise? you ask. The malaise is the pain of loss. The world is lost to you, the world and the people in it, and there remains only you and the world and you are no more able to be in the world than Banquo's ghost" (120). The world is lost, yet the world remains. On these terms one leads, like Banquo's ghost, only a fictive existence.

One lives, then, by virtue of a trick. For Binx, always, as characteristic of the aesthete, less a man of his word than he is a man of *the* word, many of his tricks are verbal ones. Words themselves are tricks played on reality. The inchoate, undifferentiated stuff of life is ordered by words into ideas or images which can be entertained or turned away, and, vis-a-vis the thing named, a namer moves from the relationship of a guest unsure of his ground to that of a host. To apply this here, the very act of naming the loss recovers a portion, however miniscule, of what was lost — "the world and you in it" — the universe. It is a type of what Percy calls the "esthetic reversal." "In the joy of naming," Percy tells us, "one lives authentically. No matter whether I give a name to, or hear the name of, a strange bird: no matter whether I write or read a line of great poetry, form or understand a scientific hypothesis, I thereby exist authentically as a namer or a hearer, as an I or a Thou — and in either case as a co-celebrant of what is."[5]

The ethical pitfalls yawning at the feet of so purely an esthetic stance are clear. It bares one to the temptations of a life of maximum sensation — intellectual and otherwise — and minimum involvement (moviegoing in its worst form). The very gusto of Binx's naming shows how easy it is to feel problems with the satisfaction of a solution. Naming, working like other arts by paradox (unlike skills), is a recognition that can easily constitute a dismissal. "Malaise," for example, is a recognition of loss that helps Binx to ignore it with astonishing zest. Kate Cutrer, Binx's fiancee, tells him, "You remind me of a prisoner in the death house who takes a wry pleasure in doing things like registering to vote. . . . all your gaiety and good spirits have the same death house quality. . . . I've had enough of your death house pranks" (193). A death house prisoner, as displaced and disenfranchised as a fetus outside the womb, Binx, by his verbal tricks conjuring the bars away, insists on exercising his rights as a sovereign citizen of the state. Like the movie actor a nobody nowhere, he pretends, with much of the actor's perfection of gesture, to be a somebody somewhere.

Action — the simple achievement or non-achievement of a worthy goal in a dignifying, stimulating, profitably exhausting way — is today a piece of nostalgia. For, to adapt a phrase from Camus, "the divorce between the mind that desires and the world that disappoints" is complete.[6] Binx is born into a world that finds its model in the stock brokerage where he is employed — a world not responsible for or to any product, depending on excitement largely on luck and dedicated to possibility. It is a world, in short, not of action but of transaction. To the esthete, who, characteristically, remains aloof from concrete commitments the better to broaden the space of his intellectual playground, the peculiar gift of the modern loss is simply this: one need not act as a doer, only as an actor. When Binx is a little boy, his brother dies, and Aunt Emily tells him, " 'Now it's all up to you. It's going to be difficult for you but I know you're going to act like a soldier.' This was true. I could easily act like a soldier. Was that all I had to do?" (4).

In a world bottomed on the principle not of fulfillment but of performance, one especially need not be. For the modern person adrift, engulfed, on the tide of history, shapes of power far more eloquent and persuasive than he could create on his own can be struck from the air. The world of *The Moviegoer* is a bazaar of lifestyles, a costume room. There is an attire for every enterprise. Need a seductive voice on the phone with your ex-girlfriend's roommate? Try on "Old confederate Marlon Brando — a reedy insinuating voice, full of winks and leers and above all pleased with itself" (230). Need the right pose for supervising a construction project? Consider the "old Gable: . . . he knew how to seem to work and how to seem to forget about women and still move in such a way as to please women: stand asweat with his hands in his back pockets" (95). To act like Brando or Gable is to act like someone who is also acting. It is to be the shadow of a shadow.

Such a world hangs together only by some tacit mutual consent to accept each other's acting as action. One makes *do*: that is, he makes the idea of doing. Hence the significance of Binx's main "trick, . . . making money" (30) — and women: "I think of Sharon and American Motors. It closed yesterday at 30¼" (117). The sentence shows the central balancing act that helps to keep Binx's life free of "the old longings" (9). "Money is a good counterpoise to beauty. Beauty, the quest of beauty alone, is a whoredom. Ten years ago I pursued beauty and gave no thought to money. I listened to the lovely tunes of Mahler and felt a sickness in my very soul. Now I pursue money and on the whole feel better" (196).

Binx's shrewd, persistent checkmating of beauty's dangerously seductive moves with the ruses of wealth takes several forms. For example, his current girlfriend is always, in addition, his secretary at the brokerage.

Holding beauty hostage in a Grubstreet setting, he plays the esthetic off against the utilitarian. He maintains what is for him a salutory sense of how nearly his Marcias and Lindas and Sharons resemble money. Their names interchangeable, they are, like money, sheerly and irredeemably representative. Like money, they are valued for their promise of something whose reality is always in doubt and therefore open to the wildest kinds of speculation. Again, like money, they are ideas, mere figments, which are accepted as facts and pursued as truths. Sharon is made beautiful by hopes that exceed Binx's designs on her: "How beautiful she is. She is beautiful and brave and chipper as a sparrow. My throat catches with the sadness of her beauty" (130). But the "sadness" bespeaks a saving recognition: one can have beauty only as one has money — at an eternal remove from whatever essential being it may seem to allude to. To insist on experiencing the reality of something only symbolic is to set one's cap for the goddess death. But schooled in the brokerage rigorously to observe the distinction between symbol and reality, Binx keeps the girl concealed behind her "beauty." The counterbalancing reference to the "sparrow" is both a reinforcing denomination of Sharon's symbolic function and a continuing investment in the vulgarization of quest which here pays such dividends. For what emerges here is Binx's controlled enjoyment of the old metaphysical and apocalyptic longings and hungers. The girl functions as an occasion for his sorrow over the world. The sadness is therapeutic: it is "rinsing" (133): and it is an estimable achievement. Sadness may be inspiring. Anxiety — another response to the modern loss — never: it cripples the imagination. Binx's sadness, lending itself so easily to esthetic ventures, helps keep the creative possible.

This reflex-quick formalization that converts incipient anguish or anxiety into sadness works by the ministry of humor and wit. Take for example, Binx's description of the filling station he considers buying: "It is easy to visualize the little tile cube of a building with its far flung porches, its apron of silky concrete and, revolving on high, the immaculate bivalve glowing in every inch of its pretty styrene (I have already approached the Shell distributor)" (112). This is more than his professional appreciation of quality merchandise, the complacent squint of the knowing appraiser: "good pipe in a good slab" (93). It is more than his almost sumptuous delight in say the polished metal of a playground ocean wave and jungle gym: "How shiny and strong and well-set are the steel pipes, polished to silver by thousands of little blue-skirted and khaki-clad butts" (87). His filling station summons forth a lyricism that in its lush cadence and high solemnity and esprit befits an Adoration of the Virgin or a The Building of the Temple. The object of the description warrants only visualization, but what we get is a vision. The humor and the sadness lie precisely in this excess of language to the occasion. It's funny that so keen an observer is so enamored of the things of this world; funny that so ironic an observer can unabashedly seek the consolations of melodrama; but not so funny that he can find no object, in Fitzgerald's wonderful phrase, "commensurate to his capacity for wonder." But his achievement is that he wonders anyway: "not for five minutes," he says, "will I be distracted from the wonder" (42).

How does he do it?

Surely the sadness redeeming the humor of frivolity and the humor redeeming the sadness of misery help make wonder possible. But presiding over the flash point of Binx's contact with the world is a complex of other safeguards and aggressions. To see the world again, to bring the given things of our surroundings, extinguished by use, back again in their forgotten strangeness, Binx, like the clown, stands the world on its head. "Everything," he says, "is upside-down for me. . . . What are generally considered to be the best times are for me the worst times, and that worst of times [when he was wounded in Korea] was one of the best" (10). Despite the seeming passivity of these remarks by Binx concerning his antithetical variations on stereotypes, his reversive perspective is not finally passive at all. It is astonishingly active, arrogant, and subversive. In the filling station description, for instance, he unsettles that agreement of ours about what is real, which we call truth, by flying full in the face of Romantic tradition in specific and Western hierarchical dispositions of reality in general. Shelley, moralizing his song in *A Defence of Poetry*, pronounces thus: "Poetry, and the principle of Self, of which Money is the visible incarnation, are the God and Mammon of the world."[7] Here, in his high poetical celebration of a projected money-making venture, Binx creates, and exuberantly exercises, his freedom from a tradition by his very outrage of it. Yet we should note the composure of his assault on this long cherished valuation of orders. Decisive controls are carefully built into the iconoclastic drive and thrill of the rhetoric. The lyric intensity of feeling is, after all, in excess of the object because it can be. The post-Romantic esthete is in little danger from a filling station. Just as Binx is peculiarly free to estheticize Sharon because their romance, if we may call it that, is never threatened by marriage, so here too his poise is founded in the esthetic distance that makes the commonplace beautiful. Every control risks its own excess: here, specifically, the sentimentality of melodrama. The additional necessary control present is the irony. For implicit too in the discomposing disproportion of emotion to object is Binx's mockery of, his embarrassment of, his own unfulfilled longings.

Embarrassment is the main feeling that the filling station description arouses in the reader, and it is perhaps the dominant and most unstudied feeling of our age. *The Moviegoer* is suffused with the embarrassment endemic in existing at the "dead end of a traditional hypothesis."[8] More or less related to this are the exquisitely excruciating and droll social and personal embarrassments Binx encounters in various forms: the transparency of people's performance needs, their bare-faced solicitation of your help in getting their act right: the hideous enthusiasm of mistaken people, the earnestness of inadequacy; and the embarrassment of others depending on you to maintain, in some stoical act of pretense, an exhausted or otherwise defunct relationship. To survive in any hopeful way so embarrassed and embarrassing an age, to fend off the rigidities consequent to a monstrously overactive self-consciousness, a person needs be ironical. Aroused, intelligent, combative, Binx's irony is in a very real way his saving grace. Against the preachers of lifeways, whether the high-minded spokesmen of outworn creeds or the grossly ardent devotees of fashionably and sentimentally conceived self-concept systems, Binx mounts a counterattack. He embarrasses the embarrassers by taking their words to heart. For instance, his aunt sends him advice on how to live based on a quotation from Marcus Aurelius: "Every moment think steadily as a Roman and a man, to do what thou hast in hand with perfect and simple dignity, and a feeling of affection and freedom and justice" (78). Binx's pointed but completely tacit, in fact, probably unconscious response to this comes one short paragraph later: "I switch on television and sit directly in front of it, bolt upright and hands on knees in my ladder-back chair" (78). Here Binx obeys to the letter the first two clauses of the quotation, and the TV play that follows, a saccharine Virtue Regained piece, stuffed with feelings of "affection and freedom and justice," is something Binx unabashedly enjoys. The moral of this dumb show is that the world which furnished the occasion for the old stoical virtues is irrevocably gone. As they become increasingly meaningless, their hold on the imagination becomes increasingly dangerous. Often, in particular and intelligent ways, one must be cruel to the past. Binx's stance is precisely calculated to unstopper the vial of this classical quotation — to let the life it holds die naturally as it were upon the modern air. Like Falstaff, Binx mimics the world that he is shut out of, and, in so doing, again like Falstaff, he undermines the values by which he is being judged.[9]

Such mimicry, of course, often and easily slides into or is immediately indistinguishable from mockery. For example, poring over a photograph of his romantic father for "clues" in his "search," he says, "He was commissioned in the RCAF in 1940 and got himself killed before his country entered the war. And in Crete. And in the wine dark sea. And by the same Boche. And with a copy of The Shropshire Lad in his pocket. Again I search the eyes, each eye a stipple or two in a blurred oval. Beyond a doubt they are ironical" (25). The mimicking four-point summation of the progress of Western civilization becomes under the incremental pressure of the repetitions and the doggerel chant of the lines a kind of mock-epitaph. The description of his father's death act suggests the step-by-step deliberateness of a how-to-manual for the heroic exit. But the comprehensiveness of this capsule inventory of heroic trappings bespeaks as well the remarkable breadth of Binx's confrontation with his father's morbid soul. His mother, with her usual shrewd, escapist gesture — part of her "canny management of the shocks of life" by reducing them to their homeliest common denominator, "no more heart's desire for her, thank you" (142) —

tries to dismiss his father this way: "He was overwrought" (153). But Binx perfects his father's own deficient irony. Under its protection he at once symbolically enacts his father's death and disengages himself from it. He asserts his freedom from a confining superego, his father and the traditional Western belief system he embodies, burying it in the sea of its beginnings.

Binx's mockery works, then, by a simultaneous assumption and disavowal of the world. In one of his most satiric passages he addresses himself in a mock-dedicatory manner to the radio program This I Believe: "Being a creature of habit, as regular as a monk, and taking pleasure in the homeliest repetitions, I listen every night at ten to a program called This I Believe. Monks have their compline, I have This I Believe" (108). A representative sample of this mindless pietism goes like this: "I believe in music. I believe in a child's smile. I believe in love. I also believe in hate" (109). Like a clown, who mottles himself in every coloration of the human spectrum, Binx, in putting on the world, puts the world on. He mocks the world mocking him. The bold, intimate sweep of his subversive style corrodes the going forms from within and disposes of them from without and leaves him free to muse. The ironic distance makes the esthetic distance possible. It creates a space in which the beautiful can most safely appear.

In fact, in especially important ways, Binx's wonder is sustained by a brooding and vigorous involvement with place and space that sounds some traditional themes. Here, for example, is the *locus amoenus:* "truthfully it seems that if she [Kate Cutrer] can just hit upon the right place, a shuttered place of brick and vine and flowing water, her very life can be lived" (57). Binx also invokes the *genius loci.* For place-presence is in a Southerner's bones, knowing, as he does, "all about genie-souls and living in haunted places like Shiloh and the Wilderness and Vicksburg and Atlanta" (202). But Binx eagerly, no qualms about it, sells his "patrimony" (90), the last land in his immediate family, to a contractor in order to buy his filling station. This conversion of estate into real estate is a radical venture from more viewpoints than that of the Southern agrarian tradition. The move from the land to the highway symbolizes a basic shift in the concept of the self. The belief in the fixity of the self, which is implicit in one's spiritual attachment to his place, is wearing away. Increasingly the self identifies itself to us today as much less an entity than a process. Like the Mardi Gras, in full swing during the two weeks that the book spans, our age is a season of maskers. The self it seems to demand is a protean one capable of undergoing radical changes yet withal maintaining some quintessential identity.[10] Such a new self, crossing zones and shifting its shape to renew its legibility in the role-language of strongly varying, highly articulated situations, needs a new place-base to sustain it. Binx finds, or rather founds, such a place in his style.

We can best observe his construction of this place in what surely is the loveliest passage in the book.

> Evening is the best time in Gentilly. There are not so many trees and the buildings are low and the world is all sky. The sky is a deep bright ocean full of light and life. A mare's tail of cirrus cloud stands in high from the Gulf. High above the Lake a broken vee of ibises points for the marshes: they go suddenly white as they fly into the tilting salient of sunlight. Swifts find a windy middle reach of sky and come twittering down so fast I think at first gnats have crossed my eyelids. In the last sector of apple green a Lockheed Connie lowers from Mobile, her running lights blinking in the dusk. Station wagons and Greyhounds and diesel rigs rumble toward the Gulf Coast, their fabulous tail-lights glowing like rubies in the darkening east. Most of the commercial buildings are empty except the filling stations where attendants hose down the concrete under the glowing discs and shells and stars. (73)

"The world is all sky." A space is created, pure and receptive, where something can happen that Binx can trust. What happens, essentially, is the style. The style here is remarkably about itself, hymns its own creation. The extraordinary emphasis on spatial, aerial, and kinetic phenomena is a kind of derealization of the world that, in effect, sets forward the style as the prime reality. The hovering and expansive energies of the style, each phrase as radiantly demanding as a shooting star, come finally to rest in the description of the filling stations. When we remember that Binx sells his "place," in the traditional Southern sense of an inherited piece of land — his "patrimony" — we can appreciate even more the self-declarative, self-defining nature here of Binx's style. The submerged metaphor in this passage is as accurate as it is homely: the style *is* a kind of filling station. It fills the waiting vessel of the sky: "the sky is a deep bright ocean full of light and life." The style is an ultimate poise, a station, if you will, or stationing, amid the vicissitudes of the temporal. And the style is the only place visible or possible in the space that it creates. Indeed it becomes place in its very creation of the space where it can flourish.

How, more specifically, in this passage does style materialize as place? We note that Binx, however unostentatiously, establishes himself as a point of convergence. The idea of convergence in the "broken vee of ibises pointing for the marshes" is personally appropriated and infiltrated in the descent of the swifts that "come twittering down so fast I think at first gnats have crossed my eyelids." Familiarly he greets journeying things and gives them names (e.g., "a Lockheed Connie"). They are for the moment guests, he the host entertaining them. "In the joy of naming," we recall, "one lives authentically. . . . As a co-celebrant of what is." Here, in the place of his style, Binx can trust his experiences, live his very life. His style makes the world visible to him. It transfigures: the ibises "go suddenly white as they fly into the tilting salient of sunlight," and the "fabulous tail-lights" of the evening traffic glow "like rubies in the darkening east." Reality is blocked out yet somehow heightened. In its range and concerns the style is completely cosmopolitan. It strikes its roots deep in some common human fund and reserve of strength that enable Binx to give, in Keats's words, that "greeting of the Spirit [that] make[s] things wholly exist."[11] Binx's style is the point at which he inhabits space, recovers the universe: "the glowing discs and shells and stars."

Truly to appreciate Binx's achievement here we must consider the world in which he moves. The world of *The Moviegoer* is so familiar to us, its spiritual depredations so general and casual, its despair and malaise so all-pervading, it is easy not to recognize it. It is a world where the thou of I-thou is become the thou of I "Netted better than thirty five thou this year" (207). People are extinguished, dimmed out under overloadings of assimilatory circuits. Like Nell Lovell, they are mass man — "the anonymous 'one' of 'one says' "[12] — prey to every pot-boiling whim and fad of the quack ontologists and the taste-makers. Or, like Kate Cutrer, they are nerve-worn with consciousness: Kate's every emotion is an announcement; her mind is always ahead of her feelings, canceling their value. In such a world disaster comes as a relief. ("The real anxiety question, the question no one asks because no one wants to, is: . . . What if the Bomb should *not* fall? What then?")[13] It is in this world that Binx wins through to the grace of dynamic repose in the insufficiency of the given.

On the basis of this achievement the evening in Gentilly passage seems finally one of hope, if not expectation. The sense of migration, the suggestion too, however faint, of an eastward orientation, prophesies Binx's movement into the religious mode.[14] He is not a tourist after all, dreaming in postcards, out of contact, let alone communion, with the life he consumes through the dead eye of his Kodak. Rather, he is a pilgrim in progress, however troubled and wavering, toward some untrodden prospect in the human heart. At his most mocking and satirical he is never *only* destructive, *only* iconoclastic. As he sifts the ruins, making free with sacred relics, important disentangling distinctions stand clear in the ironic light: heroism *vs.* heroics (his father's death in the wine dark sea): sentiment *vs.* sentimentality (This I Believe). The filling station passage shows especially well the therapeutic thrust of the style. Here Binx establishes with his audience a fellowship of embarrassment. For the language with its talk of "far flung porches" and "apron of silky concrete" and "revolving on high, the immaculate bivalve" is in one sense not in excess of the occasion at all. Rather, Binx only sets himself poetry's most venerable task of celebrating a nation's greatest love — here the pursuit of the Almighty Dollar. He says, in effect, let us now praise filling stations. He embarrasses us by praising our God. With rather fiendish tact he embarrasses, does not offend, us with the truth. The persuasion works through a logic not of statement but of inklings or, better, longings — aches in reflected inner spaces. Precisely because the need for spirituality is in this particular way kept active, undismissable, we feel at a loss but not lost.

The portable place that Binx, and, through him, Percy, founds in his style aspires finally to be a kind of tabernacle and ark of the covenant for a people watching in the wilderness. For in its aroused occupancy of unfolding space the style acts both as a creator and a conditioner. It reduces things to possibilities in order to fan ablaze sinking potentials, and, in so doing, it creates the chaos we must endure if we are to establish a respect-worthy cosmos. Precariously maintaining itself in its cool savvy, its puckish verve, and lyric vigor, undersung withal by the rhetoric of a lost love, the style engages the modern loss by keeping the right desires active and the courageous distinctions unblurred. In short, it keeps green the ground for renewal.

Notes

1. *Mystery and Manners*, ed. Sally and Robert Fitzgerald (New York: Farrar, Straus & Giroux, 1969), p. 159.

2. Walker Percy, *The Moviegoer* (New York: Farrar, Straus & Giroux, 1960; Noonday rp. 1967), p. 13. All subsequent references to *The Moviegoer* are to this text.

3. Ashley Brown, "An Interview with Walker Percy," *Shenandoah* 18 (1967), 7.

4. In his novel *The Last Gentleman* Walker Percy provides for his character, William Barrett, a genealogy of alienated heroes that reads like a tomb song for the Compsons: "Over the years his family had turned ironical and lost its gift for action. It was an honorable and violent family, but gradually the violence had been deflected and turned inward. The great grandfather knew what was what and said so and acted accordingly and did not care what anyone thought. . . . The next generation, the grandfather, seemed to know what was what but he was not really so sure. He was brave but he gave much thought to the business of being brave. . . . The father was a brave man too and he said he didn't care what others thought, but he did care. . . . In the end he was killed by his own irony and sadness and by the strain of living out an ordinary day in a perfect dance of honor." *The Last Gentleman* (New York: Farrar, Straus & Giroux, 1966: Noonday rp, 1971). pp. 9–10.

5. Walker Percy, "Naming and Being," *Personalist*, 41 (1960), 153. For his discussion of "esthetic reversal" see his essay, "The Man on the Train: Three Existential Modes," *Partisan Review*, 23 (1956), 478–94.

6. Albert Camus, *The Myth of Sisyphus* (New York: Knopf, 1955), 37.

7. *Shelley and Peacock*, ed. John E. Jordan (New York: Bobbs-Merrill, 1965), p. 69.

8. The phrase is Percy's in his essay "From Facts to Fiction," *Writer*, 80 (1967), 46.

9. Binx actually plays Falstaff to his Aunt Emily's Prince Hal in one of their exchanges. *The Moviegoer*, p. 32.

10. Cf. the concept of the modern Protean man in Robert Jay Lifton, *Boundaries: Psychological Man in Revolution* (New York: Random House, 1967; Vintage rp, 1970), p. 37ff. The contrast between the old and the new idea of self, in terms of place, is highly visible in the following two quotations: " 'Which is the real person, so far as an actor is concerned? Is he more real when performing on the stage, or when he is at home? I tend to think that for people who have these many, many masks, there is no home' " (Lifton, p. 45); "It was significant that we always spoke of the Carters of Ravensworth, the Carys of Vaucluse, the Buchans of Pleasant Hill. The individual quality of a man was bound up with his kin and the 'places' where they lived" (Allen Tate, *The Fathers*, Chicago: Swallow Press, 1960, p. 135).

11. John Keats, *Selected Poems and Letters*, ed. Douglas Bush (Cambridge, Mass.: Riverside Press, 1959), p. 269.

12. The phrase is from Percy, "The Man on the Train," 479.

13. *Ibid.*, 479.

14. See Martin Luschei's admirable study of Walker Percy, *The Sovereign Wayfarer* (Baton Rouge: La. State U.P., 1972), pp. 100–10 for a learned, incisive, and, I think, convincing discussion of Binx's leap into the religious sphere. Luschei cites Percy's own remarks to this effect in *Kite-Flying and Other Irrational Acts: Conversations with Twelve Southern Writers*, ed. John Carr (Baton Rouge: La. State U.P., 1972), p. 49: "But in the end—we're using Kierkgaardian terminology—in the end Binx jumps from the aesthetic clear across the ethical to the religious. He has no ethical sphere at all. That's what Aunt Emily can't understand about him. He just doesn't believe in being the honorable man, doing the right thing, for its own sake."

The Parabolic in Faulkner, O'Connor, and Percy

Sally McFague*

In an interview Flannery O'Connor once said, "I'm interested in the old Adam. He just talks Southern because I do."[1] That casual remark might give the impression that "talking Southern" was incidental to O'Connor's perception of human life, but, in fact, the opposite is the case. The mystery of human existence for O'Connor is *embodied* in manners, that is, in the specificity of Southern time and places. "Southern identity," she says, "is not really connected with mockingbirds and beaten biscuits and white columns any more than it is with hookworm and bare feet and muddy clay roads." Rather, it is "the possibility of reading a small history in a universal light."[2] O'Connor does not write allegories which use Southern manners to illustrate concepts about the nature of human life; rather, she creates, I would like to suggest, "parables" which point indirectly through concrete events and circumstances to what she believes is essential reality.

I would, in fact, suggest that elements of a peculiar form of narrative—the New Testament parable—are evident in the writings of William Faulkner, Flannery O'Connor, and Walker Percy and that the presence of these elements accounts, at least in part, for the novelty of each author's vision of the really real, or the way to be in the world, or essential reality. Each of these authors is surrealistic in the sense of upending realistic narrative forms for the purpose of saying something other than what conventional expectations say. That "something other," however, is said *through* the ordinary: the extraordinary is narrated through the ordinary. This is the way not only of the Bible in general, but

*Reprinted by permission from *Notre Dame English Journal* 15 (Spring 1983): 49–66.

of the parables of Jesus in particular. They illustrate in an extreme way a characteristic of biblical narrative — its embodiment of mystery in manners. The peculiar feature of parables which sets them apart from other narratives is their metaphorical quality. As New Testament critics widely agree now, parables are extended metaphors. They are concrete stories about particular people in particular times and places, but they are "strange" stories, stories that set the familiar in an unfamiliar context, stories which are "about" something more than they appear to be about. That something more — essential reality, the really real, or whatever — is available, however, *only* through the parable: parable is a metaphor for essential reality.

As many critics have remarked, the outstanding feature of the parables is their *extravagance*.[3] While the stories are, at one level, thoroughly ordinary and secular, events occur and decisions are made which are absurd, radical, alien, extreme. In the naturalistic or non-human parables, the ones dealing with the mustard seed, the lost coin, the buried treasure, the pearl of great price, and so on, the extreme quality appears in the passion for the kingdom of God, its overriding importance in relation to everything else. Most of the parables, however, are personal and relational, concerned with ordinary and extraordinary, or conventional and radical, ways of dealing with other people: the Unjust Judge (Luke 18:1–8), the Prodigal Son (Luke 15:11–32), the Wicked Husbandman (Matt. 21:33–41), the Great Feast (Luke 14:16–24), the Good Samaritan (Luke 10:29–37), the Laborers in the Vineyard (Matt. 20:1–16). All of these parables are stories about absurd, alien, or radical ways of relating to others, given conventional standards. New Testament critic Robert Funk has summed up the tension between these two ways in the phrase, the "logic of merit" versus the "logic of grace."[4]

Philosopher Paul Ricoeur analyzes the function of extravagance in the parables by suggesting that the parables work on a pattern of orientation, disorientation, and reorientation: a parable begins in the ordinary world with its conventional standards and expectations, but in the course of the story, a radically different perspective is introduced to disorient the listener. The interaction of the two competing viewpoints creates tension that results in a redescription of life in the world.[5] The uneasiness generated by the disorientation of a parable, introduced by the alien perspective, is nicely suggested by New Testament exegete John Dominic Crossan: "I don't know what you mean by that story, but I'm certain I don't like it."[6] A parable is, in this analysis, an assault on the accepted, conventional way of viewing reality. It is an assault on the social, economic, and mythic structures people build for their own comfort and security. If we review the central parables of Jesus, we note again and again that expectations are reversed: an elder son does not get what he "deserves"; late workers are paid the same as early ones: a feast is given for the poor and "unworthy" when the prominent guests decline: a Samaritan comes to the aid of a Jew while "religious" people walk by on the other side.

Throughout the parables, then, two standards are in permanent tension with each other, and the effect of their interaction, for anyone who allows herself or himself to be personally involved, is profound disorientation. Thus, not "liking" the parables is the appropriate initial reaction to them. Crossan says that the parables place the listener "on the edge of the raft." What this means is the end of conventional security: "You have built a lovely home, myth assures us: but, whispers parable, you are right above an earthquake fault."[7]

These very brief comments on parables suggest at least two major characteristics of the form: parable speaks of essential reality through the concrete and the ordinary, and it accomplishes this through distortion or extravagance. The relationship between the ordinary and the extraordinary in a parable, then, is one both of intimacy and of tension, for essential reality is not discovered *apart* from the concrete: yet it cannot be identified with conventional reality. One does not escape from the ordinary in order to discover what is essential: rather, the ordinary must be distorted *in order to discover* what it truly is beneath the conventions. On these two points — the concrete and distortion — Southern literature occupies a unique place in contemporary letters. Robert Heilman has said that "the Southern temper is marked by the coincidence of a sense of the concrete [and] a sense of the elemental."[8] In commenting on this remark, Frederick Hoffman wrote that the Southern adherence to concrete fact is not an adherence to the "realistic" fact but to its "essential nature" and that the *way* Southern writers preserve both the concrete fact and its essential nature is through exaggeration, distortion, and the grotesque.[9] Precisely this tension between the concrete and the essential reality in which the concrete is opened up to essential reality through distortion and exaggeration interests us in investigating three Southern writers. We hear the old Adam talking Southern in their works. This, I would suggest, is a distinctive biblical method. We see it in the Old Testament stories of God's way with human beings and preeminently in the New Testament parables, for here, more than in other stories in the Bible, we see the element of distortion and exaggeration of the ordinary and concrete for the purpose of pointing elliptically to essential, in contrast to conventional, reality.

As an aside, I would suggest that parables and narratives manifesting parabolic elements may pose an interesting counter to the current claim by deconstructionist critics such as Jacques Derrida, Michel Foucault, and Hayden White that narrative is essentially an opiate, which gives a false sense of continuity and also serves as a support for the *status quo*, for conventional forms of order, coherence, and authority. The disorientation from conventional standards and the reorientation to another way of being in the world — to a vision of essential reality which is at the heart of parables—has a transforming, if not revolutionary, potential. This dimension in the writings of our three authors suggests a way of telling stories which is not a support for the *status quo*, but, in fact, a radical critique of it.

These general remarks must now be made more specific. The choice of William Faulkner, Flannery O'Connor, and Walker Percy as illustrations of the parabolic genre in Southern fiction is a challenging one, for if they do illustrate that genre, they do so with important differences. To be somewhat schematic for a moment, we might say that Faulkner creates *Southern* parables (Malcolm Cowley says that Faulkner's labor of the imagination was to make his story of Yoknapatawpha County stand as a parable or legend of all the Deep South[10]), that O'Connor creates *Christian* parables (the Christian novelist, says O'Connor, believes that mystery is embodied in manners,[11] and hence creates stories which include *both* dimensions), and that Percy creates *modern* parables of human beings as castaways and wayfarers submerged in everydayness, alienated from themselves and others. Faulkner's Southern parables are finally, in spite of the uplifting words of the Nobel Speech and the Christian overtones in *Requiem for a Nun* and *A Fable*, humanistic (and in their positive affirmations, a Stoic, not a biblical humanism): O'Connor's Christian parables are, though never leaving the secular and human dimension, theistic, clearly in the tradition of Jesus's parables: Percy's modern parables are existential, for, following the Kierkegaard of the aesthetic writings, he gives us a phenomenology of the modern plight but only an elliptical suggestion of the leap necessary to overcome it.

We are dealing, then, with three types of parable—a parable of the South, of the Christian life, and of the modern existential crisis. Yet, different as these all are, and we shall dwell on the differences as we look at a work by each of the writers—Faulkner's "The Bear," O'Connor's *The Violent Bear It Away*, and Percy's *The Moviegoer*—they are united by an adherence to the fundamental pattern of the parable, its way of setting the familiar and concrete in a new and strange context in order to make us see the elemental in the concrete reality before us.

To venture into Yoknapawtapha County with any grand ambitions of mapping its meaning is presumptuous and risky, and my intent is not to attempt that task. My proposal is far more modest: I want merely to suggest that Faulkner at his best is a parabolist, one who creates, not fables or allegories, but stories which can be characterized by O'Connor's phrase, "a small history in a universal light."[12] What his stories "mean" is fair game for theories ranging from Calvinism to Stoic humanism, from longing for the faded glory of pre-Civil War Southern splendor to disillusionment with the decay of moral values in contemporary society, but the stories themselves *stand*, as does any good aesthetic creation, somewhat impervious to and apart from all interpretations. This does not mean that nothing can be said about what Faulkner's stories "mean," but that, because, as I want to insist, they are parables where the meaning is an ingredient in the details of the story, one must be timid about extrapolating meanings.

This warning is necessary when dealing with Faulkner, for he left himself wide open to ideological overkill in his public statements and interviews, such as the Nobel Speech and his talk at Nagano, Japan. At Nagano Faulkner gave the familiar Nobel Speech line: "Man is tough . . . nothing, nothing — war, grief, hopelessness, despair — can last as long as man . . . provided . . . he will make the effort to believe in man and in hope."[13] The vacuous humanism of this statement is only surpassed by Faulkner's definition of Christianity as "every individual's individual mode of behavior by means of which he makes himself a better human being than his nature wants to be, if he followed his nature only."[14] Horatio Alger said it better with more verve.

Faulkner's "The Bear" is neither gritting-the-teeth humanism nor is it bootstrap Christianity. It is a pain-filled, poignant parable of a young boy coming of age in the South. The heart of the story is concrete and familiar — Ike McCaslin is initiated into the hunting world of his father and forefathers through a series of annual trips to the "big woods." The purpose of these trips, apart from the booze and the companionship, is the stalking of Old Ben, a great scarred bear who has escaped the cleverest schemes of all the hunters. But Old Ben is not just "any" bear; he is indomitable, larger than life, a spiritual being, who lives in an ambiance of immortality and malevolence, reminiscent in many ways of Melville's Moby-Dick. The familiar and the ordinary — the hunting rites whereby a boy becomes a man — are given a new and strange context provided by the bear's qualities and the solitude of the ancient, untouched woods, so that while we read the story of the boy and the bear, we are aware of a new vision of reality — a new and unconventional way of being in the world — embedded in the details of the simple story.

That new way of being is one of *renunciation:* in order even to glimpse the bear Ike must leave not only his gun, but also his watch and his compass behind:

> He stood for a moment — a child, alien and lost in the green and soaring gloom of the markless wilderness. Then he relinquished completely to it. It was the watch and the compass. He was still tainted. . . . Then he saw the bear. It did not emerge, appear: it was just there, immobile, fixed in the green and windless noon's hot dappling, not as big as he had dreamed it but as big as he had expected, bigger, dimensionless against the dappled obscurity, looking at him.[15]

But even further renunciation is required of him: indeed, he must be willing to put his life into the bear's power. A year after first seeing the bear, he comes upon it again with his small dog. The courageous, feisty dog rushes toward the bear: Ike, flinging down his gun, plunges after the dog to rescue him: ". . . he was directly under the bear. He could smell it, strong and rank. Sprawling, he looked up where it loomed and towered above him like a thunder-clap."[16] Images of another Isaac, one under the sword, flicker across the mind as one reads the passage. The bear disappears, but the boy who would not shoot and who saved the little dog is marked forever. As he grows into manhood he relinquishes his patrimony: the tainted heritage of slavery, miscegnation, incest, and ill-begotten wealth — the whole Southern history in which he and his family are so deeply imbedded. Ike does not assume a heroic, much less a Christian, sacrificial stance toward this evil, bloody history: in line with the moment when he relinquished his gun, compass, and watch and in line with the moment when he foolishly saved his little dog from the paws of Old Ben, he simple goes on living. He marries and becomes a carpenter, not with any high hopes or illusions but just "because if the Nazarene had found carpentering good for the life and ends He assumed and elected to serve, it would be all right too for Isaac McCaslin. . . ."[17]

The parable of the boy and the bear is a modest one: the end is neither tragic nor comic (in the sense of a "divine comedy" ending in salvation), but ironic — not redemption nor even noble humanism but renunciation, relinquishment of the greed for property, greed for slaves and land, which was the curse of the South. In the tradition of Cooper, Melville, and Hemingway, Ike refuses to participate in civilization and its corruption. What the parable of the boy and the bear points to indirectly is held in that moment when the boy gives up all power and is given back his life: this is essential reality, a way of being in the world in tension with the conventional way. Unlike Faulkner's humanistic speeches or the Christian overtones of redemption through sacrifice in *Requiem for a Nun* and *A Fable*, our parable suggests a low, modest view of human expectations — the possibility of at least partial peace for the few who renounce the nets of conventional greed and property. Ike is no Dilsey — he is not a saint — but an ordinary though reasonably decent human being, one who stands outside his own culture and its expectations. Faulkner's Southern parable neither preaches nor elevates: it is perhaps finally pitiable, for repudiating and renouncing one's heritage and culture is possible only for a few.

Nonetheless, as parable, Faulkner's story is a success, for the story of the boy and the bear, because of the exaggeration and distortion provided by the presence of immortal, ubiquitous Old Ben, takes on a profound significance far beyond the range of the simple hunting tale. It is a story of disorientation and reorientation: two ways of being in the world are held in tension, and the unconventional way wins out. Faulkner created other Southern parables — his greatest novels are such, I believe. When he loses his sense of concrete place, however, and speaks more directly of essential reality, most notably in *A Fable*, the parables become allegories, illustrations for the Nobel Speech, platitudes about endurance, prevailing belief in humanity, and so on. To be sure, Ike endures and prevails after a fashion, but what counts in Faulkner's greatest work is the way the manners, the Southern ways and mores, form and detail these mysteries of human life: the result is neither despairing nor redemptive of human life after the curse, but rather modest and ironic.

If Faulkner's parabolic vision of human life after the fall is modest and ironic, the same can certainly not be said of Flannery O'Connor's parables. The reality which she permits us to see by opening the familiar and the concrete through distortions is nothing less than the possibility of "second birth." Her vision is patently religious, supernatural, and redemptive — an immodest envisagement of the goal of human life. What is crucial is the way O'Connor embodies her vision: that way is thoroughly parabolic.

As displayed in her creative work and in her occasional writing reflecting on that work, O'Connor had a profoundly parabolic mentality. Unlike Faulkner, who, in interviews and in speeches, manifested little understanding of what he was up to in his creative work, O'Connor's theory and practice mesh. In her critical writings she speaks of the necessity for the fiction writer to have an "anagogical imagination," by which she means "the kind of vision that is able to see different levels of reality in one image or one situation."[18] For her the most profound level of reality is neither vague nor abstract; it is, as she goes on to say, "the Divine life and our participation in it." Elsewhere, she speaks in slightly different terms of the writer's vision as being similar to that of the prophet: "The prophet is a realist of distances, and it is this kind of realism that goes into great novels. It is the realism which does not hesitate to distort appearances in order to show a hidden truth."[19] The prophet is a "realist of distances," one who sees things with their extensions of meaning, who sees far things close up. It is a double vision: the ability to see the absolute in the concrete and the particular, to hear, in Southern talk, the old Adam. O'Connor did not believe that such vision comes naturally to modern, secularized human beings: in fact, mechanized, rationalistic society makes it extremely difficult to see beneath the surface of things to the essentials, to reality. Thus, distortion, caricature, the grotesque — her "freaks" — are necessary to create the possibility of true vision. As she says in an essay, shock is necessary: "to the hard of hearing, you shout, for the almost-blind, you draw large and startling figures."[20] The centrality of seeing, of vision, in O'Connor's work provides an entree into understanding her stories as parables, as we shall see in her novel, *The Violent Bear It Away*. Before one may show how vision functions in that novel, one must say more about the way O'Connor conceives anagogical or prophetic vision.

In the first place, and of critical importance, O'Connor is a novelist, not a prophet or a theologian. "It is the nature of fiction," she says, "not to be good for much else unless it is good in itself."[21] The materials of the fiction writer are the humblest: fiction is "about everything human and we are made out of dust, and if you scorn getting yourself dusty, then you shouldn't try to write fiction. It's not a grand enough job for you."[22] Good fiction has its own criteria of excellence: good plots, developed characters, nitty-gritty detail — matters of craft, if you will. That O'Connor never relinquishes the level of the literal and the concrete cannot be stressed too heavily. It was also her belief, as well as her practice, that the good fiction writer is always concerned to embody within the manners his or her vision of reality: "Fiction should be both canny and uncanny."[23] The novelist is "concerned with ultimate mystery as we find it embodied in the concrete world of sense experience."[24]

The union we see here between the concrete and ultimate mystery is, as I have suggested, one of the central marks of the New Testament parables. O'Connor held to this intimacy of the concrete and the truly real not only because she was a consummate fiction writer, but also because she was a Southerner and a Roman Catholic. She sees these two facts about herself coming to the same thing: the awareness that mystery is always embodied in manners. For the Southerner, O'Connor claims, this awareness takes the form of storytelling. Abstractions and formulas will not do for the Southerner. A story makes a story, and for the South, the Scriptures have filled the role of a story of mythic dimensions in which everyone recognizes the hand of God and its descent: "The Hebrew genius for making the absolute concrete has conditioned the Southerner's way of looking at things."[25] As an illustration of making the absolute concrete we might mention her comment: "The Southerner, who isn't convinced of it, is very much *afraid* that *he* may have been formed in the image and likeness of God"[26] (italics added).

In addition to the Southern storytelling sensibility, O'Connor was heir to a more conceptual formulation of the relation of the concrete and the absolute, the nature-supernature understanding of Thomism. A Catholic novelist believes, she says, that the natural world contains the supernatural. The supernatural does not contain or swallow up the natural: rather, the natural embodies the supernatural. This means, of course, that the artist and the Christian in her were not at odds: on the contrary, as Jacques Maritain says, in a passage she underlined in her copy of *Art and Scholasticism*, the work of the Christian artist "will be as wholly of the one as the other."[27] Indeed, attention to concrete detail which establishes the reality of the natural order is necessary in order to sustain the thrust into the supernatural realm.[28] The Christian novelist, therefore, feels *greater* obligation to portray the natural order, "for if," O'Connor says, "the readers don't accept the natural world, they'll certainly not accept anything else."[29]

I have spoken at some length on O'Connor's understanding of what I would call the parabolic way of making essential reality concrete — her extraordinary ability to embody the mystery in the details of Southern manners and mores. But to the other crucial note of the New Testament parables—the element of distortion or shock which makes of the ordinary something extraordinary—I have only alluded. One doubts that O'Connor, given her belief in the continuum between the natural and the supernatural, would have introduced freaks and the grotesques into her stories, if she felt that ours were a time when people naturally had sacramental vision. The distortion and the grotesque in her work are necessary in times of unbelief, when statistics and facts, the surface of life, are all that most people see, when the surface *is* reality. O'Connor is concerned with a deeper kind of realism. The grotesque, violence, and distortion are necessary to press towards what is "really real," not as we have continually stressed, apart from the concrete and the ordinary, but at the center as well as at the furthermost extensions of the concrete. What O'Connor says of Hawthorne's writing could well be applied to her own:

> He's looking for one image that will connect or combine or embody two points: one is a point in the concrete, and the other is a point not visible to the naked eye, but believed in by him firmly, just as real to him, really, as the one that everybody sees.[30]

The way to bring people to see this ultimate mystery—what O'Connor elsewhere calls grace or second birth—is through violence and distortion. "Their heads are so hard that almost nothing else will work."[31] The method is the same in many of Jesus's parables: a comment on her method by Brainard Cheney could apply equally well to the parable of the Wedding Feast, the Laborers in the Vineyard, the Talents, or the Ten Virgins.

> She invented a new form of humor. . . . This invention consists in her introducing her story with familiar surfaces in an action that seems secular, and in a secular tone of satire and humor. Before you know it, the naturalistic situation has become metaphysical and the action appropriate to it comes with a surprise, an unaccountability that is humorous, however shocking. The *means is violent*, but the end is Christian. And obviously, it works.[32]

What O'Connor is concerned to be, then, is an artist of reality, not surface reality but the reality of the power of God unto salvation. This is not an abstract or far-off reality but is in and through and under ordinary reality, if only human beings had eyes to see it. The central crisis for O'Connor's characters usually involves encounters with Jesus or with the devil: each is palpable, intimate, near, and real. The characters carry on dialogues with Jesus and with the devil who hover near. Normal, ordinary people usually do not see their salvation or damnation as immediate reality, but the freaks do. They are the ones, who as O'Connor says of fiction writers, possess "the quality of having stare," for the longer they look at an object the more of the world they see in it.[33]

More, perhaps, than in any of her other writings, in *The Violent Bear It Away* O'Connor created a Christian parable of reality. This novel, surely her greatest, is the test case for her understanding of the intimacy of the concrete and the absolute brought to awareness through violence and distortion. The novel is about a fourteen-year-old boy, Francis Tarwater, who, after the death of his great-uncle, a self-proclaimed prophet, flees to his uncle Rayber in order to fulfill the Lord's "call" that he, Tarwater, baptize Rayber's idiot son, Bishop. Rayber is a secularist and a rationalist who attempts to persuade Tarwater to fight his great-uncle's vision of reality in which salvation, second birth, and the bread of life are the components. But the old prophet also sowed the seeds of his vision in Rayber and, in spite of Rayber's attempts to affirm "the great dignity of man . . . [as] his ability to say: I was born once and no more,"[34] he too is captured by the old prophet's reality. In Rayber and in the great-uncle we have the classic parabolic tension of two ways of being in the world—a conventional and ordinary way versus an unconventional and extraordinary way—with the interesting suggestion that grace, the extraordinary, is irresistible.

This novel carries, through images of vision, of seeing, awareness of the intimacy of the concrete and the absolute brought about through distortion and violence. Both Rayber and Tarwater try to make their eyes stop at the surface of things: both know that if they stare at something, anything, too long, the thing will demand to be named and named justly. They attempt to see only a part of reality, surface, conventional reality. For both of them, the freak child, the idiot Bishop, is the power that moves them beyond that safe surface reality to essential reality.

At times Rayber

> would experience a love for the child so outrageous that he would be left shocked and depressed for days, and trembling for his sanity. . . . with little or no warning he would feel himself overwhelmed by the horrifying love. Anything he looked at too long could bring it on. Bishop did not have to be around. It could be a stick or a stone, the line of a shadow, the absurd old man's walk of a starling crossing the sidewalk. If, without thinking, he lent himself to it, he would suddenly feel a morbid surge of love that terrified him—powerful enough to throw him on the ground in an act of idiot praise.[35]

The eyes of the freaks can see the extensions of the concrete into the reality that undergirds it—the love of God—for it was the grotesque old prophet whose fish-colored eyes first got to Rayber when he was a young boy. "It was the eyes that got me." Rayber said. "Children may be attracted to mad eyes. A grown person could have resisted. A child couldn't. Children are cursed with believing."[36] The eyes of Lucette Carmody, the crippled child evangelist, burn into his as she shouts at him. "I see a damned soul before my eye! I see a dead man Jesus hasn't raised."[37] Death, death-in-life, is what comes to Rayber's "successful" attempt to avoid looking beneath the surface. He was afraid that if Bishop died, then the horrifying love, held in and limited by the child, would overwhelm him. He was afraid that "the whole world would become his idiot child," that he would be thrown "to the ground in an act of idiot praise."[38] Nothing of the sort happens. When Tarwater, having accidentally baptized Bishop first, drowns him. Rayber loses his chance for life on any terms. He feels nothing: he is, for all intents and purposes, dead.

The old prophet planted seeds in young Tarwater also, and, as Rayber says, they fell on better soil.[39] But Tarwater fights the penetration into surface reality to essential reality much as Rayber did:

> He tried when possible to . . . keep his vision located on an even level, to see no more than what was in front of his face and to let his eyes stop at the surface of that. It was as if he were afraid that if he let his eye rest for an instant longer than was needed to place something—a spade, a hoe, the mule's hind quarters before his plow, the red furrow under him—that the thing would suddenly stand before him, strange and terrifying, demanding that he name it and name it justly and be judged for the name he gave it. He did all he could to avoid this threatened intimacy of creation. When the Lord's call came, he wished it to be a voice from out of a clear and empty sky, the trumpet of the Lord God Almighty, untouched by any fleshly hand or breath.[40]

Tarwater wanted a call straight from God out of an empty sky: what he got was a call to baptize an idiot boy. Tarwater fights a call that comes with the threatened intimacy of creation, wishing for one "untouched by any fleshly hand or breath."[41] A freak, Bishop, leads Tarwater to accept his unremarkable vocation as prophet. Here we see the characteristic parabolic motif of distortion opening ordinary reality to essential reality. Tarwater cannot look Bishop in the eye, but when he finally does, his decision to follow his vocation as an unremarkable prophet has been made. "He seemed to see the little boy and nothing else, no air around him, no room, no nothing, as if his gaze had slipped and fallen into the center of the child's eyes and was still falling down and down and down."[42]

After Bishop's drowning, Tarwater goes back to his great-uncle's farm. On the way he is picked up by one of the several devil-figures in the story and sexually assaulted. The possibility of keeping "his vision located on an even level," of letting his eyes stop at the surface of things is erased forever. His eyes are "scorched": "They looked as if, touched with a coal like the lips of the prophet, they would never be used for ordinary sights again."[43] His vision has been repaired: he now sees the extensions of things into another reality, the "really real," about which it is his mission to prophesy: the terrible speed of God's mercy. The last line of the book describes his "singed eyes" set towards the city "where the children of God lay sleeping."

O'Connor's Christian parable is one in which God works through violence to mold human beings towards their own salvation. As one critic has pointed out, Tarwater has his own view of how God should communicate with him—by a clear call from an empty sky—but slowly he realizes that God works through the created world.[44] Tarwater thinks he can take control of his own life through "doing," but he discovers he is done to — the involuntary baptism of Bishop, his subjection to rape, and his discovery that someone else has buried his great-uncle when he believed he had cremated the old man.[45] Only when Tarwater begins to see into the depths of ordinary reality, into the eyes of an idiot child, does he realize what ultimate reality is. The parabolic pattern is very clear here — awareness of the intimacy of the concrete and the absolute brought about by means of a distortion of the concrete.

To move from the Christian parables of Flannery O'Connor to the modern, existential parables of Walker Percy appears, on the face of it, to be a leap into another world. Although, like O'Connor, Percy is a Roman Catholic and a Southerner, he appears to get his philosophical and literary bearings from Europe and from Protestantism: he has been deeply influenced by the phenomenology of Heidegger, Jaspers, and Marcel and by the existentialism of Kierkegaard and Camus. "Whatever impulse I had towards writing," he says, "owes nothing to sitting on a porch listening to anybody tell stories about the South, believe me."[46]

These influences cannot be overlooked in Percy, especially that of Kierkegaard and of the phenomenological method, for they are central to both the craft and the substance of his novels. In fact, Percy's career as a writer began as a philosopher: only because of his philosophical insights did he turn to novel writing as the best medium for the phenomenological task of what one critic calls surprising "being in its lair."[47] In an essay entitled "The Message in the Bottle," Percy writes that the human person is a castaway who waits for news relevant to the self, not general, but particular, news. "The Christian message is the kind of news the castaway is waiting for: not a piece of knowledge *sub species aeternitatis. . . .* [not knowledge about] "a member in good standing of the World's Great Religions but a unique Person-Event-Thing in time."[48] Percy is aware that no such news can be *preached;* it can only be discovered. The outstanding characteristic of modernity, he believes, is what he calls the malaise of everydayness in which we are all submerged.[49] One can only *awaken* from the pall of the ordinary, and this awakening does not take place by direct means. Just as Kierkegaard knew that indirect means are necessary to awaken a people believing itself Christian to authentic Christianity, so Percy believes that authentic existence must be surprised in its lair by indirection, by intimation, and by ordeal.[50] Thus, his literary method is elliptical and phenomenological, investigating realities that normally lie beneath the threshold of modern consciousness: "the novelist must first and last be a good phenomenologist."[51] The writer who derided his dependence on Southern storytelling ends up telling stories as the means to articulate the concrete way of the castaway as he comes to an awareness of his or her authentic existence, which lies in shadow beneath the everydayness of life as lived in a particular time and place.

Thus we can see Percy's method is parabolic. Like Faulkner and O'Connor, he wants to bring to light the intimacy of concrete life with essential reality, and he accomplishes this by distorting the ordinary so that the extraordinary may be glimpsed. Percy says he began *The Moviegoer* with "a *man* who finds himself in a *world*, a very concrete man who is located in a very concrete place and time" and who is represented "as *coming to himself* in somewhat the same sense as Robinson Crusoe came to himself on his island after his shipwreck, with the same wonder and curiosity."[52] Percy is a phenomenologist of reality much as O'Connor believes she is. They are both concerned with elemental reality, but this is reached not by departing from the concrete and the ordinary but by cunningly tracking it down in, through, and under the everyday. When insight comes, when one finally *sees*, O'Connor and Percy agree, one has had one's vision repaired and can name things justly: Percy says such a person is "like Adam on the First Day," whose responsibility was to name all things rightly.[53] As with O'Connor, so with Percy, the grotesque, the violence, and shock are necessary for the awakening; the differences between them lie in Percy's lighter touch and in his reluctance to identify the depths of reality in traditionally religious terms or with God-talk. His characters do not become prophets of God's judgment and mercy but rather Kierkegaard's Knights of Faith, indistinguishable from the mass of ordinary human beings.

The Moviegoer is about a week in the life of one wanderer in the everyday, Binx Bolling. The novel is set in New Orleans during Mardi Gras and concerns Binx's coming to awareness culminating on his thirtieth birthday. The coming to awareness is embodied in what Binx calls his "search," an appropriate form for a castaway and a wanderer. Of the search Binx says, "The search is what anyone would undertake if he were not sunk in the everydayness of his own life. This morning, for example, I felt as if I had come to myself on a strange island. And what does such a castaway do? Why, he pokes around the neighborhood and doesn't miss a trick."[54] Binx, a stockbroker from an old Southern family and a nominal Catholic, can be compared in temperament to Meursault in Camus's *The Stranger* or to Bartleby in Melville's *Bartleby the Scrivener;* he is laconic, basically indifferent to religious and moral values. He is the ordinary of the ordinary. Unlike his Aunt Emily, who believes in the great Roman virtues of Southern aristocratic culture, or his Uncle Jules, who lives comfortably in the City of Man, finding it "an easy-going place of old-world charm and new-world business methods," Binx has few pretentions. He despises those who see life in moral terms: "to make a contribution, however small, and leave the world a little better off."[55] He wishes only to be able to settle for what he calls "the Little Way," "not the big search for the big happiness but the sad little happiness of drinks and kisses, a good little car and a warm deep thigh."[56] He appears to be sunk in everydayness:

I am a model tenant and a model citizen and take pleasure in doing all that is expected of me. . . . I subscribe to *Consumer Reports* and as a consequence I own a first-class television set, an all but silent air conditioner, and a very long lasting deodorant. My armpits never stink.[57]

His search will not stay submerged. He is an inveterate moviegoer, for the movies are a form of distortion which breaks through everydayness at least momentarily: they allow for what he calls rotation — a sense of novelty in the midst of the ordinary — and repetition — the re-enactment of past experience by isolating a time segment usually sunk in everydayness. But these intimations are fleeting; more powerful means are necessary to break through everydayness. Only the bizarre — violence and disaster — can disrupt the ordinary. The search first occurred to Binx when he was wounded during the Korean war and lay in a ditch close to death; his fiancee, Kate, also engaged in a search, felt her greatest happiness during a car accident which she survived but which killed her lover. She says, "Have you noticed that only in time of illness or disaster or death are people real?"[58] Like O'Connor, Percy creates parables in which people come to an awareness of the intimacy of the ordinary and the extraordinary only through distortion, violence, and the grotesque. The people who *do* come to such awareness tend themselves to be freaks — Binx, the odd one who spends half his life in movies, is compared by Kate to a girl she knows who searched the neighborhood for statues of deer made out of iron: Lonnie, Binx's half-brother, who is a devout Roman Catholic with an immediate awareness of authentic existence, is a cripple who dies from self-imposed starvation.

The grotesque qualities, however, do not mean a turn away from ordinary life. In fact, like O'Connor, Percy insists that the "vertical search," the search for authentic existence in abstract, general, or scientific terms, is a failure. During an earlier time when Binx read what he calls "fundamental books" like Einstein's *The Universe as I See It*, he was involved in such a search: "I lived in my room as an Anyone living Anywhere . . . and for diversion took walks around the neighborhood. . . . The only difficulty was that though the universe had been disposed of, I myself was left over."[59] It is only by surprising being in its lair, by awakening through ordeal and violence *within* the ordinary to the power that sustains it, that the search can rightly be carried on. It is what Binx calls the horizontal search.[60]

The goal is as horizontal as the search. Binx never loses hold of concrete time and place: at the end of the novel, on his thirtieth birthday, Ash Wednesday, he decides to marry Kate, to settle down, to go to medical school, and to live an ordinary life. What he has found in his search is, on the face of it, indistinguishable from other people's lives: "There is only one thing I can do: listen to people, see how they stick themselves into the world, hand them along a ways in their dark journey and be handed along. . . ."[61] After Lonnie's death he spends some time being a friend to his half-brothers and sisters, and he tries to help Kate, who is still neurotically caught up in a vertical search. He is at the most a Knight of Faith, indistinguishable from the crowd. Binx has found his vocation, his authentic existence, but it is no big deal. As one critic says:

> Percy suggests this without moralizing and without grandiose claims, by his elliptical approach and the language of understatement. The reader can accept it or not, as he prefers. There is no attempt to force it down his throat. To me that is why *The Moviegoer* is a moving novel and no small achievement.[62]

It is also, I think, what makes Percy's novel a profound modern parable of alienation and return to authentic existence. We have looked at three Southern authors who in different ways have created parables which reflect the pattern of New Testament parables. The unity among their parables rests in the insistence by Faulkner, O'Connor, and Percy that mystery must be embodied in manners, that the ordinary and the extraordinary are intimately connected. The ordinary and the extraordinary are also at odds, however, for while essential reality cannot for these authors be discovered apart from the concrete, it also can never be identified with conventional reality. Thus, distortion, violence, and the grotesque are the necessary means for bringing the new vision to awareness: one must *hear and see* it, and such does not occur without disruption of the ordinary. In each author's case, essential reality is understood differently, but is never a mere continuation of life as usual. Whether essential reality be Faulkner's renunciation, O'Connor's salvation, or Percy's authentic existence, it is a new way of being in the world in tension with conventional ways. If reality is seen only as surface reality or only in abstraction from the concrete, parables are not possible. Where reality is viewed in intimacy *and* in tension with the concrete, stories may be told in which, through shock and surprise, we suddenly hear the old Adam talking Southern.

These three authors are, I am suggesting, all "religious" writers, but of a special sort. As O'Connor would put it, they are both "canny" and "uncanny." Or as Percy says in his essay, "Notes for a Novel About the End of the World," the religious, prophetic, or philosophical novelist is a writer with an explicit and ultimate concern about the nature of humanity and the nature of reality, but, instead of constructing a plot and characters familiar to everyone, this writer "is more apt to set forth with a stranger in a strange land where the signposts are enigmatic but which [the novelist] sets out to explore nevertheless."[63] Percy explicitly mentions both Faulkner and O'Connor in his list of religious or prophetic novelists who must shock and often tell bad news in order to be heard. As Percy concludes, such novelists have visions of reality widely divergent "from the usual views of the denizens of the secular city."[64] These visions of reality, unconventional as they are, are no easier to read than the parables of Jesus. With her usual pungency, O'Connor accurately describes the reactions of readers to both Jesus's parables and the "parables" of our three authors: "When I sit down to write a monstrous reader looms up who sits down beside me and continually mutters. 'I don't get it, I don't see it. I don't want it.'" [65]

Notes

1. Gerard E. Sherry, "An Interview with Flannery O'Connor," *The Critic* (June–July, 1963), 29.

2. Flannery O' Connor, *Mystery and Manners: Occasional Prose,* ed. Sally and Robert Fitzgerald (New York: Farrar, Straus and Giroux, 1969), p. 58. Hereafter referred to in text as *(Mystery).*

3. The widespread agreement on this point by contemporary biblical scholars marks a signficant change from earlier parable criticism that focused on the conceptual or moral qualities of parables. C. H. Dodd, Norman Perrin, Amos Wilder, Robert Funk, John Dominic Crossan, John Donahue, among others, see radicalism, superabundance, or extravagance as the note that sets the parables off as different from poetic metaphors. Their extremity moves them into the religious dimension.

4. Robert W. Funk, *Language, Hermeneutic and Word of God: The Problem of Language in the New Testament and Contemporary Theology* (New York: Harper and Row. 1966), pp. 193–96.

5. Paul Ricoeur, "Biblical Hermaneutics," *Semeia* 4 (1975), 94–112.

6. John Dominic Crossan, *The Dark Interval: Towards a Theology of Story* (Niles, IL: Argus Communications, 1975), p. 56.

7. Crossan, pp. 56–57.

8. Louis D. Rubin, Jr. and Robert D. Jacobs, eds., *South: Modern Southern Literature* (Garden City, NY: Doubleday, 1961), p. 48.

9. Frederick J. Hoffman, *The Art of Southern Fiction: A Study of Some Modern Novelists* (Carbondale, IL: Southern Illinois University Press, 1967), pp. 11–12.

10. Malcolm Cowley, "Introduction to the *Portable Faulkner," William Faulkner: Three Decades of Criticism,* ed. Frederick J. Hoffman and Olga W. Vickery (East Lansing: Michigan State University Press. 1960), p. 94.

11. O'Connor, *Mystery,* p. 124.

12. O'Connor, *Mystery,* p. 58.

13. As quoted in Hyatt H. Waggoner, *William Faulkner: From Jefferson to the World* (Lexington: University of Kentucky Press, 1966), p. 232.

14. Waggoner, p. 243.

15. William Faulkner, *Go Down, Moses* (New York: Modern Library, 1942), pp. 208–09.

16. Faulkner, p. 211.

17. Faulkner, p. 309.

18. O'Connor, *Mystery,* p. 72.

19. O'Connor, *Mystery,* p. 42.

20. O'Connor, *Mystery,* p. 34.

21. O'Connor, *Mystery,* p. 81.

22. O'Connor, *Mystery*, p. 68.

23. O'Connor, *Mystery*, p. 79.

24. O'Connor, *Mystery*, p. 125.

25. O'Connor, *Mystery*, pp. 202–03.

26. O'Connor, *Mystery*, pp. 44–45.

27. As quoted in Kathleen Feeley, *Flannery O'Connor: Voice of the Peacock* (New Brunswick, NJ: Rutgers University Press, 1972), p. 14.

28. Feeley, *Flannery O'Connor*, p. 57.

29. Flannery O'Connor, "The Novelist and Free Will," *Fresco* (University of Detroit), 1 (Winter, 1961), 100–01.

30. O'Connor, *Mystery*, p. 42.

31. O'Connor, *Mystery*, p. 112.

32. Brainard Cheney, "Flannery O'Connor's Campaign for Her Country," *Flannery O'Connor*, ed. Robert E. Reiter (St. Louis: B. Herder Book Co., n.d.). p. 3.

33. Cheney, p. 77.

34. Flannery O'Connor, *The Violent Bear It Away* (New York: Farrar. Straus and Giroux. 1960), p. 172.

35. O'Connor, *Violent*, pp. 112–13.

36. O'Connor, *Violent*, pp. 170–71.

37. O'Connor, *Violent*, p. 134.

38. O'Connor, *Violent*, pp. 182, 113.

39. O'Connor, *Violent*, p. 192.

40. O'Connor, *Violent*, pp. 21–22.

41. O'Connor, *Violent*, p. 22.

42. O'Connor, *Violent*, p. 155

43. O'Connor, *Violent*, p. 233.

44. Feeley, *Flannery O'Connor*, p. 155

45. Feeley, *Flannery O'Connor*, p. 155.

46. As quoted in Martin Luschei, *The Sovereign Wayfarer: Walker Percy's Diagnosis of the Malaise* (Baton Rouge: Louisiana State University, 1972), p. 11.

47. As quoted in Luschei, p. 74.

48. Walker Percy, *The Message in the Bottle* (New York: Farrar, Straus and Giroux, 1975), p. 141.

49. See Percy, *Moviegoer*, pp. 114–15, 135.

50. See Percy, *Message*, pp. 1016, 140–49.

51. As quoted in Luschei, p. 239.

52. As quoted in Luschei, p. 15.

53. As quoted in Luschei, p. 289.

54. Walker Percy, *The Moviegoer* (New York: Popular Library. 1961), p. 17.

55. Percy, *Moviegoer*, p. 96.

56. Percy, *Moviegoer*, p. 127.

57. Percy, *Moviegoer*, p. 12.

58. Percy, *Moviegoer*, p. 78.

59. Percy, *Moviegoer*, p. 68.

60. Percy, *Moviegoer*, p. 68

61. Percy, *Moviegoer*, p. 213.

62. Luschei, *Wayfarer*, p. 110

63. Percy, *Message*, p. 102.

64. Percy, *Message*, p. 104.

65. As quoted in Feeley, *Flannery O'Connor*, p. 104.

The Eschatological Vision of Walker Percy

Thomas LeClair*

"What it means to be a man living in the world who must die," the lacuna Kierkegaard found in Hegel's system, Walker Percy adopts as his concern.[1] How close the heroes of his three novels — *The Moviegoer, The Last Gentleman, Love in the Ruins*[2] — come to achieving this meaning depends largely upon their recognition of man as the being "who must die" and who *knows* that he must die. Awareness of mortality as basic ontological condition helps free Percy's heroes from the malaise of "every-dayness" and allows them an intimation of the meaning they seek. A Catholic, Percy also presents death as a spiritual event which tests his characters' openness to God. Percy is thus concerned with both an immanent eschatology, in his Existential analysis of death as condition, and with a transcendent eschatology, in his presentation of death as event in the economy of salvation. In the recently published *Love in the Ruins*, Percy extends his interest in the Last Things to cultural eschatology or apocalypse. Because this latest novel helps clarify the ontological and religious themes in Percy's first two novels, I give it most of my attention.

In *The Moviegoer*, Percy's first novel and winner of the 1962 National Book Award, death is an efficient rather than a final cause. It is a fact or possibility which sets the protagonists — Kate Cutrer and Binx Bolling — to their tasks of evading the impersonations demanded by their time and place — New Orleans in the fetid fifties. Binx had conceived a metaphysical search while lying wounded in a Korean ditch. For Binx, death is not an event which transforms man into an honored corpse in the Bolling family annals, but a possibility which awakens him to an existence beyond his Aunt Emily's gentle aristrocratic stoicism. Kate has been set free from a Mardi Gras queen's life by her fiancé's accidental death. Both await the crack in the facade of their lives through which the next clue to their uncertain searches will come. That clue is Lonnie Smith, Binx's devoutly religious half-brother, a disease-twisted but serene adolescent whose death tests Binx and Kate. Kate tries to avoid the boy's death. Binx accepts it, and by his acceptance earns the possibility of advancement up Percy's spiritual ladder to the acceptance of God.

God has figured all along in Binx's search, but he has been embar-

*Reprinted by permission from *Renascence* 24 (1974): 115–22.

rassed by the word throughout. Early in the novel he says the reader will smile at such a notion as God. He also states ironically that he doesn't want to search for something 98 per cent of Americans have already "found." For Binx, God is a linguistic problem. The pious banalities of a *Reader's Digest* theology have covered the notion of God with a secretion of niceties. Needed is a notion or name appropriate to the freshness of being Binx experienced when wounded.[3] Although Binx remains embarrassed by the "subject of religion," his sense of religious possibility remains intact. On Ash Wednesday he sees a Black man leaving a Catholic Church. Binx first interprets the man's Catholicism as an attempt at social climbing, then thinks that perhaps, just perhaps, this man truly believes and that "through some dim dazzling trick of grace" receives "God's own importunate bonus" (235). Since Binx feels that "it is impossible to say" just what has happened at the church — and at Lonnie's death — he is left to watch and wait, remain open to a sign of grace. His mission is Hebraic: understand suffering, exile himself from the unchosen, wait expectantly for a sign. We are left with a man aware of Percy's two eschatological interests but without any assurance that he will turn toward faith and his salvation.

In *The Last Gentleman* Percy expands the themes of *The Moviegoer* by offering a variety of well-developed responses to the dying youth Jamie Vaught who functions as a locus of spiritual interest and as a mainspring for Percy's episodic plot. Jamie's New South parents and his ingénue sister Kitty evade the truth of his moribund condition by pretending that their usual social roles and acts will magically restore the family fabric. Jamie's humanistic sister-in-law Rita evades Jamie's plight by attempting to prolong his life through science. Rita's is the technician's response to death: keep the organism functioning on the level of organism. She also thinks of Jamie's death as, in Heidegger's terms, an "event of public occurrence," the importance of which can be judged quantitatively. Jamie's traveling companion, Bill Barrett, the nominal hero of the novel, avoids thinking about Jamie's certain death until the very end of the novel when he becomes the hesitant agent of Jamie's deathbed baptism. Defined in terms of possibility, Jamie and Bill are the innocent objects of the philosophical and religious skirmishing between Jamie's sister Val and his brother Sutter.

Sutter is a psychiatrist turned coroner, a pathologist of body and soul who believes that "the certain availability of death is the very condition of recovering oneself" (291). Although Sutter is a spokesman for Percy's immanent eschatology, his awareness of death as ontological condition opens no spiritual avenues for him. Frustrated by his inability to believe, Sutter can think only of suicide as a response to a God that withheld a sign of His existence and grace. A religious man without faith, Sutter is incomplete, a Virgil in a Dantean world.

It is Val, a Roman Catholic postulant, who summarizes in the novel

the Christian position Percy has developed in his philosophical articles.[4]
Val believes that God's intervention in history was an absurd scandal that
demands absurd belief. She sees man as a wayfarer between immanence
and transcendence who therefore "stands in the way of hearing a piece of
news which is of the utmost importance to him (i.e., his salvation) and
which he had better attend to" (276). She further believes that man does
well "to be afraid and . . . to forget everything which does not pertain to
[his] salvation." For her, the Church figures primarily as the guardian of
the sacraments. Its priests are "Apostles," common men with a message
and the sacraments, rather than "Geniuses," men of obvious worldly gifts.
If Val's eschatological theology is implicitly affirmed by the dying Jamie
Vaught, Bill Barrett finds it as puzzling as Sutter's philosophizing. However, Percy's ending suggests that Bill is ready to stretch his sluggish
synapses into a posture of openness to the message Val bears. Like
Wolfram von Eschenbach's Parsival returned to the Fisher King, Bill after
Jamie's death begins to ask Sutter the proper questions, questions which
may forecast the salvation of both Sutter and the awakening Bill. At the
end of the novel Bill no longer exists in the state of "pure possibility" of the
novel's opening, but in a sphere of focused possibility, turned ever so little
toward God.

In the recently published *Love in the Ruins: The Adventures of a Bad
Catholic at a Time Near the End of the World*, Percy again explores
individual eschatology, but now within an apocalyptic frame. Set near
New Orleans, the novel opens at 5:00 p.m., July 4th, 1953, with a middle-
aged psychiatrist named Thomas More waiting for the end of the United
States, perhaps the world, an event expected in about two hours. Various
signs and portents confirm his belief that the "center did not hold" and
that he lives in the "dread latter days." Mysterious suicides and mad,
violent attacks, decadent and bestial forces prowling the lowlands, the
Antichrist and his principalities present in the flesh, a Rotary banner rent
like the temple veil — all these figure forth the End. Racial, political, and
religious extremists battle for control of an America whose technology is
strangled by vines, whose people are victims of uncontrollable rages or fits
of abstraction, and whose savior — Dr. Thomas More — has proven to be
the possible agent of destruction. Shortly after 7:00 p.m. More moves from
his secure vantage to help prevent the world's end. Perhaps *he* even does
so. A short Epilogue told five years after this glorious fourth of July
weekend establishes Percy's final religious perspective. Nothing as unin-
spired as a serious warning about nuclear holocaust, the novel comically
reverses the analysis of the doom merchants by maintaining that for a
special kind of man the End would be welcome.

Percy has from the beginning had a curious attitude toward apocalypse. In "The Man on the Train," an early *Partisan Review* article which
introduced many of the ideas he later uses in his fiction, Percy stated that
the "contingency 'what if the Bomb should fall?' is not only a cause of

anxiety in the alienated man but is one of his few remaining refuges from it."[5] The alienated man, says Percy, enjoys "the old authentic thrill of the Bomb and the Coming of the Last Days," wants to "see vines sprouting through the masonry." For the alienated man, the End promises a destruction not unlike mass suicide and thus becomes a final escape from anxiety. Or the End can mean the destruction of what he sees as a dead world. Since the alienated man sees himself superior to the dead world he inhabits, he will naturally survive the apocalypse and be awarded a freedom he can use for the authentic rejuvenation of the world or for his own selfish motives. These variations on the eschatological theme Percy introduced in both *The Moviegoer* and *The Last Gentleman*. Binx Bolling had hoped for an apocalypse which only the people he respected would survive. Bill Barrett found that it was "not the prospect of the Last Day which depressed him but rather the prospect of living through an ordinary Wednesday morning" (26). Both Binx's and Bill's fathers saw war as an apocalyptic event in which "the possible becomes actual through no doing of one's own." (*LG*,16). Finally, Valerie Vaught's school for backward Southern Black children looks "like one of those surviving enclaves after the Final War" (95), a place where meaning can be recovered. And so it is, for Val's students are without language, are innocent of the world, and therefore receive her teaching without reservation.

Val properly uses an apocalyptic situation which she happens upon. Tom More welcomes his imminent apocalyptic situation because it promises — not a world of linguistic or religious freshness — but a familiar and small world of multiple fornication with the three pieces of flesh he has safely waiting for him. More's dream conforms to what Percy, in "The Man on the Train," calls "the acceptable rhythm of the Wellesian-Huxleyan-Nathanian romance of love among the ruins. . . . Far from being a free exploration, [this kind of fantasy] is in reality a conforming to the most ritualistic of gestures: that which is thought to be proper and fitting for a sexual adventure." More finally repudiates his wholly inauthentic fantasy with his last minute attempt to prevent the imminent apocalypse. His repudiation of love in the ruins begins his private rejuvenation which Percy dramatizes as an exorcism of the devil. In the end, More, a lapsed Catholic, returns to the state of grace and takes up Percy's now familiar stance for the Catholic at the end of an era — quiet, expectant watchfulness for the confirming sign of God's grace.

The apocalypse More finally foils has its causes in his personal background, which includes a failed eschatological test. Until a few years before 1983, More had been a practicing Catholic with the sacramental life of Christ in him, which allowed him placement in the world, enjoyment of his daughter, and wantonness with his wife. But the inevitable test of Percy's fiction — an innocent youth, More's daughter Samantha, dead of a horribly disfiguring disease — destroys More's faith and his marriage. Unlike Abraham called to sacrifice his child, More and his wife Doris refuse God's will even though the religious Samantha warns her father against such a refusal. The problem of evil in the grotesque physical form of Samantha elicits from Doris an angry attack on the "loving God" who would allow such things to be. Like Rita Vaught, Doris becomes spiritual in the modern way More and Percy find specious. She runs off to a deserted island with an English charlatan—a purveyor of esoteric doctrine and maker of crafts.

More's response to his daughter's disease and death parallels Sutter Vaught's response to Jamie's. More becomes abstract in his thinking, the disease he calls "angelism," and bestial in his actions. When he realizes that fornication does not recover the world lost to oneself by abstraction and that demonic activity does not retrieve one's God, More tries suicide. His failed attempt clears his vision, and he begins to live a sane—if incomplete—life in a mad world, one of Percy's favorite themes. Taking Sutter's role as diagnostician of the world's deadness, More invents his "Qualitative Quantitative Ontological Lapsometer" which uses electrical currents to diagnose the spiritual ills of man. With it, More says, he "can measure the index of life, life in death and death in life" (190). Discouraged by the medical profession's refusal to fund such an "unscientific" device, More falls to the temptation of a satanic foundation representative named Art Immelman who offers a gadget to make the diagnostic lapsometer therapeutic. Immelman tempts More by mouthing the heresy of happiness, joy, and spontaneity, by discounting "such unhappy things as pure versus impure love, sin versus virtue . . ." (214). For Percy, this is the definition of despair. In his eschatological Catholicism which, he says in one of his interviews, harks back to an early orthodoxy, man is a homeless stranger in this world, a pilgrim making his way to salvation out of this world.[6] More finally recognizes Immelman's satanic intentions and attempts to retrieve the machines. But only at the end of the book when More risks being shot and killed, foregoes the certainty of love in the ruins, and calls upon Saint Thomas More does Tom More recover the machines and himself.

More's Epilogue five years later finds him married to the only Christian of his three girls (the others represent bestial broad, angelic artist). He lives in old slave quarters instead of the ironically named Paradise Estates he once occupied. He is waiting, watching, listening. He still hopes to cure the "modern Black Death" (chronic angelism-bestialism) and thus make man a "sovereign wanderer, lordly exile, worker and waiter and watcher" (383), Percy's favorite terms for the whole man. But More's hope for others is tempered by his recognition that man is a fated sufferer and chooser who must be allowed to sin. Unlike Don Juan of Mozart's *Don Giovanni* to which More listens throughout, he repents his sins and receives communion, thus restoring life to himself. As he explains, "eating Christ himself . . . make[s] me mortal man again and let[s] me inhabit my own flesh and love . . ." (254). The Eucharist thus combines mortality and life, immanence and transcendence, to give Tom the joy he had before Samantha's death and his loss of faith. In the novel, apocalypse or social eschatology has become a test along with the immanent and transcendent eschatological tests of Percy's other novels. More fails, then passes each of the tests and ends with the sacrament which restores life in this world and promises life in the next.

Percy's novels avoid the ponderous moralizing, savage violence, and chiliastic jeremiads that a concern with eschatology can produce. He does not sentimentally dwell on his diseased innocents, nor does he overplay the spiritual events their final moments become. Even his version of apocalypse, with its devil presiding over burning sand traps on a golf course, becomes a parody of the genre. Though unquestionably serious about his heroes' orientation to their personal and social ends, Percy employs the comic mode to illustrate their failure and, finally, their successes. As form, his comedy is truncated in *The Moviegoer* and *The Last Gentleman*, for Binx Bolling and Bill Barrett are left at a point of probably turning toward a reintegration of their lives on a higher plane. They have knowledge but have not completed the comic action of which their marriages are a good sign. If these first novels are modern infernos, in *Love in the Ruins* Percy leaves his hero pointing toward Paradise. The structure of the novel follows the basic death and rebirth action of mythic comedy. Tom More suffers a dark night of the soul, expels the villain, marries, conceives children, accepts grace, and awaits the final event in the human comedy. Each of the novels is open-ended, but *Love in the Ruins* has Percy's hero further along the way toward salvation.

Sincy Percy's heroes are both more spiritually advanced than most of his other characters and something less than what they might be, his comedy cuts several ways. His heroes see some of the world's deadness, but are also seen by the reader as incomplete even when they correctly analyze the faults of others. Because Percy's view of the good man as wayfarer toward God is generalized, his comic treatment of the less than good never becomes savage. His criticism is tempered by his own tentativeness about the details of a religious life. Those who live in "everydayness" — the highway people, the doctors, businessmen, clerks and golfers of upper, middle, and lower America — Percy both sympathizes with and makes humorous. The followers of the religion of liberalism and the converts to aesthetic spiritualism, such as Rita Vaught and Doris More, take more severe punishment, but Percy allows even them their reasons. His Blacks, whether servants or professionals, receive a special kind of head-shaking pity and respect.

Because Percy believes that only linguistic freshness can retrieve the truth of being, his characters' language is a good index for his comic intentions.[7] Percy rides hard those who cover up their lives with clichés, whether old or modern. Again, the liberals have the worst of it, while the less socialized or the odd escape Percy's mockery. Emily Cutrer (of *The*

Moviegoer), Rita Vaught, Doris More, and Art Immelman, of the major characters, use verbal refuse to avoid reality. Some characters, such as Moira in *Love in the Ruins* and Forney Aiken in *The Last Gentleman* are merely ludicrous in their allowing slogans, code words, and images from popular culture to pervade their consciousness. Other characters, most particularly the Blacks in Percy's Southern settings, are caught among several languages, none of which seems to work quite right. Minor heroes in Percy's battle against enshrined platitudes, pieties, jargon, and empty symbols are Lonnie Smith in *The Moviegoer*, a simple boy whose speech impediment makes words new; Dr. Gamow, a psychiatrist in *The Last Gentleman* who brings familiar words alive with his foreign accent; Max Gottlieb, a doctor in *Love in the Ruins* who diagnoses in plain and meaningful language; and the linguist Ives, another character in *Love in the Ruins*, whose passionate hatred for the euphemistic language of his environment reduces him to silence. Minor villains are the thinly disguised novelists to whom Percy's characters allude in each of his novels. Percy's concern with language, as his essays demonstrate, goes beyond the novelist's or poet's natural and familiar theme of linguistic exhaustion. Since, for Percy, art has a cognitive function both as exploration-discovery and as communication, and language has an ontological function, art and the language it uses must be fresh if it is to help man accomplish his various ends. Percy's own style, with its medically exact description, its mixture of concrete expression and resonating abstractions, its symbolic imagery of vision and birds, its carefully modulated tone, and its parody of even the subtlest clichés, effectively dramatizes his concern.

Once the reader's expectations are aligned, through structure, character, and language, with the line of Percy's eschatological vision, the reader sees Percy's thematic incongruities as comic rather than perverse. As a Catholic writing in an age of materialistic historicism, Percy inverts over and over again the standards and values of the objective-empirical. If one believes that the acceptance of death gives one life and believes as well in the transcendent paradox, what Percy calls the "Scandalous Thing, the Wrinkle in Time, the Jew-Christ-Church business," (*LG*,241) the inversions logically follow. The traditional comic standard of happiness Percy inverts by calling it despair and replacing it with anxiety. Only those who take their happiness from a sacramental joy pass Percy's test. For others, happiness is a temptation they must overcome until anxiety leads them to grace. Other inversions include the bad environment presented as good; the conventionally sane depicted as sick, the mad as the only sane in the world; sin as an improvement over apathetic neutrality, malice as an improvement upon sentimental good will. In Percy's world turned upside down by God's intervention in time, wonder is better than certainty, forgetting better than remembering, possibility better than actuality, homelessness better than security, the absurd better than the rational. The ultimate inversion, as Berdyaev reminds us in *The Destiny of Man*, is that, in the plane of immanence, the awareness of what we most fear — death — is better than unawareness, and that for the Christian, the End is better than the beginning or the middle, that death is superior to life. The danger of this eschatological vision, as Tom More says, is the temptation "to feast on death," others' or our own. Avoiding this perversion — collapsing the immanent into the transcendent — man as wayfarer and sovereign exile can wait for the end with serenity, longing, even joy.

Notes

1. Walker Percy, "From Facts to Fiction," *Washington Post* "Book Week," 25 December 1966, p. 6; Percy speaks freely of his Existential influences in Ashley Brown's "An Interview with Walker Percy," *Shenandoah*, 18 (Spring, 1967), 6.

2. *The Moviegoer* (New York: Farrar, Straus and Giroux, 1967); *The Last Gentleman* (New York: New American Library, 1968); *Love in the Ruins: The Adventures of a Bad Catholic at a Time Near the End of the World* (New York: Farrar, Straus and Giroux, 1971). Page references given in the text in parentheses.

3. In "Naming and Being," *Personalist*, 41 (1960), 148–57, Percy comments on anxiety opening onto selfhood and says that new names must be found for being or old ones given new meaning.

4. See Lewis A. Lawson, "Walker Percy's Indirect Communication," *Texas Studies in Literature and Language*, 11 (1969), 867–68, for a partial bibliography; Percy's "The Message in the Bottle," *Thought*, 34 (1959), 405–33 is especially important.

5. Walker Percy, "The Man on the Train: Three Existential Modes," *Partisan Review*, 23 (1956), 479; the following quotation is from the same page. The third quotation is from page 493.

6. Carlton Cremeens, "Walker Percy, The Man and the Novelist: An Interview," *Southern Review*, 4 (1968), 284: alienation, "after all, is nothing more or less than a very ancient, orthodox Christian doctrine. Man is alienated by the nature of his being here. He is here as a stranger and as a pilgrim, which is the way alienation is conceived in my books."

7. Although Percy has many essays on the problem of language and being, his "The Loss of the Creature," *Forum*, 2 (Fall, 1958), 6–14, most succinctly and clearly presents his case against used up language.

The Search for Place in
Walker Percy's Novels   Mark Johnson*

For a writer whose professed view of man is that of man the voyager, wayfarer, exile and castaway, Walker Percy shows a remarkable concern for places in his three novels. At first it seems ironic, but actually such a concern is motivated by a sense of homelessness and by a need for "a place in the world." As Percy says in "The Man on the Train," the commuter who does feel "at home, seeing the passing scene as a series of meaningful

*Reprinted by permission from the *Southern Literary Journal* 8 (1975); 55–81

projects full of signs which he reads without difficulty" is unaware of his despair and is in a worse condition than the alienated commuter who at least recognizes his predicament.[1]

An alienated homelessness is a controlling concept in much of Percy's fiction, as he admitted to Carlton Cremeens: "Alienation, after all, is nothing more or less than a very ancient, orthodox Christian doctrine. Man is alienated by the nature of his being here. He is here as a stranger and as a pilgrim, which is the way alienation is conceived in my books."[2] It would be unwise to try to define too narrowly the nature of the pilgrimage of Percy's characters, but seeing one aspect of it as a search for a place in the world, a mode of existence, illuminates one of Percy's major themes while at the same time revealing his developing sense of place in his novels.

Percy has repeatedly expressed his concern for the concrete place, as in his recent interview with Zoltán Abádi-Nagy: "It is true that I am interested in philosophical, religious issues and in my novels I use the particular in order to get at the general issues. For example, *The Moviegoer* is about New Orleans, one part in New Orleans, a young man in New Orleans."[3] In an earlier interview with John Carr he directly related his philosophy to his fiction: "As I say, I fell out with philosophy and started to [write] and the philosophy I was interested in was what was then called existential philosophy. Of course, the word no longer means much. It still means a concrete view of man, man in a situation, man in a predicament, man's anxiety, and so on. And I believed that this view of man could be handled very well in a novel, and I was interested in phenomenology, which is very strongly existentialist: the idea of describing accurately how a man feels in a given situation. And that's certainly novelistic."[4]

Percy has written no aesthetic statement about place in fiction to compare with that of Eudora Welty, for example, a writer he has called "the best fiction writer in the South."[5] His essays are directly concerned with his philosophy, either existential, linguistic or cultural. Thus he also has not presented us with a piece comparable to Flannery O'Connor's "The Fiction Writer and His Country." But a close look at the use of places in his novels can show us something about his development as a fiction writer. Gaston Bachelard's statement about space pertains to Percy's use of spatial metaphors: "Space that has been seized upon by the imagination cannot remain indifferent space subject to the measures and estimates of the surveyor. . . . Images do not adapt themselves very well to quiet ideas, or above all, to definitive ideas. The imagination is ceaselessly imagining and enriching itself with new images."[6] Percy is not writing poetry, of course, but the use of places in the successive novels reveals a less cerebral control as his imagination "seizes upon" them. Certainly Percy's view of man is an integral part of each novel's action and resolution, but he has progressed to the point that his philosophy is more successfully integrated into the novelistic form.

Places are used in Percy's novels in three ways: as vehicles of his philosophy, particularly of some specific points drawn from Kierkegaard; as illustrations of artificial as opposed to authentic environments, with a heavy emphasis on the former; and finally, in each of the novels one of the structures emerges as a representative metaphor for the mode of existence of the protagonist and the condition of his society. These distinctions overlap, but there is generally an observable shift in the successive novels away from the illustration of philosophical concepts toward an integration of place into the dramatics of the novels themselves, communicating as well as underlining characterizations, themes and ironies.

Martin Luschei has done an excellent job of explicating the philosophical underpinnings of Percy's novels in *The Sovereign Wayfarer*,[7] and I have no intention of duplicating that effort. But this essay would not be complete without a consideration of three house-metaphors in particular, all attributed to Kierkegaard and all observable in Percy's novels.

The first of these is used by Kierkegaard in *The Sickness Unto Death*, in which he likens the levels of existence (aesthetic, ethical, and religious) to the levels of a house (basement, ground floor, and attic): "Unfortunately this is the sorry and ludicrous condition of the majority of men, that in their own houses they prefer to live in the cellar. The soulish-body synthesis in every man is planned with a view to being spirit, such is the building: but the man prefers to dwell in the cellar, that is, in the determinants of sensuousness."[8] Binx Bolling is the most obvious Percy protagonist to live in the cellar, as Luschei notes: "Binx is dwelling in the basement of his possibilities. . . . Binx inhabits the aesthetic sphere defined by Kierkegaard."[9] Binx is trying to escape the problems of existence in the world through his "Little Way" — absorption in business and sex, "living in the most ordinary life imaginable" in an apartment "as impersonal as a motel room."[10] In the course of the novel, because of physical events as well as his own awareness of "the search," Binx is forced to give up his little way.

Binx's aunt is the embodiment of the ethical mode, and appropriately enough she is always found on the first floor of her house. When Kate is introduced to the reader, Binx finds her fixing up a TV room for her father in the basement, perfectly apropos for one who is more at home in the city of man than in the city of God. But the most tentative approach to Kierkegaard's *bel étage* in this first novel also occurs at Aunt Emily's — not quite in the attic, but on the mezzanine: "Off the landing is a dark little mezzanine arranged as a room of furniture. It is a place one passes twenty times a day and no more thinks of entering than of entering a picture, nor even of looking at, but having entered, enters with all the oddness of entering a picture, a tableau in depth wherein space is untenanted and where from the view of the house, the hall and dining room below, seems at once privileged and strange. Kate is there in the shadows" (175). There follows one of the most sensitive scenes in Percy's fiction, one in which he is able to portray the very beginnings of the kind of intersubjectivity which is his ideal.

Kierkegaard's levels of existence are being used in *The Last Gentleman* also. It is significant that Will Barrett works in the basement of the department store, and emerging from the building he often finds himself dislocated. But attics play a more important part in this novel, for it is in his father's attic that he comes to some sense of himself and confronts his father's suicide. The scene is treated under the third heading here.

The second Kierkegaardian concept that is relevant to this study is the idea that a man without an "infinite passion," an idea for which he can live and die, is like "a man who has rented a house and gathered all the furniture and household things together, but has not yet found the beloved with whom to share the joys and sorrows of this life."[11] Each of Percy's heroes can be seen as such a character searching for an idea for which he can live or die, and each of them in the course of this search comes to occupy a house with a "beloved." The endings of each of the novels are always tenuous, ambivalent, and significant. I would again refer the reader to Luschei's explanation of the Kierkegaardian aspects of Percy's fiction, for it helps one understand some of Percy's oblique statements. Much more is involved in these endings than the simple occupation of a house with a beloved, however, as I will show.

Percy attributed to Kierkegaard the statement, "Every man has to stand in front of the house of his childhood in order to recover himself."[12] In "The Man on the Train," he speaks briefly of such a return as "the passionate quest" in which one follows the thread of the labyrinth "at any cost."[13] The function of such a return is central to *The Last Gentleman*. Long before he reaches his father's house, Barrett is compelled into the Vaught's castle attic "as if he knew exactly where he was, though he had only once visited the second floor and had not once been above it." He had been awakened in the middle of the night: "Something had happened. There was not a sound, but the silence was not an ordinary silence. It was the silence of a time afterwards. It had been violated earlier" (238). This is a cryptic scene for the reader, who has only been told that Will's father's death was "sudden," like that of most of the men in the family (16). The scene is symptomatic of the haunting power of the father's suicide and its effect on Will. Fragmentary memories also help prepare the reader for the confrontation.

Percy devotes several alternately moving and comic pages to this crucial scene of the novel, ranging from a boy's last memories of his father's desertion of him to Bill Cullen's giving cabin cruisers to ladies from Michigan City, Indiana. The house itself plays a dual role in the scene, as both the place in which Barrett must confront the memory of his father's suicide and as the concrete place in which he at least seems to approach some insight into life. I say "seems to" because Percy characteristically shies away from what he would call edification in the scene and camouflages what may be happening behind his narrator's ironies. Touching the cold metal and "the warm finny whispering bark" of the hitching post in front of the house, Barrett fingers his way toward some sort of revelation in the concrete here and now as opposed to his father's music and poetry:

> *Wait.* He [the father] had missed it! It was not in the Brahms that one looked and not in solitariness and not in the old sad poetry but — he wrung out his ear — but here, under your nose, here in the very curiousness and drollness and extremes of the iron and the bark that — he shook his head — that —
>
> The TV studio audience laughed with its quick, obedient and above all grateful Los Angeles laughter — once we were lonesome back home, the old sad home of our fathers, and here we are together happy at last. (332)

Rarely has the true homelessness of the grateful Los Angeles audience that we are been so captured. And yet this most important scene of the novel is crippled by the very narrative distance that allows Percy to make such a comment on the loss of "the old sad home of our fathers." If Barrett comes to some kind of conclusions, to a peace with the past, to a recovery of himself (and there is serious reason to believe that he does not in the light of some of his later actions), the reader never sees it. We are told only of a vigil in the night, and are given only two sentences: "After he repacked the boat, he lay on the cot and, propping himself against the wall, drew the hard scratchy army blanket up to his armpits. For two hours he sat so, wakeful and alert, while his eyes followed the yellow drizzle of light into every corner of the attic room" (334). Such sparse description lends itself to rich imaginative interpretation, but to use Percy's terms he has not described "accurately how a man feels in a given situation." His metaphysics and his Kierkegaardian assumptions are preempting "novelistic" fiction. I strongly agree with Tony Tanner when he says, "Philosophy works in its own way and makes its own constructs, but it may be said that in a work of art as direct philosophic assertion increases, reality ebbs and art dwindles. Reality should never be an excuse for offering philosophic generalizations, though it may very well provoke a man into mining for them."[14] Percy would seem to agree when he tells John Carr, "You don't have a thesis and then illustrate it. What you do is put a man down in a certain situation and see what happens."[15] At times, however, he forgets this lesson.

A more comprehensive view of Percy's use of places and a better appreciation of what he is about in the novels can be had by seeing how he uses the places in which his characters live to underline the themes and characterizations effectively. A generalization which does not do justice to the subtleties and distinctions of Percy's writing is that most of the places seem to be either artificial or authentic environments. My terminology derives from a scene in which, with characteristic irony, Percy has a "fake

Negro" berate "artificial environments in general." Such general distinctions enable Percy to illustrate more subtly character and theme through place, rather than trying to illustrate philosophy.

Binx Bolling lives "the most ordinary life imaginable" (9) in an apartment "as impersonal as a motel room" (78). Percy has referred to his life in Gentilly as living in a desert, and Binx recognizes the "forlorn sadness" of the homes in his suburb during a pre-dawn stroll:

> These houses look handsome in the sunlight; they please me with their pretty colors, their perfect lawns and their clean airy garages. But I have noticed that at this hour of dawn they are forlorn. A sadness settles over them like a fog from the lake. (84)

> I muse along as quietly as a ghost. Instead of trying to sleep I try to fathom the mystery of this suburb at dawn. Why do these splendid houses look so defeated at this hour of the day? Other houses, say a 'dobe house in New Mexico or an old frame house in Feliciana, look much the same day or night. But these new houses look haunted. . . . What spirit takes possession of them? (86)

Like Barrett, Binx recognizes the artificiality and the spiritual emptiness of modern homes compared to "the old sad homes of our fathers," and the parallel sterility of societies is clear.

The Smith's house is a particularly nightmarish place for Binx, and he contrasts it with their fishing camp, a "good place":

> It is good to see the Smiths at their fishing camp. But not at their home in Biloxi. Five minutes in that narrow old house and dreariness sets into the marrow of my bones. The gas logs strike against the eyeballs, the smell of two thousand Sunday dinners clings to the curtains, voices echo round and round the bare stairwell, a dismal Sacred Heart forever points to itself above the chipped enamel mantelpiece. Everything is white and chipped. The floors, worn powdery, tickle the nostrils like a school room. But here on the Bayou des Allemands everybody feels the difference. Water laps against the piling. The splintered boards have secret memories of winter, the long dreaming nights and days when no one came and the fish jumped out of the black water and not a soul in sight on the whole savannah. (139)

As Percy said in "The Man on the Train," "The true smell of everydayness is the smell of Sunday dinner in the living room."[16] The camp's value for Binx is as a rotation, however, and a rotation is by definition a passing event. The escape from the sterility of everyday life does not last: "But, good as it is, my old place is used up (places get used up by rotatory and repetitive use) and when I awake, I awake in the grip of everydayness. Everydayness is the enemy." No simple return to the peaceful country life is possible for Binx who, like Barrett again, carries his own particular depravity with him. ("The everydayness is everywhere now, having begun in the cities and seeking out the remotest nooks and corners of the countryside, even the swamps") (145). Whether one's problem is ravening particles or everyday-ness, an authentic mode of living in the world must be earned, not subdeveloped.

Even with Kierkegaard's metaphor of occupying a house with one's beloved, the reader expects Binx and Kate to marry at the end of the novel, particular after the mezzanine scene. What is surprising, however, is the kind of home they occupy — one of Nell Lovell's redesigned cottages. The unsympathetic presentation of Eddie and Nell Lovell is given very tersely by Binx after conversations with each of them. Eddie "is as cogent as a bird dog quartering a field. He understands everything out there and everything out there is something to be understood" (19). Eddie sounds like one of Percy's commuters reading signs without difficulty, and both he and Nell are "dead, dead, dead" (102). Going to live in one of Nell's cottages, "with its saloon doors swinging into the kitchen, its charcoal-gray shutters and its lead St. Francis in the patio," sounds dangerously close to a return to Binx's Little Way, to "the most ordinary life imagina-ble." But he has rejected an opportunity with Joyce, his secretary's roommate, and he seems to have accepted an adult's responsibility in the scene with the children and in the final scene with Kate. The cottage, despite Binx's comment "Nell has taste" (20), should be seen as an indication of the limits of the possibilities of life in this world. Binx is presumably still on his pilgrimage, though he may no longer be so bitter about its darkness. A level of intersubjectivity has been reached, and Binx has occupied a house with his beloved. He once said of his aunt's house, "The empty house above us roars like a seashell" (60). With Kate and with the realizations he has come to, life will be better than before, though this house is not a "home."

Barrett's abstracted condition at the beginning of *The Last Gentle-man* is at least partly due to his environment. He is often distracted when he emerges from his basement at the department store, and as Pappy Vaught observes, anyone would be nervous "all huddled up in the Y in the daytime and way up under a store at night." The anonymity and artificiality of his room at the Y are underlined in its description: the room "was furnished with a single bed and a steel desk varnished to resemble wood grain" (8), and later the TV room is referred to as "a room done in Spanish colonial motif with exposed yellow beams and furniture of oxidized metal" (18). It is from this scene that Barrett, "suggestible as he was, . . . began to think it mightn't be a bad idea to return to the South and discover his identity, to use Dr. Gamow's expression" (79), and the final phrase serves beautifully to limit sharply the reader's expectations of his success.

Before leaving New York, Barrett encounters another artificial envi-ronment, this one constructed by Rita. At first he is awestruck: "Once he went to look at the house they lived in. They had, Kitty and Rita, a charming cottage in a mews stuck away inside a city block in the Village.

He had not imagined there could be such a place in New York, that the paltry particles, ravening and singing, could so easily be gotten round. But they were gotten round, by making things small and bright and hiding them away in the center of a regular city block. . . . They, Kitty and Rita, got out of the wind, so to speak, found a sunny lee corner as sheltered as a Barbados Alley" (60–1). Barrett is unable to see through Rita's manipulation of Kitty yet, but the reader's clue in the word "mews," a place of confinement, should make him think twice about what is being made "small and bright" and is hidden away. Percy's ironies make it clear, throughout the novel as well as in the scene at Rita's Barbados Alley, that whatever particles are ravening and singing in one's own head are not to be "easily gotten round" at all, and Barrett is disillusioned when he drops in on Rita later: "It was not a Barbados cottage after all but an Indian hogan. Rita wore a Chamula huipil (Kitty was explaining nervously) of heavy homespun. Kitty herself had wound a white quexquemetl above her Capri pants. Brilliant quetzals and crude votive offerings painted on tin hung from the walls" (102). The passage glitters with small sparkling ironies. The cottage is a transplanted version of Rita's Rancho la Merced which Jamie and Sutter instinctively avoid. Rita's heavy homespun and her hikuli rites reveal that her dislocation is every bit as great as the engineer's — greater, in fact, to paraphrase the eipgraph of *The Moviegoer*, because she is unaware of it. One of Sutter's more trenchant observations "places" Rita perfectly: "I'm telling you now that you are wrong about yourself and wrong about what you think you want. There is nothing wrong with you beyond a certain spitefulness and pride and a penchant for a certain species of bullshit. You're a fine girl, a fine Georgia girl — did you know Rita was from Georgia, Bill? — who got too far from home. Georgia girls have no business at Lake Chapala" (246).

We see little of the Vaught's house, but it is certainly not one of the sad homes of our fathers. Barrett refers to it as a castle "made of purplish bricks which had been broken in two and the jagged side turned out. It had beam-in-plaster gables and a fat Norman tower and casement windows with panes of bottle glass" (189). Percy doesn't go into an argument for organic architecture, but form hardly allows function in this abode. Oddly enough, Barrett regards it as "a good place to live and collect one's thoughts" (191), but his words reveal the function of the house in the novel — Barrett is merely pausing here, physically as well as metaphorically, before being driven on his journey.

One of the easier targets of Percy's satire is the American Dream Home, either as the G. E. Gold Medallion Home or as Kitty's dream home in the hills. As a beloved, Kitty is a disappointment. She is a chameleon, and her dream home is a horror: "a buzzard's roost up on the ridge," complete with "waxed paving stones and the fireplace and the view of the doleful foothills and the snowfield of G. E. Gold Medallion Homes," and even "a ferny dell and a plashy little brook with a rustic bridge," all for thirty-seven five (284). Will's dream "house," as we shall see, is the Trav-L-Aire camper, but at times the American Dream tempts him, as when he wants to "marry me a wife and live me a life" and dreams of "our honeymoon cottage in a cottage small by a waterfall" (151, 166). He does tell Kitty of his dream to pick up and leave, find Jamie and "thereafter live in Albuquerque or perhaps Santa Fe, park the camper in an arroyo or dry wash" and live happily ever after. But she is blind to this way of life, and to his credit he resists her efforts to fit him into Old Cap'n Andy's role of "crusty but loveable eccentric."

Kitty's dream serves as a good counterpoint to Will's, as he sees: "But there would be the devil's own time, he saw clearly, in hemming her up in a dry wash in New Mexico. She was house minded." Unfortunately, he too is tempted by the kind of anonymous existence Binx pursued in Gentilly: "He pulled up at a G. E. model home—what's wrong with one of these—they were much more cheerful than that buzzard's roost up on the ridge" (286). At the conclusion of the novel it appears that Will fully intends to return to Kitty and live either in the buzzard's roost or in one of the Gold Medallion homes, living him a life as a Chevrolet dealer and "making a contribution, however small." He will, presumably, occupy his house with his beloved, but his beloved is "a certain someone" who can hardly be congenial to a continuation of the kind of searching and wandering life Percy's world requires. Percy has said Barrett missed the religious experience at Jamie's death that Sutter appears to have had.[17] But also his own problem of self-identification has been artifically solved by an acceptance of a false life—Barrett seems to think he can be at home in the world. "Making a contribution, however small," was Percy's ironic phrase for living on the ethical level in *The Moviegoer*. Although Percy has said, "It doesn't follow that becoming the personnel manager of Confederate Chevrolet compromises him: his values are more complicated,"[18] what we are given points toward Barrett's compromise.

One of the most curious places in all of Percy's novels is Val Vaught's school for Tyree Negro children. At one point we find in Sutter's notebook that she echoes Percy the essayist (353-4), and her "place in the world" would therefore be of particular interest to the reader. Unfortunately, Barrett's limitations as a center of consciousness leave the reader's experience of the place unrealized: "it reminded him of a lunar installation, with silvery globes supplying nourishment to each building, a place of crude and makeshift beginnings on some blasted planet. Later there remained in his poor addled memory only a blurred impression of Seven-Up machines, plastic crucifixes, and worn, gnawed-at woodwork such as is found in old gymnasiums" (302). Perhaps Percy again wants to avoid edification, but Val is by no means presented as a sympathetic character. Her mission with the Negroes sounds suspiciously like Rita's Indian project, and would seem to have the same limitations. But Percy avoids the entire issue and dramatizes his man-as-wayfarer through Barrett and his Trav-L-Aire.

Though Barrett is tempted by the American Dream home, the Trav-L-Aire is the ideal home for this traveler — Percy's rather obvious analog for his wayfarer, pilgrim, wanderer. The camper is named for Ulysses (ironically enough by Rita) who "was meant to lead us beyond the borders of the Western world and bring us home" (96). The Trav-L-Aire itself serves him well, all "glittering and humped up and practical, yet somehow airy and light on its four brand-new Goodyear jumbo treads":

> She was all she might be, a nice balance of truck heaviness, steel and stout below and cabined aluminum lightness above. . . .
>
> Now here surely is a good way to live nowadays, said he and sat down on the firkin: *mobile yet at home*, compacted and not linked up with the crumby carnival linkage of a trailer, *in the world yet not of the world*, sampling the particularities of place yet cabined off from the sadness of place, curtained away from the ghosts of Malvern Hill, peeping out at the doleful woods of Spotsylvania through the cheerful plexiglas of Sheboygan. (153. My italics)

Speaking of this passage, Tony Tanner has said, "His tone is here clearly somewhat ironic and the attitude expressed is not offered as a final one."[19] No reader of Percy should ever expect a "final" attitude, given his view of the world, and irony is certainly Percy's mode. But as distant as he often is from Barrett,[20] Percy like Barrett sees the truck as an analog for living between immanence and transcendence, to use Sutter's words, or, in Barrett's, between the zone of the possible and the zone of the realized. The Biblical overtones of living "in the world yet not of the world" are too strong to overlook and reinforce the value of the way of life symbolized by the camper, Percy's ironies notwithstanding.

The journey on the road confirms Barrett's expectations: "The camper was everything he had hoped for and more":

> Nights were best. Then as the thick singing darkness settled about the little caboose which shed its cheerful square of light on the dark soil of old Carolina, they might debark and, with the pleasantest sense of stepping down from the zone of the possible to the zone of the realized, stroll to a service station or fishing camp or grocery store. . . . He was home. Even though he was hundreds of miles from home and never had been here and it was not even the same here — it was older and more decorous, more tended to and adream with the past — he was home. (160–1)

The Trav-L-Aire is a perfectly appropriate "home" for a wayfarer and represents Percy's first attempt in two novels at presenting an authentic environment.

In *Love in the Ruins* he has in no way abandoned his fundamental philosophical beliefs, but they are more successfully adapted to the fiction. Percy's use of places in the novel is controlled by his ideas about life in the world, but those ideas are not allowed to become as intrusive as in the other novels. Tom More's "voyaging" is not paralleled by the physical traveling of *The Last Gentleman,* for the novel takes place in one locale. Percy uses places well to sketch some very broad contrasts and this should be noted before dealing with the specific structures of the novel. Clear foils are established between Fedville, with Love clinic and its Skinner boxes, and the swamp, with its absolutely anarchistic life style and "Hester's chickee." Neither is ever seriously considered as a choice by Tom More, but both provide excellent vehicles for Percy's humor and satire. He gives more detailed attention to Paradise Estates itself, particularly to three important artificial environments: More's own house, the Howard Johnson's motel, and Lola's Tara.

Luschei rightly calls the Tom More of the beginning of the book "the perfect model of Kierkegaard's man whose house is without a beloved,"[21] but Percy has put a considerable amount of energy into the places of this third novel, beyond mere vehicles of Kierkegaard's philosophy. More's home in Paradise Estates is the only house seen in great detail, and it sounds like the kind of home in the suburbs Binx and Kate and Will and Kitty were headed for at the end of the first two novels. For More, however, this dream has gone stale—we find out later, after the death of his daughter. More has already achieved an awareness of his predicament through the worst kind of ordeal, but he is still trying to escape its implications by living on an aesthetic plane, chasing women, drinking and generally being irresponsible. At one time, though, he was quite happy in his life with his first wife. He would go to mass with his daughter and come home so happy that he would "sing and cut the fool all the way home like King David before the Ark" (12). His charcoal grill and lusty, willing wife were enough for him, but even before his daughter's death problems appeared: "My wife and I lived a good life. . . . Nevertheless, I fell prey to morning terror, shook like a leaf at the breakfast table, and began to drink vodka with my grits. At the same time that I developed liberal anxiety, I also contracted conservative rage and large-bowel complaints" (23–24). The symptoms are the typical diseases he has diagnosed in many of his patients, and identify him as a victim of the pressures and paranoias of the time of "the end of the world." He speaks of the period of his decline as "also a period of lying fallow" prior to his return to daylight in triumph (24), and Percy's ironies are already at work at several levels. Tom is no more "in triumph" than Binx, nor has he "seen the daylight"—but he is on the same kind of voyage, and again the progression from artificial to authentic environments is a significant one.

Life in the house with Doris was a nightmare of artificiality, from Tom's "hunt room" to Doris's gazebo to the enclosed patio with its Pledged bricks and library of *Siddartha, Atlas Shrugged* and *ESP and the New Spirituality.* The hunt room:

> The green gloom inside smells of old hammocks and ping-pong nets.
> Here is the "hunt" room, Doris's idea, fitted out with gun cabinet,

copper sink, bar, freezer, billiard table, life-size stereo-V, easy chairs, Audubon prints. Doris envisioned me coming here after epic hunts with hale hunting companions, eviscerating the bloody little carcasses of birds in the sink, pouring sixteen-year-old bourbon in the heavy Abercrombie field-and-stream glasses and settling down with my pipe and friends and my pointer bitch for a long winter evening of man talk and football-watching. Of course I never came here, never owned a pointer bitch, had no use for friends, and instead of hunting took to hanging around Paradise Bowling Lanes and drinking Dixie beer with my partner, Leroy Ledbetter (256).

Doris's room is at the top of a spiral staircase, "a kind of gazebo attached to the house at one of its eight sides. An airy confection of spidery white iron, a fretwork of ice cream, it floats like a tree house in the whispering crowns of the longleaf pines" (256). The misty atmosphere evoked by such phrases as "airy confection" makes the room seem as intangible as cotton candy. Like ice cream, the relationship the room symbolizes has melted under the heat. It is here that she fell for Alistair: "Here in her airy gazebo in the treetops it seemed to her that things had fallen out right at last. This surely was the way life was lived: Alistair sharing with her the English hankering for the Orient and speaking in the authentic mother tongue of reverence for life and for the need of making homely things with one's own hands: of a true community life stripped of its technological dross, of simple meetings and greetings, spiritual communions, the touch of a hand, etcetera etcetera" (257). Doris listened to Alistair "breathlessly": "To her the very air of the summerhouse seemed freighted with meanings. Possibilities floated like motes in the golden light." Percy's description is none too subtle, but to readers of *The Last Gentleman* the added clue of the last sentence is unmistakable.

The artificiality of the house had been weighing down on them even before Samantha's death, as is evidenced by their frequent trips to motels at interchanges in the middle of nowhere. But where Doris was content to stay in the anonymous motel, in the zone of possibility, Tom had to go into these small hamlets for mass where he could touch "the thread in the labyrinth." Doris couldn't understand why he went to mass: "What she couldn't understand, she being spiritual and seeing religion as spirit, was that it took religion to save me from the spirit world, from orbiting the earth like Lucifer and the angels, that it took nothing less than touching the thread of the *misty* interstates and eating Christ himself to make me moral again and let me inhabit my own flesh and love her in the morning" (241–42). More's comments bear directly on the theme of the book and a hobby-horse of Percy's, man's abstraction from himself. It is in *Love in the Ruins* that Percy rides his hobby-horse most effectively, partly at least because of his tying the concepts of abstraction and angelism-bestialism to a sense of place.

Doris and Tom's outings occurred some seven years before Samantha was born, but at the writing of the book More is still on his search, still lost in the labyrinth. His life fell apart with the death of his daughter and so at the present time of the novel he is again in an artificial environment, no less than a Howard Johnson's motel, with Moira.[22]

Moira's affinity for old ruins, Rod McKuen poetry and "a soupçon of danger, just enough," alerts the reader to her shortcomings rather quickly. She works in Love and later marries Buddy Brown, director of a "termination center" for senior citizens. This is the type of person Tom can prepare to spend "the end of the world" with, in a cozy little motel — "What safer place than a motel in no man's land, between the lines so to speak?" (126). Instead of a Biblical tent curtain, there is a torn banner left by the Rotarians and inscribed, "Is it the truth? Is it fair to all concerned? Will it build goodwill and better friendships?" Once again, the ethical mode is inadequate in Percy's world. While at the motel, Moira suggests that they "do over" Tom's house, and it certainly needs it. But her ideal is straight out of *House Beautiful*, full of Shaker tableware and "simple handcrafts." She wants to take up tennis at the club, join a poetry club, and the deadend of living with her is already overdrawn.

Tom's other lover, Lola Rhoades, comes complete with the artificial environment to end all artificial environments, Tara. But this is not only a restored Southern mansion, analog for an ethical mode if there ever was one — this is the Tara of movie fame, and no better source could provide a more artificial, tinsel-and-glitter environment than Hollywood. Even the family car's tape deck plays *Hills of Home*, the Tara theme (79). Percy is particularly devastating in a brief dialogue which cannot be paraphrased. Lola's father and Tom's mother are playing cupid while Tom is looking for Lola:

> "She's not about to leave Tara," muses Dusty. "She says her roots are there."
>
> "You should have seen her over there this morning, feeding her horses, planting greens — "
>
> "Where is Lola now?" I ask them.
>
> "You'll see her this afternoon at the fish fry, it's all settled," says Mother. "But you should have seen her, standing there in that old garden, her hands potty black, her face glowing. She never looked prettier or more determined."
>
> "I still don't like to leave her there alone," says Dusty, wagging his head.
>
> "Do you remember what Scarlett said about the land?" asks Mother. "Or was it in *The Good Earth*?"
>
> "Yes," says Dusty, popping his great jaw muscles. (172)

So much for an artificial return to agrarianism. When Lola tells Tom, "When all is said and done, the only thing we can be sure of is the land. The land never lets you down," he can only reply, " 'That's true,' I say, 'though I never did know what that meant' " (265). Although Tom is tempted by the picture of life Tara represents, he is saved by his own self-conscious irony: "There are worse lives, after all, than sitting on the gallery of Tara and . . . I look at Tara, a preposterous fake house on a fake hill: even the hill is fake, dredged up from the swamp by the state of Louisiana for Vince Marsaglia. The very preposterousness of life in Tara with Lola inflames me with love, — Yes, sitting on the gallery sipping Early Times while Lola plants greens or plays *Don Quixote* or we hold hands, her cello-callused fingers whispering in my palm. Lovely Lola" (172). It is a clever turn of the screw when Tara is bought by Willie Amadie (the black golf caddy and new mayor) and the bell is given to Father Smith's chapel.

The chapel itself is a step toward an authentic environment in the novel, but a more developed treatment is given to St. Michael's Church. It is an empty shell of what once was "a surprisingly large parish, big enough to rate a monsignor" (5). Now it is "a yellow brick dairy-barn-with-silo" for Tom, because "the center did not hold" (131).[23] The church split into three divisions, and by the time of the novel the building has become the headquarters of the revolutionaries. But the important use of St. Michael's is as the scene of Tom's lengthy and somewhat comic rebirth. He breaks out of the rectory office through the air-conditioning system, "black as the womb," and kicks out the panel to the final chord of "White Christmas": "Out she goes with a heart-stopping clatter, metal against concrete, metal against car metal — now I know they'll find me — and out I come feet first, born again, ejected into the hot bright perilous world — tumbling some-how forward until I am wedged between the inner wall and the bumper of Monsignor Schleifkopf's burnt-out Buick, a hulk of rusted metal and moldering upholstery" (295). The rebirth through ordeal is merely paro-died, of course, but evidently Percy was unable to resist the opportunity to parody Tom's sincere rebirth through ordeal of these early days of July. St. Michael's, the shell of the former church, adds a dimension to this parody which must be considered in the light of the book's conclusion and the final dwelling of our protagonist in the Slave Quarters.

Tom More in the Slave Quarters with his "lusty tart Presbyterian" wife (363) and two children is as close as we come to seeing a man "at home" in the world of one of Percy's novels. His pace is much less frenetic and his time is divided between his modest practice and his collard garden. He finally seems to have achieved some amount of satisfaction with his life.

He has occupied the Slave Quarters, literal slave housing which had been restored by Paradise developers for their domestic help. In the course of the novel we see them occupied by Father Smith's incongruous congre-gation (174), and it is a significant place to be at the end of the novel both for "the remnant of a remnant" of the church, and for our protagonist. Just as the church has returned to the role of servant of modern man, our modern wayfarer has come to terms with himself and with life. The conclusion is still by no means "edifying," nor is it a picture of the ideal life. Tom is still tempted (by both his Early Times and by Mrs. Prouty) and is still subject to morning terror, but he deals with his problems in a more mature manner, and at last recognizes such problems as problems. The worst sign is that even after all that has happened, he still believes he can cure the evils of the modern world if he can just fix his machine.[24] But his goals are noble and at one point he echoes Percy the essayist: "What I want is no longer the Nobel, screw prizes, but just to figure out what I've hit on. Some day a man will walk into my office as ghost or beast or ghost-beast and walk out as a man, which is to say sovereign wayfarer, lordly exile, worker and waiter and watcher" (361).

This is the final role Tom has adopted, and it is as optimistic as any in Percy. The epilogue, "Five Years Later," begins with the words, "Hoeing collards in my kitchen garden." The echo of Thoreau is significant, from the pleasure in straightly hoed rows to his joy in new, well-made boots. Between the joy and the irony of the Slave Quarters passage, we sense that More is very much aware of the role of man as wayfarer and wanderer.

The ending is tentative, but after the ordeals of the novel and the return to a figurative father in Saint Thomas More and the church, Tom has attained his highest level. It is after his ordeals that he returns to the saint, as in a scene after his attempted suicide. "Dear God, I can see it now, why can't I see it other times, that it is you I love in the beauty of the world and in all the lovely girls and dear good friends, and it is pilgrims we are, wayfarers on a journey, and not pigs, nor angels. Why can I not be merry and loving like my ancestor, a gentle pure-hearted knight for our Lady and our blessed Lord and Savior? Pray for me, Sir Thomas More" (104). In a metaphorical sense, the resolution of the novel is a return to the house of Tom's childhood. At the same time, Tom has achieved his most honest level of intersubjectivity with Ellen, his tart lusty Presbyterian, and as the book closes he is "at home in bed where all good men belong" (379). The problems of the novel are not ignored and the ending is very tentative, but, again like *Walden*, the ending of the book is a beginning. As always in Percy, a house is not a "home": man is a voyager and can never be truly at home in the world.

From the beginning of his fiction-writing career, Percy has been concerned with the use of places to represent the condition of the protagonist or of his society. Martin Luschei tells us of Percy's first effort: "The novel was called *The Charterhouse* and had a country club as its setting. Percy's idea was that the country club with its golf course had displaced the medieval cathedral as the center of communal activity around which people lived."[25] In *The Moviegoer* he places Binx in Gentilly, and Binx himself describes the "defeated" houses of this suburb. Percy related the Gentilly setting to a desert in his interview with John Carr: "There's also a rather conscious parallel between Binx going to Gentilly and Phillip going to the Gaza Desert. A man goes to the desert to seek something. Gentilly is a desert if there ever was one. The same thing happened in *The Last Gentleman.* They end up in the Western desert."[26] But one's "own deprivation," as Barrett put it, can prevent a place's spirit from operating: Sutter laments in his notebook, "*Genius lori* of Western desert did not materialize" (349). The desert theme of *The Moviegoer* is subtly underlined in Binx's reading *Arabia Deserta,* some of whose chapter titles read "The Nomad Life in the Desert," "Life in the Wandering Village," "The Fukara Wandering as Fugitives in the Desert" and "Peace in the Desert."[27] If Gentilly is an appropriate place for a seeker to be, the Trav-L-Aire is an appropriate vehicle for Percy's second searcher, Will Barrett. But while these two seekers remain in their respective deserts at the ends of those novels, Tom More comes full circle for Percy in his return to the church and to the Slave Quarters. As Luschei notes, "From the charterhouse of Percy's apprentice novel to the Quarters is quite a distance."[28]

The sense of place affects more than the use of buildings in Percy's novels, of course. As he stated, he is concerned with "the idea of describing accurately how a man feels in a given situation." From his very first published novel, Percy has used that same given situation to work quite successfully the paradox in man's "situation" or place in the world: on the one hand, his characters are particularly concerned with their place in the world; on the other, they are never at home in the world, but see themselves as wanderers and pilgrims. With each successive novel, the treatment is better realized.

A sense of place is of paramount importance to Binx, who is continually worrying about finding himself No one Nowhere or Anyone Anywhere. For example, he needs to talk to proprietors or ticket sellers before seeing a movie: "If I did not talk to the theater owner or ticket seller, I should be lost, cut loose metaphysically speaking. I should be seeing one copy of a film "which might be shown anywhere and at any time" (75). Traveling petrifies him: ". . . if a man travels lightly to a hundred strange cities and cares nothing for the risks he takes, he may find himself No one and Nowhere" (99). His worst fears are realized when he arrives in Chicago:

> It turns out that my misgivings about Chicago were justified. No sooner do we step down from the train than the genie-soul of Chicago flaps down like a buzzard and perches on my shoulder. During the whole of our brief sojourn I am ridden by it. . . . (if only somebody could tell me who built the damn station, the circumstances of the building, details of the wrangling between city officials and the railroad, so that I would not fall victim to it, the station, the very first crack off the bat. Every place of arrival should have a booth set up and manned by an ordinary person whose task it is to greet strangers and give them a little trophy of local space-time stuff — tell them of his difficulties in high school and put a pinch of soil in their pockets — in order to insure that the stranger

shall not become an Anyone). Oh son of a bitch but I am in a sweat. (201–2).

On the other hand, Binx sees himself as an exile. "It is true that I am Jewish by instinct. We share the same exile. The fact is, however, I am more Jewish than the Jews I know. They are more at home than I am. I accept my exile" (89). The key phrase, of course, is "at home." For all Binx's efforts in Gentilly, he is not and cannot be at home. *The Moviegoer* is in many respects a more successful book than *The Last Gentleman*, but in its use of places and a sense of place it is too overt and too cerebral. Binx verbalizes like an essayist rather than as a character,[29] and his passages about "slipping out of space and time" and being "cut loose metaphysically speaking" are precisely that: metaphysical speaking.

Will Barrett's ailments, we are told, are directly connected to his dislocation, his lack of a sense of place, and his whole journey in the book is a metaphor for his search for a place in the world. Mr. Vaught, in whom Will can see "a glimpse of the shrewdness behind the old man's buffoonery," diagnoses Will's problem tersely: " 'Nervous! Hell, I'd be nervous too if I lived up here with all these folks.' He nodded down at the moraine of Washington Heights. 'All huddled up in the Y in the daytime and way up under a store all night. And peeping through a spyglass. Shoot, man!' " (78–9). Twice in the novel Will finds that "it came over him suddenly that he didn't live anywhere and had no address" (313, 122). Repeated references are made to the return to the South for a search for his identity, where he finds that, indeed, you can't go home again:

> The South he came home to was different from the South he had left. It was happy, victorious, Christian, rich, patriotic and Republican.
>
> The happiness and serenity of the South disconcerted him. He had felt good in the North because everyone else felt so bad. . . . It was impossible for him to be at home in the North because the North was homeless. There are many things worse than being homeless in a homeless place — in fact, this is one condition of being at home, if you are yourself homeless. For example, it is much worse to be homeless and then to go home where everyone is at home and then still be homeless. The South was at home. Therefore his homelessness was much worse in the South because he had expected to find himself at home there. (185–6; see 214, 320)

Percy is having some fun with Barrett's predicament, but as with all satire, the point is a serious one. The seriousness underlines another ironic passage, in which Percy undercuts his own themes by putting them in the mouth of Forney Aiken, the "fake Negro" whose speech is "rapid and slurred, for all the world like a shaky white man's": "You take your modern office building, as tastefully done as you please. What does it do to a man to uproot him from the earth? There is the cause of your violence!" Forney berates "artificial environments in general" to the confusion of Barrett, who qualifies the point: "Back to nature was the last thing he had in mind. 'Except — ahem' said he, feeling his own voice go a bit reedy, 'Except I would suspect that even if one picked out the most natural surroundings he might carry his own deprivation with him' " (126–7).

Places are most successfully used in Percy's most recent novel, which represents a major step in his development of what he himself has called "novelistic" writing. Excellent use is made of the area of Louisiana which is the setting of *Love in the Ruins*, from the contrast between the regimentation of Fedville and the anarchy of the swamp to the specific locales of Paradise Estates itself. The metaphors and the philosophy are less verbalized and are more fully incorporated into the development of the novel. Here the pilgrim hero comes as close as one can to a home in the world. Like Will Barrett, Tom More is a descendant of a family of wanderers: "All Mores, until I came along, were good Catholics and went to mass — I too until a few years ago. Wanderers we became, like Jews in the wilderness" (21). In their wandering they settled in Louisiana, and it is Tom's good fortune and his salvation that he does not forget his pilgrim's wandering and his greatest ancestor.

Each of Percy's novels remains under the strict control of his view of man. Certainly this consistent philosophical perspective provides much of the value of these novels, but in each of them, in varying degrees, cerebral passages intrude themselves and become distracting exposition. Richard Lehan complained of *The Last Gentleman* that its resolution was "both highly idealistic and totally undramatized — unrealized in the novel and probably unrealizable in fact."[30] While to a degree true, this is rather harsh, for each of the novels is an outstanding performance. While I want to repeat that I do not want to seem prescriptive, in each of the successive novels Percy's sense of place is more fully realized and enriches the novel accordingly. In Bachelard's terms, his imagination has seized upon the places. Martin Luschei is correct when he says Percy's "great achievement may prove to have been translating Kierkegaard into concrete American terms."[31] but Percy has stated that his next novel will be very different, evidently feeling that his gloss on Kierkegaard is complete. Whatever the terms of his next novel, I suspect he will still be concerned with the predicament of modern man in the world, and his sense of place will have advanced again to fuller and richer dimensions.

Notes

1. Walker Percy, "The Man on the Train: Three Existential Modes," *Partisan Review*, 23 (January 5 and 12, 1957), 478–9.

2. Carlton Cremeens, "Walker Percy," the Man and the Novelist: An Interview," *Southern Review*, n.s. 4 (Apr., 1968), 284.

3. Zoltán Abádi-Nagy, "A Talk with Walker Percy," *Southern Literary Journal*, 6 (Fall, 1973), 4. See also Percy's "From Facts to Fiction," *Writer*, 8 (Oct., 1967), 46: "I would begin

with a *man* who finds himself in a *world*, a very concrete man who is located in a very concrete place and time."

4. John Carr, "Rotation and Repetition," *Kite-Flying and Other Irrational Acts: Conversations with Twelve Southerners*, ed. John Carr (Baton Rouge: Louisiana State Univ. Press, 1972), pp. 42–3. In treating Percy's developing "novelistic" sense of place I do not want to be taken as prescriptive. Certainly, elements of both the romance and the anatomy, to use Frye's terms, are present, but the novel's characteristics as distinguished by Frye, particularly the novel's emphasis on "the link with history and a sense of the temporal context" (Frye, 307), are pre-eminent. The forms may and do overlap. See Northrop Frye, *Anatomy of Criticism: Four Essays* (New York: Atheneum, 1969), pp. 303–14. Percy's term, of course, remains "novelistic."

5. Carr, p. 55.

6. Gaston Bachelard, *The Poetics of Space*, trans. Marie Jolas (Boston: Beacon Press, 1969), p. xxxii.

7. Martin Luschei, *The Sovereign Wayfarer: Walker Percy's Diagnosis of the Malaise* (Baton Rouge: Louisiana State Univ. Press, 1972).

8. Soren Kierkegaard, *Fear and Trembling and The Sickness Unto Death*, trans. Walter Lowrie (Princeton Univ. Press, 1953), p. 176. Also cited by Luschei, p. 76.

9. Luschei, p. 77.

10. Walker Percy, *The Moviegoer* (New York: The Noonday Press, 1967), pp. 9, 78. Originally published by Alfred A. Knopf, 1961. *The Last Gentleman* (New York: Farrar, Strauss and Giroux, 1966). *Love in the Ruins* (New York; Dell, 1972). Subsequent references will be noted parenthetically in the text.

11. Kierkegaard, quoted by Luschei, p. 58.

12. Carr, 50.

13. "The Man on the Train," 490.

14. Tony Tanner, *The Reign of Wonder: Naivety and Reality in American Literature* (Cambridge: Cambridge Univ. Press, 1965), pp. 345–6.

15. Carr, p. 40.

16. "The Man on the Train," 488.

17. Carr, p. 51.

18. Ashley Brown, "An Interview with Walker Percy," *Shenandoah*, 18 (Spring, 1967), 8.

19. Tony Tanner, *City of Words: American Fiction, 1950–1970* (New York: Harper & Row, 1971), p. 262.

20. This is Percy's only third person narrative, and he spoke quite harshly of Barrett in his interview with Abádi-Nagy, 16.

21. Luschei, p. 195.

22. Percy seems preoccupied with places, both in their barrenness and their richness, both in his fiction and in his essays and interviews. He told Cremeens that motels, being "faceless and rootless," are good places to write, whereas in "Virtues and Vices in the Southern Literary Renascence," *Commonweal*, 76 (May 11, 1962), 181–2, he can laud Monroeville, Alabama, as a place that is "so haunted by presences that the unheard voices make themselves heard by any sensitive ear." In the same article he wisely warns, "A sense of place can decay to the merely bizarre."

23. See Percy's essay, "Notes for a Novel About the End of the World," *Katallagete* (Journal of the Committee of Southern Churchmen, Nashville), (Winter, 1967–8), 7–14, for a developed treatment of the world of this third novel. The role of the church in such a world is also described: see esp. 12–13.

24. Percy himself has called attention to this failing of More's. See Abádi-Nagy, 17.

25. Luschei, p. 14.

26. Carr, p. 48.

27. Charles M. Doughty, *Travels in Arabia Deserta*, 3rd ed. (New York: Random House, 1921).

28. Luschei, p. 230n.

29. Aspects of Binx's character appear in the description of the tourist in Percy's essay, "The Loss of the Creature," University of Houston *Forum*, II (Fall, 1958), 14: "He moves like a ghost through schoolroom, city streets, trains, parks, movies. He carves his initials as a last desperate measure to escape his ghostly role of consumer. He is saying in effect: I am not a ghost after all: I am a sovereign person. And he establishes title the only way remaining to him, by staking his claim over one square inch of wood or stone."

30. Richard Lehan, "The Way Back: Redemption in the Novels of Walker Percy," *Southern Review*, n.s. 4 (Apr., 1968), 318-9.

31. Luschei, p. 242.

Walker Percy: Sensualist Thinker   William Dowie, S.J.*

Walker Percy's time for recognition has come. Although his first novel, *The Moviegoer*, won the National Book Award in 1962, until recently he has been omitted more than included in writings on contemporary fiction. I doubt that this will be the case any longer. V. S. Pritchett, Wilfrid Sheed, and Thomas McGuane all have reviewed Percy's latest book, *Love in the Ruins*, with convincing praise.[1] And Alfred Kazin began his biographical series on contemporary Americans in *Harper's* with a warm, appreciative essay on Walker Percy.[2] "Covington, Louisiana's most prominent existentialist," as a friend has dubbed Percy, is here to stay.

The biggest temptation when writing on Percy is to bask in the richness of his narrative voice by quoting too liberally from his novels. His finely wrought prose now sings a paean to Southern womanhood:

> Ellen Oglethorpe is a beautiful but tyrannical Georgia Presbyterian. A ripe Georgian persimmon not a peach, she fairly pops the buttons of her nurse's uniform with her tart ripeness. She burgeons with marriageable Presbyterianism.[3]

and now attends the activity of a falcon:

> Along the cornice it would strut, cock a yellow eye down at the great misty rectangle (the eye sunk and fierce in its socket and half eclipsed by the orbit of bone), and down it would come smoking, at two hundred miles an hour, big feet stuck out in front like a Stuka, strike the pigeons in mid-air with a thump and a blue flak-burst of feathers.[4]

*Reprinted by permission from *Novel* 6 (1972):52-65.

It comes as no surprise that Percy himself spends part of his time sitting on the banks of the Bogufalaya River awaiting the arrival of a prothonotary warbler or such like guest. Bird-watching patience and precision of observation show through his writing. His descriptions read as realistically as experience itself at almost every point. What John O'Hara said of F. Scott Fitzgerald's fiction is equally true of Percy's: "The people were right, the talk was right, the clothes, the cars were real." Atmosphere too is real in Percy's narration, as on the day before the Tennessee-Ole Miss football game when there is "a grace and a dispensation in the air, an excitement and hope about the game on the morrow and a putting away of the old sad unaccomplished past" (*LG*, p. 264).

The hero of *The Moviegoer*, Binx Bolling, says that it was at the Tivoli theatre that he first "discovered place and time, tasted it like okra."[5] This strong vegetable, used heavily in creole cooking for its seasoning power, aptly represents the sensuous flavor of Percy's prose. Whether Binx is trying to fathom the secret of the Gentilly neighborhood at midnight or Will Barrett is examining a wall in New York through a high powered telescope or Thomas More is enjoying the "hot bosky bite of bourbon whiskey" (*LR*, p. 23), place, time, color, smell, and touch all saturate the Percy style. Will Barrett stands behind the Handsome Woman in the elevator and inhales "the heavy electric smell of unperfumed hair" (*LR*, p. 49). With great attentiveness Barrett, thinking of the gun which his father used to commit suicide, hopes as it were to find a clue in the feel of the hitching post:

> Again his hand went forth, knowing where it was, though he could not see, and touched the tiny iron horsehead of the hitching post, traced the cold metal down to the place where the oak had grown round it in an elephant lip. His fingertips touched the warm funny whispering bark. (*LG*, p. 332)

Percy's protagonists hear things like "the thick singing darkness" (*LG*, p. 161), the "slight muscous squeak" of a door panel (*LR*, p. 293), and the "high thin piping of waxwings" (*M*, p. 111). The sense of felt life bulges out of Percy's paragraphs. In *Love in the Ruins*, Thomas More's tryst in the bunker of the 18th hole comes alive in its vividness:

> We kiss in the grassy bunker. She kisses oddly, stooping to it, developing a torque and twisting down and away, seeming to grow shorter. Her breath catches. What she puts me in mind of is not a Texas girl at all but a smart Northern girl, a prodigy who has always played the cello ten hours a day, then one day finds herself at a summer festival and twenty-one and decides it is time to be kissed. So she stoops to it with an odd, shy yet practiced movement, what I fancy to be the Julliard summer-festival style of kissing.
>
> Now her hands are clasped in the small of my back. My hands are clasped in the small of her back. She hisses Dvořák. My hot chicken

blood sings with albumen molecules. Her hand is warm and whispery as a horn.

We lie in the grassy bunker, she gazing at the winter constellations wheeling in their courses, I singing like a cello between her knees. Fiery Betelgeuse hangs like a topaz in the south. We kiss hungrily, I going around after her.(p. 95)

In the root meaning of the word, Percy is a sensualist; for his novels celebrate the activity of the senses. His main characters respond sensually to that "cosmic sexual-religious longing" (*LR*, p. 156) that Thomas More says he has had since he was ten years old.

Unlike other novels that are devoted to capturing raw experience, Percy's work reveals the mind of the philosopher as well. Two of his three novels are introduced by citations from Sören Kierkegaard, whose influence Percy admits. "It was the religious existentialists Kierkegaard and Dostoevsky," writes Alfred Kazin, "not Faulkner the Southern genius, who influenced him."[6] I think it is more a question of degree than of strict alternatives. Percy had been re-reading Faulkner when I met him four summers ago; and with respectful admiration he cited a remark of Flannery O'Connor about Faulkner: "When the big train comes along, everybody else gets off the tracks." It is hard to imagine any Southern novelist still writing about the South not being influenced by Faulkner; and Percy is no exception.

Unlike Faulkner's fiction, however, Percy's work is controlled more by idea than by the organic growth of incident to incident. While he remains true to experience, Percy does not submit to its tyranny. "Bare experience," complained Philip Rahv twenty years ago, "is still the *leitmotiv* of the American writer, though the literary depression of recent years tends to show that this theme is virtually exhausted."[7] Rahv goes on to suggest a proper relationship between the two most important elements of a successful novel:

> Experience, in the sense of "felt life" rather than as life's total practice, is the main but by no means the total substance of literature. . . . Experience . . . is the substructure of literature above which there rises a superstructure of values, ideas, and judgments — in a word, of the multiple forms of consciousness. But this base and summit are not stationary: they continually act and react upon each other.[8]

Experience acts upon the superstructure in a peculiarly important way in Percy's novels. It is an antidote for the deadening abstractions that abound in our culture. It is a method of discovery. "The majority of men lead lives of quiet desperation," said Thoreau; and Binx-Will-Tom would agree. They see the world around them absorbed by the "spirit of abstraction." Binx hears it when Nell Lovell tells him that her goal in life is "to make a contribution, however small, and leave the world just a little better off" (*M*, p. 96). It is to avoid this abstraction that Binx tells Kate he now distrusts beauty, that "beauty, the quest of beauty alone, is a whoredom" (*M*, p. 180), and that money is a better god than beauty. Money is here and concrete. Beauty is too often a label used to avoid the realism of time and change; it is the abstraction *par excellence*, capable of glossing over the terrible mundaneness of change and death. Only by avoiding such comfortable fogs and by confronting the reality of objects can the lost hero find his way. Will Barrett realizes that his father's suicide was partly the result of the false abstractions he became locked in, that his times were:

> the worst of times, a time of fake beauty and fake victory. . . . He had missed it! It was not in the Brahms that one looked and not in solitariness and not in the old sad poetry but — he wrung out his ear — but here, under your nose, here in the very curiousness and drollness and extraness of the iron and the bark. . . . (*LG*, p. 332)

It is the very existence of the ordinary individual object, not so much the vague romantic feeling from music or poetry, that cries out there must be more; the search is justified.

Brahms and the old sad poetry become emblems of a spirit that tries to avoid the everydayness of the human condition. Will Barrett turns instead to the totally unexpected ("extraness") and unexplained ("curiousness") qualities of things, because objects have no pretense to autonomy or completeness; a rock, a tree, a bottle cap — even Clint Walker's remark to the saddle tramp in the softest, easiest old Virginia voice: "Mister, I don't believe I'd do that if I was you" — are too obviously frail not to lead into a further inquiry about the meaning of life. They bespeak contingency. However, when the movies end happily or when Kitty talks of settling down into Cap'n Andy Mickle's cottage on South Ridge, there is an implicit stance of self-sufficiency that is deadening in its weak pretense. All of Percy's protagonists become watchers, wanderers, listeners — thus opening themselves primarily to the sensual experiences of things around them. The bird-watcher's willingness to wait and watch is the archetypal image for Percy. The bird-watcher accepts the present, uses the past, and is hopeful of something to come.

Percy's protagonists have more than the naked eye to help them on their search. Immersion in immediate experience is one response to the spirit of abstraction. But it is not enough. For the habit of "seeing things as theories and himself as a shadow" (*LR*, p. 34) has so infected the individual that more is needed. Will Barrett senses that "things are not as accessible as they used to be" (*LG*, p. 31), and lavishly buys a $1900 Tetzlar telescope in order to recover the reality of things in all their particularity. He feels that "these lenses did not transmit light merely. They penetrated to the heart of things" (*LG*, p. 29). With his telescope even ordinary bricks "gained in value. Every grain and crack and excrescence became available" (*LG*, p. 31). This recovery of the reality of things means appreciating common objects for what they are in themselves. By unveiling the marvelous within the ordinary, the telescope unleashes the very surprise of existence itself.

So each of Percy's principal characters have instruments of recovery. Binx has his movies, not a perfect instrument, he realizes, for:

> The movies are onto the search, but they screw it up. The search always ends in despair. They like to show a fellow coming to himself in a strange place — but what does he do? He takes up with the local librarian, sets about proving to the local children what a nice fellow he is, and settles down with a vengeance. In two weeks time he is so sunk in everydayness that he might as well be dead. (*M*, p. 18)

In *Love in the Ruins* the situation is even more extreme. Labels, parties, allegiances carry the day: leftists, knotheads, love children, bantus, Catholic liberals and conservatives. Transcendence rules in all its absolutist fervor. Dr. More has his own invention, his lapsometer with its "way of measuring the length and breadth and motions of the very self. My little machine is the first caliper of the soul" (p. 107). With his device, More is able to measure both abstractive activity, angelism, and:

> adjustment to the environment, or, as I call it without prejudice, bestialism. . . . It is not uncommon nowadays to see patients suffering from angelism-bestialism. A man, for example, can feel at one and the same time extremely abstracted and inordinately lustful toward lovely young women who may be perfect strangers. (p. 27)

More's lapsometer is explicitly scientific. Whereas Binx Bolling gave up his chemical research in order to follow his search, More is a doctor who is absorbed by the scientific and indeed sees it as the only way of effecting a cure in the modern spirit. Percy, then, embraces the scientific more than ever in this novel, even while he satirizes the abstracted uses science can be put to, the Pit and the Love Clinic. Nevertheless, it is a use of the technology of the age rather than a flight from it into mere contemplation, which seemed to be the tendency of the first two novels. Another difference is that More's machine holds out the possibility of a cure. Basically diagnostic, the lapsometer also has medicinal potential in its ability to stimulate Brodmann Area 32 and the thalamus with heavy doses of sodium and chloride respectively. It is an instrument of power, though, and as such is dangerous, as is only too obvious in the mayhem that the diabolical Art Immelmann raises. But primarily its nature is therapeutic.

Since Percy himself admits to being a novelist whose primary and initial interest is ideas, the "superstructure of values, ideas, and judgments" which Philip Rahv referred to as half of the fictional material should not be too difficult to find in Percy's novels. Just as attention to experience answers to the problem of abstraction, so some kind of intellectual search is the only vital response to the malaise that settles in the midst of otherwise happy experiences. The basic question that underlies the novels is the rather metaphysical one, "Under what terms is the universe acceptable?" The heroes, Binx, Will, and Tom, are generally impressioniable characters who examine the terms by which others have made their peace with the world. Their observations and reactions do speak thematically about various possibilities.

One possibility presented to Binx, in *The Moviegoer*, is the traditional Southern way of his Aunt Emily, Uncle Jules, and Walter. Aunt Emily is the most articulate spokesman for this mode of life. She is an almost intact remnant of the old Southern female whose courage, *noblesse oblige*, bearing, power to inspire and comfort she embodies. Binx knows what to do when he is with her; he forgets when away. Her presence radiates the call to a community of good fellowship and shared vision. Yet she has, in her liberal upbringing, veered away from the Christian presuppositions of the Southern tradition. She "likes to say she is an Episcopalian by emotion, a Greek by nature and a Buddhist by choice" (p. 26). Her plea to Binx is framed in terms that are stoic and existential: let one do what one can and what one must, and be satisfied. Binx feels the strength of her argument and emotion when he is with her; but when alone, he simply cannot be satisfied. Aunt Emily is not troubled by theory or rational satisfaction; her feminine instinct for survival, protection, and good living join her in spirit to many of Faulkner's heroines. Indeed the exchange between Binx and Aunt Emily quite clearly is set in an expected pattern of traditional male-female roles which Cleanth Brooks rightly labels part of Faulkner's vision:

> . . . the role of man as active; man makes choices and lives up to the choices . . . the role of woman as characteristically fostering and sustaining. She undergirds society, upholding the family and community mores, sending her men out into battle, including the ethical battle.[9]

This is the pattern that Aunt Emily calls upon Binx to fit into. She wants him to decide what he will *do*. She wants him to become a man of action who will fit into the line of Southern gentlemen his family has produced. She sees her husband, Uncle Jules, as a "Cato" and her expectations for Binx run along the same lines. Her advice to Binx in memo form reads:

> Every moment think steadily as a Roman and a man, to do what thou hast in hand with perfect and simple dignity, and a feeling of affection and freedom and justice. These words of the Emperor Marcus Aurelius Antoninus strike me as pretty good advice, for even the orneriest young scamp. (p. 75)

Binx is unable to accept the advice, to take his right place. And his position outside the fold of the expected community, combined with a certain indifference and honesty, has caused him to be compared with the main character of Camus's *The Fall*.[10] The comparison is just, but there are also important dissimilarities. Binx fights against the *tedium vitae* by an active engagement in his search. He refuses to stop at the level of the absurd. In fact, Binx's search is really a rejection of the terms on which Camus tried to effect a reconciliation with the world through the myth of Sisyphus. Camus established man's total honesty as his fundamental value, justifying the struggles of man by his heightened consciousness of what he was doing, even though doomed to defeat. This courageous, unreasoning confrontation directly with harsh reality elevates man to such nobility for Camus that it effectively creates a value worth the world's weight.

This however has no appeal for the New Orleans stockbroker. If anything, his Aunt Emily more closely embodies the Camus stance. In fact, she has integrated Camus's heroics into the Southern myth to replace former religious values. She tells Binx:

> I don't quite know what we're doing on this insignificant cinder spinning away in a dark corner of the universe. That is a secret which the high gods have not confided in me. Yet one thing I believe and I believe it with every fibre of my being. A man must live by his lights and do what little he can and do it as best he can. In this world goodness is destined to be defeated. But a man must go down fighting. That is the victory. To do anything less is to be less than a man. (p. 53)

This is indeed noble, but Aunt Emily has given in to the absurd, has stopped asking questions, has decided simply to "go down fighting." Binx himself is not the absurd hero, for he refuses to accept the limits that Camus and Aunt Emily place on the human situation. Unable to judge that the world is absurd, he treats it as a mystery. Like a detective on a case, Binx seeks some clue to the mystery in individual objects. It was in the war while he lay wounded underneath a chindolea bush, watching a dung beetle scratching around under some leaves that an immense curiosity awoke in Binx: "I was onto something. I vowed that if I ever got out of this fix, I would pursue the search" (p. 15).

He is like many of Camus's heroes in his sensual appreciation of life. Whereas Camus wrote of basking in "the bay, the sun, the red and white games on the seaward terraces, the flowers and sports stadiums, the cool-legged girls";[11] Binx lies "drowsing in the sun" on a Gulf Coast beach with Sharon of the "golden thighs, such a fine strapping armful they are" (pp. 127, 124). But Binx always preserves an underlying sense of the insufficiency of the good life, an unrest that prevents him from settling down in the sensual. Even after the successful escapade with Sharon, while he is riding in his red MG along the beautiful boulevard, with "ten thousand handsome cars, fifty thousand handsome, well-fed and kind-hearted people," the malaise settles like a fall-out. Almost in desperation, he grabs for Sharon's thigh. When she stops him, he reacts indifferently, "as willing not to mess with her as mess with her, to tell the truth" (p. 166). The malaise closely resembles Kierkegaard's despair. For Kierkegaard, it was irony that led the esthetic man to despair by making him conscious of his dissatisfaction and distaste for pleasures to which he is attached. This is the case with Binx. Recall the intellectual pleasures as well as the sensual that he dabbled in: his reading and underlining liberal and conservative periodicals, his faithful listening to *This I Believe* over the radio. Toward the end of the story, however, Binx observes the same kind of dabblings by a fellow train passenger with a completely reversed attitude. The man had underlined in a magazine article the phrase, "The gradual convergence of physical and social science" (p. 175). Binx reflects that even a week ago such a phrase would have provoked no more than an ironic tingle or two at the back of his neck. "Now it howls through the Ponchitoula Swamp, the very sound and soul of despair" (p. 176). Like Kierkegaard's esthete, Binx must undergo pangs of despair as long as he fails to move into an ethical existence, which is what Binx finally does when he marries Kate in response to her needs.

Binx's family on his mother's side is Catholic and presents the other main call to his allegiance. But Catholicism has absolutely no impact on him: "My mother's family think I have lost my faith and they pray for me to recover it. I don't know what they're talking about" (p. 135); for Binx feels that his unbelief "was invincible from the beginning" (p. 136). He reflects:

> I could never make head or tail of God. The proofs of God's existence may have been true for all I know, but it didn't make the slightest difference. If God himself had appeared to me, it would have changed nothing. In fact, I have only to hear the word God and a curtain comes down in my head. (p. 136)

Binx grew up in a world no longer dependent upon God, that is, one to which God was irrelevant. This current of life in which no sign or proof of God would really make any difference anyway is an indication to Binx that something is wrong with the present settlement. God has become a meaningless abstraction to a callow world. And so, although Binx feels that "it no longer avails to start with creatures and prove God . . . it is impossible to rule God out" (p. 136).

Of course, the chief possibility of life which Binx reacts against is acquiescence to everydayness, the world of mass man absorbed by technology and rational abstraction, the living from cliché to cliché without explanation or expectation. Binx admits that he doesn't know whether he is way ahead or way behind the 98% of the people who have found God. What he does know is that he is different from them, and that saying God is the goal of his search would "amount to setting myself a goal which everyone else has reached — and therefore raising a question in which no one has the slightest interest" (p. 18). 98% of the people are immersed in patterns and habits of the quotidian that are not in the least changed by their having found God.

Binx admires his half-brother Lonnie's faith which enables Lonnie to accept his tragically early death in the spirit of a real victory. Lonnie dies at peace, and the notion of God does not appear quite so irrelevant as it previously did to Binx. Lonnie's death also takes on an aura of sacrificial efficacy for Binx and Kate. Binx has absorbed some of Lonnie's concern for those around him, as he returns to take care of the children and provide support for Kate.

Which brings us to another theme of the novel, the human need for reliance upon another's word and direction. Kate is nearly incapable of action unless she can know that someone is directing her and thinking about her all the time. Binx accepts this role. Even a simple action like going downtown on the streetcar to the Homestead requires an act of faith for Kate. Unlike the theme of *Catch-22*, which Frederick Karl summarizes as: "the only sure thing in a swamp of identity is one's own identity,"[12] *The Moviegoer* expresses the radical need for something outside oneself. For Kate, the only sure thing is faith in another. She tells Binx, "What I want is to believe in someone completely and then do what he wants me to do. . . . I am a religious person" (p. 150). The type of faith that is needed by Kate is not a content-belief specifically, a belief *that*, but rather a belief *in*, an extension of the type of dependence on the other that is implicit in all forms of conversation. Naturally a belief in someone implies a certain amount of trust in his words; but Kate's specific need is for the other to lean upon. And she finds such a mooring in Binx.

The Last Gentleman is not as neat a book as Percy's first. It is more sprawling, wandering, and experience-filled. But the basic concerns are the same. The same principal themes emerge: the necessity of a search and the movement from esthetic to ethic. The novel's only real thematic advance over *The Moviegoer* is a negative one. Williston Bibb Barrett is alive as long as he is asking questions, looking through his telescope, and responding to his friend Jamie's need for companionship. Like Binx, Will is an outsider who "became a watcher and a listener and a wanderer" (*LG*, p. 10).

The Last Gentleman asks the same root question of life's worthwhileness. And it answers it by having Will Barrett meet a family with a diversity of answers. The center of the Vaught family, mother and father, generally frame their lives in terms of the commercialized Southern tradition. They are descendants of Faulkner's Compsons. Mr. Vaught is completely absorbed in his used car business and his golf. Daughter Kitty is at first as "inward and watchful" as Barrett. Will thinks that she "might wander with him through old green Louisiana, perch on the back step of the camper of an evening with the same shared sense of singularity of time and the excellence of place" (p. 260). But Kitty becomes Miss Katherine Gibbs Vaught "and the next thing he knew she'd have her picture in the *Commercial Appeal*" (p. 261). Kitty becomes swallowed by the university life of sorority and football spirit. Daughter-in-law Rita's ideal of the good life is also peculiarly modern. It had been reached at one point in her life with Sutter; and he coldly describes the ideal:

> We were good, you and I, as good as you wanted us to be, and in the end
> I couldn't stand it. You were productive and so, for the first time in
> years, was I, and thanks to you. As you say, we were self-actualizing
> people and altogether successful, though somewhat self-conscious, in
> our cultivation of joy, zest, awe, freshness, and the right balance of adult
> autonomous control and childlike playfulness, as you used to call it. (pp.
> 245–246)

Val, the older sister, has followed the path of religion by becoming a nun
and working with the poor blacks in Alabama. Jamie is young and dying.
Sutter is the family renegade on one side just as Val is on the other — both
unacceptable to the family because they have rejected the ordinary way.
The character of Sutter is Percy's main progression over his previous novel.
Sutter opted out of his successful marriage and successful medical practice
because he decided that the ultimate satisfaction of life was free lewdness
blended with scientific speculation, thus achieving "immanence" through
fornication and "transcendence" through science. Sutter has no religion or
belief in God, but thinks of himself as a "sincere, humble, and even moral
pornographer" (p. 281). He indicts the man-on-the-street for his hypocrisy,
saying:

> Americans are not devils but they are becoming as lewd as devils. As for
> me, I elect lewdness over paltriness. Americans practice it with their
> Christianity and are paltry with both. Where your treasure is, there is
> your heart and there's theirs, zwischen die Beinen. (p. 292)

Eventually sex fails Sutter, just as it failed Binx in the train with Kate:
"Flesh poor flesh failed us. The burden was too great" (*M*, p. 183).
Lewdness is not enough to bear the weight of the absurdity of his younger
brother's death; and science just doesn't transcend it. Sutter is a stark and
honest character. His attitude toward life is rather simple: if you accept
faith in a future, other-worldly life, you should live directed by your faith
to this life; if you accept this world as all, then you should have the
courage to say no to it by suicide if the enterprise of living grows absurd.
Jamie's death is the coup; afterwards Sutter resolves to kill himself.

Will Barrett instinctively recoils from the various kinds of settling
down present in the Vaught family. Having fallen in love with Kitty, he
tries to keep her from falling into everydayness. Val is a puzzle to him, one
he doesn't like but respects. It is to Sutter that Will is drawn, Sutter the
philosopher of transcendence and immanence who also senses that "there
is something wrong with the world" (p. 78). Attracted by Sutter's
perception and honesty, Will draws back from his antinomies:

> Where he probably goes wrong, mused the engineer sleepily, is in
> the extremity of his alternatives: God and not-God, getting under
> women's dresses and blowing your brains out. Whereas and in fact my
> problem is how to live from one ordinary minute to the next on a
> Wednesday afternoon. (pp. 354–355)

Their problems are indeed different: Barrett trying to live with the quotidian and Sutter being pursued by the absurd; Barrett searching for a way to unite immanence and transcendence rather than accept Sutter's bifurcation. They are both far removed from those young men,

> Sewanee Episcopal types, good soft-spoken hard-drinking graceful youths, gentle with women and very much themselves with themselves, set, that is, for the next fifty years in the actuality of themselves and their own good names. They knew what they were, how things were and how things should be. (p. 265)

Will asks Sutter in relation to these boys, "Why do they feel so good . . . and I feel so bad?" Sutter responds, "The question is whether they feel as good as you think, and if they do, then the question is whether it is necessarily worse to feel bad than good under the circumstances" (p. 268). Sutter's answer is that Will's trouble is nothing personal, but the general state of the human condition and that Will just happens to be observant enough, and sick enough, to realize it more than most people who lead healthy lives of habit or "quiet desperation."

At the end of the story, Will is tempted to settle down, to call off the search. He argues with Sutter and with himself: "There is nothing wrong with it," that is, with living on South Ridge with Kitty, taking a position with Mr. Vaught, being a community man and making "a small contribution of good will and understanding" (p. 384). Only, the memory of the Deke from Vanderbilt who had everything but suddenly broke into a scream one fine afternoon haunts Barrett enough to leave him questioning at the end of the novel. It is to Sutter that he turns because Sutter is the scientist of the phenomena of transcendence and immanence, even though his own life resulted in a "breakdown of the sexual as a mode of reentry from the posture of transcendence" (p. 372).

Will remains a watcher, wanderer, searcher at the end. He runs toward Sutter's Edsel with "great joyous ten-foot antelope bounds" as if he had hit upon something, a "final question" (p. 409). His mode of action up until now had been directed by the immediateness of his attraction to Kitty and by the immediateness of Jamie's need. After he has fulfilled Val's, and eventually Jamie's too, wish for Jamie's baptism, and after Jamie dies, Williston Bibb Barrett once more must confront the question of what to do. The conclusion of the book leaves him in this dilemma. The choices have been sharpened by Jamie's death and Sutter's intention to follow. Will's final decision is left unanswered in the novel, almost in challenge to the reader to make the decision for him. It is also a sign that we have more to learn from the scientist-sensualist character than the suicide-bound Sutter is capable of giving in *The Last Gentleman*.

Barrett, then, is left questing rather than doing. Unfortunately, this ending does not advance the theme of the novel any further than it had been before Jamie's death. Will Barrett goes back to his old searching ways, and *The Last Gentleman* remains the most incomplete of Percy's novels thematically.

Percy's latest novel, *Love in the Ruins*, is more futuristic, apocalyptic, and satiric than the first two. Its immediate literary ancestors are C. S. Lewis's *That Hideous Strength* and Walter Miller's *Canticle for Leibowitz*, both of which are set in the future and have central religious concerns. Both deal with the question of technology *vs.* traditional wisdom, and Lewis's novel foreshadows Percy's in using sex as a central religious metaphor.

Love in the Ruins has all of the sense of reality that Percy poured into his previous work, but it exaggerates more for satirical and farcical purposes. Percy is still very much a novelist of ideas and values in his most recent book. The citation from Romano Guardini that introduced *The Last Gentleman* might serve as its scenario:

> . . . We know now that the modern world is coming to an end . . . at the same time, the unbeliever will emerge from the fogs of secularism. He will cease to reap benefit from the values and forces developed by the very Revelation he denies. . . . Loneliness in faith will be terrible. Love will disappear from the face of the public world, but the more precious will be that love which flows from one lonely person to another. . . . The world to come will be filled with animosity and danger, but it will be a world open and clean.

Love in the Ruins is thematically contiguous with the other Percy novels, but it takes things a bit further and is more explicitly concerned with religion. The subtitle is "The Adventures of a Bad Catholic at a Time Near the End of the World." And the first person narrator exposes himself quite clearly as a typical Graham Greene character with a jaunty sense of humor:

> Some years ago . . . I stopped eating Christ in Communion, stopped going to mass, and have since fallen into a disorderly life. I believe in God and the whole business but I love women best, music and science next, whiskey next, God fourth, and my fellowman hardly at all. Generally I do as I please. A man, wrote John, who says he believes in God and does not keep his commandments is a liar. If John is right, then I am a liar. Nevertheless, I still believe. (p. 6)

This tension in Thomas More, a distant descendant of the English saint, between his belief and his allegiance, runs throughout the novel. More is fully driven by a "longing, longings for women, for the Nobel Prize, for the hot bosky bite of bourbon whiskey, and other great heart-wrenching longings that have no name" (p. 23).

Like his predecessors, Binx and Will, he is aware of the danger of the spirit of abstraction and he is involved in a search. Like them also, More has an ailment that separates him from the ordinary man-in-the-street. Spending his happiest moments in the mental ward, More is at home with those who are admittedly sick. It is the mask of health — the poles of bestialism and angelism that rule the world under acceptable labels — that frightens him. When More himself starts to sink into the sickness of normalcy, "morning terror" shakes him out of it. Corresponding to the malaise of Binx and the melancholy of Will, it keeps him from settling with the everyday.

However, More is also aware of the necessity for living at some level of abstraction. His quest is within a more structured framework than either Will's or Binx's. He admits, "I . . . am a Roman Catholic. . . . I believe in the Holy Catholic Apostolic and Roman Church, in God the Father, in the election of the Jews, in Jesus Christ His Son our Lord. . . ." (p. 6); thus accepting a type of abstraction. His search is to bring his own abstractive life and his experiential life together, or, as he puts it, to achieve a blend of angelism and bestialism. With his lapsometer, he also hopes to heal the same kind of divisions in society at large:

> What if man could reenter paradise, so to speak, and live there both as man and spirit, whole and intact man-spirit, as solid flesh as a speckled trout, a dappled thing, yet aware of itself as a self! (p. 36)

Oddly enough, More succeeds, at least in his own case and at least to some degree. He comes to connect these great heart-wrenching longings to their source in God, who himself has intersected with man in the space-time of history and thus provided the model and the ground for living as man-spirits. The very space-time means of a Church and sacraments safeguard the abstraction-experience union. At one point, More prays:

> Dear God, I can see it now, why can't I see it other times, that it is you I love in the beauty of the world and in all the lovely girls and dear good friends, and it is pilgrims we are, wayfarers on a journey, and not pigs nor angels. (p. 109)

But realization is not enough; and More was able to offer this prayer rather early in the novel. It is only through the love that he finds in the ruins that More can literally put himself together and get right with God. Just as he ceased going to Communion when his first wife left him, remarriage enables him to return to the sacraments again. It is only through the particular again — love of Ellen, his lapsometer research — that More comes to feel at one with the world. After the upheaval he is much poorer than before; but wealth is irrelevant. It is only through the experience of Communion that he feels reconciled with God. This is why he is so hard on Hermann Hesse and esoteric religion and spiritualism. He reflects of his first wife Doris:

> What she didn't understand, she being spiritual and seeing religion as spirit, was that it took religion to save me from the spirit world, from orbiting the earth like Lucifer and the angels, that it took nothing less than touching the thread off the misty interstates and eating Christ

> himself to make me mortal man again and let me inhabit my own flesh
> and love her in the morning. (p. 254)

But the equation works both ways. Marriage allows More to order his sex life and so go back to Communion, after confessing and receiving the sacrament of Penance.

Confession, however, is no easy matter to him, mainly because of his haunting inability to feel sorry for his sins. He goes to see a priest anyhow; and, in the course of the confession, finds himself feeling not so much sorry as ashamed of having made so much over paltry sins. The reference of the priest to "middle-aged daydreams" apparently hit home. Also he is ashamed of whatever of his past sins are recalled by the priest's emphasis on "a bit of ordinary kindness to people, particularly our own families" and "doing what we can for our poor unhappy country" (p. 399). One has the feeling that in that sudden blush of shame, More for the first time fully grasped sin as not just imaginary black spots on the white milk bottle of his soul, but as the recognized evil done and good left undone to those around him. At any rate, he receives absolution and is left feeling "like God's spoiled child" with his "library, a laboratory, a lusty Presbyterian wife, a cosy tree house, an idea, and all the time in the world" (p. 383). He continues his scientific works to perfect his lapsometer; and he abandons ambition, drunkenness, and licentiousness — while still kept on edge by the "longing, the desire that has no name" (p. 393). Now he harbors the notion of man as "sovereign wanderer, lordly exile, worker and waiter and watcher" (p. 383).

The novel concludes with two important experiences: More's taking of Communion and his bedding down with his wife Ellen. Sex, as the greatest channel of this ineffable longing on earth, has a lordly place. As in Lewis's *That Hideous Strength*, the bed is the final setting, symbolizing man's at-oneness with this world of flesh and also his unquenchable longings. The search has not ended. "Our hearts are restless, O Lord," wrote Augustine, "until they rest in Thee." But it can be pursued under livable terms:

> To bed we go for a long, winter's nap, twined about each other as
> the ivy twineth, not under a bush or in a car or on the floor or any such
> humbug as marked the past peculiar years of Christendom, but at home
> in bed where all good folk belong. (p. 403)

This is the world Guardini spoke of, "open and clean," and one in which, as love disappears from public life, all "the more precious will be that love which flows from one lonely person to another."

By now it should be clear that Percy believes that to survive one needs to resist complete absorption in either pole of sensation or thought, that one must hold the tension somehow. His heroes still strive to maintain both sides of this pull. *Love in the Ruins* brings the struggle to greater resolution than either of the previous works. In the meantime, Percy has blended experience and idea in a manner uncommon to American fiction, which itself has fluctuated from pole to pole: bare experience and heady fantasy. Percy has succeeded in creating, in Philip Rahv's terms, both a substructure and a superstructure in his fiction; and their interaction makes for a rather impressive edifice.

Notes

1. V. S. Pritchett, "Clowns," *The New York Review of Books*, 16 (July 1, 1971), 15. Wilfred Sheed, "The Good Word: Walker Percy Redivivus," *The New York Times Book Review* (July 4, 1971), 2. Thomas McGuane, "Love in the Ruins," *The New York Times Book Review* (May 23, 1971), 7, 37.

2. Alfred Kazin, "The Pilgrimage of Walker Percy," *Harper's Magazine*, 242 (June, 1971), 81–86.

3. *Love in the Ruins* (New York, 1971), p. 155.

4. *The Last Gentleman* (New York, 1966), p. 5.

5. *The Moviegoer* (New York, 1961), p. 72. Subsequent references to the novels are included in the text.

6. Kazin, 85.

7. Philip Rahv, "The Cult of Experience in American Writing," *Critiques and Essays on Modern Fiction: 1920–1951*, ed., John W. Aldridge (New York, 1952), p. 243.

8. Rahv, pp. 240–241.

9. Cleanth Brooks, *The Hidden God* (New Haven, 1963), p. 25.

10. Brainard Cheney, "To Restore a Fragmented Image." *Sewanee Review*, 69 (Autumn, 1961), 691.

11. Albert Camus. *The Myth of Sisyphus and Other Essays* (New York, 1955), p. 105.

12. Frederick Karl, "Joseph Heller's *Catch-22*: Only Fools Walk in Darkness," *Contemporary American Novelists*, ed., Harry T. Moore (Carbondale, Ill., 1964), p. 137.

A Symbolic Structure for Walker Percy's Fiction
J. P. Telotte*

Most critics have approached Walker Percy's work, particularly his fiction, from either of two directions; they see him as an inheritor of the Southern literary tradition of Faulkner or as an exponent of modern existential philosophy after the pattern of Sartre and Camus. Of course, Percy's openness and accessibility in great part account for these critical perspectives, since in numerous interviews he has practically staked out the territory which students of his work might most profitably explore.[1] Consequently, with the publication of his collected linguistic essays in *The Message in the Bottle*, we might have expected criticism to take a marked

*Reprinted by permission from *Modern Fiction Studies* 26 (1980):227–40. ©1980 by Purdue Research Foundation.

turn in that direction, treating his fiction from the vantage afforded by his language theories. Those few essayists who have chosen to discuss Percy's linguistic work at all have, however, failed to take that next critical step and demonstrate its bearing on his novels.[2] And in light of the current vogue for semiotic and structuralist approaches to literature, such an omission must seem all the more glaring. I would here like to make a tentative effort to redress this problem by suggesting that a most profitable and illuminating approach to Percy's fiction may be had through his linguistic concerns.

Perhaps Percy is himself much to blame for this critical vacuum, for he has flatly denied that there is any connection between his linguistic work and his fiction. In fact, he has stated that his "interest in language theory" and his "practice as a novelist" have "very little to do with each other. Maybe it's just as well. God help us if a novelist was thinking of theoretical linguistics when he was writing. It'd be pretty bad."[3] Seeming to offer some substantiation to this claim is the fact that Percy's first linguistic writings appeared in 1954, seven years before his first novel was published, indicating apparently a separate and longstanding interest in language which *need* not have carried over into his fictional endeavors. Drawing upon Percy's comments on this subject, Lewis Lawson suggests that perhaps Percy has tended "to turn to fiction whenever he became stymied in his study" of language,[4] as if one were simply a respite from the other. The problem is, as we all know, that an author's stated *intentions* provide notoriously bad grounds for critical appraisals, and this may be even more the case with a fictionalist, one whose very occupation is the creation of pleasing untruths.

Complicating the issue is the fact that Percy speaks very pointedly to his own vocation in *Message in the Bottle*: that is, he does not limit himself to describing the structure of language and a pattern for its use, but he incorporates into his discussion one role of the language user, specifically the novelist's. The modern novelist, as he sees it, performs a prophetic-corrective function: "the novelist deals first and last with individuals," particularly those who have "very nearly come to the end of the line."[5] Their predicament stems from the failure of a "radical *bond* . . . which connects man with reality" (*MB*, p. 102), a bond which Percy sees as almost synonymous with the language act. It is the novelist's task to call man's attention to this breakdown; "in his confused Orphic way," he tries to "tell us something we would do well to listen to" (*MB*, p. 107). In other words, the serious novelist's task is to speak to alienated modern man, and by so doing, to effect "an aesthetic reversal of alienation" (*MB*, p. 83). The hope is that by communicating this vision, the artist may restore that vital bond, reuniting man to his world and conferring meaning where even the hope for something meaningful has been all but forgotten. In sum, the novelist as Percy describes him functions within a triadic relationship by speaking through the symbolic medium of his novel — a word writ large —

to a waiting public, hopeful for a very vital "message in the bottle." Not surprisingly, this same triadic pattern of communication has been proposed by Percy to account for the nature of language itself.

Following a schema proposed by one of the founders of semiotics, Charles Sanders Peirce,[6] Percy posits a trinary description of the language act, one consisting of a symbol, interpretant, and object:

Intrepretant in an Interpreter

Sign △ _ _ △ Object (or designatum)

According to Percy, language is primarily a "naming act," that is, the creation of a "meaning" relation between a word and its referent "by which we are able to speak and perhaps to think about something" (MB, p. 280). This notion of "meaning" derives from the unique quality of human language, the fact that every word involves an "is-saying," an assertion that in some sense there holds an identity between the word and that which it symbolizes. Mechanistically, Percy describes this relation as "a coupling of elements by a coupler" (MB, p. 166). In this sense, man himself becomes that coupling agent — the thinking, knowing being who perceives and understands his world through a symbolic medium.

As we can see, Percy has fashioned a distinctly humanistic substructure for his semiotics. He does not actually begin with the phenomenon of language but, as is consistent with his thorough grounding in existential philosophy, with man, the creature who uses language so distinctively. Percy defines man as the "symbol-monger," he who knows his world and indeed himself through the intercession of language: "we do know, not as the angels know and not as dogs know but as men, who must know one thing through the mirror of another" (MB, p. 82). Through that naming act, man asserts his knowledge of the world he inhabits and even affirms his own place in that world as knower and namer of all he encounters.

This existential approach to linguistics springs from Percy's reaction to a prevalent behaviorist interpretation of both man and his language. The behavioral view considers language primarily as a binary, stimulus-response event between two entities. As Percy describes it, "Language is held to be a kind of sign response and so understandable in behavioristic terms as an interaction between an organism and its environment — which consists, in this case, of other organisms" (MB, p. 192). Such an approach to language, he feels, must fail on two counts. For one, it misinterprets the language act by treating a word simply as another kind of environmental stimulus. A cause-effect explanation, Percy holds, cannot possibly account for the "coupling" activity language involves, that *meaning* relation created between every word and referent: "to set forth language as sequence of stimuli and responses overlooks the salient trait of symbolic behavior: Symbols, words, not only call forth responses; they also denote things, name things for . . . speakers" (*MB*, p. 194). At the same time, a binary approach tends to devalue or even omit from consideration the *human* element of language. When man is considered at all, he is viewed as little better than another reacting organism, responding like a dutiful animal to its environmental directives or like a machine, clicking off / on, yes / no according to its data input.

Percy apparently believes that any attempt to analyze language apart from its human context is doomed to failure. Without the human element, after all, there would be no language act, no purpose for naming or even a namer. Besides, he suggests, language always involves an "intentional relation"; that is, it is designed to function in a specifically human context, *intending* a listener for every speaker, "one for whom the name becomes meaningful" (*MB*, p. 256) for every "namer" or language user. To take full account of this relationship, therefore, Percy integrates into his initial triad a further three-cornered relation composed of the indispensible elements in every human communication: the speaker, the symbol, and the hearer.

In explanation of this second triad, Percy asserts that "without the presence of another, symbolization cannot conceivably occur because there is no one from whom the word can be received as meaningful." Consequently, he concludes, *"The irreducible condition of every act of symbolization is the rendering intelligible: that is to say, the formulation of experience for a real or an implied someone else"* (*MB*, p. 257). Viewed in this light, language properly functions to assert a distinctive relationship between people, the relation of "intersubjectivity." In this respect, as Robert Coles points out, Percy "is especially indebted to Gabriel Marcel" who, in elaborating his theories on human interrelationship, noted man's predilection for "designations" or meanings which are held in common as a form of intersubjective knowing. According to Marcel's terminology, symbolization is the act by which one moves "from the metaphysics of *I think* (or name, or categorize, or come up with a formulation) to the metaphysics of *we are*."[7] To add this necessary dimension to the mechanistic triad adapted from Peirce, then, Percy has formulated a complementary triangular pattern, the two of them congruently forming a coherent existential description of the human language act:

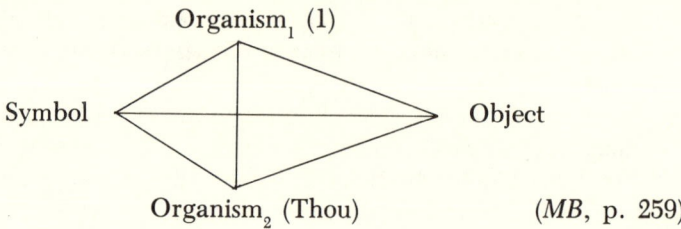

Organism₁ (1)

Symbol ⟷ Object

Organism₂ (Thou)   (*MB*, p. 259)

The Message in the Bottle, Percy says, concerns "two things, man's strange behavior and man's strange gift of language, and . . . how understanding the latter might help in understanding the former" (*MB*, p. 9). What this indicates is that Percy's primary concern is with modern man's "strange behavior," his sense of alienation. While his linguistic theories and diagrams are of value in their own right, therefore, their main function is to illuminate the condition of man. Working from his explanatory diagrams. Percy concludes that in order to function properly man must effect his natural role of "symbol-monger" and that any dysfunction of the language process could precipitate or correspond to an existential predicament. As he explains, our "need to know" is a distinctly human urge so strong that its denial may result in an acute "disability" which "can range from a simple insentience . . . to acute anxiety before a pressing something which is unformulated" (*MB*, p. 281). In short, Percy indicates that one of the root causes of modern man's alienation is the failure of his communicative abilities — a breakdown of those triadic patterns he has described. The alienation of man from his world, from his fellow man, even from his God may be explained by reference to this linguistic pattern. And conversely, that same triad apparently may function as something of an antidote. If man can but "break into the world of language,"[8] he may find himself in proper accord with his world once more as its "knower," affirming his own existence as a "namer" of all he surveys. Provided that man can open himself up to the intersubjective possibilities of communication, if he braves the risk of caring for others, the possibility remains that he may re-establish that most fundamental of human communities, "the I-Thou relation" (*MB*, p. 271) espoused by Martin Buber.

This brief summary of Percy's linguistic theories should begin to suggest some application to his fiction. Certainly several of the themes outlined above are already familiar to readers of Percy's fiction; however, as I earlier indicated, Percy has himself complicated the issue in almost the same breath by denying any connection between his linguistic work and his novels, yet in one instance going so far as to outline just such an interrelationship. For example, in the same interview wherein he asserted that these two concerns have "very little to do with each other," he freely described a triadic pattern he was trying to create in his novel *Lancelot:*

> a man finds himself in some sort of a cell — it's not clear whether it's a prison cell or a sanitorium cell. He's there for several reasons — he's not quite sure, as a matter of fact he's amnesic. But he's very much aware that the language is worn out. And in the next room there's a woman who's in a state of catatonia: she's also mute, she's retreated from language. So he conceives the idea of trying to communicate with her by knocking on the wall. It doesn't matter, except that what I had in mind was the wearing out of language and the creation of new language. . . . They're in adjoining cells, and their windows let on to

the same scene, which is a very narrow slice of New Orleans, uptown New Orleans. It's a corner of the old Lafayette Cemetery, and a slice of the levee, and a slice of a movie theatre—but you can see a lot, you know. It's a triad. . . . So this man is in this cell and he likes it there, because it's the purest kind of triadic situation—an "I" and "thou," something to look at and an opportunity to create a language, like Adam and Eve.[10]

The prison symbolizes that distancing of self from the world and others which Percy sees as a general characteristic of modern man's alienation. This man and woman demonstrate, though, that language can counter this condition, particularly by affirming that fundamental intersubjective relation of speaker and hearer. As long as the potential for communication remains open to these people, they need never fear being imprisoned within what Percy has elsewhere described as "the wintry kingdom of self."[11]

The larger narrative structure of *Lancelot* betrays this same triadic pattern, for it consists very pointedly of an intersubjective communication between the alienated title-character and Perceval, a priest and former friend. Lancelot begins this tale in alienation, locked in his asylum cell as a result of the murder of his wife and her movie company friends. But gradually, through the action of this confession-absolution dialogue with Perceval, he moves for the first time towards an affirmation of life and community. Though freed to start a new life, Lancelot clearly still has a long way to go; as Cole suggests, he must "continue to live, to ask questions, to find that answers are hard to come upon."[12] However, at least one answer is forthcoming, for the novel ends with a single, resounding "Yes" from Perceval, an affirmation totally consistent with the hope Percy holds out through his linguistic models.

Lancelot, then, offers no great difficulty in discerning the outlines of a "linguistic" structuring principle. The question is, has this same pattern infused Percy's other novels as well, or does *Lancelot* simply represent a recent marriage of his interests in fiction and language? Has he "narratized"—that is, structured a story around—those linguistic triads previously? A glance at the novel which preceded *Lancelot, Love in the Ruins*, should begin to demonstrate how pervasive this triadic pattern is in Percy's canon.

One reason for turning to *Love in the Ruins*, apart from the fact that it has so far received scant attention,[13] is that its narrative structure is unique among Percy's novels. As in *Lancelot* and *The Moviegoer*, Percy here uses a first-person narrator, Tom More, but while Binx Bolling's opening monologue derives from Camus' Meursault,[14] the alienated man talking into a void, Tom's commentary proceeds from a quite different perspective. He speaks not confessionally, like Lance, but *correctively*, "into a pocket recorder so that survivors poking around the ruins of Howard Johnson's a hundred years from now will have a chance of avoiding a repetition"[15] of the catastrophic events he sees forthcoming. Tom's warning thus represents at least a tentative intersubjective act, for with it he demonstrates a general concern for others and a genuine desire to communicate something meaningful. At the same time, by accounting for his narrative structure, Percy immediately focuses our attention on the act of communication more forcefully than in any of his previous novels, while also underscoring modern man's absolute need for such corrective messages.

Administering to such vital human needs should be only natural for Tom, since he is a healer of men who has hit upon a special diagnostic method. He diagnoses man's ills by *triangulating* electrical activity in key cortical centers.[16] Although he cannot yet cure the sickness which he thereby detects, through his diagnostic procedure Tom can at least "name" the problem, and, as he discovers, this naming itself has great restorative powers; "the very act of locating the site, touching the sore spot" (*LR*, p. 32), tends to ease his patients, as the cases of Ted Tennis and P. T. Bledsoe demonstrate.

One reason why "naming" is so invigorating is its relative rarity in that futuristic culture. In Tom's world, language has become simply a functional, directive device, merely a term in a Skinnerian stimulus-response relation. "Love," for example, is the name of a clinic which studies not human caring but sexual proficiency. In the confines of Love Clinic, Tom tries to confess his feelings for Moira, but his speech goes haywire: "Love, I, you," he stammers. In that behavioral atmosphere "love" loses its meaning and one tends "to think of the act of love as a thing" (*LR*, p. 137). Because of this devaluation of love from a mysterious, intersubjective relationship to a thing or orgasm to be measured and timed, the most vital of human communications, the asserting of care for another, cannot take place.

As Percy here depicts it, this binary, indexical language has unfortunately became the standard rather than an exception in the "ruins" of modern America.[17] In such an environment everyone wears a label, identifying himself as either liberal or conservative, Knothead or LEFT PAPASANE, and even those terms are either so inappropriate or so all-inclusive (LEFTPAPASANE = Liberty, Equality, Fraternity, The Pill, Atheism, Pot, Anti-Pollution, Sex, Abortion Now, Euthanasia) that they are practically meaningless. Moreover, these polarizing terms bring about not intersubjectivity but conflict, for they lead to name-calling and rigid mind-sets, as the exchange between Drs. Billy Matthews and Mark Habeeb demonstrates:

"Un-American!"
"Kluxer!"
"One Worlder!"
"Racist!"
"Nigger Lover."

"Knothead!"
"Liberal" (*LR*, p. 370)

Their words are simply epithets, nearly meaningless responses evoked almost automatically by a particular set of circumstances and communicating at best the intense frustrations these people feel at not being able to resolve their differences.

None of these names ever touches the ambiguous essence of the human condition, or even the situation of man in contemporary America. If this form of communication suggests anything, it is precisely how *little* real communication is actually taking place and consequently how important true communication may be for understanding man's alienation. In one particular instance, Tom feels that Max Gottlieb — whose name fittingly translates as "God's love" — actually saved his life by a "naming" act, "by naming my terror, giving it habitation, standing at the foot of my bed, knowing the worst of me, then naming it with ordinary words, English common nouns" (*LR*, p. 109), and he describes this act appropriately enough as "love." Max's simple diagnosis of "mood swings" may hardly account for Tom's larger problem, but his display of human caring and a desire to restore Tom are what underlie that naming and transform it into a regenerative act.

Of course, for communication to be successful at all there must be a certain receptivity involved. As Percy's triad stipulates, "every symbolic formation . . . requires a real or posited *someone else* for whom the symbol is intended as meaningful. Denotation is an exercise in intersubjectivity. The two are suddenly no longer related as organisms in a nexus of interaction but as a namer and hearer of a name, an I and a Thou, co-conceivers and co-celebrants of the object beheld under the auspices of a common symbol" (*MB*, p., 271). It is fitting, then, that Tom describes his lapsometer as a "listening device," a mechanism by which he can 'hear' the electrical activity" of the human brain (*LR*, p. 29). And essentially Tom throughout the novel plays the role of a "listener," one who hears other people's problems and diagnoses them, as well as one who aids others simply by taking the time to hear them out. In this age, Percy implies, man's greatest ills are often not physical and needful of medical attention. For the more pervasive problems of isolation and alienation, a different kind of physician and a new medication are required; only human communication can begin to minister properly to man in this situation. When Tom tends to Charley Parker, for instance, his wife confesses that basically "he loves to talk to you" (*LR*, p. 40), meaning that it is as much Tom's willing ear as his lapsometer or medical attention that has helped make Charley feel better. And because of the intersubjective nature of this act, it is beneficial for both physician and patient, both listener and speaker, as Tom comes to realize: "A note for physicians: if you listen carefully to what patients say, they will often tell you not only what is wrong with them but also what is wrong with you" (*LR*, p. 39).

On the whole, though, this futuristic world seems singularly devoid of both people who have something significant to communicate and listeners for any messages. There are few enough people who can even properly interpret what little they do hear. On one level, people do not care enough any more to hear what their neighbors are saying; and the other side of the problem is that few, save for a handful of priests like Father Smith, even know *what* to listen for. Tom's apocalyptic warnings of "noxious sodium vapors" and fallout thus fall on deaf ears, for his "metaphysical" terminology, his talk of angelism, sin, penance, and the life of the spirit, bears little meaning for his behaviorist colleagues who are conditioned to view things in totally concrete and physically causal terms. In their eyes Tom himself seems the abnormal one, more a patient than a doctor.

Since he has been conditioned to accept that behavioral view as the only proper one, Tom begins to suffer a linguistic dysfunction — just as Percy's triads would predict. His speech suddenly becomes defective: "No fanks," "I'm fime," "Eins upon a oncy," and "Rike," he utters. Perhaps the Director of Love Clinic is not entirely wrong in labeling him a patient, then, for his linguistic difficulties may be symptomatic of an illness, though in this case one spawned by those apparently healthy and contented behaviorists who, according to Percy, "cannot construe the assertory act of language" (*MB*, p. 230).

In *Message in the Bottle* Percy indicates that the behavioral worldview eventually binds man within a "cocoon of dread silence" which can be countered solely by "breaking into a daylight of language" (*MB*, pp. 22, 45). Obviously Tom stands in need of some such regeneration. His life is in chaos and his early promise in discovering More's Syndrome "didn't pan out. On the contrary. There followed twenty years of silence and decline" (*LR*, p. 24). In keeping with those decades of silence, Tom's house has come to resemble a "cocoon" of deathly quiet; it is enveloped in vines and even the machinery which seems to make modern life function has stopped. Silence has become all pervasive: "Nothing works. All my household motors are silent" (*LR*, p. 62). And Tom's situation mirrors the general predicament of his culture where this disease of silence has become rampant. Mr. Ives, who once "liked to talk," has become mute and "can't or won't speak," apparently because "he's too damn mad to talk" and "doesn't trust" anyone, not even Tom (*LR*, pp. 159–160). While Father Smith has not yet lost faith in humanity, even he has fallen prey to this widespread modern affliction, suddenly going silent in the midst of Mass and excusing himself with the explanation that "the channels are jammed and the word is not getting through" between man and God (*LR*, p. 184). Tom rather understates the congregation's reaction when he notes that "nothing is more uncomfortable than silence when speech is expected" (*LR*, p. 183). When even the priests, coupling agents between man and God, fall silent, the result must surely be more than discomfort. In the face of God's silence, confronted with the loss of that "good news" which triadically bonds the human and the divine, the human proposition must seem radically altered, meaning itself clearly in doubt. Tom's later conclusion, that "silence prolonged can induce terror" (*LR*, p. 184), seems a much more appropriate description of this situation.

What these people await is something to restore life—or more accurately, someone to speak to them in their silence and isolation. Old Mr. Ives who is being committed to that "anteroom to the funeral parlor," the Happy Isles of Jekyll, Georgia, primarily because he refuses to submit to behavioral stimuli in the predictable ways, symbolically suggests the way out of this plight. Like Tom and Percy's other heroes, he has been seeking a "coupling agent," that key element in both of Percy's language triads, and what others have mistaken for senility is simply Mr. Ives' intentness in his search and his disgust at the multiple, pointless interruptions he has been subjected to. In searching for a "fountain of youth," he had uncovered the "Ocala frieze," a tablet of Proto-Creek symbols, but to decipher these mysterious "glyphs" he needed a coupler, "one or two direct pairings of glyphs and Spanish words" (*LR*, p. 230). His diggings turned up just such a pairing, a coupling of language elements engraved on a golden medallion. The "fountain of youth" he sought thus had little to do with magic potions or elixirs, but was rather a linguistic "life restorer." Mr. Ives managed to couple a dead language with a living one, thereby restoring that formerly lifeless one. And this feat becomes doubly significant since it is also metaphoric of Mr. Ives' own rebirth into society. His "unnatural" silence has almost brought about his commitment, though his deafness and dumbness were only feigned to thwart the behaviorists who had interfered in his work. With the aid of Tom and his lapsometer Mr. Ives begins to speak again and thereby saves his own life. What Percy seems to suggest by this is that any rebirth of language or the communicative ability it implies also promises a regeneration of life in man, the languaging creature; a restored language may offer a true "fountain of youth" for all men.

Working against this life-restoring activity is the Mephistophelean Art Immelman, Percy's near-comic embodiment of evil who, as we might expect, acts as an anti-communication force as well. Under his spell, for example, Tom often finds himself "at a loss for words" and at one point unable to "utter a word" at all (*LR*, p., 362). When under the influence of Art's "musical-erotic" trance, Tom happily shuts out everyone else to listen to the tune running through his head, a song of human isolation: *"Everybody's talking at me. / I can't hear a word they saying. / Only the echoes of my mind"* (*LR*, p. 336).

Essentially, Art mediates against the mystery of language, especially its capacity for conveying vital information from one person to another. One evidence of this is the fact that he functions on a completely literal level, twice taking Tom's "goddamn" not as an interjection but as an actual condemnation from which he "turns white and falls back a step" (*LR*, p. 169). In fact, all of Tom's cursing—to which, as a quite ordinary person, he is freely given—escapes Art's comprehension, apparently because of its metaphoric character. When Tom shouts "Screw the pilot" and "you son of a bitch," Art stands mystified, asking, "How do you mean, Doc?" and "How is that possible?": but he is unable to puzzle out Tom's intent—"I don't understand your imputation about my mother" (*LR*, p. 328–329)—because such "colorful" language involves more than just signs and literal representation. Perhaps more obviously so than most language usage, cursing is clearly metaphoric and certainly uniquely human in character. Since he is committed to the powers of darkness, Art is unable to communicate as humans do. What Tom finds is that intersubjectivity, what should be the natural product of proper communication, is impossible with him: "It's no use trying to tell you" anything, he declares (*LR*, p. 329).

To counter this threat to human relationships—to life itself—which Art embodies, a creative act is needed. In *The Moviegoer* Binx Bolling carries out a literal "naming" process; he asserts to another that Kate Cutrer is his fiancée and by so doing gains release from his merry-go-round of pointless love affairs and inauthentic existence. Will Barrett of *The Last Gentleman* likewise carries out such a symbolic "naming": in this case he names himself for Sutter Vaught—"I, Will Barrett. . . . need you and want you to come back"—in token of his sincerity and care. Tom More also follows this pattern, as he heralds a general rebirth of human communication (for which "naming" is simply Percy's generic title, remember) by a very literal naming of himself. Only through such a linguistic, and hence human, commitment can Tom truly stand for life in the face of death, for love despite the tendency to isolation, and for communication in defiance of a pervasive silence.

To accomplish this feat, Tom is driven to what we might term the ultimate language act—prayer. As Art prepares to collect on his Faustian bargain and as Tom and Ellen fearfully watch him approach, Tom "names" himself and his ancestor, St. Thomas More, by praying for heavenly intercession in this predicament: *"Sir Thomas More, kinsman, saint, best dearest merriest of Englishmen, pray for us and drive this son of a bitch hence"* (*LR*, p. 376). The coupling which Tom here enacts is twofold and thus doubly momentous. For the first time he has clearly acknowledged both his need of spiritual aid and his love for his nurse Ellen. Tom's salvation is therefore not, like so many stereotyped versions, a denial of the physical world in favor of the spiritual; rather, by the way he exorcizes this evil influence Tom embraces both, reasserting the possibility for both physical and spiritual life.[18]

This prayer to Thomas More and its correlative, the final community prayer at Father Smith's church for the unification and regeneration of the United States, mirror the general coupling activity to which the novel moves. The marital union of Tom and Ellen has as its counterpart an ecumenical movement among the various religions of the era. United in common cause, all seeking a restoration of their community, the various religious services "overlap. Jews wait for the Lord, Protestants sing hymns to him, Catholics say mass and eat him" (*LR*, p. 396). Out of the ruins of contemporary materialism, a new spiritual life is emerging; and it is only fitting that this unified church service ends on the sounds of celebration outside where Tom's own child, first-born from his new marriage and thus the first fruit of this new community, shoots off fireworks while crying, together with the other children, "Hurrah for Jesus Christ!" and "Hurrah for the United States!" (*LR*, p. 400). In little Tom More we have an image of what the proper conjunction—or triangulation, if you will—of man and woman, of the secular and the spiritual can bring about. Through his cheers, the child reminds us of that life-affirming conclusion to *The Brothers Karamazov* and suggests that a new and better world has come into being here.

The novel ends on this obvious commitment to life and its potential. Those couplings within man's power have been achieved, each one opening up possibilities for further human contact and understanding, and those outside man's power are being prayed for. Different faiths have been brought together to worship and speak in unison that "prayer confessing the sins of the Church and asking for the reunion of Christians and of the United States" (*LR*, p. 400). Tom and Ellen are happily married and raising a family; and Tom has begun still another effort at unification, this time on a national scale, with the founding of a group with a mysterious acronymic title, SOUP—Southerners and Others United to Preserve the Union in Repayment of an old Debt to the Yankees Who Saved It Once Before and Are Destroying It Now.[19] Even Victor Charles, the black veterinary attendant, has managed a unification of sorts, gathering whites and blacks in common support of his Congressional campaign under the banner of "the old rooster," that mysterious, long-time *symbol* of Louisiana Democrats. By virtue of such multiple "symbolic" activity, unity has become the order of the day and the potential of life its decree.

What *Love in the Ruins*, like *Lancelot*, clearly demonstrates, therefore, is that, despite his disclaimers, several of Percy's novels implicitly betray the outline of his linguistic work. Moreover, the example of these novels suggests that a profitable approach to the rest of Percy's fiction might well consider the content of his linguistic investigations. Throughout his writings, fiction and language theory included, Percy obviously tries to speak directly to the predicament of modern man. What I have tried to suggest is that in so doing perhaps he cannot help but follow his own formula for the workings of a truly meaningful communication.[20] In any case, this interweaving of linguistic and fictional concerns outlined here hardly seems to represent a weakness in his work. In his canon Percy consistently displays a unity of concerns and a unity of vision, and it is precisely this integrity, I would argue, that enables him to address so articulately the fundamental problems of human existence.

Notes

1. Some of the more influential of these interviews include John Carr, "An Interview with Walker Percy," *Georgia Review*, 25 (1971), 317–332; Carlton Cremeens, "Walker Percy, the Man and the Novelist: An Interview," *Southern Review*, n.s. 4 (1968), 271–290; and Bradley Dewey, "Walker Percy Talks about Kierkegaard," *Journal of Religion*, 54 (1974), 273–298.

2. Robert Coles's recent two-part "Profile" of Percy in *The New Yorker*, 2 October, 9 October 1978, for example, offers an overview of Percy's thoughts on symbolization and even connects them to his interest in Marcel and existential philosophy; however, Coles finally reads the novels totally from the existential perspective previously mapped out by Martin Luschei in his study of Percy. *The Sovereign Wayfarer* (Baton Rouge: Louisiana State University Press, 1972). Lewis Lawson, at the close of his review-essay on *The Message in the Bottle*, "Walker Percy as Martian Visitor," *Southern Literary Journal*, 8 (1976), 102–113, suggests a tentative relation between the linguistics and the fiction, but it is clearly a connection which he sees as not yet realized: "Perhaps . . . in a future novel, acting upon his contention that consciousness is a collaboration, that thinking is symbolization resulting from intersubjectivity, that the self cannot know itself through symbolization, Percy will create a new first-person narration that will offer a radical complexity — and truthfulness — to the rendering of consciousness in fiction" (p. 113). I would suggest that *Love in the Ruins* already marks a step in precisely this direction.

3. Told to Marcus Smith in "Talking about Talking: an Interview with Walker Percy," *New Orleans Review*, 5 (1976), 17.

4. Lawson, p. 107.

5. *The Message in the Bottle* (New York: Farrar, Straus & Giroux, 1975), pp. 108, 112. Subsequent references will be cited in the text as *MB*.

6. According to Peirce, "every intellectual operation involves a triad" of sign, interpretant, and object, this threefold relation accounting for the nature of "meaning" which, he reasons, "is inexpressible by means of dyadic relations." See *Philosophical Writings of Peirce*, ed. Justus Buchler (New York: Dover, 1955), pp. 114, 274.

7. Coles, 2 October, p. 67. The correspondence between Marcel's existential philosophy and Percy's fiction has previously been detailed in John Zeugner's "Walker Percy and Gabriel Marcel: The Castaway and the Wayfarer," *Mississippi Quarterly*, 28 (1974–75), 21–53, and an often overlooked but pioneering essay by Michael Blouin, "The Novels of Walker Percy: An Attempt at Synthesis," *Xavier University Studies*, 6 (1967), 29–42.

8. Percy uses this phrase in *The Last Gentleman* to describe the Tyree children who have been taught to use language for the first time: "When they do suddenly break into the world of language, it is something to see. They are like Adam on the First Day." Significantly, Percy returns to this same phrase when he discusses the needs of modern man in *The Message in the Bottle* (p. 45).

9. For a more detailed discussion see my essay, "Walker Percy's Language of Creation," *The Southern Quarterly*, 16 (1978), 105–116, as well as the first part of Coles's "Profile" on Percy.

10. "Talking about Talking," p. 16.

11. "Stoicism in the South," *Commonweal*, 64 (6 July 1956), 343.

12. Coles, 9 October, p. 122.

13. Thomas LeClair's recent article, "Walker Percy's Devil," *Southern Literary Journal*, 10 (1978), 3–13, and Luschei's chapter on *Love in the Ruins* are the major exceptions.

14. In *The Sovereign Wayfarer*, Luschei details just how closely the opening paragraphs of *The Moviegoer* and *The Stranger* parallel one another (p. 15).

15. *Love in the Ruins* (New York: Farrar, Straus & Giroux, 1971), p. 28. Subsequent references will be cited in the text as *LR*.

16. At the close of *Message in the Bottle* Percy tentatively suggests such a "cortical" explanation of the linguistic function. Working from the findings of Norman Geschwind, he postulates that a triadic structure in the human brain, consisting of visual and auditory components as well as a third, coupling element, would account for the literary language theory he has advanced.

17. In a side note LeClair observes that "the novel is largely composed of devalued language," but he reads it as simply a "parody" of the "bogus naming—scientific, mystical, and popular—that clamors in our ears" (pp. 11, 12) so commonly today.

18. LeClair holds that "More's banishing of his devil is less than heroic," that "the immediate motivation is to protect (for himself?) nurse Ellen" (p. 7), and Luschei describes Tom's rejection of Art as "a very minor victory" (p. 228). The stark conditions surrounding this confrontation—good versus evil, life pitted against death, silence or communication—would certainly seem to belie these readings, however. After all, Art makes no "offer," as Luschei would have it, something which might be easily declined, but he demands Tom's very soul, and only a momentous act can possibly counter such a threat. If Tom's salvation here seems almost too easy, it could be because Percy wishes to suggest just how powerful the human act of communication is.

19. Curiously, SOUP is unlike the numerous other acronyms in the novel; it invokes a sense of something unknown or unaccounted for, since its letters only partially indicate the full meaning of the word. In *Message in the Bottle* Percy indicates that in all human naming "there must be a space between the name and the thing" and that is the resulting "element of obscurity about the name" which makes it so meaningful (pp. 73, 71).

20. At the close of his essay, Coles cites a conversation with Percy in which the novelist speaks directly to this question. Percy notes that "the writer explores ideas that come to him or he imagines stories, which he then develops. But the writer also reaches out to others, and if the result can't be speech, a conversation between two people, there is, I hope, another kind of exchange between him and someone else: the effort that has produced words on paper stirs a response in the reader—Pascal's 'motions of the heart' " (9 October, p. 125).

Story, Story-Teller and Listener: Notes on *Lancelot*

Simone Vauthier*

Toward the end of *Lancelot*, the eponymous character comments to the priest-psychiatrist friend who has been his confidant for five long days: "I have the feeling that while I was talking and changing, you were listening and changing."[1] The remark stressing the effects of Lance's narration points to an important dimension of the novel. Story-telling is an action which constitutes the primary frame of the narrative and is as much

*Reprinted by permission from the *South Carolina Review* 13 (1981): 39–54.

the vital center of the work as the "terrible events" at Belle Isle which Lancelot narrates in the secondary frame.

Lancelot, however, oversimplifies their respective roles. Though keeping silent is one of the ways in which Percival contributes to the exchange, he is not simply a listener. This is an illusion fostered by the narrative technique, which has the I-narrator integrate into his own utterances those of his partner in the act of communication. But we must posit an implicit addresser who projects first a manifest locutor (to whom in fact a great number of functions are delegated since he is also protagonist in the two time frames, observer, commentator, and mouthpiece for other characters) and a second locutor who is only made to speak out in the last two pages of the book but who has been participating in the interaction all along. The priest's final utterances reported in italics then anchor what I have called the primary frame. They retrospectively guarantee that a conversation has really been going on, and not taking place in Lance's deranged mind. Seen in relation to the implicit addresser of the narrative, the two speakers are on an equality although the mode of narration foregrounds Lancelot. Because they reach us through Lancelot's speech, Percival's contributions to the conversation are deemphasized, thus making it our responsibility to restore the balance.

To reconstruct Percival's end of the exchange, however, is an all but impossible task. For one thing Lance relays his friend's utterances selectively and summarily. Often his own response is the only clue we have to the priest's having spoken. For instance when Lance asks, "Then you know my story?" the remark, introduced as it is with "then," presupposes that Percival has evinced knowledge of his friend's affairs. But the only other textual indication that he has indeed spoken is the blank space that separates Lancelot's two utterances. For another thing, although Lancelot sometimes quotes his friend's speech in such a way that attribution is easy ("Did I love her, you ask?" [89]; "But we have plenty of evil around you say" [138]; "You say we are redeemed" [224]), the larger part of the confidant's sayings is assimilated into the narrator's discourse in the form of questions: "A clue to what? To the mystery of Belle Isle? No. To hell with that" (106).[2] Such a device, while making for the naturalness of the narration, at the same time blurs the distinction between the quoted speech and the quoting speech which often resorts to the interrogative. For Lance is fond of rhetorical questions ("Can one ever be sure of anything?" [130], makes bona fide inquiries from his friend ("Why did you leave twenty years ago?" [105]; "Do you think I'm crazy?" [175]), and occasionally engages in some self-questioning ("Why didn't I do something about Siobhan, not about the well, which I couldn't have cared less about . . . why didn't I do something about Siobhan" [54]). Not infrequently too the question can be taken to be oriented both toward the other and toward the self (see p. 89). In the fast-running flow of the narrator's discourse, when question succeeds question, now rhetorical, now addressed to the other and now to the self, the reader may be forgiven if he fails to pinpoint the original locutor of every utterance. A close analysis of the text would, however, show that, far from being silent as it is too often claimed,[3] Percival constantly — if perhaps briefly — participates in the exchange.

Throughout the narrative, Percival's contributions, in fact, serve to authenticate some of Lance's statements. Either directly as in the following example: "Is this a prison or a hospital or a prison hospital? A Center for Aberrant Behavior? *So that's it.* I have behave aberrantly. In short, I'm in the nuthouse" (3, emphasis mine). Or indirectly when Percival leaves uncorrected some of his friend's assertions. (Thus there is no reason to question Lance's definition of Percival as a priest-psychiatrist and see in him a fellow-inmate).[4] Although Lance's account is by no means trustworthy in its details, the priest's comments or silences provide a sort of general validation of the basic facts. On three occasions, for instance, Lance quotes headlines on the Belle Isle events (13, 60, 105), probably in an unconscious attempt to put some distance between himself and his crimes. While he quotes from memory, we may presume that his rendering is faithful to the spirit, if not the letter, of the phrases. An assumption which becomes a certainty on the third occasion. For then it is Percival who brings up the subject, as appears from Lance's questions: "Jacoby? I haven't told you about him? The headlines? BELLE ISLE BURNS! DIRECTOR MURDERED AND MUTILATED! EX-GRID STAR HELD FOR QUESTIONING! Yes, I remember all that" (105). Since none of the headlines mentioned earlier by Lance alluded to the fate of the director, Percival when introducing Jacoby's name is not simply reminding his friend of what he told him but recalling something which he himself read. Therefore the headlines are not fantasized by the protagonist. In the fictional universe they acquire objective status as they become the basis for an act of communication between the two men.

They both "know" Lancelot's "story," or rather the newspaper version of it. But there exists also another version. For Lance is less than truthful when he says that he has "refused all psychiatrists, ministers, priests, group therapy and whatnot" (5). He later casually alludes to his "monthly physical and mental examination" (62), refers to "the psychologist here" and to "my psychiatrist" in contexts which prove his familiarity with both. Certainly, lawyer that he is, we may suppose that he has kept from imparting to other people the revelations which he can entrust to Percival, true friend and priest. We are quite ready to believe him when he thanks Percival at the end: "You know that I could not have told anyone else" (253; see also 105 and 108). His recital however must be set against those two other versions of his story. Of the institutional story, there is no trace in the text.[5] All we know is that it is of the anything-goes kind: "No matter what I tell [the psychologist], even if I break wind, he gives me the same quick congratulatory look" (107). Of the newspaper story, we only have fragments. But such as they are, they suffice to put us in a situation which is not unlike that of Percival: we are aware of facts and hypotheses about the destruction of Belle Isle and the murders, long before Lance can bring himself to narrate his actions. Knowledge of the public story enables Percival to prompt his friend and ask questions that cover / uncover areas which Lance would rather leave untouched. When after the account of the murders, Percival wants to know how Lance got burned, he obliquely points out all that remains unspoken in his friend's almost compulsive stream of words. And incidentally the chilling answer ("I had to go back to find the knife") gives the lie to an earlier statement of Lance's "my hands burned trying to save Margot" (105). Similarly knowledge of the headlines alerts the reader to the most glaring gap in Lance's circumstantial narration of the arson and murders — his omitting Jacoby's mutilation. Sketchy and sensation-oriented as it is, the public story reveals the incompleteness and selectiveness of the I-narrator discourse.

But this, of course, comes into being in response to the other stories. What Lance tells the staff of the Center for Aberrant Behavior is meaningless to him because of the psychiatric attitude of "dissolving" tolerance. What the newspapers tell, Lance can recognize as his story; but it is also the story of a third person, the stereotyped "scion of old family," to whom certain feelings and actions are conventionally and generously ascribed ("CRAZED BY GRIEF AND RAGE" he "SUFFERS BURNS TRYING TO SAVE WIFE" [13]). Alienating and grossly off the mark, the newspaper account is serviceable to Lance who can exploit it as a device of affirmation / negation, yet ultimately useless in his quest for knowledge. Deprived of his identity by the institutional and journalistic versions of his case, Lancelot must reclaim his story and his identity through telling his own tale to the proper listener.

Percival qualifies as a confidant for a number of reasons. "Classmate, fraternity brother and later best of friends," Percival is Lancelot's *alter ego*, who will serve him as "a kind of catalyst." The listener, "bound by the seal of friendship if not the confessional," can even be trusted to understand that his friend gives himself "a certain license to talk crazy" (160). Because he has an image of the younger Lance, and can see him in relation to his becoming, he offers the reader the possibility to weave together past, present and future, and thus define his true nature. He is expected to help Lance look for the clue which the latter feels he has missed: "There is something I don't understand. And you are both my leverage point and my companion. Because you knew Belle Isle and you know me" (108). And he can also be told about Lancelot's grandiose mad plans for a Third Revolution: ". . . so since you understand me and my past — if you don't, nobody does, I am going to tell you my plans for the future" (156). At the same time, Percival is the confidant whom the narrator needs because as a priest-psychiatrist, he is somehow close to the Establishment, hence a fitting repository for the secret which, *qua* secret, is oriented toward those very people from whom it has been kept.[6] It is not only to disclose whatever he could not, would not tell the doctors, and thereby unburden himself that Lance tells his twice-told tale. (As a matter of fact, the gaps in his narration, his abrupt changes of subject, his frequent denials tend to prove that Lance consciously omits and unconsciously represses a good deal). He tells it also to make it, in his own words, "not a confession but a secret" (155), to create, as it were, a space of concealment, which separates him and his confidant from "them" and creates a community. In this way Lance is able to reassert his much-threatened sovereignty and assume some power over his listener. So a verbal repetition, intended to preclude repetition of past mistakes, repeats in the very structure of the act of communication, and quite apart from its contents, the process of exclusion that has been lethally operative in Lance's past and has led to his present isolation.

If the telling of any story, let alone a secret, is always affected in complex ways by its recipient (the image which the teller has of him, and of their relationship, the image he has of the listener's image of himself and their relationship, etc.), the influence of the listener in this case is all the greater because the speaker stands to him in a relation of long-established dependence. Percival is Lancelot's *mediator* in the sense René Girard gives to the word. To summarize baldly Girard's theories, desire, though it believes itself spontaneous, is always mimetic. Because it is imitation of the Other's desire, it has generated conflicts and violence from time immemorial.[7] In our egalitarian societies, mimesis has become ontological mimesis. For a dead God, modern man has substituted the Self but continues to seek for absolutes. Conscious of his own radical insufficiency, the subject turns to the Other whom he believes to be endowed with the metaphysical autonomy, the plentitude of being which *he* lacks. In short, he has renounced the divine Mediator only to depend more and more on a human mediator who is both model and rival, venerated as model, hated as obstacle to the subject's metaphysical desire. Thus receiving and sending a multiplicity of contradictory signs which urge and forbid imitation, men are caught in the vicious circle of rivalry and violence. Since in the resulting state of universal idolatry, differences between men disappear, the general mimesis becomes exacerbated and, with it, the double bind which results from ontological desire.

Now *Lancelot* seems to me to mark a departure in Walker Percy's work, precisely because the mimetic process is here very much in evidence. What with the double frame, the double plot, the double quest, the doubling of the hero *actant*, the appearances of doubles, the two movies (one of which is described as a double feature), the thematic importance of actors and the cinema, etc., the traces of mimesis proliferate at all levels. I am not trying to impute to Walker Percy ideas that are René Girard's. But Girard's theory of man, which accounts for man's[8] alienation, provides an alternative to the Christian-existentialist reading which is generally propounded of the work. Although the theory of mimetic desire accounts for much of what happens in the Belle Isle frame of the narrative, where mimesis works in more obvious ways, I will today use it as a key to what happens in the teller-listener situation where desire is perhaps less openly displayed.

Lance's relationship to his friend is conditioned by their past relationship and his view of it. In early adolescence, they seem, in the words of Lewis Lawson, to have "held the world in common by using the Arthurian legend as focus."[9] In Girardian terms, they had external mediators in common. When he recalls his nickname "Sir Launcelot" and fairly consistently addresses Harry by his, Percival, the narrator attempts to revive their mutual expectations of a high, selfless destiny, their sense of a spiritual bonding. But he is also unconsciously setting up Harry-Percival as his *internal* mediator and so he is led to emphasize at the beginning the redemptory role of Parsifal "who found the Grail and brought life to a dead land" (10). On the other hand, for the same reason, he does not later recognize the superiority of Percival over Lancelot in the Grail quest and groups the two together, mistakenly, as the "only two knights to see the Grail" (116). On closer examination, Lance's youthful memories are colored with the ambiguities of the mimetic situation. In the reporting of the *Tennessee Belle* incident, he shows himself as rescuer and follower at the same time, "I, of course, having to go after you as usual" (61). The middle-aged narrator still wonders whether Percival's reading of Verlaine, or his diving off the *Tennessee Belle* was an "act" (13, 16, 51), and whether his becoming a priest was not "the ultimate reckless lifetime thing" (61). The uncertainty about the "reality" of the Other's actions is of course a problem of the mimetic life, and in fact Lance puts forward a mimetic explanation of Percival's going to Africa: he intended to "outdo Albert Schweitzer, because of course that was outdoing even him, wasn't it, because you had the True Faith and he didn't, being only a Protestant" (61). Interestingly, all three "acts" involve a mediation: in the case of the *Tennessee Belle* stunt, Harry was doing a Huck Finn kind of rotation on Jefferson, and not Jackson's, Island and turns out looking "bluer than Nigger Jim." In his reading, the mediation is slightly more esoteric but quite obvious since Verlaine is a man who jumped from the aesthetic to the religious stage, a poet who after his conversion wrote a poem on Parzifal and another entitled "Saint Graal."[10] And though the reader may question Lance's explanation of Percival's motives for going to Africa, Schweitzer still appears as a likely mediator. But Lancelot, who is so keenly and contemptuously aware of the inauthenticity of the actors he meets, of their being "blown about this way and that, like puffballs, in and out of their roles, 'into' Christian Science, back out again" (112), seems to feel only admiration for Harry's acts which are endowed with a sort of absoluteness, whether they are "the *ultimate* show-off thing or the *ultimate* splendid thing" (61, emphasis mine). With his talent for doing the unexpected, Lance says "the uncalled for" thing, Harry has been a wonder to his friend. So when, on the priest's first visit, Lance puts on an "act" of his own, pretending he does not know who his caller is, he may be attempting to ease his way back into their relationship through imitation. At any rate, throughout his recital, the narrator in turn is clearly out to impress his listener. On several occasions, he expects to "surprise" him (10, 11, 20, 254), and when the response is not what he anticipated, he even inquires: "Are you surprised? No? Yes?" (21). His one-upmanship is revealed in casual remarks, like "I have an idea even crazier than one of yours" (62). And just as the many questions he asks Percival evince, not a real interest in Percival's ideas, but an obsessive desire to hold his attention, so his careful observation of his listener's facial and bodily expressions, his smiles, shrugs and turning toward the window, reveals not so much concern for his friend's state of mind as his own sensitivity to the impression he is making.

As mediator, Percival is both model and rival, hence the singular mixture of diffidence and (increasing) authority, of secrecy and self-revelation in Lancelot's recital, the character at once agonistic and seductive of his discourse.[11] Since his recent experience has brought him to the isolation of his cell and the vacuity of meetings with people to whom he has nothing to say, Lance wants to recreate the experience with and for someone whom he can talk to in order to "know what [he] already know[s]" (85). But though he needs to tell his friend, Lance, as a victim of mimetic desire, does not want to share his suffering with Percival and on the contrary attempts to hide it from him (and from himself). Because he is afraid he is alone in not enjoying metaphysical autonomy, and still depends on the verdict of the Other for his very being, he has to show how free he became and still is, notwithstanding the fact that he is a prisoner. His recital is a display, and a construction of a fantasy of mastery. Once "the master of Belle Isle" he imposed his order on the mishmash others made through their corruption, and now he remains master of the situation, including the situation of discourse. This must enable him to prove that, when he murdered his wife, her lover and two other people, he acted in the past, as he says he will in his Third Revolution future, "from perfect sobriety and freedom" (157).

But this illusion of mastery, in the present, can only be built at the expense of Percival, who must be cut down to size. Like any mimetic disciple, Lancelot would like to repudiate the bonds of mediation.[12] In Percival, a priest physician, that is to say "a screwed-up priest or a half-assed physician. Or both" (10), he finds an easy butt.[13] Furthermore, from their first talk, Lance is sure that "something went wrong" with his friend (see, for instance, 6, 11, 61). The phrase is all the more telling because Lance also applies it to himself (e.g. 106, 108, 137).[14] Lance's two favorite explanations of his friend's so-called "trouble" are love of a woman and loss of faith, both of which would mean of course that the priest has lost his radiant transcendence. Sometimes he baits Percival with a double taunt: "Why are you always asking about love? Have you been crossed up too? Isn't your God's love enough for you? Margot's love was enough for me" (122). Throughout, the sarcastic — and usually very cogent — comments he makes on the failure of Christianity in general and of Catholicism in particular, syntactically include Percival: it is "your Catholic Church," "your saints," "your Jewish Bible," "your sweet Jesus," and almost always "your Lord" and "your God." (Only your Virgin can easily be accepted as Our Lady.) Lance neatly turns the tables on Percival who stands charged at the very least with guilt by association ("So you fucked it up good" [177]) and is in fact summarily condemned: "Damn you and your God. Between the two of you, you should have got it straight" (176). Lancelot's antagonism towards his mediator can also be observed in his peculiar teasing, in his use of the phrase "good news" or the word "confession." From their second meeting he tantalizes Percival with the hope that he will confess: "I have a confession to make" (9), but the confessions announced never amount to more than the admission of some failure or secret. Once he lures his friend with a "Come here Percival. I want to tell you something. It is not a confession but a secret. It's not a sin because I do not know what a sin is" (155) and finally tells him about "his plans for the future." On another occasion, he admits: "A confession: [Margot] took the lead the first time" (170). Or he says: "Very well, I will make another confession: My son is a homosexual now and I can understand why" (177). (The confession here presumably bears on his ability to understand since he has already told about his son's homosexuality.) Obviously, he often owns to a thing which does him little credit but is never outrageous. Several of these "confessions," however, concern sexuality and two of them the passivity of men. Thus they finally point to Lancelot's deep-lying fear of women.

Only towards the end does he use the word "confession" in its sacramental sense, but then again he anticipates the priest's expectations — or those he ascribes to him — only to frustrate them: "No, no confession forthcoming, Father, as you well know" (253). His whole performance, the success and the failure of it, is inscribed in these two statements: "I have a confession to make"; "No confession forthcoming." This pointed rejection of Percival as a mediator in the Catholic sense of the word is the negative image of his importance as mimetic mediator (and one of the ways in which Lance can remain blind to the effects of mimetic desire in his life.)

Nowhere is this importance more striking than in the pattern and imagery through which Lancelot manages to (re)construct his story. For would Lance have shaped his story as a quest for the Unholy Grail, had not his listener been the friend whom he prefers to call Percival, even though he does "not look as if [he] found the Grail"? (176–177).[15] As a matter of fact, he seems to come only gradually to this commanding image, though allusions to the Arthurian knights crop up early. At first presenting tentatively the idea of "a search for evil" ("Have you ever considered the possibility that one might undertake a search not for God but for evil?" [51]), he eventually hits upon the metaphor that focuses various aspects of his past and present experience in the middle of his narrative: "I think I see now what I am doing. I am reliving with you my quest" (137);[16] "Do you know what I was? The Knight of the Unholy Grail" (138). By inverting the legend which referred to a Christian world-view and is doubly associated with Percival, Lancelot tries to proclaim his autonomy but in fact demonstrates once more his dependence on the mediation of Percival in a classic of negative mimetism.[17] Together with his theory of sexual love as an absolute — itself a perfect example of what Girard calls "deviated transcendence"[18] — the Unholy Grail pattern generates or magnetizes a number of religious metaphors, some of them quite provocative. In the following example, Lancelot claims he means no offense but his calling Percival, for once, Father, leaves the reader suspicious:

> She was a *feast*. I wanted to eat her. I ate her.
> That was my *communion*, Father — no offense intended, that sweet dark *sanctuary* guarded by the heavy gold columns of her thighs, the *ark* of the covenant. (171, emphasis mine)

Though he pokes fun at the film people for making the stranger in their movie, "the new Christ, of course" (153, also 148), he presents Anna as "the first woman of the new order," asking "Who else might be the new Virgin but a gang-raped social worker? I do not joke" (159). In the murder sequence, religious images cluster richly (237–38). The bed where Margot makes love to Jacoby is "like a Gothic cathedral" complete with spires, gargoyles, flying buttresses, altar screen, and "unconsecrated priest hearing an impenitent confession" (238). For the I-narrator at this climactic moment in his narrative which corresponds to a crucial experience, instead of confessing or at least expressing contrition, chooses to describe the I-actor as "kneeling in [his] confessional" (238). The mimetic character of such self-images is evident.

But even when he grandly assumes a more positive role, the narrator reveals himself the prey of mimetic desire: "I'll prophesy," says the man who, a few days before, wondered whether his friend's religious name referred to John the Evangelist or John the Baptist, "a loner out in the wilderness" (10). And prophesy he does, denouncing "the great whorehouse and fagdom of America" (176), "the defunct befouled and collapsing North and the corrupt thriving and Jesus-hollering South" (219), in fact the madness of our whole Judeo-Christian Western culture, and announcing the Third Revolution (157), "The new Reformation" (177), which will accomplish what Christianity has failed to do: "We'll take the Grail you didn't find but we'll keep the broadsword and the great warrior Archangel of Mont-Saint-Michel" (178). Moreover, in one of the major reversals of roles in his performance, Lance, with arrogant generosity, offers redemption to the priest through participation in his Third Revolution:[19] "No, it is not you who are offering me something, salvation, a choice, whatever. I am offering you a choice. Do you want to become one of us?" (179). This, however, is not the last word in one-upmanship. As a quester or even prophet, Lance is still on the same human level, as his friend, priest though he is. The transformation of model into counter-model culminates in his identification, however figurative, with Lucifer. First when he depicts himself "wheeling slowly up into the night like Lucifer blown out of hell, great wings spread against the starlight" (246) in an image which mirrors the basic inversion since the movement described is up and out of hell, whereas Lucifer was cast down into hell.[20] Then, when he asks Percival, "Why so wary? You act as if I were Satan showing you the kingdoms of the world from the pinnacle of the temple" (254). This tentative identification with him who is, for René Girard, "the very name of the mimetic process as a whole,"[21] is to be correlated to Lance's demiurgic desire to create a new order, whether a new Eden or a new Dispensation is difficult to say.[22]

The identification, however, is only the rhetorical tip of a general pattern of escalation. Lancelot who once in the past has been driven to murder — the extreme but logical outcome of mimesis — is again carried away by the mimetic process. Dismayed by the symptoms of the ontological disease which prevails in modern culture, the general indiscrimination, the indeterminacy of sex roles, the blurring of the distinction between Lady and Whore, the loss of values, etc., and unaware that he has not escaped the contagion, Lance wants a world in which "there will be no confusion" (179). In order to assert his difference, he needs to erect a barrier between himself and the madding crowd, needs to "assign responsibilities,"[23] needs to apportion guilt, and occasionally innocence. But whether he prophesies a Utopian future — a future "area of innocence which he will inhabit alone"[24] or with a chosen few — or indignantly castigates the promiscuity and corruption of the age, violence always looms in Lancelot's discourse and in fact keeps mounting. "If it takes the sword, we'll use the sword" (256). His railings against contemporary culture become rantings. The man who was reluctant to define love (81, 89) and later contended that "loving a woman" is "absolute and infinite" (129), the man who hated pornographers, comes to discover that "the secret of life is violence and rape" and "its gospel is pornography" (224; see also 239), thus proving the double bind of metaphysical desire: the more men try to be different, the more they become like one another. In fact it is partly because the will to difference can "never exorcise identity and reciprocity"[25] that Lancelot is caught in the spiral of increasing violence and incoherence. In order to assert an ever more problematic difference, Lancelot oscillates more and more rapidly between contradictory statements or attitudes: his last meeting with Percival is a dizzying example of his shifts and turns. Eventually after feeling free to condemn and absolve throughout his narration, Lance reaches a point where his justice is stricter than God's. Just as in the climax of the Belle Isle events he arrogated to himself the right of life and death, so at the end of his recital, he declares that the difference between God and himself is that he "won't tolerate the Russians or the Chinese either" for "God uses instruments. I am my own instrument." Metaphysical *hubris* can go no further: Lancelot has reached the autonomy he was seeking but at what cost? He has been led symbolically to repeat the sacrificial act of elimination, which he was actually guilty of, in order to hide from himself the reality of his murders.[26] His narrative quest before both succeeds as an existential gesture and fails as a moral quest for the very reason that he manages to bring himself to speak about his blood sacrifice and yet never faces up to his violence.

Attending Lancelot in his cognitive quest, Percival embarks upon a spiritual adventure of his own which only reaches us through faint echoes, through the ripples it makes on the surface of Lancelot's discourse, but which leaves him changed at the end of the novel.

On first meeting Lance in the hospital, Percival does not seek to renew the acquaintance. Yet, when the patient does, Percival commits himself to his friend as friend, and neither as psychiatrist nor as priest. Only gradually will he assume the priest's role. For long stretches, he acts as a sort of guide and tries to redirect Lancelot to his main narrative tracks. His questions, implying knowledge of the outward events, are not motivated by curiosity. Indeed Lance complains that "not even my sad case seems to interest you" (22; see also 20). But since Lance has just denounced the "interest" people morbidly take in the sensational, the mild abstraction of the priest may be taken as a sign that he is not completely alienated by everydayness and still has his priorities right. It looks as if Percival wanted less to hear Lancelot's story than to have him tell it. Confession may be in his mind as he insistently calls the narrator back to specifics ("What happened"; "the rest of it"), to the people involved ("Elgin?" "Siobhan?" "Jacoby"), to the circumstances ("The storm?") or even to the objects that Lance mentions too allusively ("The sword?"). Repeatedly he attempts to cut short the theorizing in which Lancelot indulges as a way both to postpone (or elude) the telling of the murders and to build a system of justification. If he does not enter into Lancelot's antagonistic little games, never rising to the bait, neither does he humor him like an insane person: his contributions to the exchange reveal genuine interest, though they are always oriented toward bringing Lance down from his high-flown generalities to a more concrete plane. He wishes to know what Lancelot's "own life will be like" (159). He asks about the relevance of Virginia to his friend's plans (219). He is not satisfied with vague pronouns: "What I can't stand is the way things are now. Furthermore, I will not stand for it. Stand for what, you ask?" (155); "We? Who are we? . . . How will we know each other" (157). Twice he points out a major oversight in Lance's Utopia and discusses the place he assigns to women (179, 22).

But Percival's interruptions, particularly his questions about love, are also intended to get Lancelot to talk about his emotions — a subject which for all his self-analysis he shies away from. As a dissociated personality who tries to solve his problems by further splitting of the self, opposing his new self to the old self, Lance ignores — except for a few brief glimpses (see 208–209) — his rage and even his suffering. The priest attempts to put him in touch with his feelings,[27] and at one point says outright that Lance is "full of hatred, anger," a remark Lance dismisses with "Don't talk to me of love until we shovel out the shit" (179).

Percival never presses Catholic doctrine upon his listener. Perhaps, at the beginning, because he is uncertain himself, but also because he avoids indulging in abstraction. Yet when asked to, he never fails to advance his experience. Challenged to show his friend a sin (52), he apparently complies. Lancelot, however, who had claimed that he would be impressed, does not accept his friend's observation: "Oh, you've seen quite a few? Well I haven't, not lately" (52). Almost the same scene occurs later when the priest adduces more general evidence: "But we have plenty of evil around you say. What about Hitler, the gas ovens and so forth? What about them? As everyone knows and says, Hitler was a madman . . ." (138). In a series of discreet references, Percival in fact outlines what his Church has to say about sin. Apart from persistently recalling the alternative of love, which Lance rejects ("Don't speak to me of Christian love" [156]), he indicates, *a propos* of incestuous grandfathers, that sinners can show penitence afterwards (55); he expresses a belief in reconciliation (200), which is also incidentally a belief in Elgin's charity. He affirms that all men are redeemed (224). And his whole behavior is evidence enough that he does not judge Lancelot. In short, he has kept proposing the Christian way unobtrusively but with increasing confidence until he is ready to tell Lancelot something he doesn't know.

Of the ordeal which the priest has suffered through his friend's recital and his failure to express the slightest regret, we can only see such traces as his interlocutor reports. Why does Percival look "pale as a ghost," "stricken," "unhappy"? Is it really because of his own troubles, as Lance speculates? Or is it perhaps because of his grief at finding Lance whom he may have expected to confess so devoid of contrition? Is it because of the strain of accompanying on his descent into Hell — or is it Purgatory? — a friend who is not even aware of being in Hell? As Dante says in the lines following those quoted in the epigraph to *Lancelot*:

> Alto fato di Dio, sarebbe rotto,
> se Lete si passasse, e tal vivanda

fosse gustata senza alcuno scotto
de pentimento che lagrime spanda.
  (Canto 30, ll 142–145)

Of Percival's pilgrimage we know only a few of the consequences. If we are to believe Lancelot's observations and interpretations, Percival prays for the dead, on his way to their last meeting, whereas he had refused to do so before the first. (This incidentally is a reminder that the dead whom Lance so casually dismisses — "his" dead in more senses than one — are also to be prayed for). He wears priest clothes instead of the "phony casuals" which he affected at the beginning, and plans "to take a little church in Alabama." All of which points to a renewed commitment to his sacerdotal vocation, i.e., to the world and to God. The rest is left for us to imagine in the light of the epigraph from *Purgatorio*.

Nonetheless a few clues to the nature of Percival's Christian behavior have been offered us — the most important of which is the contrast between the two friends in the matter of mimesis. His part in the exchange is to be a witness. A witness to Lance's hopeful youth, their shared dreams, their friendship, a witness to his friend's present quest and a witness to his own faith — however shaky it may have been at the beginning of his visits. Never does he join, as we have seen, in the rivalry which is Lance's form of relating to him, not even in the name of his Church. Thus he follows the Biblical precept: "Answer not a man out of his senses according to his folly lest thou also be like unto him. Answer a man out of his senses according to his folly, lest he be wise in his own conceit" (Proverbs, 26:4–5). Lance for his part can only see his donning his "priest uniform" as a sign that Percival is "girding for battle or dressed up like Lee for the surrender" (163), that is to say, taking part in the agonistic relation that unites / opposes them in his view in a mimetic interaction. But the attire can, and ought to, be read as confirming Percival's renewed dedication to Him who said, "I came not to judge the world but to save the world" (John, 12:47), whereas Lancelot is like the man described in Romans: "For wherein thou judgest another, thou condemnest thyself; for thou that judgest doest the same things" (Romans, 2:1). Having failed to bring his friend to a sense of repentance, Percival nevertheless accepts him in an act of love and faith evidenced in their final exchange. Such acceptance proves that Percival's way is at once totally unlike Lance's way or "their way out there," which are both the ways of mimesis. Without ever mentioning Christ, he points the way out of the pseudo-dilemma set up by Lancelot, since he practices Christian love in "imitation of the only model who can never turn into fascinating rival."[28]

Perhaps only the device of keeping Percival away from the reader's direct observation could serve to create a fictional character as free as he is from mimetic rivalry, while yet presenting (or absenting) him as a double of Lancelot. If the two characters may be considered as "a splitting of the authorial *persona*,"[29] and as incarnations of the two traditions, Stoic and

Christian, with which much of Walker Percy's fiction is concerned,[30] they also embody the doubling that structures human experience as a result of the mimetic process.[31] But unlike much fiction of the double which usually maintains the shadow — whether it be for instance Dr. Jekyll or Dorian Gray's picture — in the background until the final take-over, here it is the darker sides of the Ego that are foregrounded so that the movement is toward revelation of the lighter figure. Through Lance's quest of the Unholy Grail, Percival finds the Lance that enables him to cut through everydayness and the grail, the vision that redeems him and enables him to speak out, presumably in order to deliver Christ's good news.

Because of the narrative technique, the reader is at first primarily involved in Lance. Engrossed in his (re)construction of the protagonist and his cognitive quest, the reader must of necessity *judge* him. Whether he naively accepts Lance at face value, regarding him, for instance, as the writer's spokesman, or stands at a critical distance, making perhaps some sort of diagnosis, psychological or sociological, of his illness, he repeats Lancelot's mistake and falls into the trap the narrator has set. Our puzzlement at Percival's final response is a measure of our entrapment. Only when we realize that Percival has avoided yielding to mimetic fascination and why, can we be redeemed *qua* readers. (Whether we take the message to heart in our lives outside the book is an altogether different matter, although Walker Percy, a Catholic novelist possessed of all the "cunning" he says the Christian novelist must display nowadays,[32] presumably writes in the hope that we will.) Escaping from the snares of the narration into the freedom which the novel provides for us, if only we recognize that in our guilty pride we are creatures ridden with the ontological disease, we then can embrace Lancelot in a new paradoxical relationship in which like Percival we must respond yet not respond to what he says. From the pages of the closed book, Lance's voice keeps addressing the reader, *hypocrite lecteur, mon semblable, mon frère.*

Notes

1. Walker Percy, *Lancelot* (New York: Farrar, Straus and Giroux, 1977), p. 254. This edition is cited hereafter in the text.

2. Percival's remarks may themselves be quotations of Lance's speech: "Yes you're right. I did say that there was something that still bothered me. What? Sin? The uncertainty that there is such a thing? I don't remember" (163).

3. Joyce Carol Oates, in "*Lancelot* by Walker Percy," claims that "Percival is never allowed into the story, nor the past; he does not figure in the narrative at all" (*New Republic*, Feb. 5, 1977, p. 31). See also Robert Towers, "Southern Discomfort," *N.Y. Rev. of Books* (March 31, 1977); Robert Brinkmeyer, "Percy's Bludgeon: Message and Narrative Strategy," *The Southern Quarterly*, 18, 3 (Spring 1980), 88. A significant exception is Lewis Lawson's stimulating essay: "Walker Percy's Silent Character," *Mississippi Quarterly*, 33 (Spring 1980). But I do not accept some of its deductions, including one of its major premises, namely that "there is no behavior by Father John that reveals that he has any more knowledge of Lance's recent history than does the reader" (130).

4. See Lawson, p. 130.

5. It is to be noted however that these institutional confidences apparently win for Lance his discharge, the confirmation that he is "psychiatrically fit and legally innocent."

6. Andreas Zempléni, "La chaine du secret," *Du Secret, Nouvelle Revue de Psychanalyse*, numéro 14 (automne 1976).

7. "Le sujet qui ne peut décider par lui-même de l'objet qu'il doit désirer, s'appuie sur le désir d'un autre. Et il transforme automatiquement le désir modèle en désir qui contrecarre le sien. Parce qu'il ne comprend pas le caractère automatique de la rivalité, l'imitateur fait bientôt du fait même d'être contrecarré, repoussé, rejeté, l'excitant majeur de son désir. Sous une forme ou une autre, il va incorporer toujours plus de violence à son désir. Reconnaitre cette tendance, c'est reconnaitre que le désir à la limite, tend vers la mort, celle de l'autre, du modèle obstacle, et celle du sujet lui-même," in *Des Choses Cachées depuis la Fondation du Monde* (Paris: Bernard Grasset, 1978), p. 436. *Des Chases . . .* is Girard's latest statement of theories which he has elaborated from the early *Mensonge Romantique, Vérité Romanesque* (Paris: Bernard Grasset, 1961), in *La Violence et la Sacré* (Paris: Bernard Grasset, 1972), and in *Critique dans un Souterrain* (Lausanne: l'Age d'Homme, 1976).

8. "A theory of man must account for the alienation of man. . . . Judeo-Christianity did of course give an account of alienation not as a peculiar evil of the twentieth century, but as the enduring symptom of man's estrangement from God. Any cogent anthropology must address itself to both, the possibility of perennial estrangement of man as part of the human condition and to the undeniable fact of the cultural estrangement of Western man in the twentieth century," says Walker Percy in *The Message in the Bottle* (N.Y.: Farrar, Straus and Giroux, 1975), pp. 23–24. Let me add that Girard's conception of man was originally derived from his reading of literature and singularly of Dostoevski, whose influence Walker Percy has acknowledged and whose *The Possessed* has been mentioned in connection with *Lancelot*.

9. Lewis A. Lawson, "The Fall of the House of Lamar," in Panthea Reid Broughton, ed., *The Art of Walker Percy, Strategems for Being* (Baton Route: Louisiana State University Press, 1979), p. 221.

10. Paul Verlaine, *Oeuvres Poétiques Complètes* (Paris: La Pléiade Gallimard, 1954), pp. 306–307.

11. "How come you're wearing your priest *uniform* today? Are you *girding for battle* or dressed up like Lee for the *surrender*" is his greeting one day (163, emphasis added).

12. *Mensonge Romantique*, p. 19.

13. He will jibe at him for being "the doctor-scientist and soul expert as well," while apparently consulting him (89), or ask ironically "Are you playing the priest now?" (97), or complain "Why can't priests stick to being priests for a change?" (159).

14. "Obviously something went wrong, because here I am, in a nuthouse, or is it a prison? recovering from shock, psychosis, disorientation" (108).

15. To my knowledge he never addresses him as Harry, his real name, nor as Father John. He very occasionally calls him Father, but one use of the word is certainly ironical (155) and another can be understood as such, too (253).

16. Of course, seeing what he *is* doing is at the same time seeing, interpreting what he *was* doing, since the past quest exists only through the present attempt to put it into words, through the ongoing quest.

17. See Girard's analysis of *The Possessed* in *Mensonge Romantique*.

18. "La négation de Dieu ne supprime pas la transcendance mais elle fait dévier celle-ci de l'au-delà vers l'en-deca. . . . La transcendance déviée est une caricature de la transcendance verticale," *Mensonge Romantique*, pp. 65, 67.

19. He will also delegate functions to Percival if the latter is ready to act: "Why do I tell you all this? As a warning if you like" (160).

20. Lancelot seems to have a Nietzschean conception of the falling theme as something positive, leading not to loss of being but to ontological increase and greater freedom.

21. "Satan c'est le nom du processus mimétique dans son ensemble: c'est bien pourquoi il est source, non seulement de rivalité et de désordre mais de tous les désordres menteurs au sein desquels vivent les hommes," in *Des Choses Cachées*, p. 185.

22. To settle the question one would have to examine all the allusions to Christmas (the Christmas bonfires, the crib, etc.) and the function of the Christmas tree.

23. "L'indignation scandalisée est toujours fébrile de différencier le coupable et l'innocent, d'assigner les responsabilités, du dévoiler l'ignominie jusqu'au bout et de la chatier comme elle le mérite," in *Des Choses Cachées*, p. 449.

24. "Ce sout toujours des armes que chacun aiguise contre le voisin dans un effort désespéré pour se ménager quelque part, serait-ce dans un avenir utopique indéterminé une zone d'innocence qu'il habitera seul ou en compagnie d'une humanité régénérée," in *Des Choses Cachées*, p. 462.

25. "Si la volonté d'absorption et d'assimilation ne conquiert jamais la différence de l'autre, la volonté de différence, qui revient au même, n'exorcise jamais l'identitét la réciprocité," in *Des Choses Cachées*, p. 325.

26. "Il faut tuer et toujours tuer, pour ne pas savoir qu'on tue," in *Des Choses Cachées*, p. 186.

27. "You were asking me how I felt when I discovered that Margot had been unfaithful to me" (41).

28. "Les Evangiles et le Nouveau Testament ne prêchent pas une morale de la spontanéité. Ils ne prétendent pas que l'homme doive renoncer à l'imitation: ils recommandent d'imiter le seul modèle qui ne risque pas, si nous l'imitons vraiment comme les enfants imitent, de se transformer pour nous en rival fascinant," in *Des Choses Cachées*, p. 452.

29. John Towers, "Southern Discomfort", *N.Y. Rev. of Books*, March 31, 1977, p. 68.

30. Lewis A. Lawson, "The Fall of the House of Lamar," 243.

31. *Des Choses Cachées*, "Les doubles et l'interindividualité," pp. 323–329 and passim.

32. Zoltan Abadi-Nagy, "A Talk with Walker Percy," *Southern Literary Journal*, 6, 1 (Fall 1973), 11.

Walker Percy and Modern Gnosticism
Cleanth Brooks*

It is dangerous to impute to one man ideas that belong to another, and as one reads the pages that follow, this may seem to be precisely the course that I am pursuing. But that is not at all my intention. I am not aware that Walker Percy has ever mentioned Gnosticism in any of his writings. Nor is it necessary, for what I have to say, that he should have done so. After all, why should any modern writer mention an ancient heresy of the first centuries of the Christian era?

Gnosticism, however, is far from dead. There is plenty of hard

*Reprinted by permission from the *Southern Review* 13 (1977):677–87.

evidence that it pervades Western civilization. Consequently, the study of it, far from being a subject of merely antiquarian interest, could be indispensable for an understanding of the great intellectual movements that have convulsed our own century. Such at least is the contention of Eric Voegelin, whose monumental five-volume book, *Order and History*, is being published by the Louisiana State University Press. If Percy never mentions Gnosticism, neither has he, so far as I know, ever mentioned Voegelin and may never have read him. But again, that possibility does not figure in my present design which amounts to no more than pointing out some highly interesting and, I think, significant parallels between the writings of these two men. Yet if the parallelisms are genuinely significant, the readers of either Percy or Voegelin may benefit from the widened perspective effected by broadening for them the cultural context of each writer's work.

The basic resemblance between Percy and Voegelin that first struck me was the fact that both writers see modern man as impoverished by his distorted and disordered view of reality. As for Percy, I noticed it first in his novels. There, since he is a genuine novelist, the view is simply implied. It is, of course, spelled out in the essays that make up *The Message in the Bottle*. A comparable account of man's distorted perspective and an account of how it developed is the very theme and subject matter of all of Voegelin's writings for the last thirty years.

In all of Percy's novels the hero inherits what amounts to an orthodox Christian view of man and his relation to reality, but the world inhabited by the hero is dominated by ideas that are powerfully twisted away from any orthodox view. In the first three novels the heroes finally achieve, despite the age they live in, a religious apprehension of their own stance in the world. In the fourth novel, however, the protagonist is maddened by what he sees as the ineffectuality of Christianity in a world he finds intolerable. Vowing to take matters into his own hands, Lancelot becomes a modern Gnostic.

As I have remarked, the essays collected in *The Message in the Bottle* spell out Percy's estimate of the situation in which modern man finds himself. In the very first essay, Percy argues that a "theory of man must account for the alienation of man," but points out that the dominant ideas of the twentieth century do not and cannot. That is because they define alienation as a phenomenon located in this time and place, rather than recognize it as the necessary condition of man. But the anthropology of Judeo-Christianity has always seen alienation as man's essential condition. That tradition accounts for alienation through the doctrine of the Fall. According to this doctrine there occurred at the beginning of human history a separation or alienation of man from God, an alienation that accounted for, as Percy sees it, the "homelessness of man who (in this world) is not in fact at home." Moreover, the Judeo-Christian scheme provided, in its own terms, ways and means for man's becoming reconciled with God; but it did not promise him any heaven on this earth. The bliss of perfection and peace was to be recovered elsewhwere, in eternity, and not in the world of time.

By contrast, the modern view regards man as only "a higher organism satisfying this or that need from its environment." Man thus can be made happy by a more perfect adjustment to his environment. Through the efforts of our marvelous technology, man can now hope to make radical modification of his environment and so perfect his adjustment to it.

Our scientists and humanists, therefore, have erased the notion of the Fall and have promised to take Man back to Eden; that is, to the perfect environment from which the Judeo-Christian account claimed that he had been expelled. But the new Eden will be real, no mere fable. It will be a place—as Percy rather sardonically puts it—"where scientists know like angels, and laymen prosper in good environments, and ethical democracies progress through education."

Unfortunately, however, this promised utopian Eden remains unrealized. Man remains alienated. As Percy explains in "The Delta Factor."

> The scientists were saying that by science man was learning more and more about himself as an organism and more and more about the world as an environment and that accordingly the environment could be changed and man made to feel more and more at home.
>
> The humanists were saying that through education and the application of the ethical principles of Christianity, man's lot was certain to improve.
>
> But poets and artists and novelists were saying something else: that at a time when, according to the theory of the age, men should feel most at home they felt most homeless.
>
> Something was wrong.

Percy's view is that on this issue our poets and artists and novelists have been dead right. On earlier pages of this essay he asks a number of searching questions:

> Why has man entered on an orgy of war, murder, torture, and self-destruction unparalled in history and in the very century when he had hoped to see the dawn of universal peace and brotherhood? . . .
>
> Why have more people been killed in the twentieth century than in all other centuries put together? . . .
>
> Why do the young people look so sad, the very young who, seeing how sad their elders are, have sought a new life of joy and freedom with each other and in the green fields and forests, but who instead of finding joy look even sadder than their elders?

Percy has his own way of answering these questions. His readers will already know, or by further reading of his work, can learn, what his answers are. What I want to do here is to turn to Voegelin's description of the way in which modern man conceives of himself.

Like Percy, Voegelin interprets the various powerful drives of the modern age as heading up in a belief that utopia can be achieved. A perfect society of one sort or another is the goal, according to Voegelin, of all the modern manifestations of Gnosticism. But in this matter they inherit from the ancient Gnostics, who are their forebears in unbroken continuity. Like the modern scientists and humanists, the ancient Gnostic cults sought to erase the idea of any Fall of Man. They could not agree with what was proclaimed in *Genesis*, namely, that the Creation was essentially good—that it was the handiwork of a good God, who, in viewing his handiwork, had pronounced that "it was very good."

On the contrary, the ancient Gnostics held that the Creation was the work of a demon—of a cruel demiurge. The world—with its mutability, sexuality, wickedness, and violence—is woefully imperfect, but man has the potentiality to be perfect if he does not confound himself with this imperfect world. Man had the misfortune to be placed in this flawed world not by his own error but by an evil god. His task then is to extricate himself from this evil world, partially at least by throwing off the bonds of his own evil flesh. Then he can get back, in spite of the obstructions set up by the demiurge, to the true god and achieve the more perfect order for which he was originally designed.

Two crucial aspects of Gnosticism are worth emphasizing here: (1) Man the creature is not responsible for the evil in which he finds himself. He has a right to blame it on someone or something else. The assumption that "In Adam's fall / We sinned all" is to the Gnostic pure nonsense. And (2) Man's salvation depends upon his own efforts. He must rely not upon faith but on gnosis, the secret knowledge that makes it possible for him to evade the snares and entanglements of the demon and to reunite his soul with the divinity from which he has come.

These two traits, Voegelin points out, continue to characterize Gnosticism, even in its present-day secularized form. Dissatisfied with the nature of reality, man can now the more confidently hope that, with his increasing knowledge, he can remake the world to suit himself. As Voegelin puts it, what is common to the profusion of "gnostic experiences and symbolic expression" is "the experience of the world as an alien place into which man has strayed and from which he must find his way back home to the other world of his origin." The divine spark within him is "an alien in this world and the world is alien to it."

The continuity of Gnosticism from the ancient Gnostic sects of the classical world on down to modern manifestations of this kind of speculation was worked out as early as the first half of the nineteenth century, largely by German and French scholars. That history is highly interesting, but it can have no part in this abbreviated essay. More to my purpose here are the names of some of the modern thinkers whom Voegelin regards as Gnostics and their different formulas for eliminating modern man's sense of alienation.

It will be interesting, for example, to compare with Voegelin's view what Percy has to say about Karl Marx. Man has always been alienated, Percy writes: "By the very cogent anthropology of Judeo-Christianity . . . human existence was by no means to be understood as the transaction of a higher organism satisfying this or that need from its environment, [either] by being 'creative' or enjoying 'meaningful relationships.' . . ." Rather, human existence was to be understood "as the journey of a wayfarer along life's way." Not so for Marx. For him, as Percy puts it, "the experience of alienation was . . . an inevitable consequence of capitalism." So Marx hoped to get rid of capitalism, and expected that man's alienation would subsequently disappear; without capitalism, man could be beautifully adapted to his environment and reconciled with himself.

According to Voegelin, "Marx is a speculative gnostic." Marx has convinced himself that he has penetrated the secret of history and therefore knows the way in which it must go. The perfect society of the classless state will be achieved through "the revolution of the proletariat and the transformation of man into the communist superman." But, according to Voegelin, like all Gnostic utopians, Marx misrepresents the nature of man and for his own purposes deforms the nature of reality.

Or consider Georg Friedrich Hegel. Martin Luschei writes that Percy once told him that "After twelve years of scientific education . . . he felt rather like Kierkegaard when he finished reading Hegel: 'Hegel,' said Kierkegaard, 'explained everything under the sun except one small detail, what it means to be a man living in the world who must die.' " Furthermore, Luschei quotes, with reference to Percy's reaction against abstraction, Kierkegaard's statement that Hegelian idealism had abolished "individual man," for "every speculative philosopher" had confused "himself with humanity at large." In short, as Percy puts it with an amplitude that will cover Marx, Hegel, and many another philosopher, German philosophy had for a long time suffered from an "old interior itch" which turns too heavily to abstraction and as a consequence lets "the world slip away."

Voegelin would add further names — not limited to the German philosophers and thinkers who had let "the world" and reality itself "slip away." In fact, he would define the "old interior itch" as Gnosticism itself. "All gnostic movements," he writes, "are involved in the project of abolishing the constitution of being, with its origin in divine, transcendent being, and replacing it with a world-immanent order of being, the perfection of which lies in the realm of human action." But specifically, what does Voegelin say about Hegel? For him, Hegel is another of the moderns who have, by willfully ignoring certain elements of humanity, promulgated a deformed conception of reality. Voegelin says, among other things, that the "factor [that] Hegel excludes [from reality] is the mystery of a history that wends its way into the future without knowing its end.

History as a whole is essentially not an object of cognition; the meaning of the whole is not discernible." Nevertheless, Hegel's interior itch set him to constructing a history of man that was "fully comprehensible."

One could go on with Voegelin's roll call of other great Gnostics of later times—Hobbes, Comte, Nietzsche, Freud, Heidegger, et al. But I am here not writing an essay so much as setting down notes for an essay to be written. I shall limit myself therefore to only one more example, one that is the more interesting because it is highly problematic.

Saint Thomas More wrote a Utopia—indeed, coined the word. Does Voegelin regard him as a Gnostic? Well, no; but his treatment of More is very interesting.

> In his *Utopia* [Voegelin writes] More traces the image of man and of society that he considers perfect. To this perfection belongs the abolition of private property. Because he had the benefit of an excellent theological education, however, More is well aware that this perfect state cannot be achieved in the world: man's lust for possessions is deeply rooted in original sin, in *superbia* in the Augustinian sense. In the final part of his work when More looks over his finished picture, he has to admit that it would all be possible if only there were not the "serpent of superbia." But there *is* the serpent of superbia—and More would not think of denying it.

Is the protagonist of *Love in the Ruins*, Dr. Thomas More, a descendant of the Saint—is he a Gnostic? Well hardly, but Percy has been very careful not to make him a saint and, even more important, not to make him merely the embodiment of an abstract idea, even of an idea to which Percy is himself devoted.

Dr. Thomas More is a Roman Catholic, but Percy does not present him as a model of Christian piety. More enjoys bourbon whiskey—Early Times is clearly his favorite brand—and he is strongly attracted to a pretty girl—almost any pretty girl. He admits that he is a "bad Catholic." He says that he is like the Saint's second wife, a woman "who believed in God but saw no reason why one should disturb one's life [for Him], certainly not lose one's head."

In his novel, Percy has made the issue more complicated still—and thereby rendered his protagonist more thoroughly human—by having him invent the lapsometer, an instrument for making miraculous diagnoses of the human psyche, with the promise of reshaping humanity and, with it, the world. When More says, near the end of the novel, "I still believe my lapsometer can save the world," he sounds rather like a Gnostic himself. But the saving clause that follows—"if I can get it right"—and, still more, the sentence that follows in which he tells what he considers is wrong with the world, together indicate that he is no utopian. He has no ambition to create a new Adam. Apparently his modest ambition is to help with a highly necessary repair job on the old Adam, who now suffers from "chronic angelism-bestialism that rives soul from body and sets it orbiting the great world as the spirit of abstraction whence it takes the form of beasts, swans and bulls, werewolves, blood-suckers, Mr. Hydes, or just poor lonesome ghost locked in its own machinery."(René Descartes, thou shouldst be living at this hour — to witness where your classic riving of soul from body has left the modern world.)

Dr. More's vocation is that of a healer — so is Dr. Percy's — which is one way of saying that both are in the human repair business and that neither is a quietist or a defeatist, waiting for the civilization to collapse. But then, of course, neither is Eric Voegelin. There is a difference between (1) trying to put back together a world that is "broken, sundered, busted down," and (2) junking the world in favor of a fool-proof model that you have thought up in your own head.

All right, all right, the skeptical reader may say, but is there any positive justification for raising in Dr. Thomas More's case the complicated issue of Gnosticism? I think so, and the best way to show it is to listen to More's talk. He may be a "bad Catholic" — he may, for example, have let eleven years elapse before coming again to his father-confessor — but his theological orthodoxy is genuine, and he is himself quite conscious that it constitutes his anchor against the undertow of the powerful currents of modernity. What do we hear him saying — and what are some of the things said to him?

More says of the connection between revolution and totalitarianism: "Students are a shaky dogmatic lot. And the 'freer' they are, the more dogmatic. At heart they're totalitarians: they want either total dogmatic freedom or total dogmatic unfreedom, and the one thing that makes them unhappy is something in between." (Voegelin's "metaxy" is the "in-between state" — between the animal and the divine, between the immanent and the transcendent — which is the peculiarly human realm.)

More, speaking of his first wife, remarks that "What she didn't understand, she being spiritual and seeing religion as spirit, was that it took religion to save me from the spirit world, from orbiting the earth like Lucifer and the angels, that it took nothing less than touching the thread off the misty interstates [Voegelin's metaxy again] and eating Christ himself to make me mortal man again and let me inhabit my own flesh and love her in the morning."

More is addressed by a revolutionist as follows: "Let me put it this way, Doctor. You know what we're going to do. We're going to build a new society right here." This statement has what Voegelin would call the genuine Gnostic ring: the speaker's absolute confidence that he knows the true state of affairs, an equal certainty about the soundness of his motives, and a genuine relishing of his sense of power.

The same accent is to be heard in what a revolutionary professor says to More, though his speech also exhibits the not uncommon Gnostic ruthlessness. The professor is voicing his praise of a certain (mythical) Latin-American dictator. He says: "He's the George Washington of Ecuador, the only man beloved north and south and the only man capable of uniting the country." When More asks whether he "didn't kill several hundred thousand Ecuadorians who didn't love him," the professor is at no loss for a reply: "Yes, but they were either fascists or running dogs or lackeys of the American imperialists. Anyhow, the question has become academic."

In this general connection, it will be interesting to cite More on the subject of what he calls "angelism," which, as I interpret it, arises from the human being's impatience with the limitations of the mortal mind — impatience with perceptions mediated through the senses, the progress of thought from the known to the unknown, and dependence upon common sense and reason. A man who has fallen into "angelism," Dr. More tells us, "will fall prey to the first abstract notion proposed to him and will kill anybody who gets in his way, torture, execute, wipe out entire populations, all with the best possible motives and the best possible intentions, in fact in the name of peace and freedom, etcetera." Angelism, then, is essentially Gnostic and potentially violent. Thus, Voegelin's account of twentieth-century Gnosticism in action includes, along with those of milder Gnostics, the names of very violent ones like Stalin and Hitler. The point is that a Gnostic impatience with human limitations can easily convert into a hubristic denial of one's own limitations and an amoral disregard for ethical systems demanding decency in the human community.

That seems to be what happens to Lancelot Andrews Lamar, the character whom Walker Percy has presented as the complete twentieth-century Gnostic — a millenialist through and through — confident that he knows how to reform a corrupt world and willing to kill if he cannot cure. In Percy's latest novel, *Lancelot*, the protagonist says of his own quest: "So Sir Lancelot set out, looking for something rarer than the Grail. A sin." But Lance discovers only "buggery," not sin. (Of course, he fails to look within himself.) His basic assumption is that "Original Sin is not something man did to God but something God did to man. . . ." In other words, Lance, like an ancient Gnostic, would blame God — or a cruel demiurge — for the world's imperfections, rather than take any of the blame upon himself.

Lance sees his task as dissociation from and purification of this evil world. He decides: "I cannot tolerate this age. What is more, I won't. That [when he destroyed Belle Isle and four people on it] was my discovery: that I didn't have to." Instead, "there is going to be a new order of things and I shall be part of it." He will begin a "new Reformation," a "Third Revolution" in America, the first having been "won at Yorktown," the second "lost at Appomattox." Lance then believes both principal tenets of Gnosticism — that man is not responsible for evil and that his salvation depends on his own efforts.

At several points in *Lancelot*, Percy juxtaposes Lance's answers with

Christianity's. Lance himself explains his extremism in terms of the church's apparent defection: "I cannot tolerate this age. And I will not. I might have tolerated you and your Catholic Church, and even joined it, if you had remained true to yourself. Now you're part of the age." The church, in Lance's Gnostic vision, has confounded itself by being a part of this world. In the book's ending, Lancelot and his friend Percival, a Roman Catholic priest, agree, not on that issue but on the absoluteness of their own alternative visions: Lancelot says, "One of us is wrong. It will be your way or it will be my way." And the priest answers *"Yes."*

The ending of *Lancelot* is ambiguous, but I think that Percy juxtaposes the speaker and the auditor, the Gnostic and the Christian, in order to suggest that we are indeed in an either / or situation. *Either* we accept alienation as our necessary condition — acknowledging the world's evil condition and helping to ameliorate it, but never presuming to believe that we can eliminate it — and live in faith, *or* we will find our own theories inviting and condoning the Hitlers, the Idi Amins, and the Lancelots of the world.

For many readers, the millenialism of Lancelot Lamar will be obscured by the fact that his condemnation of the modern world may easily appear to be Walker Percy's own. This well may be. Many who share Percy's values also share Lancelot's belief that we are living in Sodom. The priest Percival evidently concurs with Lancelot about the corruption of the modern world. But one can agree with Lance that the world is corrupt without agreeing at all with his single-minded resolution: "I will start a new world single-handedly or with those like me who will not tolerate [the present world]. . . . We know what we want. And we'll have it. If it takes the sword, we'll use the sword." He is completely prepared to get rid of the world itself, for he is confident that he can devise a better one. Percival, however, is not so presumptuous nor so self-righteous — and neither, for that matter, is Walker Percy.

There is hardly need to go on. Clearly Percy and Voegelin are more than superficially alike in their diagnosis of the present state of the culture. Modern man has a disordered notion of what he is and therefore a deformed conception of reality. For a succinct account of the modern situation and how it developed, one might well look at the Introduction to Voegelin's *Science, Politics, and Gnosticism.* But I am not using this essay to ask Percy to adopt Voegelin's terms or to suggest to Voegelin that in his studies of modernity he give more attention to some of the special problems so brilliantly dramatized in Percy's novels. Indeed, I would consider it presumptuous to offer counsel to either man. My more modest intention is to suggest to Walker Percy's readers that the basic themes of Percy's novels are not merely the private and special insights of an important novelist, and are certainly not to be regarded as the privileged crankiness of a somewhat eccentric Roman Catholic intellectual. They have a close relation to a powerful and searching criticism of the modern world, of which Voegelin is clearly the major exemplar, but which in the last decade has begun to claim the attention and the endorsement of an increasing number of modern scholars.

The Semiotics of Memory: Suicide in *The Second Coming*   J. G. Kennedy*

Much that shapes human culture and individual experience derives ultimately from two mental traits unique to man: the ability to deal in symbolic abstractions and to contemplate the overwhelming fact of one's own mortality. These conditions seem integrally related; in *The Denial of Death*, Ernest Becker concludes: "Everything that man does in his symbolic world is an attempt to deny and overcome his grotesque fate."[1] Leaving aside questions of origin and relationship, which open upon the fields of psychology, anthropology, and theology, we see that these traits account in large measure for both systems of meaning and the need to use them. Among other results, the symbolizing tendency and the dread of death may be said to have produced writing itself, in the desire to perpetuate manifestations of consciousness beyond the limit of conscious existence. To the memorable formulation of Descartes, *"je pense; donc je suis."* one is tempted to add, *"je meurs; donc j'écris."* In a seminar given a year before his own untimely death, Roland Barthes retracted his earlier notions of *écriture* and stressed the human connection between writing and death in noting that Dante began to inscribe his *Divina Commedia* "in the middle of life's way" — at the point which can be defined as "the middle" only through a sense of the end.[2]

These reflections seem apposite to a discussion of Walker Percy's most recent novel, *The Second Coming* (1980), a work suffused by a consciousness of signs and symbols and by a preoccupation with the problem of death. As I hope to demonstrate, these conditions form the thematic axes of the novel, and their convergence — in an emblem of suicidal despair — forms its imaginative center. Once again, Percy's hero is Will Barrett, described in *The Last Gentleman* (1966) as a "watcher and a listener and a wanderer," belonging to that class of spiritually displaced persons who "do not know what to do and so live out their lives as if they were waiting for some sign or other."[3] Much of Barrett's confusion, in the earlier work, seems related to the suicide of his father, an event recalled during Will's return to the scene of death, the family home in Mississippi. Afflicted by amnesia throughout most of *The Last Gentleman*, Will experiences a sudden remembrance of things past in *The Second Coming* and obsessively

*Reprinted by permission from *Delta* 13 (November 1981):103–25.

reviews a childhood episode (prior to his father's suicide), which he now understands to be "the most important event in his life." As I shall attempt to argue, the singular force of this novel — arguably Percy's best — springs from his Proustian evocation of guilt, despair, and death-anxiety, as mediated by the enigmatic signs by which memory speaks.

From *The Moviegoer* (1961) onward, Percy has displayed a quasi-scientific, quasi-theological interest in the phenomenon of language and, more broadly, in man's curious habit of trafficking in symbols. This concern manifests itself in his novelistic attention to dialects, to speech impediments and aphasic behavior, to the implicit rules of "small talk," to the vacuity of popular words and expressions, and conversely to the miraculous import of certain utterances in certain situations. This interest extends to nonverbal signs and symbols; as a trained physician who thinks of his fiction as diagnosis, Percy often refers to signs of illness, either to designate the psychophysical condition of a character or to note the effects of the malaise afflicting the Western world. As a critic of popular culture, he understands the symbolic codes expressed by rooms, houses, clothing, gestures, and cars (the suicidal Sutter Vaught drives an Edsel); he has a keen eye for mannerisms which signify social class, regional identity, or character type. His deftness as a satirist owes much to his grasp of the conventional meanings attached to such artifacts as movies, television programs, consumer products, and advertisements. And as a novelist oriented toward Christian eschatology, Percy expresses a recurrent fascination with the prophesied signs of the Last Days; his fictional protagonists typically reconcile themselves to "watching and waiting" for portents of the apocalypse.

To be sure, these signs differ markedly in form and consequence, but they illustrate the surprising extent to which the writer grounds his work in the general field of semiotics. Accepting Cassirer's theory of the symbolic nature of human cognition, Percy proposes in his essay, "The Delta Factor," that the species *Homo sapiens* ought properly to be called "*Homo loquens*, man the talker, or *Homo symbolificus*, man the symbol-monger."[4] For it is man's fate, the author observes elsewhere, that we "must know one thing through the mirror of another" — that is, the "mirror" of the sensuous symbol by which we conceive of our world.[5] For Percy the fundamental "act of symbolization" is the naming process, considered to be "unique in natural history because for the first time a being in the universe stands apart from the universe and affirms some other being to be what it is."[6] This coupling of word and object, [*signifiant* and *signifié*,] comprises both the "instrument of knowing" and the basis of human intersubjectivity. Only under the aegis of commonly-held symbols can human beings interact with each other: "Every symbolic formulation, whether it be language, art, or even thought, requires a real or posited *someone else* for whom the symbol is intended to be meaningful. Denotation is an exercise in intersubjectivity."[7] The logic of this theory seems questionable (Does intersubjectivity occur when the posited "someone else" is the self-as-reader?), but its importance for Percy's fiction seems clear: the novelist regards the symbol as man's sole means of understanding and the medium of all human intercourse; it is also (as we shall see) the instrument of grace for Percy's despairing protagonists.

While loosely applicable to his earlier novels, this approach assumes particular significance in Percy's most densely semiotic narrative, *The Second Coming*. Here the writer expands his treatment of signs and symbols to explore the code of images inscribed in human memory and recalled through both deliberate and involuntary recollection. Early in the novel, Will Barrett realizes during a round of golf (itself a figure of circular return) that he has reached a state of total remembrance and pure semiosis:

> Today for some reason he remembered everything. Everything he saw became a sign of something else. This fence was a sign of another fence he had climbed through. The hawk was a sign of another hawk and of a time when he believed there were fabulous birds. . . . Even the wheeling blackbirds signified not themselves but a certain mocking sameness.[8]

Every object in Will's immediate experience has become the emblem of an object in past experience, and in this strange condition (the opposite of the amnesia that once plagued him), he imagines that "there is no mystery," that "his entire life lay before him, beginning, middle and end, as plain as the mural of Jack Nicklaus blasting out of the sand trap" (p. 79). But in reaching the stage of memory, Will makes the further discovery that the images of remembrances are themselves signs, hieroglyphs in a code which initially cannot be deciphered.

Though he wanders through a dark wood, perplexed by inscrutable correspondences, we see his deliverance ultimately secured through what Gilles Deleuze has called an "apprenticeship" in the decoding of signs.[9] A semiotic perspective marks the novel's opening sentence: "The first sign that something had gone wrong manifested itself while he was playing golf." In fact, the opening page introduces two signs: one a physical symptom (Will's falling down in a bunker) and the other an auditory sign, recalling "an event that had happened a long time ago." Actually, the first sign proves to be a function not of the second sign but of its absence: Will periodically faints (a classic Freudian syndrome) because he has repressed the memory of a traumatic childhood event evoked by the sound heard on the golf course. Moreover, the falling down, which on one level seems a reminder of man's mythic Fall, indirectly reveals a portent of the Last Days; still sprawled on the ground, Will notices a huge cloud: "As he gazed at it from the bunker, it seemed to turn purple and gold at the bottom while the top went boiling up higher and higher like the cloud over Hiroshima." The cumulus cloud over North Carolina becomes the sign of a cloud over Japan, which has itself become an emblem of death, nuclear holocaust, and the end of the world. That Will perceives the cloud as the conventional sign of the modern Armageddon is symptomatic of his apocalyptic imagination. But an ambiguity besets him: he cannot be certain whether his anxiety is a response to the world's absurdity (and imminent collapse) or to his own unnameable despair. This resembles the predicament of Tom More (*Love in the Ruins*) and Lancelot Andrewes Lamar (*Lancelot*), and it epitomizes a fundamental problem for the Percy hero: his inability to know whether the observed signs of the Last Days comprise a coded, divine inscription or a self-generated delusion, a symptom of alienation and madness.

Percy juxtaposes this larger interpretive dilemma, signified by the mushroom-shaped cloud, against the more immediate and personal question posed by the auditory sign:

> As he searched for the ball deep in the woods, another odd thing happened to him. He heard something and the sound reminded him of an event that had happened a long time ago. It was the most important event in his life, yet he had managed until that moment to forget it. (p. 3).

The novel's opening page thus adumbrates the twin spheres of anxiety — global and personal — within which Will attempts to live his life. And it implicitly represents the two conditions (identified at the outset) which define the matrix of human experience: the symbolizing instinct and the consciousness of death. The depressed protagonist confronts at the beginning of his quest a pair of signs — one public and conventional, the other private and esoteric — which convey the idea of human self-destruction. Indeed, upon encountering these signs, Will becomes "even more depressed" and on the next page (p. 4) decides to shoot himself.

Percy makes it clear, however, that Will's suicide ideation develops principally in response to the second sign, a sound evocative of the forgotten event. As the scene on the golf course unfolds (Will has sliced two tee shots into the woods), we see that the repressed episode begins to force its way into the hero's consciousness even before his perception of the sound as a sign. Actually, Percy defers an explanation of the sound until Chapter III, where in shifting the action back to the golf match, he first calls attention to Will's odd handling of the 3-iron as he crosses a wire fence that "creaked and popped against the fence posts": "even as he was climbing through, he had shifted his grip on the iron so that the club head was tucked high under his right arm, shaft resting on forearm, right hand holding the shaft steady — as one might carry a shotgun" (p. 44). Still withholding a clarification of the sound as sign, Percy recounts conversations earlier in the golf match before returning, six pages later, to the fence scene; here he depicts Will entranced by a hunting fantasy but now half conscious of his gesture with the 3-iron as a sign or clue: "Now, carefully, as if he were reenacting an event not quite remembered, as if he had forgotten something which his muscles and arms and hands might remember, he swung the shaft of the iron to and fro like the barrel of a shotgun" (p. 51). At the threshold of memory, Will then hears the sound of the fence as an echo and recognizes its semiotic nature:

> The guitar sound of the fence wire stretched above him and the singing and popping of the vines against his body were signs of another event. Stooping now, he was trying to make his body remember what had happened. Suddenly it crossed his mind that nothing else had ever happened to him. (p. 52).

In *Proust and Signs*, Deleuze speaks of the way in which signs can lead us unexpectedly toward truth: "There is always the violence of a sign which forces us into the search, which robs us of peace. The truth is not to be found by affinity, nor by good will, but is *betrayed* by involuntary signs."[10] Such is the effect of the fence sound for Will: it thrusts him instantly into the memory-world of childhood and forces upon him the task of recovering and decoding the most crucial event in his life.

The ensuing recollection (pp. 52–62) forms the imaginative crux of *The Second Coming*, and its complex, veiled meaning preoccupies Will for much of the novel, since his compulsion to kill himself (as he gradually comes to see) derives from that early experience. The long-repressed scene concerns a boyhood hunting incident in a Georgia swamp, in which Will's father, ostensibly shooting at quail, wounds his son and then nearly kills himself with the double-barreled Greener, an English shotgun. Though Percy's narrative reconstruction produces the illusion of a regained past, a flow of undifferentiated but chronological impressions, Will actually recuperates the event (as we see in subsequent flashbacks) through the mediation of discrete, static memory-signs which contain in coded form the signification of the moment. Early in the novel, Percy posits a neurological analysis of remembrance: "The brain registers and records every sensation, sight and sound and smell, it has ever received. If the neurones where such information is stored happen to be stimulated, jostled, pressed upon, any memory can be recaptured" (p. 6). Will's search implies that memory consists of separable perceptions, stored not according to an absolute chronology but according to associational clusters, in which certain images predominate and assume a synecdochic function. Thus while Will's first recollection of the "hunting accident" unfolds as a linear sequence of actions, Percy suggests that remembrance actually occurs within a network of fixed images; the sense of *déroulement* in memory is a consciousness of the mind's movement from one sign to another.

In the shooting episode, a handful of specific perceptions dominate the recollection and subsequently become the memory-signs by which

Will recaptures and deciphers the event. The implications of each can be indicated summarily:

1. THE FENCE. As we have noted, Will's sudden recollection has been precipitated by the sound of a wire fence. The memory sequence begins: "The boy had gone through the fence first, holding the new Sterlingworth Fox double-barreled twenty-gauge ahead of him, while the man pulled up the top strand of barbed wire" (p. 52). But before Will can crawl through the fence, his father grabs his shoulder, forces him back, and curses him for holding a loaded shotgun carelessly. The warning seems absurd, since (as we shortly realize) the father has already decided he must kill his son to save him from the despair of "knowing too much." For both father and son, the fence-crossing marks a change, a fundamental redefinition of the relationship: "*Here*, said the man, handing him the shotgun and stretching up the top strand of barbed wire. The wire creaked. *I trust you now*" (p. 53). The sound of the wire remains in Will's memory because the moment signifies a passage, an initiation into a new state of consciousness; the father's gesture of opening the way through the fence has become, in effect, a sign of his desire to share with the son "the one sure sweet exodus" (p. 324), a shotgun blast. Just after Will crosses through the fence, his father seems to sense the symbolism of the act and he promises, "*I'm going to see to it that you don't have to go through what I am going through*" (p. 53). Will has come through the fence, into an emerging recognition of his father's despair; but only in retrospect does he become aware of the fence as a symbolic boundary, a sign of his own entrance into the world of death-anxiety and suicidal compulsion.

2. GLITTERING EYES. Four times prior to the shooting, Will refers to the strange look in his father's eyes. He remembers that when the elder Barrett handed him the shotgun, "his eyes glittered but not in the merry way they did when the hunt went well" (p. 53). The glittering eyes, said to be "too bright," signify an unnatural urgency: Will's father is possessed by his own fatalistic vision. The eyes are thus the sign of a curse (one thinks of the Ancient Mariner), the mark of an absolute and inexplicable transformation. They betray a terrifying *difference*, the absence of the known, familiar father and the presence of an unknown, demonic double. The eyes also suggest a visionary power: "The man sounded almost absentminded and his glittering eyes seemed to cast beyond him [Will] to the future, perhaps to the lawsuit Monday" (p. 53). What the father envisions is not the lawsuit but the hopeless future, in which he foresees his son driven to the same desperate self-destruction. But for Will, the preternatural brightness of his father's eyes becomes in retrospect a sign of the violence and rage soon to express itself: a consuming indignation at the absurd, naturalistic fate of the human animal.

3. GESTURES OF AFFECTION. What puzzles Will most is his father's sudden display of affection: "Now, as the boy stood beside him, the

man gave him a hug with the arm not holding the gun. He felt the man's hand giving him hard regular pats on the arm" (pp. 53–54). The gesture leads Will to reflect on "the strangeness of it, getting an awkward hug from his father, as they stood side by side in their bulky hunting clothes in the wet cold funk-smelling pin-oak swamp." He relates the behavior to the hugs and kisses exchanged at weddings and funerals, perhaps intuiting the formal, ritualistic significance of the moment. But he shrinks from his father's kiss as "a kind of violation" and "a cheapening" and he wonders about the semiotic purpose of such gestures: "Italians and Frenchmen and women hugged and kissed each other and what did it signify?" (p. 54). As Will's father continues to caress him with "regular hard pats," he discloses the underlying meaning of his actions:

> *You and I are the same,* said the man as if he were speaking to the gun. . . . *You are like me. We are two of a kind. I saw it last night.* Here come the pats again, hard, regular slow, like a bell tolling. . . . *I saw the way you lay in bed last night and slept or didn't sleep. You're one of us, I'm afraid. You already know too much.* (p. 55)

The union signified by the father's gestures is precisely the awareness of a common doom imposed by superior knowledge, which will culminate in suicidal despair: the bell tolls for both of them. The signs of affection also express, for the elder Barrett, an implicit death pact, a bond to be sealed by the murder-suicide attempt which follows. As Will recalls the scene, his father's gestures become a sign of betrayal, a Judas-kiss marking him for death and hence a "violation" of his being. The hugs and kisses, expressive of intimacy and consanguinity (shared "death genes"), only intensify Will's sense of distance from his father and the "strangeness" of his death-dealing tenderness.

4. "SHIT". As a father gives his son the "last hard pat, sock, wham, on the shoulder," he says, *"Oh shit"* (p. 55). The expletive strikes Will as "curious" because he has never before heard his courtly father use the word. Years later, the son recalls the oath and understands it as a sign: "Now standing with the three-iron in the glade, he was thinking: he said that one and only *shit* in exactly the same flat taped voice airline pilots use before the crash: *We're going in. Shit*" (p. 55). The word lodges itself in Will's memory as a sign of surrender, a recognition of imminent and inescapable death. It further expresses chagrin at the awkward humiliation of dying: one imagines his body as an object of disgust. Behind the comic incongruity (one expects last words to be memorable, valedictory), Will reads in the expletive a coded nihilism, a sense of self as excremental waste, thoughtlessly jettisoned. This interpretation gains credence later when Ewell McBee, a neighbor, confides to Will the definition of man once articulated by the elder Barrett: "You want to know what a man is? I'll tell you. A man is born between an asshole and a peehole. He eats, sleeps, shits, fucks, works, gets old, and dies. And that's all he does. That's

what a man is" (p. 176). The grim naturalism (and fatalism) signified by the father's use of "shit" initially fascinates Will, for in his darker moods, he shares that assessment of the human condition. Indeed, he cannot throw off the hold of these memory-signs until he has completed this stage of his apprenticeship and fully decoded the "hunting accident."

5. RELOADING SOUNDS/ SHOTGUN SHELLS. The riddle of that episode is bound up with the puzzling relationship between two signs: the spent green Winchester Super-X shotgun shells and the "geclick, gecluck" sound of the reloading process. In his recollection of the shooting sequence, Will describes three shotgun blasts: the first, at a single quail; the second (which hits Will), supposedly aimed at another bird; and the third, which wounds his father. Yet he has also heard the gun breech opened after the first and second shots, and he discovers *four* expended shells — three retrieved by the hunting guide and a fourth still in the gun barrel. The belated realization of a disparity ("only now, thirty years later, did he do the arithmetic") between gunshots and empty shells confounds Will until he tests the Greener (which is still in his possession) and finds that both barrels can be discharged at once. The disruptive effect of the reloading problem illustrates perfectly what Deleuze called "the violence of a sign which forces us into the search"; it also demonstrates the force of Percy's claim that man can only "know one thing through the mirror of another."

> There were four empty shells, three the guide had picked up and put on the quilt beside me in the Negro cabin, and one in the breech of the Greener. "Here yo bullets," the guide said, not even knowing that spent shells are worthless.
> *Wait a minute.*
> Then you had to have fired both barrels at the second single.
> Why? You don't unload two Super-X's on one small quail.
> *Wait a minute. There was no second single.* If there had been, I'd remember, because I remember everything now. I'd have heard him get up before you shot, heard the sudden tiny thunder. I knew that all along. Why didn't I know that I knew it? Then both barrels were for me, weren't they? (p. 147)

For the first time Will understands that his father was not simply trying to warn him; he was trying to kill him. This knowledge instigates a further search, as Will seeks to learn through an imagined dialog with his dead father the origin of the elder Barrett's despair and the ultimate meaning of the "hunting accident" as a coded clue to Will's own self-destructive impulses. For even as he struggles to decipher the past, he finds himself drawn almost irresistibly toward a repetition of his father's fate; the moment he solves the riddle of the spent shells, Will rehearses his own suicide: "Hm. Why do I feel relieved, even dispensed, as if somehow I were now free to do what I am going to do? Smiling, he turned the carbine-length shotgun, swinging the muzzle toward him. Easily done: you can even put both thumbs on both triggers" (p. 147).

6. THE SHOTGUN. The Greener provides a physical link between past and present, being both a memory-sign (the recollected instrument of violence) and a memento of his father, the suicide, and the family tradition of "death dealing." Will's involuntary remembrance of the "hunting accident" in Chapter 3, his puzzlement about the extra shell, and his mounting temptation to shoot himself prompt him, in Part One, Chapter 5, to unpack the Greener, which has been hidden in a closet for years. This lengthy chapter marks a turning point in Will's suicidal crisis; his contemplation of the long-repressed scene becomes a virtual obsession, as Percy suggests through repeated flashbacks. By this time Will has become partly convinced (ambivalence being common to suicidal thought) that he must follow his father's example, and the Greener therefore also becomes the tangible bond between them, intensifying Will's sense of a mutual destiny. After retrieving the shotgun from the closet (where it has lain for twenty years), he breaks the breech and discovers that "there was a faint reek of gun oil and powder from the last shot" (p. 46), which scattered his father's brains across the attic of their Mississippi home. The smell of the gunpowder brings back the suicide in a thoroughly Proustian way, and Will's handling of the shotgun, his testing of the triggers, gives him an insight into his father's "love of death." In an imagined dialogue with his father (the "old mole"), Will appears to choose death:

> Did you not then believe, old mole, that these two things alone are real, loving and dying, and since one is so much like the other and there is so little of the one, in the end there remained only the other?
> Silence.
> Very well, old mole you win. (p. 162)

At this point, then, the Greener functions as a sign of necessary death, a sign of the despairing nihilism which the elder Barrett had attempted to explain prior to the "hunting accident." In the Georgia swamp, Will had sensed only the strangeness of his father's words and actions; years later, holding the Greener in his own hands, he decodes the event and understands the shotgun as the key emblem of his father's desire for death. Indeed, as an instrument of desire the Greener eventually becomes a sign of sexual power (we recall that Freud posited a relationship between suicide and sexual wish–fulfillment); a self-destruction reveals itself as an ultimate, autoerotic experience:

> In the case of love, more is better than less, two twice as good as one, and most is best of all. And if the aim is the ecstasy of love, two is closer to infinity than one, especially when the two are twelve-gauge Super-X number-eight shot. And what samurai self-love of death, let alone the little death of everyday fuck-you love, can match the double Winchester

> come of taking oneself into oneself, the cold-steel extension of oneself into mouth, yes, for you, for me, for us, the logical and ultimate act of fuck-you love fuck-off world, the penetration and union of perfect cold gunmetal into warm quailing mortal flesh, the coming to end all coming, brain cells which together faltered and fell short, now flowered and flew apart, flung like stars around the whole dark world. (pp. 148–49)

The shock of this passage derives in part from the implicit play on the novel's title: the "coming to end all coming" — suicide as the ultimate orgasmic sensation — presents a radical secular solution to the human desire for love, for transcendence, for absolute experience. The apparent absence of any such encompassing, redemptive power leads Will toward the same deadly narcissism, and we see him at this point the captive of the very signs he has deciphered. But he makes one additional discovery, which ultimately saves his life: he perceives that his father's suicide may have been based on a misreading, on a failure to recognize and interpret the signs of his own despair or — more importantly — to search for a truth beyond the immanent signs of his unhappiness.

> It dawned on him that his father's suicide was *wasted*. It availed nothing, proved nothing, solved nothing, posed no questions let alone answered questions, did nobody good. It was no more than an exit, a getting up and going out, a closing of a door. (p. 182)

Finally, it is Will's apprenticeship to signs that impels him to continue his quest, to find the truth which with either justify self-destruction or liberate him from the prison house of memory.

As noted at the outset, Will's private crisis occurs within the context of an apocalyptic anxiety; he feels oppressed not only by the phantasm of his father's suicide but by an acute sense of the death-in-life of the twentieth century:

> The name of the enemy is death, he said, grinning and shoving his hands in his pockets. Not the death of dying but the living death.
> The name of this century is the Century of the Love of Death. Death in this century is not the death people die but the death people live. Men love death because real death is better than the living death. (p. 271)

This perception, which calls to mind Binx Bolling's attack on the modern age as the "century of merde, the great shithouse of scientific humanism," clarifies the nature of Will's search: he seeks signs of life amid ubiquitous indications of death. Alienated from all forms of belief and unbelief in the late twentieth century, Will desires an ultimate sign, a self-sufficient emblem, which will confirm the existence of God — and thus the possibility of surmounting death. He seeks this revelation in Lost Cove Cave with an "experiment" calculated to establish the presence (or absence) of God;

the scheme involves the risk of death but seems an improvement upon the famous wager of Pascal ("the last French intellectual who was not insane"). Will explains, "My experiment is simply this: I shall go to a desert place [the cave] and wait for God to give a sign. If no sign is forthcoming I shall die. But people will know why I died: because there is no sign" (p. 193). The cave strategy thus has a patently semiotic object: it aims to resolve the suicidal despair evoked by the worldly sign, the Greener, through the evocation of a transcendent sign. If the latter fails to manifest itself, the hero will accept the fate signified by his father's shotgun; he will know that "what is at hand are not the Last Days but the last days, [his] last days" (p. 213).

Although Will's descent into the cave seems not to yield the sought-for sign, a raging toothache leads him (providentially?) toward deliverance as he tumbles — surely a Fortunate Fall — through an opening in the rock into the greenhouse abode of Allie Huger, the gracile nymph who becomes his salvation. A runaway mental pateint, Allie suffers from amnesia and intermittent aphasia; she lives in the greenhouse — an evident emblem of life and growth — with her prize possession, a huge iron stove ("not old but surely new, transformed, reborn") which she has "hoisted" out of the ruins of a burned-down house. Her relationship with Will grows from reciprocal need: "He would remember for her if she forgot. She would hoist him if he fell" (p. 253). Will's sudden fall into the greenhouse is not, however, his first encounter with Allie. That meeting occurred, significantly, at the very moment that Will recalled the "hunting accident": the lost golf balls, which caused him to cross the creaking fence, were returned to him by the girl. This apparent coincidence (to be examined shortly) offers an important clue to the semiotic aspect of Will's experience. In effect, the antipodes of his life-death ambivalence are expressed by the Greener and the greenhouse; he must choose between the allure of his father's "coming to end all coming" and the simple love offered by Allie.

But at this point Will fails to see the choice as a choice, because he also fails to understand Allie's very presence as a sign. And so even after he has (literally) fallen in love, he continues to brood upon self-destruction; returning home from the cave episode, he checks to make sure that the Greener and the Luger his father brought back from the war are still in the closet. Later he transfers these weapons to the trunk of his car, apparently taking a perverse comfort in their availability. The force of his lingering desire for death becomes explicit, however, when he tells a stranger that he has "unfinished business in Georgia." He feels compelled to return to the site of the "hunting accident":

> [Will] was going back to Georgia to find something he had left there, to find a place where something had happened to him. Or rather hadn't happened to him. All these years he had thought he was in luck that it didn't happen and that he had escaped with his life and a triumphant life at that. But it was something else he had escaped with, not his life.

His life — or was it his death? — he had left behind in the Thomasville swamp, where it still waited for him. (p. 296)

Any ambiguity present here is dissolved by a subsequent vow: "It was in Georgia that he would do it" (p. 297). Despite his developing attachment to Allie, Will seems at this point sunk in despair, anguished by the death-in-life of leisure living in North Carolina and possessed by the memory-signs of the violent incident.

From a psychological perspective, Will's crisis occurs as the inevitable culmination of a process. Unresolved feelings about his father's death form an essential element, for as Robert Jay Lifton has explained,

> If a family member, especially a parent, has committed suicide, one is likely to form a strong image of that act, an image which can take on great relevance for one's own struggles. Experiences of separation and loss, whether or not originally associated with the parental suicide, can readily infuse the suicidal constellation. Just as imagery of death equivalents in general are in back-and-forth association with that of actual death, a similar interaction can develop between death equivalents and the suicide construct. Whenever one feels abandoned, torn apart, or immobilized, an image of suicide may be evoked. . . . It is quite possible that where parental suicide has loomed large, a child can almost come to equate death with suicide.[11]

Significantly, Will's remembrance of the "hunting accident" and his bout with suicidal despair follow upon two experiences of "separation and loss": the death of his saintly first wife, Marion Peabody Barrett and the betrothal of his daughter, Leslie. These events apparently trigger the recollection which befalls Will on the golf course; as we have seen, the recovery of that scene evokes a set of images embedded within the "suicidal constellation." We see that the specific "suicide construct" Will develops — the conceptualization of his own death — typically involves a gunshot to the head, thus duplicating his father's suicide plan. Percy suggests the intensity of this identification when, during the cave episode, Will seems to merge with the elder Barrett: "he became his father" (p. 215). Believing that he cannot separate his fate from that of his father, Will finally concludes that he must return to the Georgia swamp to complete the action which his father tried (but failed) to carry out.

This motif of the return to a site of violence further underscores the determinism at work upon Will. In terms of Freudian theory, he seems bound to kill himself for a host of reasons.[12] First, as we have noted, Will identifies so closely with his dead father that he feels a need to join him in death and suspects that he is biologically doomed to do so by his "death genes." Second, he has, in recollecting the "hunting accident," acknowledged his ambivalence toward his father, as revealed by his avoidance of physical contact, his aversion to kissing his father, and his refusal of friendship ("We're not buddies. I don't want to be anyone's buddy."). Such latent antipathies, Freud observed, can produce guilt feelings in surviving children, who develop the need to punish themselves, even to the point of suicide, for once harboring symbolic death wishes toward parents. Third, Will feels in some sense abandoned by his father: "You, old father, old mole, loved me but loved death better" (p. 272). Freud concluded that suicidal feeling can develop from a loss of libidinal gratification (here, parental love) either through a refusal to accept the loss or as an act of revenge (one kills himself to spite the absent, rejecting parent). Fourth, after solving the problem of the shotgun shells, Will realizes that his father had attempted to kill him; among the conditions identified by Freud as predisposing one to suicide, Robert Litman notes the "disease of the superego due to cruel parents, dead parents, parents that wished the person dead."[13]. Finally, Will plans his suicide as a call for help; he wants to kill himself, but he simultaneously wants to be saved from that fate by a friend or loved one. Thus he makes a veiled reference to his scheme when he leaves his daughter's engagement party; he allows his friend, Lewis Peckham, to find him contemplating the shotgun; he discusses suicide with his doctor, Vance Battle, and he composes a letter to Sutter Vaught, outlining his patently suicidal cave experiment. As Freud realized, the suicidal person often seeks life by gambling with death and considers the attempt the only means of communicating his urgent appeal for help. In sum, these various motives produce a crushing pressure upon Will to risk annihilation.

But as the hero travels toward the Georgia swamp for his rendezvous with death, an extraordinary thing happens. He sees in the passing landscape an image which brings to mind the lovely but vulnerable Allie: "his eye traveled along the ridge and came to a notch where in the darkness of the pine and spruce there grew a single gold poplar which caught the sun like a yellow-haired girl coming out of a dark forest" (p. 297). The sunlit poplar becomes a sign evoking his first, hallucinatory glimpse of the girl:

> Deeper in the pine forest, beyond the chestnut fall, the poplar made an irregular cone of sunlight and leaves. He had been gazing at a figure behind the poplar. Was someone standing there or, more likely, was it a trick of light, a pattern in the dappled leaves? . . . The figure moved behind the poplar, or perhaps a breath of air stirred the leaves. (p. 71)

The recollected scene reminds Will of his concern for Allie, and immediately he perceives his journey to Georgia — to another forest and another haunting figure — as a mistake: "Once again his heart was flooded with sweetness but a sweetness of a different sort, a sharp sweet urgency, a need to act, to run and catch. He was losing something" (p. 297). In this critical passage, Percy superimposes one memory-sign upon another and suggests that the remembered image of Allie saves Will from the "dark forest" of suicidal obsession, from the beckoning image of his dead father.

But although Will returns to his woodland nymph, he has not yet won a clear title to life; the past continues to exert a deadly influence. At the beginning of the novel's final chapter, he again recalls the example of his father and makes a telling revelation:

> South Georgia, Alabama, Mississippi, he thought, . . . And my father and his near death in the Georgia swamp and my near death and later his death in Mississippi and my being at his death and his wanting me to be there, his wanting me to see his brain exploded, expanding like the universe and plastering the attic with neurones like stars in the night sky. Why did he want me to be there? To show me what? Now I know. To show me the one sure sweet exodus. (pp. 323–24)

Although Percy implies in *The Last Gentleman* that Will simply watched his father go in the house and heard him fire the fatal shot, this passage reveals that the boy actually witnessed the suicide. In this stunning acknowledgement, we discern the most compelling reason for Will's long repression of violent memories and his subsequent fixation upon his father and the idea of suicide. Present at his father's death, he suffers from a profound sense of guilt at having failed to intervene and at having survived the death his father had wanted him to share. He muses, "I have been living yes, but it is a living death because I knew he wanted me dead. Am I entitled to live? I am alive by a fluke like the sole survivor of Treblinka, who lived by a fluke, but did not really feel entitled to live" (p. 324). This classic survivor guilt, about which Lifton has written so extensively,[14] continues to oppress Will despite Allie's restorative influence.

Near the end of the novel, the hero thus experiences a final suicidal urge, this time in the form of an imagined appeal from his dead father:

> Come, it's the only way, the one quick sure exit of grace and violence and beauty. Come, believe me it's the ultimate come, not the first come which we all grow up dreaming about and which is never what we hoped, is it, but near enough to know there is something better, isn't it, the second, last and ultimate come to end all comes. (pp. 336–37)

This blandishment recalls Will's earlier meditation on the "logical and ultimate act of fuck-you love" (p. 148) and touches upon a problem fundamental to Percy's writing: the relationship between erotic love and depression. Sutter Vaught, Will's friend and counselor in *The Last Gentleman*, uses autopsy reports to document "post-orgasmic despair" and establish his theory of suicide as a desire for "pure transcendence" after temporary coital ecstasy. For Sutter, "lewdness" figures as the "sacrament of the dispossessed"; hence the pattern of orgasm-despair-suicide signals both the longing for transcendence and the failure of the secular/sexual order to provide it. But Sutter, like Will's father, sees no alternative and flirts with suicide as one seeks a perfect lover. Will himself feels the seduction of death, and this invitation to experience "the second, last and ultimate come to end all comes" forces him to choose between life and death, between a love directed toward the Other and a love rooted in orgasmic self-delight.

When Will leaves the motel room (where he is bedded down with Allie) the issue seems much in doubt; this paragraph, the undeniable climax of his ordeal with the memory-signs of suicide, dramatizes a definitive choice:

> He rose and dressed in the dark, walked out to the Mercedes, unlocked the trunk, took out the leather case containing the Greener and the holster containing the Luger. It was a cold starry night. The mists of summer and fall had all blown away. He walked down the highway holding the Greener like a businessman with a briefcase. When he reached the overlook the Holiday Inn looked over, he did not even pause but swung the case like a discus, the throw turning him around and heading him back. He did not hear the Greener hit bottom. As an afterthought, he pitched the Luger back over his shoulder and went away without listening. (p. 338).

The symbolism is obvious but effective. By disposing of the guns, Will has simultaneously abandoned the "quick sure exit of grace" and exorcised the ghost of his "death-dealing" father. He at last achieves that pre-condition of well-being alluded to by Kierkegaard (and presented as a headnote to *The Last Gentleman*): "If a man cannot forget, he will never amount to much." The discarding of the Greener is itself a sign of Will's successful apprenticeship to signs; he has broken the code inscribed in memory, deciphering and finally resisting its fatal message. He has thus won a conditional freedom from the tyranny of an image-repertoire signifying death. But he has yet to discover an order of signs promising life.

However, the very action which sends the Greener crashing down into the gorge turns Will away from the past and toward his new life with Allie. Her role in effecting Will's deliverance is neither coincidental nor trivial; a further reexamination of the moment when Will remembers the "hunting accident" reveals that Percy foreshadows the girl's eventual replacement of the dead father as a source of signs. Abstracted by his sudden remembrance, Will unconsciously confuses the actual, visual image of Allie with the recollected image of his dead father:

> Of course, he said, holding the three-iron across his arm like a shotgun and smiling at the figure dappled by sunlight beyond the poplar, of course. Ever since your death, all I ever wanted from you was out, out from you and from the Mississippi twilight, and from the shotguns thundering in musty attics and racketing through funk-smelling Georgia swamps. (p. 72)

Significantly, the "figure dappled by sunlight" provides a way out, an escape from the darkness of his father's vision, but only after Will recognizes the sign which he initially fails to see, the sign originally obscured by the memory-sign of the absent father: the presence of Allie.

Percy alludes to this emerging insight through another device, a metaphor used recurrently in *The Second Coming*. This is the figurative reference to "treasure" or "buried treasure," which first pertains to "the treasure Captain Kidd was supposed to have buried" (p. 39) on the island Allie has inherited (along with the greenhouse) from her Aunt Sally. But a more revealing reference occurs at the end of the sequence describing the "hunting accident," when Will first seems to perceive the significance of the shooting: *"Ah, I've found it after all. The buried treasure"* (p. 61). The treasure, Will explains, is the realization that his father "had a secret" and was trying to communicate it. Here, the "buried treasure" is the covert meaning of the Georgia episode, the essential truth of which the memory-signs are the coded expression. The treasure in effect signifies the tacit revelation that Will is destined to "come to the same place" his father reached, to see death as a boon. But Percy uses the treasure metaphor in association with Allie to suggest the idea of unanticipated restoration; of the wondrous, cast-iron stove the girl retrieves from the ruins, Percy writes, "She had found a treasure" (p. 92). The lavish description of the stove (pp. 203–204) clarifies its function as a symbol of renewal and recovery after disaster. Similarly, Percy uses a version of the treasure metaphor when Will, en route to Georgia sees the sunlit poplar and remembers Allie: "He was losing something. Something of his as solid and heavy and sweet as a pot of honey in his lap was being taken away" (p. 297). Fear of losing Allie, his "pot of honey," recalls Will from his suicidal mission: his desire for the treasure of life overcomes his longing for the treasure of death. Will completes his apprenticeship, therefore, when he recognizes Allie as a treasure and asks himself, "Is she a gift and therefore the sign of a giver?" (p. 360). In regarding Allie as a sign, Will implicitly exchanges the semiotics of memory for the semiotics of grace. He has at last perceived the sign he hoped to find in Lost Cove Cave and through this insight arrives at the stage of belief. Rejecting the suicidal nihilism of his father and Sutter Vaught, Will commits himself to Allie and to the Lord: "Am I crazy to want both, her and Him? No, not want, must have. And will have" (p. 360).

In *The Moviegoer*, Binx Bolling identifies the "only possible starting point" for his search as "the strange fact of one's own invincible apathy — that if the proofs were proved and God presented himself, nothing would be changed." He carries the problem of faith a step further, into the realm of semiotics, when he remarks:

> Abraham saw signs of God and believed. Now the only sign is that all the signs in the world make no difference. Is this God's ironic revenge? But I am onto him.[15]

Abraham's capacity for belief sprang from his perception of signs, whereas the despair of modern man, according to Percy, derives precisely from his inability to recognize a sign as a sign. The only apparent "sign" is his "invincible apathy" to tokens and portents, his blindness before signified truth. For Will Barrett, the search for truth begins with the recollection of signs; he has forgotten these images because they signify the truth he wants most deeply to deny: the fact of his own mortality. In the despair and suicide of his father, Will sees a prefiguration of his fate; his own compulsion to kill himself may be seen as a desire not for death per se but for an end to the anxiety of dying. Yet in decoding the hunting episode and accepting his suicidal tendencies, he also paradoxically clarifies and strengthens his will to live. In facing the problem of death, as mediated by memory-signs, Will opens himself fully to the horror of man's creaturely destiny ("he eats, sleeps, shits, fucks, works, gets old, and dies"); but this consciousness, as Ernest Becker has remarked, also endows man with "full humanness," generates an unrepressed passion for life, and enables one to avoid the death-in-life existence which depends upon "tranquilizing itself with the trivial."[16] Hence, Will's apprenticeship to the signs of mortality awakens a desire for new life and forces upon him the search for a sustaining truth. Perhaps most importantly, his encounter with death teaches him to recognize a sign as a sign. And the story of his search becomes the signifier of a larger meaning: only by decoding and coming to terms with the complex symbolism through which we conceive of death can we begin to discern the essential signs of Life.

Notes

1. *The Denial of Death* (New York: Free Press, 1973), p. 27.

2. Collège de France seminar, "Preparation du Roman," Dec. 2, 1978. See my essay, "Roland Barthes, Autobiography and the End of Writing," *Georgia Review*, 35 (Summer 1981), 381–98.

3. *The Last Gentleman* (New York: Farrar, Straus and Giroux, 1966), p. 6.

4. *The Message in the Bottle* (New York: Farrar, Straus and Giroux, 1975). p. 17.

5. "Metaphor as Mistake," in *The Message in the Bottle*, p. 82.

6. "The Mystery of Language," in *The Message in the Bottle*, p. 155.

7. "Symbol, Consciousness, Intersubjectivity," in *The Message in the Bottle*, p. 271.

8. *The Second Coming* (New York: Farrar, Straus and Giroux, 1980), p. 51. All subsequent references to the novel correspond to this edition.

9. *Proust and Signs*, trans. Richard Howard (New York: George Braziller, 1972), p. 4, pp. 25–37.

10. *Proust and Signs*, p. 16.

11. *The Broken Connection* (New York: Simon and Schuster, 1979), p. 254.

12. The following summary is based upon the essay by Robert E. Litman, "Sigmund Freud on Suicide," in *Essays in Self-Destruction*, ed. Edwin S. Schneidman (New York: Science House, 1967), pp. 324–44.

13. "Sigmund Freud on Suicide," p. 338.

14. See *Home from the War: Vietnam Veterans — Neither Victims nor Executioners*

(New York: Simon and Schuster, 1973) See also the chapter "Guilt," in *The Broken Connection*, pp. 132–46.

15. *The Moviegoer* (New York: Alfred A. Knopf, 1961), p. 146.

16. The latter phrase is Kierkegaard's, cited by Becker, *The Denial of Death*, p. 81.

Walker Percy's Wager: *The Second Coming*

Sue Mitchell Crowley*

> According to the doctrine of chance, you ought to put yourself to the trouble of searching for the truth; for if you die without worshipping the True Cause, you are lost. — "But," say you, "if He had wished me to worship Him, He would have left me signs of His will." — He has done so; but you neglect them. Seek them, therefore; it is well worth it.
>
> Pascal, *Pensées*, 236[1]

I

The Last Gentleman is quite clearly an unfinished novel. And Walker Percy means it to be. But beyond finding the ending ambiguous, the reader may find it also strangely dissatisfying. The intimation that Will Barrett may return to marry Kitty, establish residence in Cap'n Andy's picturesque cottage and become the scion of the Confederate Chevrolet agency is deeply at odds with the character of this young man who is not only the last gentleman but, above all, the wayfarer. The Will who interests us is the seeker who pursues Sutter Vaught to prevent him from driving off in his Edsel into the desert to keep his date with his own suicide. There in Santa Fe, the City of Holy Faith, Will demands that Sutter "wait" for him because, as he repeatedly says, he "needs" him. This need arises because Will has "a final question" — he perceives that Sutter, although an atheist, understands what has just occurred at the death-bed baptism of his younger brother, Jamie. Will asks, "What happened back there?"[2]

The word "happen" occurs in its various forms, albeit unnoticeably, with startling frequency throughout Percy's work. Far from being a weak verb, it is crucial to an understanding of the way in which Percy's fiction works. His philosophy and theology, as well as his conception of plot, depend on this seemingly insignificant word. Percy says that when "a non-believer like Sartre writes, nothing happens," but that "when we [believers] write, we wait for something to happen. And when it does," he continues, "what happens is grace."[3] This motion of grace occurs first for the writer's hand, his pen, if you will, and the writing is a gift; and then it

---

*This essay was written specifically for this volume and appears here for the first time.

occurs for the plot he creates, for the characters themselves. And, this, Percy believes, is how Christianity enters a novel.

The reader of *The Last Gentleman* simply wants to know what *happens* to Will Barrett. Will exists as *homo viator* in Kierkegaard's religious mode. He is the communicator of the salvific message from Father Boomer to Jamie — a kind of "transistor," Percy calls him. But Will "did not know how he knew" (406). Poor Will has, Percy insists in several interviews, "missed it."[4]

So *The Second Coming* is a sequel, not only because it marks a return for Will Barrett and certain members of the Vaught family, but because the new novel attempts to answer the very questions raised by the earlier one: what is the nature of faith and how does one receive it? In this sense, *The Second Coming* is a title that points to the return promised in the New Testament; but it points to revelation that is not written as well.

Percy, too, seems to have wondered, if unconsciously, about what happened to Will. He claims, however, that he had written over two hundred pages of this novel before he realized that his hero was indeed Will Barrett.[5] His hero has now "married him a wife" and "lived him a life." Will ponders himself as sequel:

> I went as far as I could go, married a rich hardheaded plain decent crippled pious upstate Utica, New York, woman, practiced Trusts and Estates law in a paneled office on Wall Street, kept a sailboat on the North Shore, played squash, lived at 76th and Fifth, walked my poodle in the park, went up an elevator to get home, tipped three doormen and four elevator men at Christmas, thought happily about making money like everyone else (money is a kind of happiness), made more money than some, married a great deal more money than most, learned how to whistle down a cab two blocks away and get in and out of "21" in time for the theatre. . . . I even tried to believe in the Christian God. . . . Yes, I did all that and succeeded in everything except believing in the Christian God.[6]

Now Will has returned to the South, to North Carolina where his wife Marion has before her death founded St. Mark's, an Episcopal home for the elderly, and his born-again daughter Leslie is about to be married and turn her mother's estate into still another philanthropic institution, a "love community" for the aged. But, Will muses, the whole twenty years (the time intervening between the novels) could just as easily have been "a long night's dream." Will is still the man who had to know everything before he could do anything, who still insists on engineering his own life. He is the wanderer who pursues anyone who might know something he doesn't know, anyone who might be, as Binx Bolling would say, "onto something."

Near the end of *The Second Coming* Will says to the ancient Father Weatherbee, "I perceive that you seem to know something" (p. 358). The priest's knowledge is, in Percy's terms, the form that faith takes. Will comes, as we shall see, to demand an empirical sign on which to base his faith. He does receive signs but, as Pascal knew so well, they are not signs that prove, for then faith has no reason to be. They are signs incarnated, rather, in history as event, in words as Word, in persons as sacraments. "The spirit of grace, the hardness of heart; external circumstances" *(Pensées,* 507): these comprise the plot of Percy's novel. The fiction is, as he would say, "the fleshing out"[7] of a definition of faith.

Percy's nonfictional exploration of faith, "The Message in the Bottle," was first published in *Thought* in 1959 and then became the title essay for his collected essays in 1975. The basic debate in the essay is discernible in its epigraphs. Is faith a form of knowledge? Thomas in both *The Summa* and *De Veritate* defines faith as belonging to the cognitive faculty, as originating in the speculative understanding. The enlightening of the mind causes the will to seek the good, which, in turn, moves the intellect to affirmation. Søren Kierkegaard, on the other hand, believes this to be impossible, for "No knowledge can have for its object the absurdity that the eternal is the historical."[8] For Kierkegaard, then, the Incarnation is "The Scandal." Percy, who most often regards Kierkegaard as his mentor, sides here with the Scholastic position that reason supports faith. In a recent interview he states the content of faith: "that God exists and that man is created in his image."[9] And he makes it clear that his views have not changed since he wrote "The Message in the Bottle":

> [Faith] is different from scientific knowing, but it is a form of knowledge. I tend to agree with Aquinas there, even though I am more sympathetic with Kierkegaard. I am on his wavelength, I understand his phenomenology, his analysis of the existential predicament of modern man. Aquinas did not have that, but I think Aquinas was right about faith. It is not a leap into the absurd, it is an act of faith, which is a form of knowledge.[10]

Will Barrett recapitulates in both novels the role of the castaway in "The Message in the Bottle." The young Will has "lost his memory in the shipwreck" (MB, 119), and the older Will is still Percy's very "special sort of castaway": a well-educated, useful member of the community, one who is curious about the world. The castaway comes upon bottles washed up by the waves and containing messages that, Percy explains, are sentences expressing different forms of knowledge. There is, on the other hand, a piece of knowledge *sub specie aeternitatis* that "can be arrived at anywhere by anyone and at any time," and if it comes as a message, is received by one, such as a scientist or a philosopher, who is "objective-minded," removed from his own concrete situation. On the other hand, there is "a piece of news" that expresses an event or a state of affairs "peculiarly relevant to the concrete predicament of the hearer of the news." A castaway, because he is in need, stands in the way of hearing the news.

He must, however, have criteria for evaluating a piece of news. Percy offers four canons of acceptance that are not subject to the procedures of verification such as one would employ for a piece of ordinary knowledge. First, the news must be relevant to one's predicament in the world. Percy's example cannot be lost on readers of his fifth novel. There are two commuters on a train. One is self-satisfied and leads a meaningless life, the other suffers from acute anxiety and knows that something is terribly wrong. If a stranger approaches the first and says he has news of the utmost importance for him, that commuter will reject it out of hand since he does not believe he is in a predicament. But, Percy writes, "The second commuter might very well heed the stranger's 'Come!' . . . Indeed it may well be that he was been waiting all his life to hear this 'Come!' " (134). Second, the newsbearer must have the proper credentials. He is a brother or a friend who knows one's need and approaches in sobriety and good faith. And if he should be a stranger it is but the more extraordinary that he understands one's predicament — and still more pressing that one should heed him. "It was enough," Percy writes, "for Jesus to utter the one word *Come* to a stranger — yet when he uttered the same word in Nazareth, no one came" (136). Again the title of the novel takes on new resonances. Third, the news must be both possible, that is, not absurd — this is one of Percy's critical areas of difference with Kierkegaard — and true. Fourth, the response of the hearer is not merely to confirm the knowledge but to take action appropriate to his situation. Percy gives still another example that seems pertinent for a reader of *The Second Coming*. Should a fire break out at a conference of eminent scholars in the Aspen Auditorium, the single sentence "Come! I know the way out" (138) will be of far greater import than all the others uttered at the conference.

In the last analysis, however, such island news, while relevant to the survival of the castaway in his everyday world, is still somehow incomplete. Percy notes also that "Kierkegaard, of all people, overlooked a major canon of significance of the news from across the seas — the most 'Kierkegaardian' canon," that of the "hearer of the news" (147). To be a castaway, as Percy would have it, is to be "a stranger who is in the world but who is not at home in the world" (142). If he imagines he is at home, he is in despair. To be a castaway means to hope for news from across the sea and to know that, if a message should come, one must recognize it as the sign of the one who sent it.

If Percy disagrees with Kierkegaard as to the intellectual nature of faith — that one can show belief to be reasonable — he agrees with him perfectly as to the object of belief. Christianity is finally a belief in a Teacher rather than a teaching. The newsbearer of that crucial news from across the sea is the one Kierkegaard calls "The Apostle,"[11] the one whom we believe because he has been given the authority to deliver the message (146–47). The news he bears must answer the castaway's deepest needs: "news of where he came from and what he must do." Such news is not Paradox. And if the newsbearer should also bring the means by which the castaway may do what he must do, then, writes Percy, "the castaway will, by the grace of God, believe him" (149).

One believes not a doctrine but the unique Person-Event-Thing in history. As Gabriel Marcel, the Catholic existentialist to whom Percy owes much of his own theological perspective, holds, one should not "have" belief but "believe-in." Percy's "Message" integrates faith with grace and providence so that affirmation must become action. He concludes that in our era, when everyone is an apostle of some product or some cause, all saying "Come," it may be that the best way to say "Come!" is in silence (148). (Certainly this is the mode of Percy's Percival.) The implication is that the call may take the form of signs or revelations in everyday life.

In *The Second Coming* Will Barrett demands an empirical sign, a knowledge *sub specie aeternitatis*, that God exists. The signs he receives, however, are of the nature of news; they are relevant to his concrete situation. They take the form of language, of symbol, of event, as in "what happens," of gift. All are modes of knowing, all are revelations, the very basis of faith.

II

Since the publication of *The Moviegoer* Percy has been recognized as a philosophical novelist. One may wonder, then, if his fiction finds its inception in an idea, as for example Camus's does, or in a character or situation, a Jamesian germ. Percy's readers have only to look at his opening sentences, where they can discover his heroes "thrown into existence," to understand that his existentialism and his fictional method are one and the same. These sentences — and he lavishes great care on them — set the terms for the novels. *The Second Coming* begins: "The first sign that something had gone wrong manifested itself while he was playing golf." Will's predicament is manifested, not only in his slice, but in his continual falling. Like Binx Bolling of *The Moviegoer*, Will suffers from what Heidegger calls everydayness, but Percy develops the notion even more explicitly in this novel according to Heidegger's explanation of what "being-there" means. Dasein, Heiddeger explains, has fallen away from itself as an authentic potentiality for Being its Self. It has fallen into the world in the sense of being lost in the public "they."[12] Will repeatedly calls the "they" of contemporary America "farcical." His falling has been diagnosed as spells of "petty-mal trance," a term not inappropriate for Will's sense of the malaise. But his loss of self has occurred on an even deeper level. Like the young Will of *The Last Gentleman*, he has a sense of having experienced a very private event, the most important of his life but one he cannot remember. His authentic coming to himself seems to depend on a return to that event. Strangely enough, while he cannot recall this unique event, his new condition has created a reversal of his old amnesia: now he remembers everything else.

Primarily he remembers Ethel Rosenblum, his first love in high school, and wonders over and over why "all the Jews have left North Carolina." His late wife had believed that the endurance of the Jews in the world is "a sign of God's plan working out" (12). Will wonders if this absence is indeed a sign. While all the churches in this most Christian town in the most Christian state in the most Christian nation in the world sport signs, none of these are signs for Will, who can neither approve of the unbelievers nor of the believers he observes (13–14); the latter are, in fact, very like the crowd of Kierkegaard's Christendom. On Sunday morning, Will, who perennially sees himself objectively and wants to cure "the great suck of self," stands, not in church, but "on the edge of a gorge in old Carolina, a talented agreeable wealthy man living in as pleasant an environment as one can imagine" and thinking nonetheless of "putting a bullet in his brain" (14).

The reader is only gradually made aware of the source of Will's despair. Percy begins chapter 3 with the revelation that "Undoubtedly something was happening to him" (44). Will still has his golf slice, but he discovers that he does not care about it. What he does care about is the hawk that drops like a stone in the woods – it reminds him of something (47). On this day "Everything he saw became a sign of something else" (51). And suddenly it crosses his mind that the guitar sound of the wire fence and the popping of the wires against his body are "signs of another event," and that "nothing else had ever happened to him" (52). The reader then begins to guess why Will carries the Luger, why, to borrow from Heidegger, he is being-towards-death, why he feels inauthentic and quests for an authentic understanding of his own end and what it is that he wants so desperately to rediscover.

In *The Last Gentleman* Will returns to the scene of his father's suicide and recalls how his father, years before, walking under the water oaks, listening to Brahms's Great Horn Theme and explaining his own disillusionment with the farcical evils of the world, took leave of his son. As he would do with Sutter years later, the boy Will begs him to "Wait!" but his father proceeds to load his twelve-gauge Greener, go to the attic, and shoot himself (328–32). Upon his return to the house as a young man Will discovers the skull of his namesake Williston Bibb Barrett, and we see him as Hamlet pondering the "to be or not to be" of suicide and, like Hamlet, referring to the haunting figure of his dead father as "old mole." (162).

The Second Coming reveals a related, but still earlier, and even more terrifying incident in the young Will's life. What the older Will Barrett finally not so much remembers as agonizingly reconstructs – and what Percy describes in some of the finest prose of his career – is the dark truth that what had come to be thought of as "the hunting accident" in

Thomasville, Georgia, had, in fact, been his father's attempt to kill both his son and himself—to save his son from the despair he himself has known. *This* was the only thing that had ever "happened" to him. Smiling, the older Will muses: *"Ah, I've found it after all. The buried treasure"* (p.61). And he realizes that he has inherited his father's anger as well as those genes that seek nothingness rather than life. He discovers that it is not physical death he abhors but the living-death, Kierkegaard's sickness unto death, his own despair. It is his father's "death-dealing" he has tried to escape by going North to live, and it is the discovery of it he has sought in returning South. Now he knows what his father knew and what he had hoped out of a curious kind of love to spare him. Percy's title means many things in the context of the novel, but here "coming" becomes a ghastly metaphysical conceit of sex and death. Death in Heidegger's vision is the end of coming-to-be. Percy describes Will's epiphany as brutally autoerotic:

> the double Winchester come of taking oneself into oneself, the cold-steel extension of oneself into mouth . . . the penetration and union of perfect cold gunmetal into warm quailing mortal flesh, the coming to end all coming. . . . (148–49).

At the same time that Percy has been giving us Will's story, writing his sequel so to speak, he has been creating in alternating chapters a true counterpoint, Allie's story. If Will is towards-death, she is towards-life, coming-to-be. If he remembers everything she remembers almost nothing. He is the complete man of his world, possessing all, but being toward "nothing." She has lost everything, has virtually nothing, not even language, but is open to "all," to Being itself. He has a mountaintop home but is homeless; she is homeless but making a home. Allie, too, is in need of signs. Since she has descended into herself until she has become schizophrenic and been given shock treatments, she must rediscover language. Once again Percy is raising the question: who is really sane in an insane world? Both Will and Allie are in need of a cure; both come instead in the end to find their cure by curing.

But something has also "happened" for Allie, a bequest. As she overhears her mother's account of her good fortune she ponders: "Everyone listens when someone tells the news of a happening" (118). It seems that Sally Kemp, the elderly friend of Allie's Aunt Grace, has left Allie two valuable pieces of property. Kitty explains: "What had happened of course was that she and Grace had had a fight and she had changed her will so Grace should have gotten it but we'll take care of Grace—" (119). Percy's play on the word "grace" here is reminiscent of Flannery O'Connor's brand of salvific humor, what Nathan Scott calls *"coincidentia oppositorum."*[13] But grace it is, even Providence. (Like O'Connor, Percy says he cannot, however, use words of this sort, because either they are worn out, bankrupt, or they scare people off.[14]). In *The Second Coming* the gift is the event that is essentially the beginning of the action. Had Allie not been able to escape from the mental hospital to the Kemp place, Will could never have met her there or "fallen" into the world of the greenhouse.

Allie is very much there; in fact, she seems to be being itself, one of her own growing things. She is Eve in a new garden, Allison in a glass house wonderland of words, surrounded by and reflecting sunlight at every turn. She is also utterly alone, *allein*. When Will first happens upon her he does not yet know her story, does not know that she is the daughter of Kitty Vaught, his old flame, and Buddy Huger, a reactionary dentist, or that they are conniving at "plans" for Allie. They will have her permanently if nicely committed so as to take over her North Carolina and island properties. Allie, who has been an A student but "flunked ordinary living," must now re-create her life. Before leaving the hospital she has written "INSTRUCTIONS FROM MYSELF TO MYSELF" so she will know what to do after she has had electro-shock therapy. Now she finds she is free to act and gradually she begins to have what Heidegger calls projects; she projects herself into the future, though she has trouble remembering the past. She has bought the necessities and taken possession of her house.

When Will, having sent a golfball through the glass, first approaches Allie's home in the making, the setting sun gives it the appearance, by turn, of an ark and a cathedral, Old Testament and New Testament emblems of salvation. The first thing Allie senses about Will is his anger, his need for salvation. He suffers a shock of recognition, aware that she is seeing all of him, and "For one odd moment she was as familiar to him as he himself" (77).

Before Will returns again Allie begins pondering words and their meanings. She takes out her Scripto pencil and carefully writes *"I am here"* (85). For Percy the discovery of the self depends on standing at a particular point in the world, a point from which one can declare one's identity. Besides learning words, Allie's other great project involves the magnificent old Grand Crown stove she has found in the greenhouse. She is as resolved to move it alone as she is to live her life alone. She begins planning how to hoist the stove with pulleys and levers so she can reposition it in her glass house. Archimedes, inventor of those devices, said "Give me a place to stand on, and I will move the earth"; Descartes, quoting Archimedes, finds his place to stand with his "Cogito";[15] Allie, twentieth-century Heideggerian, pronounces that she can hoist anything if she has "a fixed point and time to figure" (252). The Grand Crown, as opposed to the Ben Franklin, brand name of the stove undoubtedly refers to the legendary Archimedean experiment to determine the weight of gold in the king's crown. Percy's elaborate allusion not only reminds the reader that the discovery of the real treasure of the self depends on having a place to stand, but it hints as well what that point may ultimately be for Will. In what is often called the Grand Pensée (792) Pascal compares Archimedes and Christ. Despite his achievements in science and mathematics and his princely rank, Archimedes never acted the prince. In the same manner, "It would have been useless for our Lord Jesus Christ to come like a king, in order to shine forth in His Kingdom of holiness. But He came there appropriately in the glory of his own order." Christ the King who came in lowliness will come in glory at the Second Coming, and it is both in an awareness of everydayness redeemed and in the hope of that Second Coming that Percy would have Will Barrett stand.

But it is in an I-Thou relationship that the Christological point can be discovered. When Will returns he again falls and explains: "Lately I tend to fall down." Allie replies, "That's all right. I tend to pick things up. I'm a hoister." To which he replies, "We'd make a twosome" (113). Along with avocados he brings her the gift of the words she needs. Allie is like the children Val teaches in *The Last Gentleman* who suddenly break into the world of language. She is also like "Adam on the First Day" (301). She and Will proceed to re-create each other, Will saying: "I need you for hoisting and you need me for interpretation" (329).

Will has not, though, found his place to stand, still falls. He is, on the one hand, haunted by the fact that his father's suicide has been in vain, that it proved nothing. Since for Will his father had made no Great Discovery, his suicide had been *"wasted"* (182). On the other hand, Will continues to ponder the fate of the missing Jews. They are for him the sign his father had missed. He demands of Jack Curl, the jump-suited, ecumenical-minded Episcopal chaplain of St. Mark's, whether he believes that the Jews are a sign and whether God exists. Curl, realizing he faces a God seeker, can respond only tritely that he finds God "in other people" (137). Will finds his answer meaningless and, good Gnostic that he is, resolves to put the question directly, "once and for all" in such a way that a "yes" or "no" answer is required. He recalls that before he had married the believing Marion he had pondered: "Wasn't it possible to believe in God like Pascal's cold-blooded bettor, because there was everything to gain if you were right and nothing to lose if you were wrong?" (156). But, unlike the bettor, Will demands certitude, that God reveal himself. He begins to contrive his own wager, insisting on his own variations. He devises a plan by which God will either rescue him from starvation or let him die. He seeks proof, knowledge *sub specie aeternitatis*. Pascal regards "proofs" for the existence of God only as apologetic aids to bring a man to faith and of a distinctly different order of knowledge from faith itself. The Wager in its own context is only a final attempt to catch the attention of one whose thought is already on eternity and whose feet are on the road, a man, in fact, very like Will Barrett. For Pascal the existence of God is incomprehensible, but just as incomprehensible for him is the belief that God does not exist: incomprehensibility is no criterion for truth or falsity. Therefore the man who is embarked, the wayfarer, must wager. "It is not optional," Pascal argues: "If you gain, you gain all; if you lose, you lose nothing. Wager then, without hesitation that He is" (*Pensées*, 233). But when one wagers one does not demand proof; one seeks rather, Pascal believes, to be cured of an ill. God is the *deus absconditus* and, while one can show a man why it is reasonable to believe, he must finally go to Scripture where God reveals himself. "Faith is different from proof; the one is human, the other is a gift of God" (*Pensées*, 248). Faith is knowledge for Pascal, but knowledge of a different order. It is immediate apprehension, suprarational, but not irrational as it is for Kierkegaard. Such a gift is *le coeur*.

The metaphysical proofs for the existence of God are unconvincing, even futile for Pascal — they relate to the God of the philosophers, not to the God of Revelation. Sister Val has explained to Will in *The Last Gentleman* that she never could remember the five proofs for the existence of God but that she "believes it all," the "whole business: God, the Jews, Christ, the Church, grace, and the forgiveness of sins . . ." (301). Certainly Val speaks for Percy here. But it is proof, knowledge *sub specie aeternitatis*, that the engineer Will Barrett seeks when he goes to Lost Cove Cave. He demands a sign from God, failing to realize, as Pascal says, that God conceals himself from those who tempt him and reveals himself to those who will choose him. Marcel, like Pascal, sees the proofs as a means to an end. The efficacy of the proofs, Marcel believes, resided within a particular tradition, a particular framework of values, in which the acceptance of the proofs existed as faith a priori to the proofs themselves. The proofs merely register the conformity between faith and what is conceived as the demands of reason.

Shortly before his daughter's wedding Will carries out his scheme. He writes Sutter Vaught, explaining that should he fail to return from the cave it will be because of "the absence of God" (187). He describes his venture as the "ultimate scientific experiment . . . because God is the subject under investigation (186). This, it would seem, is the ultimate vertical search in Percy's fiction. Will, condemning the present-day Christians as "offensive and fanatical" and the present-day unbelievers as "crazy," looks for a *tertium quid* (189–90). He believes that the wager of Pascal, "the last French intellectual who was not insane," (191) was the last practical proposal made in history. Will fails, however, to differentiate between Pascal's bettor and the author himself, whose end is apologetic, and sees the wager as ludicrous and frivolous. Will's own wager will be scientific and his death will depend on whether or not the hidden God manifests himself, speaks a clear "yes" or "no" (192). Will arms himself with enough Placidyl capsules to enable him to "wait and watch and listen" (207). Then he "set forth on the strangest adventure of his life, descended into Lost Cove Cave looking for proof of the existence of God and a sign of the apocalypse like some crack-pot preacher in California" (198).

The cave from the first seems like a womb, and in places Will "had to turn his head sideways like a baby getting through a pelvis" (209). During this time in utero Will moves from his rationalistic demand that "God speak" to a series of memories and fantasies because "unfortunately things can go wrong with an experiment most carefully designed by a sane scientist. A clear yes or no answer may not be forthcoming, after all. The answer may be a muddy maybe. In the case of Will Barrett, what went wrong could hardly be traced to God or man, Jews or whomever, but rather to a cause at once humiliating and comical: a toothache" (213). The toothache is not the sign Will asked for, but it is the one he gets. And one is reminded here that Kierkegaard perceives the comical to be the stage just prior to the religious. Anyone with a toothache must acknowledge that he is a creature. "Whether it was God's doing or ordinary mortal frailty, one cannot be sure. What happened in any event, happened after seven or eight days" (213).

What happened is the rebirth of Will Barrett, his emergence from the cave into reality, an episode based clearly on the Plato parable that compares the world of appearance to an underground cave and depicts the progress of the mind from the lowest state of unenlightenment to knowledge of the Good. In "The Allegory of the Cave and *The Moviegoer*" Lewis Lawson reminds us that there is recurring reference in both Percy's fiction and nonfiction to Arnold Toynbee's *A Study of History,* and that the allusions are most often made to volume 3 in which Toynbee treats the movement of Withdrawal and Return.[16] Toynbee employs the Simile of the Cave to demonstrate the Hellenic understanding of this concept. In *The Second Coming* Percy is making very explicit use of both Plato and Toynbee.

Will Barrett enters a cavernous underground chamber with an entrance open to the light and a long passage. He has been a prisoner of his own quest to know the nature of death. The shadows that pass before him depict the major events of his life and his times, particularly those with his father. He even imagines he is buried under the earth with "old mole" (215). (The nicest bit of satire in the novel may be the inclusion here of John Erlichman emerging from prison, hardly the ideal statesman of the Republic [231–32].) Like Plato's prisoners, Will has mistaken the shadows for reality. But when the toothache abates he, like the unique prisoner who is set free, turns his head and sees a shadow on the rock, one not caused by his flashlight (Percy's substitute for Plato's firelight). He drags himself to the sunlight and, like the prisoner, is delivered from the cave. In the Allegory the free man is then able to look at the Sun and contemplate its nature, and he decides that he would "endure anything rather than go back to his old beliefs and live in the old way."[17] Though his eyes are dazzled by the light, he at last perceives the Good and can then act with wisdom.

Will Barrett struggles toward the sunlight and falls into the existence of Allie's greenhouse. Like the Grand Crown stove he is "reborn." A fire burns behind "amber mica bright as tiger's eyes" (228). Archimedean that she is, Allie hoists him and moves him, as she has the stove, by herself. When he awakes from a long sleep, the newborn Will pronounces, however tentatively, his own being there: "Don't tell anybody I'm here" (229). Unlike the prisoner of the Allegory, Will need not return to the cave. There is a clue to the reason in the fact that upon awakening he has mistaken the greenhouse for a church. Percy's world, as Lawson has so cogently argued is, like Augustine's, post-Platonic. And the reality into which Will falls is more than Heideggerian, it is being redeemed.

Toynbee follows his section on Platonic thought with one on Christianity that develops the idea that, while the Hellenic and Christian paths to enlightenment are identical, the spirit in which that path is taken is not. The enlightened Greek would rest in his philosophic contemplation (the Greek word for contemplation is that from which the English word "theory" is derived; Percy would term such a state "abstraction"). The mystical experience of the Christian, on the other hand, includes the virtue of love, which enables him to pass directly from "the heights of communion to the slums, moral and material of the unredeemed world."[18] In the life of Christ there is a recurring movement of withdrawal and return, and Toynbee concludes: "In the concept of the Second Coming the *motif* of Withdrawal-and-Return attains its deepest spiritual meaning,"[19] and death is overcome. The material of Toynbee makes its way into Percy's novel, but, taking care to disguise his religious language, Percy often puts it in the mouths of his most secular characters. Will realizes that it is Kitty with her comical newfound belief in reincarnation who is uttering ultimate truth about his own spiritual life. She says that after trial and exile his "destiny is the Return" (286). Will returns from the cave smelling of the grave but "smeared head to toe with a whitish grease like a channel swimmer" or a newborn (233–34).

Until now Allie's relation to reality has centered on her dog, "a true creature of the world," whose sheer creatureliness is one of the reasons she has not sunk more deeply into her Sirius self. There are two Sirius stars, one the Dog Star, very near, brightest of all the stars and twice as bright as the sun itself; the other, its companion star Sirius B, is a white-dwarf star whose light is pulled back into itself. Allie imagines that if one sinks deeply enough into oneself one will find company waiting. When Will falls into her greenhouse company has truly arrived and she, like Plato's Good, radiates light outward rather than pulling it back into herself. Will, too, focuses on the dog; he *sees* now, not the idea dog, but Allie's dog. He saves the creature and this is his apocalypse.[20] As he becomes open and committed to being, the ordeal of the cave begins to seem less important. When Allie inquires if he found the answer, he replies "yes" but that he doesn't know if the answer is "yes" or "no" (246). He does know, however, what he must do. And, just as Binx had instructed Kate, he tells Allie what she must do. As she goes about her business ordering their lives, she is pleased to have a proper job of her own. If he can tell her what to do, she can, despite her fear that "a name would give him form once and for all" (249), name him, give him identity.

They begin a life of what Marcel calls creative fidelity. Fidelity is a word that implies an affirmation of a need and a standing in relation to the object of one's faith. Allie, expressing this fidelity, endows it with irreducible simplicity and power. "Now she knew what she did not want: not being with him. 'I do not want him not being there' " (253). Any fidelity, Marcel writes, begins with the "I believe," which entails the "I exist."[21] To be is to "be-with." By "being-with" one can verify simultaneously another's existence and one's own. (Marcel's debt to both Buber and Heiddeger is apparent here.) Will and Allie become "fellow-*creatures*," a term Marcel finds incomparably precious.[22] The "existential" is for Marcel — and for Percy, for Will and Allie — the moment in which existence is discovered as Thou. Thus does their intersubjectivity become possible.

Percy bases his conception of symbol on Marcel's intersubjectivity, which the novelist defines as "that meeting of minds by which two selves take each other's meaning with reference to the same object held in common" (MB, 265). "The very essence of symbolization is an entering into *mutuality* toward that which is symbolized" (MB 256). A symbol demands co-conceivers, a namer and a hearer, and Percy notes that "conceive" means "to take with" (MB, 257). Like Binx, Will must "hand someone along." Such knowing depends on a metaphysic of "we are" rather than "I think" (MB, 271). Only after the "we name," Percy's place to stand, does the "I think" become possible (MB, 275).

In *The Message in the Bottle* Percy graphs this symbol-making as a diamond.[23] In their conversation before the dark glass of the train window Kate and Binx "sit knee to knee and nose to nose" forming a diamond, a symbol for a symbol, and thus see "face to face" (M, 191–92). Lancelot and Anna, the girl in the next room who cannot speak, see different halves of the same sign, and thus they are two deltas that form a complete diamond. In *The Second Coming* words become a way of making love. Will wants to explain to Allie what he has learned in the cave, but first he falls silent:

> He turned back. Their foreheads touched. Their bodies made a diamond. . . . When he began to talk she found that she could not hear his words for listening to the way he said them. Was he saying the words for the words themselves, for what they meant, or for what they could do to her? . . . Though he hardly touched her, his words seemed to flow across all parts of her body. Were they meant to? A pleasure she had never known before bloomed deep in her body. Was this a way of making love? (261–62).

Both characters realize that each has had an Archimedean spiral passage, he down into the cave, she down into her star, each one an attempt to get back to the self. Now they find that they are on the same journey. As he explains his passage through the cave, she can hardly hear him because of the fierce electrical storm that rages outside the greenhouse. "His voice seemed to be inside her head." The lightning creates facets of glass which flash blue and white: "It was like living inside a diamond" (264). Allie plays joyously with basic words, realizing what it is to "fall" in love, that this is "being in love" (264–65). Then lightning strikes again and the "glass house glittered like a diamond trapping light" (265), like in fact, the crystal temple of the Apocalypse.

Allie, the sun that warms the "dead planet" of Will's life, is the mode of his knowing himself, of his return. Marcel believes we must actively make ourselves more permeable to "the Light by which we are in the world," so that death will not fascinate us to the extent that it invades our entire experience and extinguishes our joy.[24] A man unto-death is a man unto infidelity. A blinded consciousness such as Will's will unfold toward the light. The light of the Dog Star radiates outward. The effect of this generosity is immediate; knowing, then, results in action. Will declares that he will "Take care of the people who need taking care of." He will return to see Leslie, whose wedding he has missed. He will become Allie's legal guardian so that her parents cannot control her fortune. Then he thanks Allie for taking "care" of him (265–66). Both Will and Allie have been in need of cures; now both in caring begin to cure. For his part he will tell her what to do and give her language. Allie, caretaker of the greenhouse, is caretaker, rescuer of Will. The words "care" and "cure" occur with the frequency and regularity of a refrain throughout the novel.

In one of the most extraordinary and moving passages in *Being and Time* Heidegger speaks of Dasein's very being as Care, *Sorge*.[25] "Being-towards one's ownmost potentiality-for-Being" means that Dasein is already ahead of itself. This includes one's falling and one's Being-alongside, being-with. Care may mean simply one's worry, one's anxiety or one's anxious exertion. But "cura" is the root word for care, so that *Sorge* may also mean "devotedness." In this dual sense of care, angst and fidelity, *Sorge* is the two-fold structure of *The Second Coming*, as it is of being-in-the-world. Allie escapes for the first time the "everlasting self sick of itself" when she feeds and bathes Will after his fall from the cave. Enclosing his body to warm him, she feels "as if her body had at last found the center of itself outside itself" (257). She gives him the life by which to deny what he calls "the living death in all its guises." He defies his dead father and chooses "to be" (272–74).

But Percy knows that Will must return not simply to the idyllic world of the greenhouse but to the complex web of social relationships and responsibilities that comprise his everyday life. Without Allie, however, the living-death still haunts him. Removed from Allie's presence and care, preparing to go to sleep in his Mercedes, Will once again realizes that "something is going to happen," once again the memory comes flooding back, the only thing that had ever happened to him. But this time D'Lo is there. The old family housekeeper cares for him, telling him that "the good Lawd got something special in mind" for him. She knows this because "he got the whole world in his hand, even a mean little old boy like you." When Will wonders how she knows that, she says, "Because, bless God, I know" (276), an example pure and simple of what Percy means by faith as knowledge.

As he returns to the empty house to begin to put his everyday life in order, the sun now seems to follow and surround Will as it does so many of Flannery O'Connor's characters. And in a fictional mode identical to hers, Percy has Will say, "Christ, I'm weak from hunger . . ." (288). Then in a startling series of events, things begin to "happen." Driving back to town in the dark Will sees a light out of the corner of his eye "as if a runner with a lantern were keeping pace" (292). Thinking he is on the Interstate Will wrecks the Mercedes, waits in the car until morning and then, wayfarer still, sets off walking down the highway. In the bus station he meets a man who is returning to Georgia. Still uncured, he decides that he has left something unsettled in the Thomasville swamp. It was not his life but his death he had left behind. It was "in Georgia that he would find it. And it was in Georgia that he would do it" (297). He boards the bus, but on the way he suddenly sees "a single golden poplar which caught the sun like a yellow-haired girl coming out of a dark forest," and his heart fills with a sweetness and a need and a fear that he is losing something (297). In his effort to force his way off the bus — to return — he is injured and wakes to find himself in the Duke University hospital. He is diagnosed as having *wahnsinnige Sehnsucht*, "inappropriate longing" (302). His longing is for Allie, "to see her face," as if to see "face to face." Percy's phrase is theologically crucial.

Percy, like O'Connor, sees nature as a "sacramental kind of existence," a quality of vision he owes to Gerard Manley Hopkins's "inscape." He believes that Hopkins saw "in a very sacramental and religious way, which owes a lot more to Aquinas than it does to the Kierkegaardian tradition."[26] It is out of this same sense of the sacred that Percy conceives of Kate, of Ellen Oglethorpe, of Anna — and most of all of Allie. Percy says quite forthrightly that they are sacramental.[27] A sacrament, an outward sign of inward grace, is a mode by which meaning becomes incarnate in reality. A sacrament is the ultimate sign. Allie's sign is the light, the radiance by which Will knows and can be. And as grace she is "the sign of the giver" (360).

His pH up again, and thus his longing, so that things take on "significance," Will returns to Allie, who stands "holding her hand against the sun" (326). He takes her to the Holiday Inn to protect her and care for her. He resolves to take up the practice of law once more, to marry Allie, to buy a garden home, to have a child to walk to school. Only after he takes the Greener and the Luger and hurls them into the gorge to avoid once and for all the ultimate "come," to cancel forever the awful impregnation of death, does he return to Allie in the Holiday Inn (the name, surely, being one of Percy's etymological puns). Three times he says, "Come here" and she, answering "I'm here," came against him with the "effect of flying up to him from below like a little cave bat and clinging to him with every part of her." Then Percy creates the perfect antidote, the cure for the old conceit of sex and death and adds still another resonance for his title: "Entering her was like turning a corner and coming home" (339). Allie in wonder says that she now has a needfulness she didn't until that moment know she needed: "It is now evident that whatever was wrong with me is now largely cured. Quel mystery" (340).

III

Will goes to the ancient Father Weatherbee to ask him to perform their marriage ceremony. He is grateful that Jack Curl, off reuniting the Church, has, in a comic fulfillment of D'Lo's prophecy, left him in the "damn good" hands, "better than Allstate," of Father Weatherbee. The old priest has two unusual interests — in fact, according to Jack Curl, he believes in only two things in the world: the Seaboard Air Line, one of the model trains in the attic at St. Mark's, and Apostolic Succession. Both become signs for Will. Still with what the world would call inappropriate longings, still the Will who wanted to know what Sutter knew, he sees something in Father Weatherbee's eyes. He confronts him with his persistent question: "In any event, the historical phenomenon of the Jews cannot be accounted for by historical or sociological theory. Accordingly, they may be said to be in some fashion or other a sign" (357). Will pursues his own argument, serving as his own apologist: Apostolic Succession goes back to Christ who was, of course, a Jew. The Jews are the common denominator between him and believers — he is "on the track of something." Will says he refuses to believe all of the old Episcopal priest's dogmas, "Unless of course," he has "the authority to tell me something I don't know" (358). What Father Weatherbee knows, and, as the apostle, has the authority to proclaim, are the very ideas Pascal, in the seventeenth century, offered to men who are in darkness and "estranged from God" but who seek him with their whole hearts (*Pensées*, 194). First, he offers the visible Church, a sign of God for those who seek. Second, he offers the good news. Pascal writes that the *deus absconditus* "gives himself in the Scriptures." The Seaboard Air Line is at once a mode of travel for the true wayfarer and at the same time evocative of the beach where one may find a message in a bottle. Father Weatherbee fails to understand present-day America and prefers to tell of his Christian community on Mindanao, which believes "the Gospel whole and entire, and the teachings of the Church." The old priest continues: "They said that if I told them, then it must be true or I would not have gone to so much trouble" (359) Father Weatherbee is a newsbearer, Kierkegaard's apostle, quite literally, of the news from across the sea.[28] Like Lonnie, Sister Val, Father Boomer, Percival, D'Lo, and Father Smith of *Love in the Ruins*, now come back as the prophetic stylite of *The Thanatos Syndrome*, he is simple, unpretentious, even unattractive.[29] His authority rests solely on his being appointed and sent by God. Will grips the old man's wrists "as if he were a child": "Do you believe that Christ will come again and that in fact there are certain unmistakable signs of his coming in these very times?" (360). The priest, his "bones like dry sticks," asks, "What do you want of me?" and looks at Will with a new expression, a shock of recognition. Then Will thinks of Allie in her greenhouse, so evocative for the reader of the scriptures that culminate in the book of Revelation.

> His heart leapt for joy. What is it I want from her and him, he wondered, not only want but must have? Is she a gift and therefore a sign of the giver? Could it be that the Lord is here, masquerading behind this simple silly holy face? Am I crazy to want both, her and Him? No, not want, must have. And will have (360).

Percy's Kierkegaardian man of infinite possibilities has "willed," he has chosen, and he is on the brink of the religious stage. What Will is only just beginning to realize is that no modern millennium is impending, but that certain unmistakable signs of the Second Coming are being revealed to him nevertheless.

His own return, his resurrection, has occurred. It is the result of all the seemingly gratuitous things that have "happened" to him. Now he is projecting, being-ahead of himself. He is planning a construction company and a greenhouse orchid business so that the old men of St. Mark's can have a proper job of work. In the light of Allie's presence he is nurtured and growing like the corn of the primordial myth Toynbee cites.[30] He seems to understand with Pascal that if one would have faith one must do the works of faith. Will has given Allie words and then recognized in Father Weatherbee a sign of the Word and his own need of that particular message in the bottle. Finally, he has heard her *Liebesbotschaft*, Love's Message (354), and received the sacrament of Allie.

One senses Percy's delight in this his most happy ending. One senses, too, a broadening of his definition of faith as it is incarnated in fiction, from the Thomistic affirmation of the existence of God to include the existential definitions of those later Catholics — Pascal for whom faith is *le coeur* and Marcel for whom faith means to stand in relation to the one of whom one has most need. And is this, finally, not simply to "know," to have received the news from across the sea.

Notes

1. Blaise Pascal, *Pensées* and *The Provincial Letters* (New York: Modern Library, 1941), no. 236. Hereafter, numbers will be cited in the text.

2. *The Last Gentleman* (New York: Farrar, Straus and Giroux, 1966), 407. Hereafter, page numbers will be cited in the text.

3. J. Donald and Sue Mitchell Crowley, an unpublished interview with Walker Percy, 12 March, 1982, Covington, Louisiana.

4. In the following interviews Percy discusses the ending of *The Last Gentleman:* Zoltan Abadi-Nagy, "A Talk with Walker Percy," *Southern Literary Journal* 6 (Fall 1973): 12, 14; Ashley Brown, "An Interview with Walker Percy," *Shenandoah* 18 (Spring 1967): 8; Charles T. Bunting, "An Afternoon with Walker Percy," *Notes on Mississippi Writers* 4 (Fall 1971): 46; John Carr, "An Interview with Walker Percy," *Georgia Review* 25 (Fall 1971): 329; Jan Nordby Gretlund, "An Interview with Walker Percy in His Home in Covington, Louisiana, January 2, 1981," *South Carolina Review* 13 (1981): 4–5. These interviews are reprinted in *Conversations with Walker Percy*, eds. Lewis A. Lawson and Victor A. Kramer (Jackson: University Press of Mississippi, 1985).

5. Crowley interview. *The Second Coming* had its genesis in the arrival of one of Percy's old friends who, despite the fact that he was a man of means and a great success, was in a deep depression, and, having gone to church, got on a bus and inexplicably showed up at the Percys' door.

6. *The Second Coming* (New York: Farrar, Straus and Giroux, 1980). 72–73. Hereafter, page numbers will be cited within the text.

7. Crowley interview.

8. *The Message in the Bottle* (New York: Farrar, Straus and Giroux, 1975), 119. Hereafter, page numbers will be cited within the text.

9. Gretlund interview, 4.

10. Gretlund interview, 4. See also Bradley R. Dewey, "Walker Percy Talks about Kierkegaard: An Annotated Interview," *Journal of Religion* 54 (1974): 291.

11. Søren Kierkegaard, *The Present Age and Of the Difference Between a Genius and an Apostle* (New York: Harper Torchbooks, 1962), 89–108.

12. Heidegger, *Being and Time*, trans. John Macquarrie and Edward Robinson (New York: Harper and Row, 1962), I.5, 38.

13. "Flannery O'Connor's Testimony," *The Added Dimension: The Art and Mind of Flannery O' Connor*, ed. Melvin J. Friedman and Lewis A. Lawson (New York: Fordham University Press, 1966), 150.

14. Crowley interview. See also Marcus Smith, "Talking about Talking," *New Orleans Review* 5, no. 1 (1976): 17.

15. Lewis Lawson, "The Allegory of the Cave and *The Moviegoer*," *South Carolina Review* 13 (1981): 14.

16. Ibid., 13–18.

17. Plato, *The Republic of Plato*, trans. Francis MacDonald Cornford (New York and London: Oxford University Press, 1945), 230.

18. Toynbee, *A Study of History*, Abridgement of Vols. 1–6 by D.C. Somervell (New York and London: Oxford University Press, 1946), 220.

19. Ibid., 223.

20. See Percy's "The Loss of the Creature" in *The Message in the Bottle*.

21. Marcel, *Creative Fidelity*, trans. Robert Rosthal (New York: Noonday Press, 1964), 168–69.

22. Marcel, *The Mystery of Being 2* (Chicago: Henry Regnery, 1960), 20.

23. See J.P. Telotte, "A Symbolic Structure for Walker Percy's Fiction," in this volume.

24. Marcel, *Creative Fidelity*, 173.

25. Heidegger, *Being and Time*, Chapter 6, 41 and 42.

26. Dewey interview, 294–95.

27. Crowley interview.

28. Dewey interview, 284–85. Percy confirms that not only is Father Boomer based on

Kierkegaard's Apostle, but that the vertical and horizontal searches in his fiction are patterned after *Of the Difference Between a Genius and an Apostle.*

29. Can Percy mean us to think of these characters as "Whether-Be" and "De Lord?"

30. Toynbee, *A Study of History*, 220–21.

Walker Percy's Prodigal Son   Lewis A. Lawson*

The unusual noise was heard by the maid. In the attic she discovered that her employer had just used a shotgun to end his life. The afternoon newspaper of 9 July 1929, dutifully blamed "ill health" for the "rash act" by Leroy Percy, forty, one of the most prominent citizens of Birmingham, Alabama.[1] Thus was the old life of the Percy family, of Fairway Drive, New Country Club Road, blasted.

Leroy Percy's widow took her three sons—Walker, thirteen, Leroy, twelve, and Phinizy, eight—to her mother's home in Athens, Georgia. There they stayed for a year or so, until they were invited by William Alexander Percy, Leroy's first cousin, to share his home in Greenville, Mississippi. After Mrs. Percy's death in an automobile accident, 2 April 1932, "Uncle Will" took the three orphans as his sons.

There were resemblances between the cousins, Leroy and Will. They were roughly of the same age and appearance. Both had gone to good colleges—Leroy to Princeton, Will to Sewanee—and to Harvard Law (Leroy made the *Review*). Both served in the Great War—Leroy as a training pilot, Will as an infantry officer in combat. Both had notable fathers—Leroy's, Walker, had been a lawyer, a member of the Alabama legislature, and a magnetic force during Birmingham's early years as a steel city; Will's Leroy, had also been a lawyer, served as U.S. senator from Mississippi, and continued the strong leadership in Greenville provided by his father, William Alexander Percy, grandfather to both Leroy and Will.

There were also differences, perhaps resulting as much from environment as from innate characteristics. Leroy seems to have had more of that singleness of purpose that Southerners discern in Yankees: both he and his father prospered in the substantial world of the Tennessee Coal, Iron, and Railroad Company and in the city and country club world it nourished—until they took their abrupt leave of them. Will ranged wide in his interests—he was a poet, an editor, a man with a rare appreciation for the beauty and nobility of both the world of ideas and the world of nature: he (a little more so than his father) seems always to have been away from Greenville, even if he conscientiously attended to the world of men when he got back.

*This essay appears here for the first time and is published by permission of the author.

Beneath the uniformity of the Percy appearance, then, there was a fractured person: a tendency (to thrive and, despairing, die young) poised against a tendency (to despair and, despairing, thrive). The eldest of Leroy's sons, Walker, must have noticed this tension in his heritage, as someone who, looking long enough, might detect a hairline crack splitting a facade. His decision to major in the sciences — not a Percy interest — at the University of North Carolina — not a Percy school — and later to study medicine — not a Percy profession — at Columbia's College of Physicians and Surgeons may announce an attempt to escape a fatal dilemma.

Walker Percy was entranced by the scientific method. But while it provided an admirable method for organizing matter and general knowledge, it evidently did not resolve his specific distress. For he was obliged, during medical school, to submit himself to three years of psychoanalysis. He says now that he and his analyst were not "sure" what "ailed" him, even when therapy was discontinued.[2]

He had never lost the ability to function successfully, so that he graduated from medical school and began his internship in pathology at Bellevue Hospital. Just about the same time that Uncle Will died — 21 January 1942, of a stroke — Walker was felled by tuberculosis. There is a theory that organic illness can result from psychological causes — that a certain psychological type has at least a predisposition to a specific organic illness — but since it is more acceptable in literary speculation than in medical diagnosis, it will not be argued here. All that can be said with any certainty is that Walker Percy spent the war years alone and flat on his back at Lake Saranac.

In that position he discovered the full meaning of *Dasein:* Here I am! Here I am? Here I am. He must have spent countless hours studying the distance from his mind to his hand — his essays frequently describe that sick person's measurement. In several places Percy has indicated that he discovered his grand theme in the sanitarium, that human existence is not "explained" by rational explanation, even — especially not — by modern science.

Percy made one attempt to resume an active life as a physician. He quickly suffered a relapse and returned to bed. When he was able, he moved to Santa Fe. The climate would undoubtedly be good for his health. That short stay in New Mexico — a year or so — provided an image of place that occurs continually in his works, though it has been missed by most critics, who never leave the Interstate when they go through Percy. It is most easily seen as a locus for the rotation, Percy's description of that surge into the future in search of freedom. The Southwest, once attained, though, turns out to be the testing ground on which modern science has constructed a means of achieving the Apocalypse. Thus, ultimately, death rather than life haunts Percy's Southwest. Such a discovery at the heart of brightness may have triggered Percy to encounter another presence in the desert. And then another.

In short order Percy returned to Mississippi to marry, moved to New Orleans, and became a Catholic. After a while, the Percy family moved to nearby Covington, Louisiana, where it has remained. In a charming essay[3] Percy has explained his choice of Covington as a place to live: some places, like Santa Fe, are so exotic that he would never feel at home there; other places, like Greenville, are so concrete that he could survive there only by pretense; Covington is something of a compromise. There one is neither without context nor overwhelmed by it; thus one is reasonably free to think about how one relates to a world that permits neither extreme, freedom or captivity.

In short, Percy tries to clear his mind of prior assumptions when he begins to think of the life-situation. He has spoken of his modus operandi for writing a novel:

> I begin with a *man* who finds himself in a *world*, a very concrete man who is located in a very concrete place and time. Such a man might be represented as *coming to himself* in somewhat the same sense as Robinson Crusoe came to himself on his island after his shipwreck, with the same wonder and curiosity.[4]

Such a man must scout the island, of course, to inventory and utilize its contents and to locate any other inhabitants. At the same time, though, he should not become so involved in his island activities that he ceases to listen for news from across the water. Nor can he forget that he was on a voyage when he was shipwrecked.

Percy had always been a reader, and when he went to live with Uncle Will he was with someone who was passionately concerned with books and music, who had created books himself, who had houseguests who were at that very moment creating books. No academic drudge, Percy had continued to read, appreciate music, and (perhaps especially) go to the movies during his college years. When he was in the sanitarium, he could be a free reader, could read not only a book, but a book's book-network. Probably enough has been said elsewhere about one kind of reading that he did at Saranac: much of it was phenomenological, that is to say, existential analysis and fiction. But he also continued to follow scientific developments, for he had not lost his love of and respect for empiricism and intellectual generalization merely because they did not provide any information about individual human experience. In Santa Fe and after marriage he read (an inheritance provided an income). There are those passengers who read for dear life during the first thirty seconds of an airliner's takeoff; there are some people who always seem to be reading with such intensity.

In time Percy began to write, first publishing essays and then *The Moviegoer*. It should be no surprise that his writing reveals just as much intensity. These days of insatiate demand for fiction offer examples of the person who writes novels because, shrewdly practiced, fictioning can be a very lucrative career. Although Percy has been quite popular, it is not because he set out to write formula fiction. But neither did he start out to write *serious* fiction, an antisocial act by the intelligentsia that ought to be criminalized. Although he quickly got a reputation as a thinker (he was interviewed by William F. Buckley, Jr.), a satirist, and an existentialist, it is equally false to regard him as one who — having reasoned out a philosophy — condescends to contribute to the shelf of Great Books. Percy needed to make neither a living nor a statement, but a life. Like his Robinson Crusoe, Percy had come to himself, washed up on a beach; he had to account for the voyage that he had been on when the storm hit and to explore the strange island. Unless he got busy he would perish. The themes in Percy's fiction reveal an unceasing effort to order and control those forces that lurk in the jungle back of the beach. The Percy novels, that is to say, are much more personal than many have thought them to be — behind that public world so brilliantly perceived is a private world that demands to be confessed.

The most visible conflict in *The Moviegoer* (1961)[5] is between Binx Bolling and the worldview provided by the scientific establishment. He has done those things that are supposed to enhance a person's life: he has followed the "vertical search" (M, 70), Plato's ascent from the cave. Thus Binx should be happy, his life clarified by generalization. But his success has only induced in him an illness that modern science cannot treat because it does not understand the condition or its symptoms.

He has become a lonely spectator, a moviegoer of life, who — caught up in bad faith — thrives and despairs in a horizontal world, hiding his *Arabia Deserta* in a Standard and Poor binder. He would like to be content with the world that is caught by the objective-empirical camera; as he tells a ticket-seller (who has no ticket for him, of course), he would like to live in Arizona (M, 74). Perhaps it would be possible to live like Clint Walker, sustained by mesquite and rotations (M, 143). He would like to be a Robinson Crusoe who comes to himself on the beach at Ship Island with a "10", Sharon — happily named — an *Erdgeist* from Eufala.

But on day one, by virtue of the memory of an old ordeal, he comes to himself, thrown onto the ground, as in Korea (M, 10). Taking an inventory of his tools (M, 11), he has this impression: ". . . I felt as if I had come to myself on a strange island. And what does such a castaway do? Why, he pokes around the neighborhood and he doesn't miss a trick" (M, 13). Even so, Binx continues to dissemble.

Binx's quest in the present is all too effectively frustrated by his contradictory past. It would be hard enough to settle his account with one past, but he has two, both of which dun him regularly.

His Aunt Emily represents the tradition of Southern stoicism, of despairing and thriving. Her way of living is to view the present as merely the last sorry phase of the decline of the West; overwhelmed by the " . . .

barbarians at the inner gate . . ." (M, 33), she (as almost the sole survivor of a race of giants) can only withdraw to the citadel and protect the relics as long as possible. Her cabinet of family bibelots (M, 175) and her mantel of family photographs (M, 24–25) indicate her intention to stop time. But that is not enough. The past must be reconstructed: Binx understands that her view of the past is an aesthetic repetition, the creating of a home movie in which all the embarrassing and deadend sequences have been edited out (M, 49), so that the remainder — history — is a singular story of high-relief absolutes.

At the same time, there is a dark family tradition, more to be inferred than observed. At the age of twelve Binx had lost his father, who suffered so severely, apparently from endogenous depression, that only the onset of World War II (which could be seen as the Apocalypse) could stimulate him to become functional again. Volunteering to serve with the Canadians, he died during the battle for Crete. Binx's bitterness at twenty-nine suggests just how deeply he had been hurt at twelve by his father's abandonment of him — having asked his mother what his father was like, Binx is provoked by her evasive reply:

> Sure he was cute. He had found a way to do both: to please them and please himself. To leave. To do what he wanted to do and save old England doing it. And perhaps even carry off the grandest coup of all: to die. To win the big prize for them and for himself (but not even he dreamed he would succeed not only in dying but in dying in Crete in the wine dark sea). (M, 157)

Binx as much as says that his father sought his death. Yet his recognition of his father's depression and self-destruction does not chill his interest, but rather compels him to seek an answer from those irony-stippled eyes in the mantelpiece photograph.

So Binx makes an effort to wander his island during the week that precedes his thirtieth birthday. He analyzes the many forms that the "vertical search" takes and implicitly admits a continuing fascination for it. He seeks the past, as at the family hunting lodge and in Chicago. He dreams of opening a service station, of being of help to others who are wayfarers. Literally on a trip himself, the man on the train, he discovers another inhabitant, Kate Cutrer, and realizes that love offers an opportunity to escape the confines of subjectivity.

Is it possible that the movie they see in Chicago, *The Young Philadelphians* (M, 211), is a sneak preview of their future? Is human love all that is needed to make the island habitable? A call from the past quickly dashes such fond hopes: Aunt Emily, with the aid of the police (!), has found them, and "ten thousand williwaws" (M, 212) sweep the island.

Binx must return to stand before his Aunt Emily, who berates him for failing to abide by the tradition that she has fabricated. Despairing, she refuses even to contemplate the effort that a despairing person might make to escape his sickness. It is permitted only to despair and thrive, is her message, as she sits at her desk, casting her accounts (M, 226).

When he is dismissed, Binx is given that all-important Percy word by Kate, "wait" (M, 227). But after he has waited, he despairs: love is either nonexistent or impotent to withstand other island forces. Consequently Binx has a vision that he credits to his father: a glimpse of the world as Hell, as a vast shithouse. He can understand now why his Aunt Emily secretly yearns for the Bomb, after which an Oppenheimer-like messiah (M, 181) could slouch across the desert to inaugurate the millennium. He can understand why his father sought an Apocalypse off Crete.

The strong implication is that Binx is in a fit state to commit suicide. He attempts to call Sharon, to connect through sex (M, 228). But the despair of that act should be understood: the research of Dr. Sutter Vaught has established that all too often male suicides show spermatozoa at the meatus. Then Kate comes, at the same time that Binx notices the church activity of Ash Wednesday. Could it be possible that human love, as much as it is, is more than just itself, that it is an emblem of divine love?

The epilogue does not "close" the novel. Binx marries Kate, enters medical school. Human love is celebrated; a genuine repetition, going back to the beginning and starting over, is revealed. But how it stands with the fathers is left unstated.

The Last Gentleman (1966)[6] continues the exploration of alienation. A shift in point of view, from Binx's first-person to Will's (generally) limited third-person, argues that the author is making an effort to write a more "objective" novel. So, too, does the employment of a much broader humor suggest an effort to keep the material more in the world established by consensus. But the meaning conveyed by action and setting quickly confesses that Percy is once again sorting out his own life.

The descendant of a once-influential Southern family, Will Barrett lives in New York City, works as a humidification engineer at Macy's, and has spent much of his estate on five years of analysis. He would like to accept the world pictured by the empiricists and the generalizers: his control board at Macy's tempts him to think that life is simply circuitry. But once he emerges on Thirty-fourth Street Will discovers that the world withdraws from his fingertips.

Consequently he has just spent his last $1,900 for a telescope, which, he hopes, will bridge the distance between his eye and the object. He is delighted at the enhancement of the individual thing and the many new things that he observes, must hope to capture the thing-in-itself. Almost at once he becomes a bird watcher, spotting a peregrine. Several days of watching for the wayfarer should suggest that he feels the need to go some place himself, but it is not until his telescope catches sight of a girl, with whom he falls in love at first sight, that he acts.

The girl, Kitty, leads him to her family, the Vaughts, who immediately awaken Will's memories of the South. Chandler Vaught disarms him by talking as if he and Will have known each other for years. Will cannot resist father Vaught's bait: he must ask the question (LG, 52). Of course Chandler Vaught had known lawyer Ed Barrett, had hunted with him, had admired his actions as a Congressman. Mrs. Vaught, in her turn, knew Will's mother: ". . . Lucy Hunnicutt, the prettiest little thing I ever saw" (LG, 53). Will is to be forgiven, if he begins to think of family (LG, 56). Maybe he can go home again. And maybe the past is as innocent and colorful as the Vaughts, who constitute an aesthetic repetition, a time warp, "a film of bygone days in which, by virtue merely of the lapsed time, the subject is invested with an archaic sweetness and wholeness all the more touching for its being exposed as an illusion" (LG, 45). If it were not for Kitty's brother, Jamie, who has a fatal illness, the Vaughts might convince Will that time in the South really does stand still.

Will agrees to take Jamie home, but it is clear that he has persuaded himself that he, too, can go home. Since Will comes from Ithaca (LG, 51), where else would a camper named "Ulysses" (LG, 95) take him, eventually? Bidding farewell to his psychiatrist, Dr. Gamow, ". . . a father of sorts" (LG, 41), Will escapes the Empire State.

There are several clues that reentry will not be quite so easy. Will had not been able to graduate from Princeton in the family tradition (LG, 13); betraying his heritage altogether, he did not make a good soldier (LG, 18). Of course he cannot become a lawyer. Then, too, there are his illnesses: he has had "spells" (LG, 11) since childhood, attacks of amnesia, tremors, and such psychological phenomena as déjà vus; he is also deaf in one ear.

The Vaughts live in Atlanta, just off the number 6 hole of the country club fairway, but subsequent events suggest that Percy has Birmingham in mind.[7] Wherever it is, it is definitely prelapsarian; in Percy's world the golf course is not a showcase for Snopes sons, but rather an integral part of Paradise Estates. Of her youth Val Vaught remembers "the golf links and the pool": "I spent every warm day of my girlhood at the pool, all day every day, even eating meals there" (LG, 207).

Yet Will is not peaceful in this place of childhood. He is strangely moved by the fruity steel smell of Hoppe's gun oil (LG, 217). He dreams his "blocked" dream of his father (LG, 237–238) and, awakened by an unheard sound, is drawn to the attic. Soon he cannot be sure that he is living his life, and not his father's, as he cannot remember which of them had actually met Senator Underwood (LG, 347–348, 351).[8]

Moreover, he meets Vaughts who are quite unlike those whom he had met in New York. There is Val, who, upon learning of Jamie's illness, became a nun. Her religious name, Johnette Mary Vianney, hints that she had studied *The Varieties of Religious Experience*. There is Sutter, a failure as a physician, whose response to the diagnosis of Jamie's leukemia was to get them lost in the desert in New Mexico. When his plan is frustrated by their rescue, he attempts suicide—but botches that. Together, Val and Sutter provide Will with opposing options: Val is intent that Jamie be baptized—posing herself with a hawk (LG, 296), she manifests her faith in the peregrine nature of Christianity (as Sutter recognizes [LG, 353]); Sutter is intent that Jamie should face the absurd without sedation of any kind (LG, 373)—and so he takes him off to New Mexico again. After Jamie's death, Sutter implies, he will be free to complete his suicide.

All the while Will has business in Ithaca, which is an image of Greenville. Throughout his return to the South Will has been unable to complete a sequence of memories about his father. Now, though, standing in front of his childhood home, he leaves childhood by admitting that his father had committed suicide, *just after* saying that he would not leave him (LG, 331).

According to Will's recurrent memory, Mr. Barrett despaired because the world was no longer clarified by absolutes. He seems to have spoken much about morals, when he really meant classes. Thus he killed himself in bitterness over the breaching of a system of social control (such an overreaction encourages the speculation that the real motivation was internal). Will suddenly realizes that the past was never unequivocal—as myth has it—and that his father killed himself simply because he could not accept ". . . the very curiousness and drollness and extraness . . ." (LG, 332) of evolving reality.

Anyone who *stops*, who settles upon a particular moment as the eternal present, shields himself from reality with a myth. To illustrate: Will goes to Shut Off, Louisiana, where a surviving uncle, Fannin, lives as a twentieth-century Silas Phelps. Though he appears a great innocent, who loves Captain Kangaroo, Paladin, and his faithful servant, a whole society of such innocents would be about as harmless as South Africa.

Any high seriousness left in his father's act is undercut by his uncle's high jinks. As Will leads out for the Territory, the wide-open future, he must feel that he is finally free of the closed past. When he gets to Santa Fe and has to settle for Cream of Wheat, instead of grits (LG, 358), he has crossed the divide; he no longer even gets excited about Civil War battles. Apparently now unhindered from following another creed, he immediately sees Sutter, who senses that Will has faith in him and jokes about it by reversing the roles of the story of Philip and the eunuch.

Jamie is dying. The question is, how shall Will look at that fact, through Val's or Sutter's eyes, as a mystical or a molecular event? He resents having to choose between Val and Sutter, that ". . . exotic pair" (LG, 393). All the same, Will arranges for Jamie to be baptized. The tension between a transcendent and an immanent version persists: even as he receives the sacrament, Jamie is spuing ". . . the dread ultimate rot of . . . molecules" (LG, 401). As the sacrament is being completed and Jamie is dying, Will sees a ". . . Holsum bread truck pass under the street light" (LG, 404), but attaches no meaning to it, is not looking for a sign. That is, he does not choose Val's way of looking at things; it remains, therefore, for him to follow Sutter, who stops when he shouts, "Wait" (LG, 409).

What has happened? The ghost of family history/Southern past seems to have been vanquished. Will has escaped to the Southwestern desert, to possibility. But there the choice is either faith (being baptized, like the chamberlain) or science (despairing at ultimate death and therefore in love with easeful death). Percy's ending is again "open."

Love in the Ruins (1971)[9] begins where *The Last Gentleman* left off. There was a time when Tom More lived an idyllic life in Paradise Estates, one of those modern developments that hug a golf course. To complete his Adamic existence there were Doris — his Apple Queen from Winchester[10] — and Samantha, their daughter. In a section of Louisiana apparently not unlike the area around Covington, Paradise Estates is not overwhelmingly one thing or another (LR, 15). It is dominated by a television transmitter, which rises above the tower of the now-abandoned St. Michael's Church. All perceptions of life have been reduced, that is to say, to the standards of public time and public significance and therefore lack any sense of time as a continuum or of event as anything but a spectacle for diversion. With this "screen" for the novel, time is always disjointed and "gappy" and human actions are always just the least bit self-conscious and phony.

Tom More is not bothered by family history or Southern past. His mother, Miss Marva (sounds like a vocalist for Lawrence Welk) is alive and well: prospering as a Gnostic real estate agent, she truly moves heaven and the dirt. His father was a doctor, who apparently did not make much of an impact at all on Tom and who, if he did commit suicide, did it a drink at a time.

Rather, Tom is bothered by the phenomenon that did not faze Will Barrett, the death of an innocent. Tom had apparently successfully joined faith and science: he was a Roman Catholic and a physician. When Samantha died from a brain tumor, Tom lost his faith to the point that he attempted suicide. He became a drunk, his drink of choice — Early Times — revealing his nostalgia for that greatest aesthetic repetition, Eden. Soon enough, Doris first departs and later conveniently makes him a wealthy widower.

Tom reacts to bad news by attacking the messenger: although his daughter died of a brain tumor he pursues research in the brain as the locus of consciousness. Death will undoubtedly keep its sting, but the consciousness can be deadened. Thus he takes the route of modern science: man must *adjust* to the reality principle. He begins by measuring the degree of maladjustment, but, after he gets Faustian ambitions, he aspires to modify consciousness by technology — divorced of its high-tech, ray-gun glamour, his approach is the old shock treatment and chemical therapy used for mental illness, a temporary lobotomy.

At the same time that Tom is perfecting his perfection-machine, the lapsometer, the worldview fostered by institutions of consensus has fallen apart. Both political parties have been captured by extremists; the Catholic Church has split three ways. Tom is fond of thinking of Yeats — "the centre did not hold" (LR, 18) — and Yeats's conclusion, that at the end of a cycle it is time for the coming of another savior, must also occur to him. Since he has also read his Toynbee, Tom, seeing himself as one who has Withdrawn and is now ready to Return, fancies himself that world savior. Although it is 1983, he will save the world from 1984.

His own worldview is as fragmented as the world he views. His affections are torn between Moira Schaffner, whose every move is a rotation, and Lola Rhoades, an aesthetic repetition of incredible proportions. Moira — faery of openness is she — promises that Tom will meet his destiny in the desert; Lola, hissing Dvořák, offers the lure of going home, recapturing the past at Tara. If the girls seem to be caricatures, it is because Tom sees them as banal objects, as if life were nothing but a day-long Donahue show.

No wonder that Tom has become a drunk. Now, on the day of the novel, he has gotten a real load on, for the Fourth of July, a grand old American custom. Then lays himself down by the Interstate to dream a drunken dream of how he will save the world. The dream, not a deep sleep, but a semiconscious state in which empirical observation is distorted by very subjective interpretation, mostly covers the last few days. The conclusion to be drawn from the dream is that he has very nearly gone to the devil. When he awakens, he is able to save himself only by admitting the need for intercession — he is, to labor the point, not a savior, if he needs to be saved — and by relying upon the help of Ellen Oglethorpe, his nurse and soon-to-be wife, a beautiful, but stern Presbyterian, who accepts the Protestant argument that faith alone is not sufficient. The epilogue, five years later, reveals that Tom, although still hoping to produce his great contribution to man, is living a life of reduced circumstances, but of a marital happiness that must prefigure heaven. He himself knows it: "Poor as I am, I feel like God's spoiled child. I am Robinson Crusoe set down on the best possible island with a library, a laboratory, a lusty Presbyterian wife, a cozy tree house, an idea, and all the time in the world" (LR, 383).

In this novel does Percy say anything to himself? Certainly the family-history / Southern-past element is rather slight and lightly treated; there is neither a father-suicide nor a father-Stoic. Tom More has everything that a human being could hope for — family, health, employment, status, wealth. Then his daughter is afflicted with a material malfunction and his confidence crumbles. Beneath the surface action there is the story of Tom More's reaction to total adversity; for all the satiric humor of the social world of the novel, the personal world of Tom More is a very serious retelling of the Job story.

Rather than being a son haunted by a father, Tom is a father haunted by a daughter. He will not accept her death as a mystery to be grieved;

thus he cannot receive a restoration to a life inspired by faith. Instead he focuses on knowledge — but gradually his research into organic illness becomes an effort to alter man's basic nature by eliminating his sense of alienation. He does not wish to improve man's estate so much as to restore Paradise Estates. His success is diabolical, therefore, for it robs mankind of the freedom to choose.

There has been a past — even a father figure — rejected: Tom has from time to time spoken of his ancestor, Sir Thomas More. Obviously he had thought himself superior to Sir Thomas, for he had actually provided the technology for achieving a Utopia, while Sir Thomas had only written a book. But when the technology causes everything to act exactly opposite to his intention, he is forced to pray to Sir Thomas as an intercessor. Then he is saved: five years later he has been, like Job, rewarded with a second family. He knows enough, too, to confess his sins and to wear his sackcloth and ashes, to accept the world offered by a father, Father Renaldo Smith. The novel, then, could be something of an admonition, a reminder that the cause for depression is not always back there in the past, but out there in the future. The future is not always escape, any more than the past is always captivity.

In a way *Lancelot* (1977)[11] reverses *Love in the Ruins.* Tom More winds up confessing to Father Smith on Christmas Eve and then going to bed with his wife; Lance Lamar mockingly confesses to Father John his actions after finding his wife in bed with another man. As the novel opens, Father John enters the cell of his childhood friend, in a Center for Aberrant Behavior. Since he has been invited, the priest has reason to think that Lance might need him for some religious purpose; it is, after all, All Saints' Day. Lance is aware that the priest might anticipate, for he begins the second visit: "I have a confession to make" (L, 9). That it is, but not in any religious sense.

Instead, Lance begins to narrate the story of his life a year ago — his wife's infidelity and his response, spying on her, entrapping her, murdering her lover, and being the cause of her death. During the five days of the narration, Lance increasingly interpolates speculation, generalization, and fantasy into his circumstantial material. Gradually he builds up a myth of "phased" history — family, Southern, American, and universal. At the same time he reveals, without knowing it, that the whole complex is stimulated by an unresolved childhood problem: his father, a weakling and ultimately a convicted bribe-taker, had apparently condoned Lance's mother's infidelity. At least that is the interpretation that Lance now places upon his parents' behavior; he therefore acts savagely to prevent such an event from repeating itself. So alienated from his father is he that he acts with the kind of severity that, he says, his legendary ancestors had employed: he leaps the actual to imitate the apocryphal. The result is a fusion of private need and fantasy fulfillment that rivals that in *Absalom, Absalom!.*

Much of the response to the novel has tended toward one extreme or another. Some reviewers have admired Lance as the modern man of wrath, who has had *enough* and whose great-hearted explanation of his private code is more than sufficient to justify his actions. Others, assuming that Percy must identify with Lance, are incensed when Lance violates some aspect of fashion or manners that they cherish.

Both responses fail to understand the structure of the novel, Percy's most daring, in that it relies on a concept almost forgotten in contemporary America. Only half of the novel is written; the other half must be inferred. The audible stream of narration, conveying a Gnostic worldview, must be contrasted with the silent stream of audition, conveying the unchanging Christian message. Lance may prate of the idyllic past that his name connotes and think that wrath will restore it; Father John, obviously taking his name from the Evangelist, can only remain silent or speak of the one thing that will save mankind, love. The final scene, which could not be more "open," thus rises from the personal to the allegorical: man will remain mired in the wrath of his fathers or he will accept the love of the Father.

As majestic as the theme of the novel finally becomes, it maintains an intensely personal meaning. Lance Lamar's recollections of family deeds — before he begins to apply *his* exaggeration to them — sound more than a little like the family deeds in *The Last Gentleman* and, before that, in William Alexander Percy's *Lanterns on the Levee*. Father John, whose name is apparently Henry Percy, comes from a family in which the men "tended toward depression and early suicide" (L, 15). This novel, then, could be another admonition. That legendary Stoicism is a part of the Percy tradition, as Walker Percy has himself indicated. Such stalwartness must have been especially appealing to a youth who had been so abruptly abandoned. But the tradition simply did not suffice — and Walker Percy took the leap that Lance accuses Henry Percy of taking (L, 61). It is instructive that Walker Percy read Kierkegaard as he was translated in the forties, as he lived in a "cell" at Saranac. It was soon after that he confessed his faith in Christianity. He has continued to confess, directly in his interviews and indirectly in his writing, both his fiction and nonfiction.

But he has not forgotten the other tradition, nor should he, for it has many exemplary qualities. The important thing is to keep it — and the tendency toward depression that it apparently breeds — under control. Writing about that tradition is thus for Walker Percy a confession that a pull toward stasis still pervades his consciousness. But writing is, even more, proof for himself that faith still animates his being.

Although he may write more fiction, in *The Second Coming* (1980)[12] Percy must have completed his story of the son who lost a father. The protagonist, a middle-aged Will Barrett, has seemingly captured all of the images of possibility that have enticed Percy's other protagonists. After the death of Jamie Vaught, Will had not remained with Sutter, who became a television-watching burnout. Rather, he returned east, finished college and law school, and married Marion Peabody, a hefty heiress. In New York City, of all places, Will had successfully practiced law and marriage (one daughter). Now, after Marion's death, Will lives in early retirement in the resort area around Asheville, the topmost circle of Appalachian paradise. There he spends his days playing professional-level golf, beloved by the community (he has just received the man of the year award from the Rotary Club).

But he has begun to suffer from falling spells — which suggests that fallenness Heidegger discovers as a symptom of the inauthentic life.[13] Subpar golf may indeed accompany a subpar life. The first falling scene (SC, 3) is the standard Percy scene of coming-to-oneself, nose in dirt, acute awareness of bird or bug and of sky. In addition, Will has begun to slice out-of-bounds, as if some part of his being realizes that unless he gets off the fairway, he will remain in his hell of satisfaction.

As a person will, Will, when he senses his disconnectedness, begins to cast backward, to discover that point at which the lapse was first (or perhaps first) apparent. He is stimulated by the late summer spores to think of Ethel Rosenblum, a girl whom he had desired back in high school. So fierce had been his frustration at not connecting with her that he had fallen into the goldenrod and rabbit tobacco of a Mississippi vacant lot. Falling, then, may be the experience of a lack, but it is for that very reason the awakening of hope. O fortunate fall. Although the Bermuda grass of the golf course does not show any beating, it is nevertheless a beaten track, Percy readers will know, that Will must get off of, in order to cross a zone, stumble upon Pier Angeli or some similar angel.

Who turns out to be Allie Huger — praise the Lord — daughter of Kitty Vaught. Thus connecting with Will's deep past, Allie is an avatar of Ethel Rosenblum: with such Edenic responsibilities she, appropriately, lives in a greenhouse just off the golf course.

Always before, Percy has created his Eve out of Adam's rib; the female has been seen only through the male's eyes. This time, though, the narrative structure consists of counterpoint — first a chapter of Will's consciousness, then one of Allie's. In this way, when they eventually become one body by making love, they also make one mind by being in love. Thus they illustrate one of the major points of Percy's anthropology. Pure consciousness is not the isolated Cartesian awareness, which might occasionally suffer adulteration in some nonscientific activity, such as love. Instead, in Percy's view, consciousness is defined by its etymology — "knowing with." Isolated awareness is thus *deprived* consciousness, good for measuring, certainly, but inadequate for building worlds.

Allie has just escaped from Valleyhead Sanatorium, committed there by her parents for having flunked ordinary living — although she had made straight A's in everything else. She is another Kate Cutrer, in that she has lived her life in anxiety over her role. When given a part, she has been able to play it; when there has been no direction she has retreated into immobility. At Valleyhead, she has been subjected to electro-shock treatment, for her immobility has been interpreted as depression. It is at the prospect of yet another "buzzing" series that she plots a successful escape to an estate which has been bequeathed her. Since the house has burned, she must fashion a habitation in its greenhouse. There, amnesiac from her shocking treatment, she becomes a Robinson Crusoe.

So, too, is Will a Crusoe, who must rise from the beach of *"befindlichkeit,"* who must recover himself and scout the woods. Out-of-bounds is not just a *Tempest* setting, a locus for love in the ruins, though, for that place is haunted by the ghost of his father. Will knows his *Hamlet*, refers to his father over and over as "old mole" — a very apt description, for nothing has done more damage to the greens of Will's course, the ground of his being.

Will has lived with the version of his father's suicide that can be reconstructed in *The Last Gentleman*. What he has blocked is his experience of a hunt when his father had tried to kill both Will and himself. Now, though, venturing off his adult (amnesiac) life's course means that Will begins to struggle with that episode. If he would recapture the joy of connection, he must first deal with the horror that had originally alienated him.

Slowly, in a sequence of reconstructions, Will realizes that his father had fired both barrels of a shotgun at him, then reloaded one barrel to kill himself. Although his father had failed to kill his son, he had so traumatized him that Will's life has been spent in death-in-life, in hovering so close to the ordinary that he has had no real feelng. Thus he has hankered after the apocalyptic moment, as in the Ewell McBee episode (LC, 15–18), for that interruption of everydayness that produces a sense of genuine experience. And, lately, he has begun to flirt with his own destruction, fondle his father's Luger pistol and Greener shotgun.

Meeting cute, the unexpected encounter, the rotation with Allie has not overcome Will's domination by the dark past. There comes the time, then, when he decides to concoct the ultimate test: he will seclude himself in a cave, where only God can save him, if He exists and if He lists. For all the intricacy of his plot to trick his insurance company, Will is actually motivated by a simple idea: he will retreat to the womb, go back before the moment of desire or alienation, renounce his will, put it into God's hands as to whether he will or will not be born again. But, after about a week of being buried, he experiences such a toothache that he cannot keep from coming out of the cave (the toothache then goes into some sort of authorial remission).

Who can fathom the mysteries of Grace—this is no ascent from Plato's cave, but a tumble into Allie's greenhouse! She, who has hoisted a stove, has no trouble lifting him. Mothering him, she gives him his second life. Formally, love, the second life, succeeds death, is part 2 of the novel, which occupies more than a hundred pages. Fortunately Percy stresses love as an action, rather than exclusively as a state of mind; as a result, the novel does not turn sentimental but instead becomes even more concerned with ordinary details. First she must care for him, attend to his bodily well-being; then he must care for her, attend to her legal and financial well-being. In a Heideggerian care-relationship they build a world.

Even yet, though, there is one more threat to the union of Will and Allie (or Grace, as she could be called). What if one has struggled successfully to oppose all external detrimental forces and to welcome any external help (used will and accepted grace), yet harbors an enemy, himself? Will has on occasion wondered if his fundamental state of mind is inherited (LC, 10), if "it does come down to chemistry after all" (LC, 78). Even after he has been restored to life by Allie, he finds himself out of control, attempting literally to return to the patch of Georgia swamp in which his life became haunted. Thus he is discovered wandering the Interstate, as befuddled as his twenty-year-old self somewhere between Cross Keys and Port Republic. It turns out that he suffers a very slight chemical imbalance, which, when corrected, controls the impulses that interfere with his willful control of his actions. "Did it all come down to chemistry after all?" (LC, 307)

Praise the Lord, no. He realizes that he still loves Allie, that his feeling for her was not merely a symptom of his unbalanced condition. Thus he goes to her, lifts her up, this time, and takes her off to a Howard Johnson's. Then, even when his pH goes out of control and drags him out to a desert place (LC, 337) with the Greener, he withstands the temptations, flings the guns into the abyss, and returns to Allie's bed. It is, be sure about it, love, not medication, that conquers death. With that love, Will and Allie will marry, tend to each other (LC, 341), join those partialities, Messrs. Arnold and Ryan, to become Crusoe, Incorporated, in order to build cabins all over Sourwood Mountain.

The title is a brilliant epitome of the novel. In one sense, it refers to Yeats's poem, the Apocalypse fondly awaited by the Southern Stoic, which has enticed each of Percy's protagonists. It also refers to the orgasm, for both Allie and Will discover a sense of incarnation in sexuality that neither has felt before. The sexual meaning, in turn, suggests another theological meaning, that the communion of two persons in love making love is but a token of that available in the divine relationship. That He created love for humans to experience is proof that He is a loving God. Yet again, the title refers to that experience so meaningful to Percy, "coming to oneself." One comes into the world, but it is a lifetime later that one experiences a second "coming to oneself," when one becomes aware of himself, really aware for the first time, of time.

Percy frequently illustrates this experience by citing Robinson Crusoe. But an older illustration, that he surely knows, is that of the Prodigal Son

(Luke 15:17), who "came to himself,"[14] after having wandered away from his father in pursuit of the things of this world. In despair the son suddenly sees that all he has to do is to return. In his novels Walker Percy has always been creating parables of the Prodigal Son, who comes to himself, then starts on the road back. That the Father will receive him is a Truth outside the scope of novels, which concern human actions.

Percy's novels themselves are the confessions of a Prodigal Son. Something happened to Walker Percy in New Mexico in 1945–46: it may not have been an act, only a state of mind. But something happened, which is objectified in atomic and desert images that in each novel hint of soul sickness. In a recent article, Percy writes, "A novelist these days has to be an ex-suicide."[15] Walker Percy does not engage in idle talk, especially in an interview of himself; he must intend that statement to be taken seriously. Then something else happened in Santa Fe (there is sometimes an uncanny aptness in language): he must have "come to himself." Straightforth he came to Mississippi to marry and to become a Catholic. His writing has traced his interior road back: the alienation in which he found himself, the temptation to rely upon science for answers that it cannot give, the lifelong uncovering of a past inadequate because of its pagan pride, and — with great deception — his Christian faith. Yet for all the personal meaning to his novels, there remains, finally, yet another meaning, available only because of the personal meaning. he has written, "The highest role of the educator is the maieutic role of Socrates; to help the student come to himself not as a consumer of experience but as a sovereign individual."[16] Walker Percy is an educator: because of his experience as a Prodigal Son, he has been able to help many another Prodigal to come to himself.

Notes

1. The suicide was front-page news on 9 July 1929 in both the *Birmingham Post* and *Birmingham News:* the *New York Times* printed a notice of the death on 10 July, 10. Leroy's father, Walker, also committed suicide with a shotgun, 8 February 1917. The *Birmingham Age-Herald*, 9 February 1917, 1, termed the death an accident, but the *Birmingham News* that same day reported the coroner's verdict of suicide and gave melancholia as the cause (1). In *Lanterns on the Levee*, William Alexander Percy describes the suicide of the original American Percy, Captain Charles B., Walker Percy's great-great-great-grandfather.

2. See Robert Coles, *Walker Percy: An American Search* (Boston: Little, Brown and Company, 1972), 62–63. That "ailed" is a word associated with Harry Stack Sullivan's interviewing; Percy's use of it in conversation with Coles suggests just how vivid is his recall, no doubt a useful capacity for a novelist.

3. Walker Percy, "Why I Live Where I Live," *Esquire*, 93 (April 1980): 35–36.

4. Walker Percy, "From Facts to Fiction," *Book Week* 4 (25 December 1966): 6, 9. He is speaking here only of *The Moviegoer*, but what he says applies to all of his novels.

5. Walker Percy, *The Moviegoer* (New York: Noonday Press, 1967). Page references are incorporated into the text as (M).

6. Walker Percy, *The Last Gentleman* (New York: Farrar, Straus and Giroux, 1966). Page references are incorporated into the text as (LG).

7. See "Bourbon," *Esquire* 84 (December 1975): 148–149.

8. The relationship between the Percy family and Oscar W. Underwood is briefly sketched in Evans C. Johnson, *Oscar W. Underwood: A Political Biography* (Baton Rouge: Louisiana State University Press, 1980).

9. Walker Percy, *Love in the Ruins* (New York: Farrar, Straus and Giroux, 1971). Page references are incorporated into the text as (LR).

10. Walker Percy must have enjoyed his vacations at "Uncle Will's" summer place at Sewanee, for he consistently employs the Southern mountains as an image of the idyllic place.

11. Walker Percy, *Lancelot* (New York: Farrar, Straus and Giroux, 1977). Page references are incorporated into the text as (L).

12. Walker Percy, *The Second Coming* (New York: Farrar, Straus and Giroux, 1980). Page references are incorporated into the text as (SC).

13. See Heidegger, *Being and Time*, trans. John Macquarrie and Edward Robinson (New York: Harper and Row, 1962), 210–24.

14. J.A. Findlay, "Luke," in *the Abingdon Bible Commentary*, eds. Frederick C. Eiselen, Edwin Lewis, and David G. Downey (New York: Abingdon Press, 1929), 1048b, points out that in the Greek the expression has a medical meaning, to be restored to consciousness.

15. Walker Percy, "Questions They Never Asked Me," *Esquire* 88 (December 1977): 184. Percy also speaks of discovering a knack for writing, of which he speculates: "Maybe it's inherited, maybe it's the result of a rotten childhood—I don't know." The two may not be mutually exclusive ideas: a fear of inheritance might have made for the rotten childhood; the writing has been the restoration to, the preservation of, health.

16. See "The Loss of the Creature," in *The Message in the Bottle* (New York: Farrar, Straus and Giroux, 1975), 63. Not to labor the point—but Percy's novels constitute a message in a bottle.

Walker Percy: The Continuity of the Complex Fate

J. Donald Crowley*

> It's a complex fate, being an American, and one of the responsibilities it entails is fighting against a supersitious valuation of Europe.
>
> Henry James, *Hawthorne*

> Yet like Emerson, Poe, and many Americans before him, he [Wallace Stevens] sought in other writers and in other cultures the means not to have ideas but to express them. He sought the means of validating his own insights and doing his own work.
>
> Roy Harvey Pearce, *The Continuity of American Poetry*

Virtually ever since the early 1960s, when *The Moviegoer* and *The Last Gentleman* won for Walker Percy the reputation of being one of our

*This essay was written specifically for this volume and appears here for the first time.

most gifted contemporary American writers, the criticism — oftentimes masterfully and, frequently, aided by Percy himself in interviews — has interpreted and evaluated his work by way of the perspective of European influences. And quite properly. Much of the best criticism, following the example of Martin Luschei's *The Sovereign Wayfarer: Walker Percy's Diagnosis of the Malaise* (1972), has extended the analysis of Percy's fiction and nonfiction alike as dramatizations and elaborations of the ideas of Kierkegaard and other existentialists. A fuller list of "influences" would have to bow not only to Camus, Sartre, Gabriel Marcel, and Dostoyevski, Mann, and Joyce, but to Wittgenstein, Heidegger, Pascal, Augustine, Aquinas, and then take note (as the criticism has not yet done) of Percy's being steeped in the writers of the Catholic Renascence — Leon Bloy, George Bernanos, Romano Guardini, Francois Mauriac, Jacques Maritain — before going on to Jaspers and a host of language theorists. Percy's, clearly, is a marvelously eclectic literary-cultural carpetbag of foreign items.

Conversely, Percy's direct indebtednesses here at home have been thought to be remarkably few, and only in very recent years has the criticism seriously qualified Luschei's view that Percy "was simply never under Faulkner's influence. . . . He leapfrogged Faulkner and other writers Southern and American, with the sole exception of Mark Twain, . . . and went to Europe. By the time he came home he could see and speak for himself" (9). The sole exception was for years not even Twain in general but the author of *Adventures of Huckleberry Finn*, Percy consenting to the large truth in Hemingway's encomium that Twain's classic is the one book "all modern American literature" comes from. Recent studies of influence and similarity have linked Percy with Faulkner, Hemingway, Flannery O'Connor, Caroline Gordon, Allen Tate, Robert Penn Warren, even Hawthorne, among others.[1] But the relatively little commentary on Percy's use of Charles Saunders Peirce, whose triadic theory of the nature of words, language, and communication is central in most of Percy's essays on semiotics and present, too, in his fiction, is an index to the work still to be done in these areas. Relatively little has been said, for example, about what Percy might have absorbed from the work of other American writers he has praised: Bellow's, Styron's, Cheever's, Carlos Williams's, Heller's *Something Happened*, Walter M. Miller, Jr.'s *A Canticle for Leibowitz*, whose protagonist Percy appropriates for *Lost in the Cosmos*. Most of all, perhaps, given Percy's riffing on *Life on the Mississippi* in descriptive and digressive passages of *The Thanatos Syndrome*,[2] the extent to which all his novels juxtapose wide varieties of spoken American idiom — regional, social, racial, scientific, pseudoscientific — might very well be found to have its primary precedent in Twain's brilliant playing with the possibilities of vernacular speech.

My interest here, however, is not with "influences" — direct or indirect, explicit or implicit — but with the larger and more ranging question of Percy's essential Americanness and his relation to the longest-lived literary tradition of his native land. Extrapolating from Roy Harvey Pearce's comment about the relevance of European poetry for Stevens's work, we can see that Percy, in going so often abroad to school, is, far from being unusual, engaged rather in a characteristically American artistic exercise. As much critical insight as still remains to be discovered by way of genetic and source studies, it seems time for the criticism to heed Percy's request in his 1977 *Esquire* self-interview — "Please don't ask me about Dostoevski and Kierkegaard"[3] — and come upon some newer, refreshing ways to view his art. I mean not so much to reverse Luschei's reading here, except insofar as he asserts that "American" is a critical category of virtually no value in elucidating Percy and substitutes for it "an existential sensibility . . ." that for him is the mark of Percy's "uniqueness" (viii, 242–43). My purpose is instead to qualify and add to the criticism as it has already developed beyond Luschei, and to do so in the manner of suggestive prolegomenon: to unbend the subject, as Henry James would say, so as to broaden the terms of the discourse.

My thesis, then, is that the signatures of Percy's art and thought are, at last, indelibly American: the arduous terms of his calling, the intense and steady pressures between the life and the work, his attitudes and assumptions about the basic nature, function, and, finally, limits of art, his extraordinarily passionate attention to language, his angle of vision on the word's relation to reality, numerous of the most typical elements of his style, his recurrent themes — all these have an American stamp of character. As Percy himself asked, "how it came to pass that a physician turned writer and became a novelist,"[4] so we might inquire, even at the risk of referring too little to Percy himself, how does it come to pass that a late twentieth-century Southern Catholic writer takes his place in the history of an American consciousness that stretches back through Ralph Waldo Emerson and many of those other nineteenth-century New England abolitionists to find its earliest roots in a seventeenth-century Puritanism that, in "breaking away once and for all from Roman Catholic authoritarianism" (Pearce, 39), stands in dynamic opposition to several of Percy's primary articles of belief? The question might be asked if only because Percy himself, writing about Herman Melville in 1983, asked why the South had no Melville in the 1840s and 50s and answered, "It's just that the post-Christianity and alienation of the Massachusetts writer [he's speaking of Melville's stay in the Berkshires] took a hundred years to reach the Mississippi."[5]

To read Percy in terms of American antecedents is to read him as Malcolm Cowley years ago read Whitman's 1855 *Leaves of Grass*, whose leading ideas Cowley found to share large similarities with Eastern thought and Indian philosophy with which the poet surely had no acquaintance. It is to call to mind, too, Harold Bloom's remark regarding the tyrannical influence of Emerson on later American writers: "many contemporary Americans still pay something, whether or not they have read Emerson, since his peculiar relevance now is that we seem to read him merely by living here, in this place still somehow his, and not our own."[6] Percy, clearly, has had to pay no tax to, or fret any anxiety about, the influence of Emerson or his contemporaries. Quite the opposite. What I suggest is that those earlier writers came into possession of some stark and enduring truths about the nature of New World experience and that Percy, being himself a mighty noticer of things great and small in American culture, has, with remarkable self-reliance, come upon his own latter-day versions of many of these same insights independently. No less than Whitman, Percy is a writer engaged in his own language experiments, and he has created a style with which to give those insights an incisive life for the present postmodern phase of New World conditions. If the evolution of European existentialist thinking unquestionably derives from Kierkegaard, it is nonetheless true and of no little consequence that Kierkegaard's American contemporaries, Percy's native predecessors, were constructing out of their indigenous experience responses profoundly existential. Indeed, Luschei hints at as much when, discussing Kierkegaard's *Either/Or*, he simply notes in passing that "The parallels with Emerson are striking, especially with regard to the necessity of action for the whole man. Kierkegaard's Knight of Faith at times looks remarkably like a Danish cousin of Emerson's American Scholar" (59, fn. 111).

It is this Percy — the Percy who, however many radical differences there are between him and the Sage of Concord, has his own parallels with Man Thinking — that the criticism has not attended to even in recent essays that make American comparisons. To see him is to see a writer and thinker who knows, by native instinct as it were, that the one right use of books, even books by Dostoyevski and Kierkegaard, is, as Emerson pronounced, "but to inspire." It is to see the writer who, however much on the borrow, acknowledges more happily than most the gleanings he has taken from his representative men and women and is finally, like Emerson, beyond influence. Percy himself tells it best in explaining how he was able to write *The Moviegoer*, after two earlier unsuccessful efforts to put together a publishable novel:

> It is not like learning a skill or a game at which, with practice, one gradually improves. One works hard all right, but what comes, comes all of a sudden and as a breakthrough. One hits on something. What happens is a period of unsuccessful effort during which one works very hard — and fails. There follows a period of discouragement. Then there comes a paradoxical moment of collapse-and-renewal in which one somehow breaks with the past and starts afresh. The slate is wiped clean. It is almost as if the discouragement were necessary, that one first has to encounter despair before one is entitled to hope. Then a time comes when one takes a pencil and paper and begins. Begins, really for the first time. . . . One begins to write not as one thinks he is supposed

to write, and not even to write like the great models one admires, but rather to write as if he were the first man on earth ever to set pencil to paper.[7]

Whatever else the statement implies — say, about living itself — it is without doubt expressive of that Adamic impulse that Pearce defined as the dominant mode of American poetry. And this time it comes, most curiously, from a Mississippian, a Papist no less. There is in Percy — such are the swirling transformations in American history and culture — a new-fangled version of the antinomianism of those original Puritans, a reversal of the terms of their rebellion against authoritarianism. Paradoxical, to be sure, and tricky, but, in the post-Christian technological world as Percy sees it, true. However much Percy is a devout believer in, say, apostolic succession, "what he sees first in the Western world," as he put it in "A Novel about the End of the World," "is the massive failure of Christendom itself."[8] And then, when he specifies the terms of that failure, they have an American edge to them and an American application: Christendom's "vocabulary is worn out" and Christendom (Percy seems careful here to distinguish between that and Christianity) has suffered an "egregious moral failure" (MB, 116, 117). It's useful to let him speak at some length here because the words bear on every aspect of his vision:

> It is significant that the failure of Christendom in the United States has not occurred in the sector of theology or metaphysics, with which the existentialists and the new theologians are also concerned and toward which Americans have always been indifferent, but rather in the sector of everyday morality, which has acutely concerned Americans since the Puritans. Americans take pride in doing right. It is not chauvinistic to suppose that perhaps they have done righter than any other great power in history. But in one place, the place which hurts the most and where charity was most needed, they have not done right. White Americans have sinned against the Negro from the beginning and continue to do so, initially with cruelty and presently with an indifference which may be even more destructive. And it is the churches which, far from fighting the good fight against man's inhumanity to man, have sanctified and perpetuated this indifference. (MB, 117)

Two points need to be made here. One is that to seize upon a failure of vocabulary, of words — especially when mentioning the Puritans, however casually, in the same breath — is, I propose, a very American thing to do. The other, more to the present issue, is that when Christendom is so thoroughly discredited ecclesiastical authoritarianism can hardly be the dominant hierarchy to be opposed as it had been, centuries ago, for the Puritans. Percy's Catholicism, especially as Mississippi Catholicism, comes closer to being only one more of the latest forms of infidelity given the reigning gods of the age. Those "hierarchies" to be opposed are there for Percy, as they always are for the American writer, though now of a radically different sort:

what has happened is not merely the technological transformation of the world but something psychologically even more portentous. It is the absorption by the layman not of the scientific method but rather of the magical aura of science, whose credentials he accepts for all sectors of reality. Thus in the lay culture of a scientific society nothing is easier than to fall prey to a kind of seduction which sunders one's very self from itself into an all-transcending "objective" consciousness and a consumer-self with a list of "needs" to be satisfied. It is this monstrous bifurcation of man into angelic and bestial components against which the old theologies must be weighed before the new theologies are erected. Such a man could not take account of God, the devil, and the angels if they were standing before him, because he has already peopled the universe with his own hierarchies. When the novelist writes of a man "coming to himself" through some such catalyst as catastrophe or ordeal, he may be offering obscure testimony to a gross disorder of consciousness and to the need of recovering oneself as neither angel nor organism but as a wayfaring creature somewhere between. (*MB*, 113)

Defining the current lords of life reigning over his life is one thing. Another is to know how to proceed as a writer "having cast his lot with a discredited Christendom and having inherited a defunct vocabulary" (*MB*, 118). Percy's response was, in effect, to utter himself what has long since been the prayer of American writers since Emerson—"Oh, to find a language!"—and then, like his Mr. Ives in *Love in the Ruins* (who plans, upon his release from a Skinnerian Geriatric Rehabilitation Clinic, to return home and " 'Write a book, look at the hills, live till I die' " [234]), get on about the mission rather than the business of writing and living. And, like Emerson, in that order. To be sure, there are gaping differences between these two, Percy and Emerson, some of them no doubt of a defiant and contradictory character—just as there are between Emerson and all those other writers, Thoreau and Whitman included, who must be said in Bloom's terms to be "after Emerson." I deliberately hold them in abeyance here, being as I am out for Percy's (and Emerson's) favorite American language game of "like,"[9] of simile and similarities in Emerson's (and Percy's) beautifully, profoundly pluralistic worlds. Emerson, that is to say, when he defined the American Scholar as the whole Man Thinking, "educated by nature, by books, and by action" and exercising his duty to "cheer, to raise and to guide men by showing them facts amidst appearances," wrote, long before the fact, an apt shorthand gloss on Percy's primary aspirations as a writer. When Percy, in "The Loss of the Creature" (*MB*, 63), declares that "The highest role of the educator is the maieutic role of Socrates: to help the student come to himself not as a consumer of experience but as a sovereign individual," he is speaking in an American vein whose resonance is distinctly traceable to Emerson and beyond. The insight he urges, at this very late stage of our capitalistic enterprise, is his own version of the persistent and perennial American impulse toward the testing of the possibilities of individual metamorphosis.

It is the insight that Emerson—complaining all the while, at a much earlier stage of American materialism, that "Things are in the saddle"— reinvented out of the older Puritan urge toward regeneration even as he was rejecting Puritan belief. Daniel Shea puts superbly the way in which this subject of metamorphosis seems to choose the American writer rather than being created by him:

> Emerson is the crucial figure in a tradition that has helped identify American literature, the celebration and testing of the proposition that "men are convertible"—an institutionalized article of faith to the Puritans but one that has been vexed by second thoughts ever since. By raising again the question of grace, Emerson gave extended life to the seventeenth-century spiritual autobiography. By precept and example he challenged the American writer to deliver up out of his experience a transformed language and imaginative structures more nearly organic with an American conception of man as endlessly capable of regeneration. Such a challenge ought not to yield the novel's standard progression, in which a central character, interacting with a society both alluring and problematic, comes to rest in increased self-understanding. The kind of becoming suggested in the symbol of the transparent eyeball [Emerson's own notorious transformation in *Nature*] is metamorphic, not simply a change of status but a change of state; the attainment of a newly given self, not simply the regaining of identity through recognition. Without Ovid's recourse to the gods, the American writer after Emerson is challenged to induce belief that something extrinsic to character has, in a transforming moment, become intrinsic to him. Something apparently not in the system of the protagonist's growth, but deriving from his natural environment, perhaps from the American spirit of place, invades and transforms the self. From such a point of view, American books may well appear as so many varieties of religious experience and William James a better guide to them than the literary historian.[10]

Thus seen, the body of Emerson's work is given over to addressing the difficulty of the fundamentally existentialist task of placing oneself securely in the concrete situation of the world. His essential subject, before Heidegger, is in many ways Heidegger's *Dasein*. Thus the starkness, the spatial blankness of the question with which he begins the essay "Experience," originally entitled "Life:" "Where do we find ourselves? In a series of which we do not know the extremes, and believe that it has none. We wake and find ourselves on a stair; there are stairs below us, which we seem to have ascended; there are stairs above us, many a one, which go upward and out of sight." For Emerson the universal plight is that, always doubting the accuracy of our perceptions, we become "Ghostlike [as] we glide through nature, and should not know our place again." What Emerson names here I take to be a closer than rough equivalent to Percy's diagnosis of "everydayness" as the root cause of the postmodern malaise. Emerson, for all the transcendental optimism behind the buoyant question in *Nature*—"Why should not we also enjoy an original relation to the universe?"—also had, like Percy much later, a fearful conception of man, New World man, as in danger of being lost in the cosmos.

Emerson, of course, did not so much invent the idea as he simply gave voice, pointedly and powerfully, to a condition or a risk endemic to the American territory. It is not until the very conclusion of *The Prairie* (1827) that James Fenimore Cooper can let his epic hero Natty Bumppo find himself with his "Here!" in his dying breath. Still earlier, in 1821, Washington Irving had concocted a (the?) model American tale of Rip Van Winkle's eighteen-year-long dream sleep through the American Revolution. And by 1835 Hawthorne followed with the slender sketch of Wakefield, surely an American type though a Londoner, who, out of affectless whim, absents himself for twenty years from wife and home and becomes the "Outcast of the Universe" as he gazes down in orbit from a nearby apartment window on her and his own missing self. The European eyes of Alexis de Tocqueville had also in the early 1830s anticipated much of Emerson's essential vision about the difficulties of "being there:" he sees the American as "Man himself, taken aloof from his country and his age and standing in the presence of God and Nature. . . . Man [who] springs from nowhere, crosses time and disappears forever in the bosom of God; . . . seen but for a moment, wandering on the verge of two abysses, and there he is lost."[11]

And the body of Percy's work, fiction and nonfiction alike, belongs in this catalog of attempts to address the American existential necessity of placing the self as being-in-the-world. His subtitle to "The Delta Factor" epitomizes well the bent in all his writing: "How I Discovered the Delta Factor Sitting at My Desk One Summer Day in Louisiana Thinking about an Event in the Life of Helen Keller on Another Summer Day in Alabama in 1887." Put in the context of his early predecessors' versions of the New World predicament, the little fable with which Percy begins that essay has an aboriginally American stamp: "In the beginning was Alpha and the end is Omega, but somewhere between occurred Delta, which was nothing less than the arrival of man himself and his breakthrough into the daylight of language and consciousness and knowing, of happiness and sadness, of being with and being alone, of being right and being wrong, of being himself and not himself, and of being at home and being a stranger" (*MB*, [3]). The statement constitutes a recognizably American definition—recognizable because in extremis—of the utter crux that the *word* has been in the New World. Sacvan Bercovitch makes the brilliant and initially astonishing claim, for example, that the New England Puritans' "distinctive contribution" to American culture "is not religious, moral, or institutional" but instead "lies in the realm of rhetoric"; that, being "inveterate believers in words," the Puritans "provided the scriptural basis for what we have come to call the myth of America."[12] In equating their individual and national destinies with the prophetic pre-text of Holy Scripture—building their "City upon a hill" for the rest of the world to witness and then imitate — the Puritans, so Bercovitch insists, did nothing less than accommodate the Bible to themselves by rewriting it: *"In the beginning was the word, and the word was with the New England way, and the word became 'America' "* ([219]). Which is to say that, whatever metamorphoses American language would undergo, the Puritans had fixed the word as uniquely pivotal in virtually all New World experience. The effects have been such, as Bercovitch points out, as to have long outlived Puritanism itself: "Washington Irving," he says, "surveying the new republic in the guise of a visiting Muslim," concludes quickly that the young American "government is a pure unadulterated logocracy, or government of words" [219].

No wonder, then, that later still Emerson, organizing *Nature*, made "Language" his middle, mediating chapter between "Commodity" and "Spirit" and everything else in the visible and invisible worlds. As the Puritans had appropriated to themselves the sacred scriptures, Emerson, in his transformation of their ideal of Logos, transplanted the Bible's revelatory powers in Nature as the source of the Spirit's ministering to man in the present. Taking Nature to mean in some large part the American landscape, that landscape he arrogated to himself as the measure of the possibilities of his own being.[13] And since Nature is at once "the symbol of Spirit," no wonder he would add later, in "The American Scholar," that "Life is our dictionary" and then, in "The Poet," that "The world being thus put under the mind for verb and noun, the poet is he who can articulate it" and that, taking another leap, "America is a poem in our eyes." No wonder that Whitman, in his 1855 preface to *Leaves*, exulted that "The United States themselves are essentially the greatest poem." Whatever else, these are extraordinary curiosities as definitions of life and poem and country never seen before, and we would do well to compare to them the American extravagance of Percy's subtitle, *How Queer Man Is, How Queer Language Is, and What One Has to Do with the Other (The Message in the Bottle)*.

Bercovitch's astute analysis of the false rhetoric of the American myth does not stop until he examines the current postmodern threat to it; and the relevance to Percy, his time and place, needs to be made clear:

> The rhetoric implies that America's future, and by extension the fate of humanity, hinges on the efforts of the individual representative American. And the social effects have been plain enough: a persistent anxiety about "making it" (along with a pervasive tendency to violence about *not* making it), a constant emphasis on the need to "do it yourself" (and to "do it now"), countless pieties (and handbooks) concerning the duties, pleasures, and benefits of "self-realization." . . . The future itself . . . depends on a procession of representative Americans — in any given generation, a community of individuals who will fulfill the myth, and a succession of such communites from one generation to the next, even

unto the end of the world. But what if the individuals do not want the myth, or successive generations, or the world? . . . What happens when history severs the symbol from the nation, the logos from the logocracy? It is a prospect that returns us full circle to the Puritan discovery three centuries ago: *I have been to the Bible and America does not exist.* What happens when history separates "America," divine plan and all, from the United States? (226–28)

Readers of *Love in the Ruins* and *Lost in the Cosmos* will share, I hope, something of my sense that Bercovitch, seeming to have read them as well, is writing here as if prophetically about Percy's next book. Percy's conjunction of the moral failure of Christendom and the betrayal of the promise of America is one evidence of his commitment to his own modest version of a myth of America as redemptive. So too is the antic epilogue of his comic-apocalyptic novel, where he conflates those two texts in collapsing together, in the Southern manner, July Fourth and Christmas: shooting off fire-crackers outside the ragtag church, the children shout "Hurrah for Jesus Christ!" . . . "Hurrah for the United States!" and a minor black character Victor Charles "wishes [Tom More] merry Christmas and tells [him] he's running for Congress" (400). But if Bercovitch anticipates Percy's American interests and concerns, Percy's *Lost in the Cosmos* has anticipated Bercovitch's speculations. There the small remnant of survivors from the year 2069's World War III have to look square in the face their leader Captain Schuyler's pronouncement about their present political circumstances: "America? What America? There is no America" (260).

Nor is it in just these two of his works that the Americanness of Percy's vision declares itself. Nearly all his central characters have the aspect of being what Bercovitch calls the "individual representative American," and though their separate questions of destiny are always in the foreground, there is nonetheless present, and never too far off, the question of the fate of a larger community. In one way or another they all participate in the native egocentric predicament that made de Tocqueville nervous about America: "In democratic communites," he observed, "each citizen is habitually engaged in the contemplation of a very puny object, namely, himself. If ever he raises his looks higher, he then perceives nothing but the immense form of society at large, or the still more imposing aspect of mankind. His ideas are all either extremely minute and clear, or extremely general and vague; what lies between is an open void" (184). De Tocqueville here names some of the perils of an existential lostness he perceived to have in the 1830s an exclusively American intensity, and in doing so he anticipates, inevitably, so many of our primary twentieth-century American themes: those, certainly, of Fitzgerald's *The Great Gatsby*, a book that seems to define that point where Percy's pick up to continue the essential American fable, now of the postmodern and deracinated self. Binx Bolling, Percy's first protagonist, is like no one else so much as he is Nick Carraway at the end of *Gatsby*. Nick, totally deprived of anything on which to spend his own wonder, has to face as a twin loss the passing of the feast that was Gatsby's life: first, through the grimness of a thirtieth birthday that stretches out before him in the shape of a dreary, desolate decade holding little or no prospect of metamorphosis; secondly, in the end of the nation's own celebration, registered menacingly on an old railroad timetable dated "July 5th," and the despoliation of a continent he could still imagine as having been, originally, "a fresh green breast of the new world." What we last know of Nick is that, telling Gatsby's story, he drifts aimlessly "somewhere back in that vast obscurity" of the Midwest without even the consolation of Natty Bumppo's minimal "Here!," his interest in "bonds" (a pun worthy of Thoreau) now as dead as Gatsby.

Also a stockbroker, Binx too drifts aimlessly around New Orleans, another example of the familiar figure of the American as unemployed consciousness. The only feast available to him is a meretricious Mardi Gras, the only refuge from boredom — except for a number of charmingly lyrical, ineffectual efforts to enjoy the secrets of a series of secretarial thighs — a ghostly perch in spectatordom from which to observe moviegoers watching movies and tourists touring. He is more stripped of future even than James's John Marcher. But finally for Binx the American metamorphic place and moment come: absenting himself from Fat Tuesday, he returns in time for the muted and mysterious — but authentic — feast of Ash Wednesday, his own thirtieth birthday, and the new season of family deaths, most anguishingly that of the fifteen-year-old Lonnie, whom Binx has referred to up until the end only as his "half-brother," even though the boy is Binx's alter ego and the sole entry for him into the world's, and the word's, reality. There is in Binx's recovery no fanfare or manifest triumph; nor is there an expiatory note, self-conscious or otherwise, that would have been anathema to the self-reliance of an Emerson. There is, however, the insinuated recognition that an involvement with persons and events in time necessarily presupposes an unfolding series of such ordeals and thus the need to come by further metamorphic moments. As Emerson might have said, "up again, old heart!"

Each of Percy's fictions successively intensifies and escalates the terms of the ordeal to be endured and tests still more constrictively the possibilities of recovery and transformation. Thus, in the space-odyssey conclusion of *Lost in the Cosmos* Percy's representative American is the marvelously composite figure Marcus Aurelius Schuyler: stoic astronaut of Dutch descent, heir alike to Rip Van Winkle and Flying Dutchman, a master of the American technique of role-playing and very much "like a Christian who had lost his faith in everything but the Fall of Man" (228–29). His mission is to captain a starship voyage so to decode an extraterrestrial message thought by NASA to be real. Not incidentally, the journey is exactly the duration of Rip's old deep sleep. Nor is it mere coincidence that Schuyler, as he takes leave of what is now the very old new world, sees

Long Island, not as Fitzgerald had Nick have those "old Dutch sailors' eyes" see it — the embodiment of "the last and greatest of all human dreams" — but rather as "Long Island nuzzling into the continent like a great whale" (229). The world to which Schuyler and his crew return is one which has only a few thousand known survivors of a nuclear holocaust, and they are scattered about on several continents. Schuyler's group can remain in the radically reduced environment of what is left of "America," whose surviving children are "mostly genetically malformed and misbegotten" (242); or, since they are still possessed of free choice and the book being cast in the debased form of *The Last Self-Help Book*, they can orbit away again without the children and "colonize Europa, one of the Galilean satellites of Jupiter" (246), change its name to New Ionia," and, according to a eugenically inspired utopianist called Aristarchus Jones, begin building

> a society based on reason and science, and to do so without repeating the mistakes of the past, for example, the Dark Ages, two thousand years of Plato and Judaism and Christianity — a free and peace-loving society where the sciences and arts can flourish free from the superstitions and repressions of religion — . . . . There is no reason why we cannot start a new society on another planet just as we started a new society in the New World. (246–47)

Percy makes clear that Aristarchus's hopes are ill-conceived and steeped in as much hubris as those of Lancelot Lamar; indeed, both men might profit from a close reading of the first chapter of *The Scarlet Letter*. But Percy leaves the choice completely to the reader — he has no other habit here — by creating two scenarios, the one here at home, the other metaphorically, existentially spaced-out. They are his worst-case alternatives, the ultimate nature of the catastrophe in this brief science fiction now embracing man generically and containing the larger society of the world's population itself. Secondly, Percy's perspective here is his most blatantly American. His allusions put side by side for the attentive reader images drawn from what is perhaps our greatest elegiac vision about our country — Fitzgerald's — together with an unmistakable hint of Melville's awesome conception of the nature of evil. This he does for the purpose of taking us full circle again to the story of Rip Van Winkle, now in space-age dress, so that we might once again "come to . . . know [ourselves] as sovereign individuals" and then know better, among other matters of wisdom and practicality, how to write and live our stories of ourselves more fully.

More needs to be said of Percy's reference to Irving's hero, but here we might pause briefly to note Percy's American style. His parody of self-help manuals in *Lost in the Cosmos* is only the most obvious instance of his basic mode, which is in all its parts deeply collaborative, always bent on inviting the reader into the writing as joint enterprise: there is in it the old American urge, surely a consequence formally of the Emersonian pronunciamentos already cited, toward a style as point-of-view that would compel the reader to engage actively in a mutual, communal creative process with the writer. Hawthorne's strategies in his prefaces, his presenting to the reader a blossom plucked from the rosebush just outside the prison ("so directly on the threshold of our narrative, which is now about to issue from that inauspicious portal") Hester emerges from; Melville's making the narrator of "Bartleby" the very type of his own middle-class reader; the involuted first sentence of "The Beast in the Jungle"; Whitman's first grand declaration in "Song of Myself"; Faulkner's collective "we" in "A Rose for Emily" — these I mention as typical examples, suggestive I hope of innumerable other instances, of a dominant tone and rhetoric decisively American. It is not to be confused with the Trollopian or the familiarity of the rhetoric of the Victorian novel. No writer has named the difference more compellingly than Whitman did when, in *Democratic Vistas,* he proposes as "the sole course open to these United States . . . a new theory of composition for imaginative works of the very first class":

> Books are to be call'd for, and supplied, on the assumption that the process of reading is not a half-sleep, but, in the highest sense, an exercise, a gymnast's struggle; that the reader is to do something for himself, must be on the alert, must himself or herself construct indeed the poem, argument, history, metaphysical essay — the text furnishing the hints, the clue, the start or framework. Not the book needs so much to be the complete thing, but the reader of the book does. That were to make a nation of supple and athletic minds, well-train'd, intuitive, used to depend on themselves, and not on a few coteries of writers.

Where we see such "queer" definitions — redefinitions — of life and poem and country, we should not be surprised by radical revisions in the role of the reader. That Percy shares affinities even with the good gray poet might seem to be what Huck Finn would call "a stretcher." But then one asks what Whitman means in that same long essay in citing a remark of the Librarian of Congress: "The true question to ask respecting a book, is, *has it helped any human soul?*" What, indeed, if not an assertion of the maieutic role of the writer? — the American writer. The affinities are not only apparent but profound, even in the face of differences equally profound.

The extraordinary burdens Whitman places on the faithful American reader are in lovely correspondence with the severe demands he has already put on the devoted American writer. For Whitman, after Emerson, to be a poet was nothing less than a profession of faith, an answering to a still small voice urging vocation. By no means unique to Whitman, this sense of urgency is such that from one perspective American literary history is a charting of the varieties of calling. It has, as we should expect, a sweepingly pluralistic nature. There is, for example, the sweet piety of the first sentence of John Woolman's Quaker *Journal* (1774): "I have often felt a motion of love to leave some hints in writing of my experience of the goodness of God, and now, in the thirty-sixth year of my age [1756–57], I begin this work." At least one of the things that makes Irving's tale such a paradigm is that all Rip did upon finally returning home was to tell and retell the story of his absence and that the telling, in fact, became and remained his vocation. Instead of being one of the varieties of religious experience, Rip's vocation seems a sad and comic pastime since, though all his auditors come to know his story by heart, they remain unsure of its actual truth but continue yet to wish that his story were, or might become, theirs. That story-telling is substantially more than a traditional "literary" pursuit for Hawthorne is evidenced dramatically in "The Custom-House" by his musing about his Puritan ancestors' transgressions and their chagrin over his being merely "A writer of story-books!" Such pressures between the life and the art, the art and the life, as I am referring to have been steadfast in our literature and have announced themselves freshly in recent works as diverse as, say, John Updike's *Under the Dogwood Tree* and Alice Walker's *The Color Purple.*

As Henry Nash Smith and Richard Poirier have noted, it was Emerson who gave to the mission of the American writer the stamp of vocation: "The Man is only half himself," as he put it in "The Poet," "the other half is his expression." The effect of this injunction on Thoreau was, of course, charismatic, and his response to it issued in that sui generis American fable, *Walden.* It gave rise, too, to that richest of abiding American dilemmas about the relationship between life and art: "My life has been the poem I would have writ,/But I could not both live and utter it." The richest and most abiding, that is, if the little couplet does indeed outstrip Gertrude Stein's later aspirations to write the biographies of each and every American. At any rate, as singular as Thoreau's statement is, it becomes, in its very singularity, the very type of the tradition. American literature always reminds us that its subject is man and language: language in the Whitman way when Whitman can say simultaneously that *Leaves of Grass* "is only a language experiment" and that it is his "attempt, from first to last, to put a *Person*, a human being (myself in the latter half of the Nineteenth Century, in America,) freely, fully, and truly on record."

Walker Percy takes his place in this continuity of American writers who, in having such heightened expectations of the powers of the word and therefore put almost incredible burdens upon it, keep writing their historically unfolding versions of the oldest conception of the possibilities of language on this continent. Speaking of the practice of poetry in America, Herbert Schneidau points out that "The true Puritan heritage consists not of poetic achievements as such but rather with a strenuous wrestling with the problems of language and symbolism, a profound investigation of the techniques by which God's will was made manifest in words and related labors, which served to carry forward the Puritan

veneration of the Bible's imaginative writing while allowing later generations to abandon cautious scruples about the dangers of worldly art."[14] The
end of the American literary enterprise has been, since the Puritans, not
the making of well-wrought urns, but the pursuit of radical redefinitions
of poetry and fiction themselves. Hear again Whitman on this score, his
words in "A Backward Glance O'er Travel'd Roads:" "No one will get at
my verses who insists upon viewing them as a literary performance, or as
aiming at art or aestheticism." However high the artistic achievement of
various of our greatest works has been, they still characteristically, in their
Americanness, declare a willingness to sacrifice, if necessary, traditional
formal unities in the service of the higher cause of their American subject.
Percy's comments in "Notes for a Novel about the End of the World"
announce again this steady native predisposition:

> Let me define the sort of novelist I have in mind. I locate him not on a
> scale of merit — he is not necessarily a good novelist — but in terms of
> goals. He is, the novelist we speak of, a writer who has an explicit
> ultimate concern with the nature of man and the nature of reality where
> man finds himself. Instead of constructing a plot and creating a cast of
> characters from a world familiar to everybody, he is more apt to set
> forth with a stranger in a strange land where the signposts are enigmatic
> but which he sets out to explore nevertheless. One might apply to the
> novelist such adjectives as "philosophical," "metaphysical," "prophetic,"
> "eschatological," and even "religious." I use the word "religious" in its
> root sense as signifying a radical *bond*, as the writer sees it, which
> connects man with reality — or the failure of such a bond — and so
> confers meaning to his life — or the absence of meaning. (*MB*, 102-3)

Here Percy mentions only those writers he takes to be his predecessors
in that class of novel he describes — Dostoyevski, Tolstoy, Sartre, Faulkner,
Flannery O'Connor, Camus — and he justifies Sartre's inclusion because "his
atheism is 'religious' in the sense intended here: that the novelist betrays a
passionate conviction about man's nature, the world, and man's obligation
to the world" (103). And then, like so many of his American antecedents,
he goes on to "exclude much of the English novel," content in the
concession that both Austen and Richardson are "better novelists" than
either Sartre or O'Connor. Inquiring into the nature of the recurring
preoccupation of the American novelist — and it is, finally, the American
novelist of whom Percy speaks — he finds a clue in the "complaint of British
critics" that American writers are predisposed toward "philosophical
megalomania":

> Certainly one can agree that if British virtues lie in tidiness of style,
> clarity and concision, a respect for form, and a native embarrassment
> before "larger questions," American failings include pretension, grandi-
> osity, formlessness, Dionysian excess, and a kind of metaphysical omniv-
> orousness. American novels tend to be about everything. Morever, at the
> end, everything is disposed of, God, man, and the world. The most

frequently used blurb on the dust jackets of the last ten thousand American novels is the sentence "This novel investigates the problem of evil and the essential loneliness of man." A large order, that, but the American novelist usually feels up to it. (103–4)

Percy's definition here of the content and the style of the American novel — and his own style in uttering it — are quintessentially American. They are also a reminder that Percy is out there ahead of his readers in the discovery of himself as "one of them." His definition is, after all, not new: whatever originality it has is that of personal restatement. For it takes us all the way back to de Tocqueville and his judgment a century and a half ago that, although "The inhabitants of the United States have then, properly speaking, no literature," their literature, when it did appear, would be characterized by a style "frequently . . . fantastic, incorrect, overburdened, and loose, — almost always vehement and bold," by a poetry generally in which traditional form would "ordinarily be slighted, sometimes despised" (177).

Although Percy has a large knack for the ambience of the novel of manners, his attachment to nontraditional and mixed modes of narrative all readers of his work will recognize as a donnée. His exploitation of the trivialized nature of the self-help manual in *Lost in the Cosmos*, a thing half-horse and half-alligator from one end to the other, is but the most antic of many examples. The impulse to odd forms or angles of telling declares itself virtually everywhere in Percy's work. Just as Irving used Muslim eyes to get a fresh perspective on his native land, so Percy, in "A Theory of Language" (*MB*, [298]–327), gives himself a Martian persona. His novels are likewise testimony to the fact that, however laughable and grotesque it was and is, Emerson's "transparent eyeball," embodying the metamorphic moment as an act of seeing, defined in permanent ways so many American literary strategies. One thinks of Binx Bolling's freshness of view beneath the Korean chindolea bush, of the young Will Barrett surveying Central Park with his telescope, of Tom More's planting himself, in the opening scene of *Love in the Ruins*, in "a pine grove on the southwest cusp of the interstate cloverleaf," of Lancelot Lamar's stripped minimal cell-window view of cemetery and fragmented sign, of the older Will Barrett Georgia-bound by bus catching sight of "a single gold poplar which caught the sun like a yellow-haired girl coming out of a dark forest" (297), of the older Tom More in *The Thanatos Syndrome*, "one of those rare birds who sees things out of the corner of his eye, so to speak" [3]. Percy's protagonists all have the aspect of standing in for one of Rouault's Kings turned one-eyed Jack. And, as in Emersonian thought, their "seeing" compels their "saying," their view becomes inseparable from, manifest in, their voice. Lance, for example is literally reduced to, has become, a view and a voice only; and his hearer — with whom the reader stands in silently — is a priest listening to an anticonfession, Lance's life now relived as almost unspeakable story. The question posed here is a familiar American one, a brutal one: can Lance, telling his story, escape out of his unnamed hospital/prison and the solipsism of the story itself and gain reentrance into life and living again? Can the very language that constitutes his prison-house become a way out? Not, one suspects, unless he has heard his friend Percival's unspoken words that have throughout made up the variant, alternative text to his own demented narrative.

This double dilemma of both Lancelot and the hearer/readers of his story we might keep in mind in picking up again the question of the Emersonian stamp of the American writer's vocation. It is but another name for that quietly, profoundly passionate attention that Percy's most astute readers have already sensed in his work: the ways in which, as Frost might have said, Percy "carries himself toward his ideas and his deeds."[15] The essential biographical outlines of Percy's early ordeals have long since been known.[16] The drama of these earlier years is enough to equip any sensitive person with a Jamesian imagination of disaster. Together with the long years of Percy's arduous initiation as a writer they have a shape that calls to mind other, similar American literary callings: one thinks of Emerson's turning away not only from the ministry but from the biological sciences as the repository of the answers he first felt he most needed, of Hawthorne's dozen anonymous years, of Whitman's fitful struggles, of the collapse of Melville's popularity with the publication of *Moby-Dick*. The paradigm of the American writer's unroutine efforts somehow, to use again the words of Frost, to make his vocation and his avocation one constitutes perhaps our native literary tradition's most absorbing scheme, its relentless involvement with the enigmatic questions: What is Life, after all? What is the relationship between Life and Art, anyway? What, also, is Man?

Explaining "how a physician turned writer and became a novelist," Percy in effect shows how much of his own experience closely replicates Emerson's disappointment in biological science: "If the first great intellectual discovery of my life was the beauty of the scientific method, surely the second was the discovery of the singular predicament of man in the very world which has been transformed by this science. An extraordinary paradox became clear: that the more science progressed and even as it benefited man, the less it said about what it was like to be a man living in the world" (22). The problem becomes for Percy, out of his own original insight, what it has always been for the American imagination—the defense of the idea of Man, an adequate theory of human nature: "it is man himself," he continues, "who is called into question and must be defended, and it is the very nature of man which must be rediscovered and re-expressed in fresh language of a new poetry and fiction and theater" (46). One can almost hear Emerson as refrain here, mumbling his complaints about "this half-sight of science" and its hobgoblin "Statistics." And Percy himself, in describing these shocks of recognition, describes as well his own Emersonian metamorphic moment: "Then came the cataclysm, brought to pass appropriately enough by one of these elegant agents of disease, the same scarlet tubercle bacillus I used to see lying crisscrossed like Chinese characters in the sputum and lymphoid tissues of patients at Bellevue. Now I was one of them" (28). Metamorphic, clearly, and momentous in every way: the physician put, kicking and screaming, as it were, into the world of his patients and their — and his — disease. Being in 1941 the right age, Percy might very well have repeated the words in which Melville had summed up *his* metamorphic experience: "I date my life from my twenty-fifth year." Metaphorically the ordeal contains a psychological reenactment, too, of Emerson's discovery of his tragic sense: "It is very unhappy, but too late to be helped, the discovery we have made that we exist. That discovery is called the Fall of Man" ("Experience").

Readers who know well both Emerson and Percy's *Lost in the Cosmos* might object strenuously here that the whole point of Percy's book is to assert that it is definitively *not* "too late to be helped" and that Percy seems dedicated to contradicting the Emerson who proclaimed in his journals that the one "doctrine" he promulgated was "the infinitude of the private man." That idea would seem to smack of the post-Nietzchean twentieth-century "autonomous self" that is indeed — whether in his role as scientist, artist, or passive consumer — the central target of Percy's satire. But reading Emerson well is, as anyone who has tried that experiment knows, extremely difficult, and to get at the Emerson I speak of here is to sift through the numerous layers of assertive self-reliance to the realization that they rested, finally, on the man's utter faith in god-reliance. It is to sift through, too, the many layers of his "saying" to what was for him the higher reality of experience, "doing." To so sift, then, here is John Updike overcoming his initial skepticism about Emerson's contemporary relevance to us. He is quoting one of Emerson's traveling companions during his 1871 trip to northern California:

> "How *can* Mr. Emerson," said one of the younger members of the party to me that day, "be so agreeable, all the time, without getting tired!" It was the *naive* expression of what we all had felt. There never was a more agreeable travelling companion; he was always accessible, cheerful, sympathetic, considerate, tolerant; and there was always that same respectful interest in those with whom he talked, even the humblest, which raised them in their own estimation. One thing particularly impressed me, — the sense that he seemed to have of a certain great amplitude of time and leisure. It was the behavior of one who really *believed* in an immortal life, and had adjusted his conduct accordingly; so that, beautiful and grand as the natural objects were, among which our journey [to Yosemite] lay, they were matched by the sweet elevation of character, and the spiritual charm of our gracious friend.[17]

There is that Emerson, then, who, in spite of his protestations about a coldness of temperament and his chilling regrets that even the death of his son Waldo could not touch his "inmost me," was truly the friend of those who would live in the concrete here and now. "Now I was one of them," he too had a genius for saying, as he tried to discharge his solemn obligations, not to his thinking and his writing, but—in Percy's words—to the world, and thus his duties to man. Indeed, Updike's recovered Emerson sounds— and acts—very much like Percy's ideal psychiatrist, Harry Stack Sullivan, and his student-protege Tom More in *The Thanatos Syndrome* (16–17, 368–72). If Emerson was sadly forced to write that "our relations are oblique and casual" ("Experience"), once away from his writing table and in the company of other people he seems, according to this filtered account, to have had an uncommon ability to create, to incarnate the conditions of community: the sage on paper may appear to go off in the direction of self-assertion and renunciation of family and friends in favor of solitude and nature, but the experiential person acted out his being relationally. The California episode is a reminder that, paradoxically, the ideal that dominates both his thinking and his doing is community. In "The American Scholar," an essay that expends its vision on each person's re-creation of the Ideal Man, Emerson declares extravagantly in closing: "A nation of men will for the first time exist, because each believes himself inspired by the Divine Soul which also inspires all men." It is an astonishing claim, but no more visionary than Arthur Dimmesdale's Election Sermon: a reminder that Emerson's ultimate worldly concern in the bulk of his writing is the possibility of New World community, of society resting on an authentic pluralism rather than on those coercions that de Tocqueville called "the tyranny of the majority." Nor was his in any way a Gnostic ideal.

The movement of Emerson's thinking, then, is from self to selves together and, simultaneously, from ideas and thinking to the world of deeds and action, from writing and the making of poems (and of definitions of the poet serviceable for other, better poets) to the ultimate mission of becoming again a being-in-the-world of actual social circumstances. I refer to Emerson as a way of talking about essential aspects of Percy: the way lies in indirection and, as Emily Dickinson would say, "circuit." The Emerson retrieved by Updike is the Emerson who sustained for others his disciplined and demanding generosity of spirit. What that capaciousness of heart means and does is very like the exercise that Percy, in his generosity, sets out to do in his novels and essays: "I begin with a *man* who finds himself in a *world*, a very concrete man who is located in a very concrete place and time. Such a man might be represented as coming to himself. . . ."[18] What Emerson's companions felt him doing existentially—making their own selves realer to themselves—conforms closely to Percy's complex supra-aesthetic endeavors in pursuing the creation of fictional characters. The American novel, as Percy has perceived, is that sort of deadly serious concern: the novel, to cite James's objection to the British mode of Trollope and others, "is not a novel as a pudding is a pudding." This concern is the essence I mean in referring to the heightened pressures between the life and the art, the existential and the aesthetic, and vice versa.

Following are two comments about those relationships that put Percy and Emerson side by side. First, Emerson in "The American Scholar," having just defined life as "our dictionary":

> I learn immediately from any speaker how much he has already lived, through the poverty or splendor of his speech. Life lies behind us as the quarry from whence we get tiles and copestones for the masonry of to-day. This is the way to learn grammar. Colleges and books only copy the language which the field and the work-yard made.
>
> But the final value of action, like that of books, and better than books, is that it is a resource. That great principle of Undulation in nature . . . [is] the law of nature because . . . [it is] the law of spirit.
>
> The mind now thinks, now acts, and each fit reproduces the other. When the artist has exhausted his materials, when the fancy no longer paints, when thoughts are no longer apprehended and books are a weariness, — he has always the resource to *live*. Character is higher than intellect. Thinking is the function. Living is the functionary. The stream retreats to its source. A great soul will be strong to live, as well as strong to think. Does he lack organ or medium to impart his truths? He can still fall back on this elemental force of living them. This is a total act. Thinking is a partial act.

So much for thinking, and writing, and the making of art. On to the unfinished task of Living, which Emerson leaves, in his writing, noticeably undefined. He *assumes* the definition of living, and his powers and capacities, truly, to live are in the testimony of his traveling companions. Here, now, is Percy, addressing in "The State of the Novel" the mission again of the artist in terms of his own sense of the greater mandate to live: "It is the artist who at his best reverses the alienating process by the very act of seeing it clearly for what it is and naming it, and who in this same act establishes a kind of community. It is a paradoxical community whose members are both alone yet not alone, who strive to become themselves and discover that there are others who, however tentatively, have undertaken the same quest" (365). Percy goes on to note that novelist and reader alike are aware of the peculiar postmodern dangers of "the passive consumership of technology" and of the "loss of personal sovereignty" that occurs when we come to be made to feel that our happiness, in our talk-show culture, "depends on . . . [our] exposure to this or that psychology or this or that group encounter or technique." But he is not finished before he takes up the "similar danger attendant upon literature and art," and here—the remarks are the justification of my long digression on Emerson—Percy seems to reinvent the man in voicing his own values:

> If it is true that the poet and novelist are in the vanguard in their foreboding that something has gone badly wrong and in their sketching out of the nature of the pathology, let the reader both rejoice and

beware, rejoice that the good novelist has 'the skill to point out the specters which he, the reader, had been only dimly aware of, but beware in doing so of surrendering the slightest sovereignty over himself. If one happens to be a good writer or a scientist and lucky enough occasionally to hit on the truth, or if one is a reader or a consumer and lucky enough to benefit from a great medical discovery or a novelistic breakthrough which excites him — well and good. Well and good, that is, as long as one never forgets that the living of one's life is not to be found in books, either the reading of them or the writing of them. (372–73)

This branch of being "after Emerson" has the American writer propelled Adamically into his art as if by a veritably sacred calling and propelled, also, to invent endless strategies of word and rhetoric that would draw his reader into his text as active collaborator so that together they can test that language's ultimate powers of communication. The process involves an heroic ordeal of attempting to blur and dissolve the differences between the facts and the fictions and then, not surprisingly, a gracious admitting of the failure to have done so. In his next loving act, that American writer removes himself and his reader alike from the art by way of a pressing invitation to reclaim that higher mode of being themselves very concrete persons in the concrete here and now. "I stop somewhere," this writer seems to say, with Whitman, to the reader, "waiting for you." The process involves that old familiar American pattern of withdrawal and return, the ritual enactment of the going into solitude as the very avenue, paradoxically, to community. The force of that pattern is such that both these writers — Emerson, he who gave up the ministry because the Unitarian observance of the Lord's Supper had failed him, and Percy, he who as a Catholic finds the Eucharist a source of meaning for both art and life — embody it, incarnate it.

Percy defines the proper modes of novelistic writing as "cognitive" and still more as "diagnostic" as it comes to grips with the postmodern American malaise. Speaking of Joseph Heller's *Something Happened*, trying to specify that pronoun, Percy writes: "It is more like some aboriginal disaster, the original sin of the twentieth century. But where do we locate the disaster? Has something dreadful happened to Bob Slocum or to the society in which he lives? or both?" ("The State of the Novel," 365). And then he characterizes the literature of the last century as having "registered a massive dissent from the modern proposition that with the advance of science and technology and education, life gets better too" (365). His questions, his comments provide the occasion to place him still more firmly in a national, native context larger than and different from those addressed by source studies. The context of these words, for example, so Percylike:

For my part, I would alarm and caution even the political and business reader, and to the utmost extent, against the prevailing delusion that the establishment of free political institutions, and plentiful intellectual smartness, with general good order, physical plenty, industry, etc. (desirable and precious advantages as they all are), do, of themselves, determine and yield to our experiment of democracy the fruitage of success. . . .

I say we had best look our times and lands searchingly in the face, like a physician diagnosing some deep disease. Never was there more hollowness at heart than at present, and here in the United States. Genuine belief seems to have left us. . . . I say that our New World democracy, however great a success in uplifting the masses out of their sloughs, in materialistic development, products, and in a certain highly deceptive superficial popular intellectuality, is, so far, an almost complete failure in its social aspects, and in really grand religious, moral, literary, and aesthetic results. . . . Is there a great moral and religious civilization—the only justification of a great material one? Confess that to severe eyes, using the moral microscope upon humanity, a sort of dry and flat Sahara appears, these cities, crowded with petty grotesques, malformations, phantoms, playing meaningless antics.

These words are taken, not from *Lost in the Cosmos* or *The Thanatos Syndrome*, though with a few fairly simple changes of diction here and there a good many readers might think they come from either. They are, of all things, the words of Walt Whitman in *Democratic Vistas* (1871). And wherever Percy and Whitman differ, it nonetheless remains that the bulk of Percy's writing can be seen — and gains in significance when so seen — as another original American refrain on conditions pressingly American. What is the issue desperately on the line for Whitman is the future of American democracy and thus, for him, the future of the world: "The United States themselves are destined," he says, "to surmount the gorgeous history of feudalism, or else prove the most tremendous failure of time."

Percy's voice, like Whitman's here, contains a capacity for jeremiad in focusing on comic-apocalyptic and postapocalyptic vision. And for Percy, as for Whitman, the avoidance of catastrophe depends on the willingness of individuals to undergo the ordeals involved in such metamorphic acts of self-discovery as prepare them for the unfinished task of making society possible. Thus Binx, at the end of *The Moviegoer*, returns from his evasive travels to marry Kate and extend himself to "my brothers and sisters call[ing] out behind me." Thus, too, the total lack of closure in *The Last Gentleman*, which has the still more deeply disoriented Will Barrett chasing after personal sovereignty, however problematically, through human relationship. Catastrophe at last avoided in the comic-apocalyptic *Love in the Ruins*, the old social order now overturned and anticly reversed, the same fallen but regenerate conditions continue to prevail as both the life of personal domestic love and the political life of the nation are, if mutedly, renewed. *Lancelot* is Percy's exploration of the novel as jeremiad, his boldest experiment with reductive point of view as well as circumstances. Lancelot, cuckolded and having seen his home, his world of Belle Isle, debased into a pornographic movie set, has, in acting out with meticulous efficiency his murderous revenge, blown himself into psychologically undefinable space. A character who makes Poe's Montresor pale by comparison, Lancelot plans out of an almost maniacal stoicism to remove himself, upon his release, to a new home in Virginia, "a small solid two-hundred-year-old barn" (252). There he will later be joined by another patient, a young woman victim of a brutal rape whom he has helped recover from a catatonic state. The two of them, and a child she implies they will later have, will, returning to this very old place, take up the task of building again a larger community. It will be a humanizing one, however, only if Lancelot achieves his own uncertain metamorphic moment. In *The Second Coming* the same patterns of disorientation, ordeal, and recovery lead still another time to the effort to renew community. The older Will Barrett — his name announcing again the doubleness of his American burden of enduring and revealing — discovers the terms of himself and being outside himself in Allie. Barrett's gift to her is the words she has, as a result of electro-shock therapy and aphasia, lost touch with; hers to him is herself, her being as deed and action. Possessed of enormous wealth they are free at the end to begin once more anew in the old new world, once again for self and other: "I want well-built log cabins, enough land for privacy, and gardens, and at a price young couples, singles, and retired couples can afford" (346).

That there is in Percy's, as there is in much classic American writing generally, a noticeable repetitiveness in spite of all his lively variations on the theme is — this need to keep finding new ways to say much the same thing — the result of the urgency of the American quest after the very possibilities of society as much as it might been seen, too, as the necessary effort to avoid anxieties of influence. As William Carlos Williams put it, the question is "how to begin to begin again." That is the question that, at once, leads Percy into such deliberate exercises in experimental forms of narrative and into the naturalness for him of repeatedly inclusive and open-ended last scenes in his fictions and last sentences in so many of his essays. It may also be the question that has now prompted him to write a second explicit sequel in *The Thanatos Syndrome*. And where does this sequel "end"? Just where *The Second Coming* did — back at still another old new beginning. The final chapter with the first provides a kind of framed narrative as Dr. Tom More and Mrs. LaFaye — called Mickey, though her real name is Jeanie — share still another counseling session and, in a perfect dramatization of Percy's ideal of triadic, indirect communication, succeed with full mutuality as physician-patient and patient-physician in bringing themselves to themselves. The novel is Percy's most deeply self-reflexive, even metafictional work. It is filled with games, competitions, sport — some of them wholesome, but most of them killing perversions — and at the center of this metaphorical fabric is the great art of word-play, but one thread of which involves a design of references to "okay," "all right," and, climatically, the simple Anglo-Saxon "well." The last words of the novel, unspoken but loud—a sequel themselves to Percival's studied silence in Lancelot—are "Well well well." Those words I take to be Percy's, the fiction's doxology, one not handed down in outworn liturgical formulae, but instead bubbling up out of the most commonplace words available and now rescued by Percy's art from their status as long-since dead metaphor. It is as if with the thought of them Tom More and Mickey LaFaye—and Walker Percy with them—make their light escape from this novelistic world back into the beautiful reality of existential being. Having "come to themselves," Percy seems to say here as elsewhere, each of them is now ready, not for further art, but for life and living. If there is more than one gloss on this story's "ending," surely one of them is Percy's own Emersonian admonition that one should never forget that "the living of one's life is not to be found in books, either the reading of them or the writing of them."

It may be objected that to say that fictional characters and their creator can take leave of the aesthetic realm and land in the existential is nothing but still another fiction, another "mere illusion." But at least it's a difficult illusion to try to pull off: some such statement might be offered up as the first line of its defense. On the other hand, however, it is an illusion central to that pressure of the art and the life, the life and the art, that has so long reigned in the American literary imagination. And it is, after all, that very illusion the one book, as Hemingway had it, "All modern American literature comes from" does indeed create: not only in its last sentences, its epistolary close, and Huck's signature but also in its opening statements—"You don't know about me, without you have read a book by the name of 'The Adventures of Tom Sawyer,' but that ain't no matter. That book was made by Mr. Mark Twain, and he told the truth, mainly."

Now Twain, in taking up his own centennial investigation of the viability of American society, takes up Huck Finn's very odd point of view and in that act of American spiritual autobiography can be said to put so much of himself into the book only paradoxically, by so mastering Huck's voice that he *removes* himself from it before the fact.[19] Percy also asks, in effect, what Roy Harvey Pearce calls the central question of American literature: "What are we that we no longer find communitas guaranteed in the nature of things?" (290). Asking that question in *Lost in the Cosmos*, Percy risks still another original organic form and creates a dictionary definition of an American tour de force by putting himself this time literally within the world of his writing: "You are *Ralph* to me and I am *Walker* to you, but you are not *Ralph* to you and I am not *Walker* to me. (Have you ever wondered why the Ralphs you know look as if they ought to be called Ralph and not Robert?)" (107). So he notes here, in his native manner of collaboration, as he creates anticly his equivalent of Hawthorne's "neutral territory, somewhere between the real world and fairy-land, where the Actual and the Imaginary may meet, and each imbue itself with the nature of the other." Percy's conversational bent is a reflection of that quality of mind and sensibility he shares with the Emerson of the California sojourn, a quality that for Percy issues forth from an insistent definition of consciousness: *"Conscious* from *con-scio,* I know with. . . . Consciousness is that act of attention to something under the auspices of its sign, an act which is social in origin. What Descartes did not know: no such isolated individual as he described can be conscious" (105). One can see that a consequence of such a definition is to grant a primacy of place to the reader in any literary discourse: indeed, *Lost in the Cosmos* fits perfectly within Whitman's sense of the sort of American books to be called for. Percy's own presence there, a necessary consequence of what it means to "know [and say] with," is evidence of that capaciousness of spirit allowing Percy to avoid what Lionell Trilling defines as "the great sin of the intellectual: that he never really tests his ideas by what it would mean to him if he were to undergo the experience that he is recommending."[20] Percy's metamorphic moment, in 1941, of discovering himself in the test tube and as "one of them" was without doubt the occasion of a lasting self-definition both for writing and for living.

American literature is, among other things, a history of the variety of ways writers put themselves in their books. The attentive reader of Percy will share the impression that his marriage to Mary Townsend in late 1946 formalized still another metamorphosis for Percy, this one of falling in love and plighting one's troth. Though their stay at Uncle Will's cottage on the Cumberland Plateau in Tennessee was brief, one speculates that it was long enough for Percy to have enjoyed his first full sense of place as social space — his first full realization of being there, truly in the world of his and her shared consciousness. Percy's abilities to describe place and the placement of his characters have often been praised as major achievements in his fiction, and by no means merely for reasons just stylistic. His use of place, finally, in *Lost in the Cosmos* is a reminder of Shea's suggestion of American possibilities of transformation "deriving . . . perhaps from the American spirit of place" as well as of those pressures between life and art that require such statements as, say, Whitman's pronouncement that "Whosoever touches this book touches a man." In the space odyssey at the end of *Cosmos* Captain Schuyler still hangs on late in the twenty-first century with his little band of survivors, each of them a veritable species unto himself and herself. And where are they — at least if they have made the free choice that Percy would devoutly wish for them? Back there in Lost Cove, Tennessee, on the Cumberland Plateau, a point in place that marks Percy's intitiating personal and communal life, perhaps the world both of his best root memories and locus, too, of his firmest dreams of the future. Place there, surely, is no less than benediction.[21]

Percy's proto-fiction here is a radical epitome of all his work. In its depiction of the possibilities of *communitas,* to be gained by radically differentiated and dedicatedly pluralistic selves engaged once again in the endless call to personal sovereignty and then to society in a "knowing with" through the word. In interesting ways, particularly in the character of Schuyler and his fatherly role as ring-bestower of the community, *Lost in the Cosmos* has claims almost equal to those of *Love in the Ruins* as the predecessor of *The Thanatos Syndrome*. It "closes" with the survivors receiving a mysterious extraterrestrial message, unidentified, but in down-home and heightened "broadcastese," a latter-day Puritan plain style not without its self-reflexive word-play: "Repeat. Do you read? Do you read? Are you in trouble? How did you get in trouble? If you are in trouble, have you sought help? If you did, did it come? If it did, did you accept it? Are you out of trouble? What is the character of your consciousness? Are you conscious? Do you have a self? Do you know who you are? Do you know what you are doing? Do you love? Do you know how to love? Are you loved? Do you hate? Do you read me? Come back. Repeat. Come back. Come back" (262). It is a voice that would not write odes to dejection but, like Thoreau's, "brag as lustily as a chanticleer in the morning . . . if only to wake my neighbors up." An American voice, it is, as a good friend of mine who brings ideas into deeds reminds me, like the voice of Roethke, who would teach us that "My heart keeps open house."

Notes

1. See my "Introduction" to the present volume for a full survey of such studies.

2. Walker Percy, *The Thanatos Syndrome* (New York: Farrar, Straus, Giroux, 1987). See 23, 276–81 especially. The novel also includes many other references to Twain as well as numerous other American writers and fictional characters.

3. Walker Percy, "Questions They Never Asked Me," *Esquire* 88 (1977): 170.

4. Walker Percy, "From Facts to Fiction," *The Writer* 80 (October 1967): 27.

5. Walker Percy, "Herman Melville," *New Criterion* 2 (November 1983): 39.

6. Harold Bloom, "The Freshness of Transformation: Emerson's Dialectic of Influence," *Emerson: Prophecy, Metamorphosis, and Influence*, ed. David Levin (New York and London: Columbia University Press, 1975), 142.

7. Walker Percy, "From Facts to Fiction," 46.

8. Walker Percy, *The Message in the Bottle* (New York: Farrar, Straus and Giroux, 1975), 111. Other citations to this volume will be made within the text as *MB*.

9. I refer here to the series of similes Percy uses to describe his plight as a Christian novelist (*MB*, 116–17).

10. Daniel Shea, "Emerson and the American Metamorphosis," in *Emerson: Prophecy, Metamorphosis, and Influence*, 31–32.

11. Alexis de Tocqueville, *Democracy in America*, ed. Richard D. Heffner, abr. ed. (New York: New American Library, 1956), 183; hereinafter cited parenthetically in the text.

12. Sacvan Bercovitch, "The Biblical Basis of the American Myth," in *The Bible and American Arts and Letters*, ed. Giles Gunn (Philadelphia: Fortress Press, 1983), [219], 221.

13. See expecially Sacvan Bercovitch, "Emerson the Prophet: Romanticism, Puritanism, and Auto-American-Biography," in *Emerson: Prophecy, Metamorphosis, and Influence*, [1]–27.

14. Herbert Schneidau, "The Antinomian Strain: The Bible and American Poetry," in *The Bible and American Arts and Letters*, 15.

15. For a sharply differing assessment see John F. Zeugner, "Walker Percy and Gabriel Marcel: The Castaway and the Wayfarer," *Mississippi Quarterly* 28 (1975): 21–53. Zeugner is one of the earliest critics, but by no means the last, to find snobbery and "a sneering petulance" at the heart of Percy's views. For other such judgments see my "Introduction."

16. For a sketch of those see my "Introduction" and references to the most reliable studies of the life.

17. John Updike, "Emersonianism," *New Yorker*, 4 June 1984, 127–28.

18. Walker Percy, "The State of the Novel: Dying Art or New Science?" *Michigan Quarterly Review* 16 (1977): 372–73; hereinafter cited parenthetically within the text.

19. Huck's initial words in his own book, that is, create the illusion that he had a historical existence prior to Mr. Twain's book about Tom Sawyer.

20. Cited as an epigraph in Gerald Graff, *Literature Against Itself* (Chicago: Chicago University Press, 1979).

21. Twice before this Percy had put Lost Cove to fictional use. In *Love in the Ruins* it is the name of a farm near the village of Sherwood, Tennessee, owned by Mr. Ives (234); in *The Second Coming* Percy moves the whole place to North Carolina and makes it available to Will Barrett as Lost Cove cave.

INDEX

Only Walker Percy's works are cited, other author's works are cited under own names.